Vineyards & Vaqueros

BEFORE GOLD
California under Spain and Mexico
Volume 1

Rose Marie Beebe & Bob Senkewicz
Series Editors

Vineyards & Vaqueros

*Indian Labor
and the Economic Expansion
of Southern California, 1771–1877*

GEORGE HARWOOD PHILLIPS

UNIVERSITY OF OKLAHOMA PRESS
NORMAN

ALSO BY GEORGE HARWOOD PHILLIPS
Chiefs and Challengers: Indian Resistance and Cooperation in Southern California
 (Berkeley, 1975)
The Enduring Struggle: Indians in California History (San Francisco, 1981) *Indians and Intruders in Central California, 1769–1849* (Norman, Okla., 1993) *Indians and Indian Agents: The Origins of the Reservation System in California,
 1849–1852* (Norman, Okla., 1997)
*"Bringing Them under Subjection": California's Tejón Indian Reservation and Beyond,
 1852–1864* (Lincoln, Nebr., 2004)

LIBRARY OF CONGRESS CATALOGING-IN-PUBLICATION DATA
Phillips, George Harwood.
  Vineyards and vaqueros : Indian labor and the economic expansion of Southern California, 1771–1877 / George Harwood Phillips.

   p. cm. — (Before gold : California under Spain and Mexico ; v. 1)
   Includes bibliographical references and index.
   ISBN 978-0-87062-391-2 (hardcover) ISBN 978-0-8061-6745-9 (paper)

 1. Indians of North America—Employment—California—Los Angeles Region—History—18th century. 2. Indians of North America—Employment—California—Los Angeles Region—History—19th century. 3. Working class—California—Los Angeles Region—History. 4. Social change—California—Los Angeles Region—History. 5. Indians of North America—California—Los Angeles Region—Economic conditions. 6. Indians of North America—California—Los Angeles Region—Social conditions. 7. Los Angeles Region (Calif.)—Economic conditions—18th century. 8. Los Angeles Region (Calif.)—Economic conditions—19th century. 9. Los Angeles Region (Calif.)—Social conditions. 10. Los Angeles Region (Calif.)—Ethnic relations. I. Title. II. Series.

E78.C15P48 2010
331.6'997—dc22

2010008251

Vineyards and Vaqueros: Indian Labor and the Economic Expansion of Southern California, 1771–1877 is Volume 1 in the series Before Gold: California under Spain and Mexico.

The paper in this book meets the guidelines for permanence and durability of the Committee on Production Guidelines for Book Longevity of the Council on Library Resources, Inc. ∞

Copyright © 2010 by the University of Oklahoma Press, Norman, Publishing Division of the University. Paperback published 2020. Manufactured in the U.S.A.

All rights reserved. No part of this publication may be reproduced, stored in a retrieval system, or transmitted, in any form or by any means, electronic, mechanical, photocopying, recording, or otherwise—except as permitted under Section 107 or 108 of the United States Copyright Act—without the prior written permission of the University of Oklahoma Press.

Contents

List of Illustrations	7
List of Maps	8
List of Tables	9
Preface	11
Acknowledgments	13
Introduction: Against the Grain	15
1. Working the Land	37
2. Missionary Intrusion	57
3. Competing Institutions	81
4. Missionary Expansion	95
5. Urban Magnet	115
6. New Management	129
7. Emancipation and Secularization	159
8. Urban Unrest	183
9. Land of Opportunity	201
10. Skilled Labor	219
11. Aftermath	233
12. Violent Vineyards	259
13. A Useful People	297
Conclusion: Crosscurrents	321
Glossary	337
Bibliography	343
Index	377

Illustrations

Stations of the Cross, no. 4	102
Stations of the Cross, no. 6	103
Mural depicting Indians picking grapes	108
Wall design depicting an Indian hunting a deer	109
"California Vaqueros Returned from the Chase," 1854	137
Mission San Gabriel in 1833, by Ferdinand Deppe	154
Detail of *Mission San Gabriel in 1833*	157
Detail of *Mission San Gabriel in 1833*	157
"Californians Throwing the Lasso"	221
"Grizzly Bear Hunt" (1858)	222
"Bull Fight (after High Mass) at Mission Dolores"	225
Picking prickly pears near San Fernando	238
Pico and Indians at Rancho San Fernando	243
Andres Pico at Ex-mission San Fernando	244
Los Angeles in 1853	265

Maps

Los Angeles River Drainage Area As It Once Was	47
The Tongva and Their Neighbors, circa 1771	56
Missions, Pueblo Tract, and Spanish Concessions, 1771–1821	92
Changing Courses of the Los Angeles River	123
Mexican Land Grants, 1822–1846	160
Los Angeles, circa 1836	188
Los Angeles, circa 1847: Vineyards and Indian Village	197
Agricultural Lands of Los Angeles, 1849	276
Zanja System of Los Angeles circa 1880	287

Tables

1. Village headmen baptized at San Fernando, 1802–1804 — 98
2. Los Angeles harvests, 1790s (in fanegas) — 116
3. Indians residing in Los Angeles, 1830 — 126
4. Ranchos and Indian residents, 1836 — 163
5. Mission origins of Indians in Los Angeles, 1836 — 184
6. Mission origins of Indians in Los Angeles, 1844 — 195
7. Mission origins of rancho residents, 1844 — 231
8. Selected ranchos with Indian residents, 1844 — 232
9. Livestock and implements at Rancho Ex-mission San Fernando, January 1, 1846 — 235
10. Agricultural expansion in Los Angeles County, 1867–1868 (in acres) — 288

Preface

Los Angeles! These two words conjure up the split image much of the world has of this famous city: sunshine and smog, expansive beaches and congested freeways, great universities and failing schools, modern architecture and urban sprawl, international sporting events and periodic race riots, and—at the opposite ends of wealth and the alphabet—the communities of Beverly Hills and Watts. But when pondering the contradictions of the city and its region, Indian labor and economic expansion hardly come to mind. Yet these are what this book is about. Because it neither extols the dignity of labor nor concentrates solely on the victimization of workers, it is not a labor history per se, even though it deals primarily with a distinct class of laborers who became victims. Because it bypasses much conventional cultural and political developments, it does not qualify as a history of Los Angeles County, even though much of the activity described took place within the county's first boundaries. Because it is concerned with Indians from throughout the Los Angeles region and takes into account those who entered it from beyond, it cannot be labeled a tribal history, even though most of the people it deals with belonged to a "tribe" initially called the Gabrielino, later the Gabrielino-Tongva, and more recently the Tongva. Rather, it is a history of Indians incorporated into foreign-imposed institutions who became a laboring class instrumental in the economic expansion of a truly vast region.

Acknowledgments

Research on this book began many years ago, only to be put on hold as other projects took precedence. Thus it is impossible to identify all the librarians, archivists, and colleagues who provided assistance and inspiration. Because most of the unpublished primary data were obtained at the Bancroft and Huntington libraries, I owe their former and present staff members special gratitude. Because many of the published primary and secondary sources were found in the California Room of the San Diego Public Library, the staff members there deserve equal appreciation. Moreover, the library's microfilm collection of nineteenth-century newspapers provided rich data easily photocopied. Because many of materials not found elsewhere were obtained at the Mandeville Special Collections Library at the University of California–San Diego, thanks go to the staff for their kind and efficient service.

I thank Michael K. Lurch, Chester King, John Johnson, Harry Quinn, Stephen O'Neil, Julia Costello, and John D. Goodman II for sharing materials, and Blake Gumprecht for granting me permission to use the maps from his book *The Los Angeles River*. I am in their debt and hope some day to reciprocate. Thanks also to Jo Griffith who drew the original maps. Those reading part or all of the manuscript and offering valuable advice for its improvement include Michael Bernstein, Richard Carrico, Natalie Kuhlman, Barry Anderson, and John R. Johnson. Finally, seldom does a scholar benefit from the expert advice of individuals who not only created and edited a journal about California but also have an impressive publishing record themselves. Editors Rose Marie Beebe and Robert M. Senkewicz have improved the quality of this book in incalculable ways. Thank you very much.

Introduction
Against the Grain

Until recently, researchers investigating the histories of California's missions, pueblos, and ranchos have concentrated mainly on missionaries, settlers, and rancheros. When mentioned at all, Indians have been assigned an insignificant role in the functioning of these institutions. Such an approach is understandable because it is much easier to write about those who produced the historical documents than about those mentioned intermittently in them. Cutting against this grain, however, are scholars from various disciplines who are producing a literature about the historical roles of Indians at a rate far greater than what would be expected for a region of little importance in the Spanish Empire and later the Mexican Republic.[1] By discussing Indian resistance, adaptation, and survival, scholars have moved beyond victim history, in which Indians are viewed as passive observers of those taking over their territories, to a more integrated history in which Indians, if not always given

---

1. See Haas, *Conquests and Historical Identities*; Lightfoot, *Indians, Missionaries, and Merchants*; Sánchez, *Telling Identities*; Silliman, *Lost Laborers*; Bouvier, *Women and the Conquest*; Chávez-García, *Negotiating Conquest*; Sandos, *Converting California*; Hackel, *Children of Coyote*; González, *This Small City*.

leading roles in the drama, at least have important parts to play. Of course, balancing what Indians did with what was done to them may never be fully achieved, but it is certainly a goal worth seeking. It is especially worth seeking when considering Indians as workers.

A first step toward this goal is to challenge some long-held opinions regarding Indian labor practices prior to European contact. As Patricia C. Albers has written, "In popular discourse, the work that is considered a 'real' expression of the Native American experience is marked and separated symbolically from most other forms of labor. Woodcarving, basketweaving, and potterymaking are among several productive activities that are so isolated. Treated in legendary terms as part of a timeless, sacred tradition and ancient lore, the so-called authentic work of Native Americans is situated in a popular play of mythic images rather than in a progression of actual historic events."[2]

This situation is nowhere more true than in California, whose Native inhabitants are still known and renowned as some of the world's greatest basket makers. Great basket makers they were, but the label implies that their product was more an artistic than a utilitarian endeavor. Moreover, from a modern, Western perspective, collecting and processing of wild plants, which was mainly undertaken by women, and hunting and fishing, which were largely the tasks of men, do not resemble what is usually thought of as work. Indians did something else to survive.[3]

If, however, we accept archaeologist Stephen W. Silliman's definition of labor as "the social and material relations surrounding any activities that are designed to produce, distribute, or manipulate material items for personal use or for anyone else," then basket making, collecting, hunting, and fishing were types of labor.[4] Not only did the hunter-gatherers of California labor, but their labor often produced a surplus that resulted in leisure time. Moreover,

---

2. Albers, "From Legend to Land to Labor," 248.
3. That Indians labored before contact is a concept hardly new to anthropology. See, for example, Willoughby, "Division of Labor."
4. Silliman, "Theoretical Perspectives," 380.

traditional labor practices did not disappear with the arrival of Europeans. At some sites where the missions, ranchos, and pueblos once existed, archaeologists have uncovered ceramics, stone tools, soapstone vessels, grinding stones, shell beads, and other objects representative of the Indians' material culture. In other words, incorporation into foreign-imposed institutions did not destroy traditional forms of labor, although new labor practices were introduced.[5]

Silliman has suggested that "although colonial labor schedules and burdens may require particular activities or may prevent individuals from enacting desired or pre-contact cultural practices, the labor regime and its implements also provide opportunities for native individuals to maintain social continuity or to build and express new practices or identities." Too often anthropologists and historians have ignored this aspect of imperial history, and peoples "constrained by colonialism are often seen as pawns in colonial games or faceless automatons in a controlling system." Indians, in fact, sometimes used labor to their advantage: "The involvement of Native American groups in any of the standard colonial institutions in the Americas—missions, ranchos, trade outposts, presidios, forts, and secular towns—revolved around labor, even in contexts of frequent interethnic marriage. Sometimes colonial groups forced labor on native societies; other times, indigenous peoples found colonial labor opportunistic and capitalized on it. In either case, labor constituted one of the primary and most influential interpersonal and intercultural relations in pluralistic colonial communities."[6]

The importance of Indians as workers in the California mission system may have been more obvious to those living a few decades after the system collapsed than to those writing 150 years later. In 1870, for example, an individual clearly described the roles and abilities of the Indian workers: "Each mission had its own community of Indians, industrious, orderly, self-supporting, not

---

5. See Greenwood, "The California Ranchero"; Silliman, "Missions Aborted"; Frierman, "The Pastoral Period in Los Angeles."
6. Silliman, "Theoretical Perspectives," 379–84.

destitute of capacity for improvement, with a fair proportion of farm laborers, herdsmen, and mechanics. In the works of irrigation, the remains of which still exist around so many of the mission buildings, the Christianized Indians particularly excelled. They showed a remarkable native talent for the engineering required by those works. With little or no instruction of any kind, they were able to find grades, to lay out ditches, and to manage irrigation as well as the most scientific engineers."[7]

This aspect of the mission system, however, has been downplayed by both its defenders and its denigrators.[8] Maynard Geiger, historian and priest, either has the padres at Mission San Gabriel doing the work—"In 1807 the padres began to build houses for the Indians"—or, by writing in the passive voice, simply has things getting done: "In 1819 a hennery was built and on the second story a dovecot. Two mills were commenced in 1820.... In 1821, two adobe rooms were built for preserving seeds.... In 1823, a building was erected for housing a machine for cutting wood.... In 1825, the mill for grinding corn was finished."[9] Regarding this mill, Glenn S. Dumke appeared to be on the right track when he insisted that his interest was "not in its bricks and mortar but rather in the human beings who built it and used it."[10] His "human beings," however, were not the Indians who actually constructed the mill but those who managed them. Three times he stated that Father José María Zalvidea built the mill. Obviously, Geiger and Dumke understood that Indians worked at the missions, but by downplaying or bypassing this aspect of the mission system, they inadvertently overlooked what may have been one of its more positive aspects—the development of a large and often efficient labor force.

Many defenders of the system, however, have uncovered, translated, published, and analyzed much valuable data, data upon which the denigrators have heavily relied. Some of the denigrators,

---

7. Speech by U.S. Senator Gasserly, Senate, June 4, 1870, in *Los Angeles Star*, July 16, 1870.
8. Other historians have used "Christophilic Triumphalist" and "Christophobic Nihilist" to identify those with pro- and anti-missionary viewpoints. See Sandos, *Converting California*, 5.
9. Geiger, "The Building of Mission San Gabriel," 38–39.
10. Dumke, "The Masters of San Gabriel's Old Mill," 261–62.

moreover, have fostered distortions as harmful as those created by the defenders. By concentrating on those doing the mistreating, they have neglected the responses of those experiencing the mistreatment, and "bad" missionaries have become historically more important than "good" Indians. This perspective prohibits an appreciation of the often complex interplay between the colonizers and the colonized. As David Sweet has explained, "Impassioned denigrators of the frontier mission enterprise sometimes confuse genocide with ethnocide when appraising its disastrous consequences for Native American history, but such incendiary argumentation casts more heat than light on our subject. Missionaries sought to exterminate Indian culture, not Indian people."[11]

Steven W. Hackel is equally critical of those scholars who

> have argued that Indian laborers suffered incapacitating psychological disorientation when they tried to reconcile Spanish tools, technologies, and schedules with their own world views. This approach calls attention to the difficult transitions that the mission workplace demanded of Indians, but it hobbles the scholarship on labor in the mission by depicting Indian people as static, immutably bound to a wild landscape and a savage mentality. By arguing that Indians could not make the difficult transition to the modes of labor and forms of technology that the mission brought to Alta California, scholars—like the Franciscans—have largely disregarded or misunderstood the Indians who did adjust to mission labor.[12]

By examining how Indians adjusted to the new work regime and by describing how many became efficient workers, the focus remains on the Indians themselves. Recognizing adaptation and efficiency, however, is far different from approving the system in which they were achieved.

---

11. Sweet, "The Ibero-American Frontier Mission," 43. The most extreme denigrators of the system can be found in a collection of articles and statements edited by Rupert Costo and Jeannette Costo, *The Missions of California: A Legacy of Genocide*. An appendix contains a few interviews with those who challenge the premise of the book, but it is merciless in its condemnation of the missionaries. In an otherwise balanced and well-researched book, *Iñigo of Rancho Posolmi: The Life and Times of a Mission Indian*, Laurence H. Shoup and Randall T. Milliken also have promoted the genocide theme, arguing that because the missionaries failed to change policy when witnessing the deaths of so many Indians at the missions, they must have sought to eliminate a race of people.
12. Hackel, "Land, Labor, and Production," 124.

Sweet has proposed that we reread the missionaries' "accounts more critically than has sometimes been done, with an eye primarily to what they have to say about the dimly viewed Indian 'other'; and we must learn to distinguish their high ideals and aspirations ... from what we can reconstruct of their actual practice."[13] What the missionaries viewed were two distinct types of Indians: *gentiles* and *neófitos*. Before being incorporated into a mission, or remaining unincorporated, the Indian was a gentile, or "wild" person. Upon baptism, the Indian became a neophyte and thus "civilized." Although the terms made eminent sense to those using them in the eighteenth and nineteenth centuries, they need qualification today. On the one hand, "neophyte" implies a total absorption of Spanish culture, when in fact, many if not most neophytes adopted only aspects thereof. James A. Sandos has argued that baptism may have turned gentiles into neophytes, but it did not make them converts in the sense that they rejected all aspects of their spiritual traditions.[14] On the other hand, "gentile" implies an Indian who remained unchanged from pre-contact times, when in fact, many adopted various aspects of Spanish culture, especially animals, crops, and implements while living outside the mission system. Depending on time and place, both gentiles and neophytes worked for the missionaries.

The economic importance of the Indian workers cannot be appreciated unless the programs and conditions under which they labored—programs and conditions introduced and perpetuated by the missionaries—are comprehended. These programs, according to David Hurst Thomas, exhibited great diversity:

> Too often, anthropologists and ethnohistorians have viewed Hispanic religious objectives as a monolith. We must distinguish between the Hispanic master plan for missionization and the way missions actually functioned throughout the borderlands. No longer can we proceed from Bolton's abstract notion of "mission as a frontier institution," because multiple mission strategies were involved. The missions of California were different from those in Texas and New Mexico, and so were the life-styles of the Native American neophytes involved. The purposes of

---

13. Sweet, "Ibero-American Frontier Mission," 9.
14. Sandos, *Converting California*, 6.

Jesuit missions in Baja California differed from those of the Franciscan missionaries to the north. Strategic and tactical difference engendered dissimilar Native American responses to the mission effort.[15]

Even within a particular region, such as California, the way each mission was managed and the particular economic programs introduced—and thus the quality of life experienced by the Indians—varied. Those missions concentrating on agriculture organized a different kind of workforce than did those emphasizing stock raising.

Although the degree of economic success varied from mission to mission, it is difficult to find one that failed to produce enough food to feed its residents. "The prodigious agricultural and pastoral production of the Alta California missions had little to do with technology," Robert Archibald has written, "but rather was attributable to fertile and abundant land, good climate, and a labor intensive system. . . . Land was an expendable resource. Few attempts were made to conserve fertility when pastures and fields could simply expand into virgin areas, thus increasing declining yields. Because of a plentiful labor supply, herds and acreage under cultivation could be expanded practically without limits." But Archibald overstated his case in arguing that even though the missions were an economic success, they "tended to destroy the Indians" for whom they were created.[16]

The missions radically altered Indian culture, but they did not destroy Indian people. Even secularization—the systematic breakup of the mission system in the 1830s—was not designed to destroy Indians. In fact, Indians played an important role in this crucial event in California history, a role downplayed by some historians. To Hubert Howe Bancroft, "the mission, broken up and despoiled, no longer afforded shelter to its children, save a few of more solid character. . . . The rest had been dispersed to seek refuge among the settlers or in the wilderness."[17] Robert

---

15. Thomas, "Columbian Consequences," 11. Herbert E. Bolton is the author of "The Mission as a Frontier Institution in the Spanish American Colonies," first published early in the twentieth century and republished and analyzed many times since.
16. Archibald, *The Economic Aspects*, 180–81, 184.
17. Bancroft, *California Pastoral*, 241.

Glass Cleland suggested that secularization "scattered the partly civilized neophytes like sheep without a shepherd."[18] Upon losing these lands, wrote Andrew Rolle, "the Indians stood apathetically by as deeply confused, helpless witnesses."[19] According to Jessie Davies Francis, an economic historian, "Had the neophytes, upon their emancipation, assimilated in any considerable numbers with the [Mexican] population, . . . a working and consuming class would have developed." Most, however, dispersed and became "vagabonds or renegades."[20]

These views can appeal to both the defenders and the denigrators of the mission system. The former can argue that the missions protected the neophytes; the latter can insist that they failed to prepare them for life outside the system. What they do not say is what the neophytes did during and after secularization. Without question, secularization drastically altered the lives of thousands of neophytes, often for the worse. But even though some of them, especially those located along the Central California coast, found refuge in the "wilderness," they were not necessarily "dispersed" there. Many chose to leave and once in the interior successfully reordered their lives. Certainly some "of more solid character" occupied for a time the lands promised them in the secularization law, while others remained "deeply confused witnesses." But for hundreds the Los Angeles region offered opportunities. Instead of being scattered like "sheep without a shepherd," they intentionally relocated there, seeking work in the pueblo and on the ranchos. There they became the region's predominant working class, especially on the ranchos.

Although cattle ranching emerged soon after the first missions were established, the first private ranchos founded in California were little more than grazing permits issued by the governor to soldiers, artisans, settlers, and government officials who came to California with the missionaries. Once Mexico gained its independence from Spain, true land grants were issued, resulting in the legally

---
18. Cleland, *The Cattle on a Thousand Hills*, 22.
19. Rolle, *California: A History*, 157–58.
20. Francis, *An Economic and Social History*, 637.

sanctioned and privately owned rancho. And even though the rancho system survived long after the American takeover of California, the decade and a half preceding that event has received most of the attention from popular writers and professional historians.

Not nearly as divisive as that of the mission, the literature about the rancho can be divided between romantics and realists. To the former, the ranchero, living in bountiful, beautiful land, residing on an estate the size of a principality, and benefiting from a docile Indian workforce, seems to have mastered a lifestyle approaching pastoral perfection. Ironically, this image was created not by the rancheros themselves but by foreigners who visited California in increasing numbers during the 1830s and 1840s and who described in their letters and journals a people they thought were living in isolated splendor. James H. Carson, for example, arrived in California in 1847 and wrote:

> Surrounded by plenty, blessed with health, money at command, no sheriff or tax gatherer to make professional calls on them, in the midst of their happy children, they passed their time amongst their flocks, breathing the balmy air which is always laden with the fragrance from the flower clad fields. They may be said to have sung and danced their time away. Picnic parties were frequent, to which the young and old repaired, and made the dells in the wild woods ring with merry peals of laughter; fandangos were also of frequent occurrence, and the sound of the violin and guitar scarcely ever died away at the old homesteads. After skimming over the broad plains on their fine horses during the day, they joined in the giddy waltz at night. It was of no unusual occurrence to see the little black eyed girl of seven or eight summers and her great grandmother going through the intricacies of a Spanish dance together.[21]

Working with documents such as this, no wonder Nellie Van de Grift Sanchez wrote in 1929 that "for the real romance of California's story we must turn to the Mexican period, the days of the cattle barons when the *ranchero* galloped over his broad domains on his beautiful Arabian horse, the freest and happiest man on earth."[22]

---

21. Carson, "Early Recollections of the Mines," 110.
22. Sánchez, *Spanish Arcadia*, vii–viii.

This picture of California life, lamented Robert Glass Cleland in 1944, "long ago created by romantic writers and deeply embedded in popular tradition, will probably never be greatly changed by historians of a more realistic school."[23] The romantics, however, have given some ground to the realists, who view the rancho as an institution plagued with familial and legal disputes and economic uncertainty. Because emphasis remains on the rancheros and their families, however, the Indian workers are either ignored or reluctantly acknowledged as having some importance. For example, writing at the end of the nineteenth century, an individual unable to accept the well-known fact that most of the herdsmen were Indians could state only that "every wealthy old Don, in the days before the Gringo came, had upon his estate men who were more capable than their fellows in this particular vocation."[24] According to a local historian, no matter how "inefficient and lazy they [the Indians] may have been, they could learn or had already learned to ride, to help in herding, corralling and branding cattle, and in killing and skinning them; and the Indian women and children could wash and cook and do the simple work of servants in the house."[25]

Views such as this have prompted Jay D. Frierman to complain that even those writing in recent years are still "looking back on the pastoral interlude as an idyllic period" and give only a "cursory notice to the vital contribution of the Indians. It is indeed tragic that they who supplied most of the labor for the entire pastoral period should be reduced to a footnote to the 'romance' of the missions and ranchos. Without the labor of this abused population neither institution could have existed, nor could the 'dashing dons' have had the leisure to pursue those activities that gave them their cachet."[26]

Roberta S. Greenwood has written that "through the processes of fiction, legend, art, and film, an archetypal figure of the

---

23. Cleland, *From Wilderness to Empire*, 139.
24. Loughead, "The Old California Vaquero," 109–10.
25. Brackett, *History of Pomona Valley California*, 52. In Pauley, ed., *Rancho Days in Southern California: An Anthology with New Perspectives*, only one scholar mentions the importance of Indian labor. See Bakken, "Rancho Cañón de Santa Ana."
26. Frierman, "The Pastoral Period in Los Angeles," 11.

California ranchero has emerged that reflects an idealized image, which is accurate—at most—for only a few individuals, and during a limited period of time." Moreover, "the California rancheros did not live on a frontier as usually defined: They produced a single commodity dependent on a foreign market, they needed to import or impress a labor force, and they were part of a stratified society. The rancho system was not even an innovation in Alta California since both the social and physical attributes derived from the missions: the choice of place, irrigation, routes of travel, production for trade, organization of the labor force, and elements of the architecture."[27]

Her points are well taken, but the social and family life, hospitality, and equestrian skills of the rancheros make criticizing them difficult even for realists such as myself and for Douglas Monroy, who wrote: "The Californios occupied center stage of California history for only a short while. They were a people who began utterly inauspiciously, forged themselves places on the landscape as owners of great landed estates, and created a singular identity of themselves." But Monroy acknowledged that, "while we behold many of the compelling manifestations of life in the rancho era in these descriptions, one of the bases of Californio society has only dimly emerged here: this was a society based on the work of others." That society was constructed on "the continuing destruction of California Indian society."[28]

As will become apparent in the following pages, some ranchos in Southern California actually contributed to the preservation of Indian culture, but Monroy is correct to note that the basis of Californio society was Indian labor. And the importance of that labor cannot be fully appreciated without some comprehension of the personal characteristics of the rancheros and some knowledge of the programs they introduced. Indeed, the success of a rancho depended in large part on the managerial skills of the ranchero and his foreman in dealing with their Indian workers. Much more than at the missions, Indians on the ranchos had options, and

---
27. Greenwood, "The Californio Ranchero," 451, 463–64.
28. Monroy, "The Creation and Re-creation of Californio Society," 173, 190.

the economic well-being of a particular rancho often hinged on what its workers chose to do or not to do. "Anthropologists and historians need to account for Native intentions and strategies in joining or leaving ranchos," Silliman has argued, "and they need to recognize efforts of Native workers to mold their lives within rancho regimes."[29]

Some of the workers risked their lives defending the ranchos against Indian stock raiders. This aspect of rancho life has largely escaped the attention of both the romantics and realists and needs to be addressed. The raiders sought to obtain horses, mules, and to a lesser extent, cattle, rather than kill or capture human beings, and this profoundly affected many of the ranchos. Indians on both sides lost their lives in these encounters. And even though few ranchos in the Los Angeles region were abandoned because of the raids, many experienced economic hardships. The loss of horses affected the management of cattle. Pursuing stock raiders, moreover, was a labor-intensive activity. The energy expended could have been put to better use. As one historian put it, "It seems likely that a large part of the time which the picturesque 'Arcadian' *caballeros* spent in the saddle was devoted to fighting Indians."[30]

Unlike those who have written about the missions and ranchos, those who have investigated the history of Los Angeles are not so easily categorized. But regarding the early history of the town, scholars can roughly be divided between Hispanicists and Americanists; that is, between those focusing on Spanish settlers and Mexican residents and those finding foreign immigrants, mainly Americans, of more interest. The perception of the Spanish settlers has evolved from the negative to the positive. J. Gregg Layne, writing in 1934, called them "a motley lot. There was not a full-blooded white family among them, but they were pioneer stock, and with three exceptions they stayed and built the town that was later to receive better blood to thrive upon."[31] Views such as this have largely been replaced by those extolling the racial diversity of

---

29. Silliman, "Missions Aborted," 11.
30. Francis, *An Economic and Social History*, 438–39.
31. Layne, "Annals of Los Angeles," 102–3.

the founders of the pueblo. Thus fifty-eight years later, Antonio Ríos-Bustamante wrote: "The ethnicity of the *pobladores* reflected the dynamic reality of ethnic intermixture which was resulting in the formation of a new ethnicity."[32]

As for the image of the foreign immigrants, Americanists have taken it in the opposite direction, from the positive to the negative. J. M. Guinn wrote in 1895 that "the discovery of gold and the rush of immigration to the mines aroused the sleepy old 'ciudad' of Los Angeles from its bucolic dreams. A stream of immigration by the southern route, poured through its streets and gold flowed into its coffers from the sale of cattle that covered the plains beyond. With increasing prosperity the city became ambitious to make a better appearance."[33] Quite a different picture was painted by Robert W. Blew in 1972. "More than a frontier town," Los Angeles "also served as a staging place for drifters. Fur trappers, the remnants of mountain men, overland herders from Santa Fe, and soldiers from Forts Tejon and Yuma found the first taste of society and civilization here." Many of the drifters and dwellers "were young, aggressive bachelors hoping to improve their fortunes. Many of the married men were without their wives and families." Among the southerners, especially those from Texas, "personal honor was not a trifle, and any slight or injury, real or imagined, required atonement."[34]

Some Hispanicists have found the post-1850 period of greater interest than the earlier one. Their works have added greatly to our understanding of the conditions and challenges faced by Mexicans under American rule. Because they have focused on the difficulties faced by one ethnic group, however, they have had little to say about the conditions and challenges confronting the other major group—the Indians.[35] Criticism is not being leveled here, because inclusion is always accompanied by exclusion. But exclusion can inadvertently produce historical distortions. Most scholars

---

32. Ríos-Bustamante, *Mexican Los Ángeles*, 43–44.
33. Guinn, "The Plan of Old Los Angeles," 44–45.
34. Blew, "Vigilantism in Los Angeles, 1835–1874," 12.
35. See, for example, Ríos-Bustamante, *Mexican Los Ángeles*; Griswold del Castillo, *The Los Angeles Barrio*; Romo, *East Los Angeles*.

writing about early Los Angeles have overlooked the length and degree of violence that racked the pueblo. The violence is absent because Indians are absent. Overlook a large residential group, and an important, if tragic, aspect of history is also overlooked. During much of its first century, Los Angeles had a large, fluctuating Indian population that became increasingly violent because of Spanish, Mexican, and American exploitation.[36]

Ignoring this aspect has produced additional distortions—in particular, the stereotype of the "lazy" Spanish settlers of California. The stereotype was first created by missionaries who in their letters and reports had little to say that was positive about the settlers. It was then perpetuated by foreigners who observed a people they thought incapable of properly using time.[37] Many of the settlers did spend a considerable amount of time in leisure activities, but not because of some kind of genetic defect. Soon after the pueblo was founded, they employed Indians to work in their homes and fields. Indian labor allowed the settlers the leisure time some viewed as indolence. In other parts of New Spain, where Indian labor was unavailable, the settlers were noted for their industriousness.[38]

That said, in Los Angeles, leisure time and exploitation were definitely linked. W. W. Robinson deserves recognition as one of the first scholars to call attention to the exploitation of the Indian residents when in 1938 he published selected documents from the Los Angeles Archives revealing the mistreatment of the Indian residents under Mexican rule. Some of the documents deal with Indians working on various projects, but most reveal the ways they were treated.[39] Fourteen years later, Robinson cobbled together some of these documents into a monograph that focused mainly on what he called the liquidation of the Indians. But Robinson also acknowledged, if only briefly, their economic importance: "As

---

36. An exception to this neglect is González, *This Small City*.
37. For a discussion of this topic, see Langum, "Californios and the Image of Indolence"; Clark, "Their Pride, Their Manners, and Their Voices"; and Mann, "The Americanization of Arcadia."
38. See Jones, *Los Paisanos*.
39. Robinson, ed., "The Indians of Los Angeles."

time went on local Indians became the best of workers, skilled in all kinds of field work and excellent herdsmen and horsemen. They became household servants and cooks. They were indispensable to the development of the Pueblo and the ranchos."[40] Overlooked was the rapid rise of intra-Indian violence and crime.

In 1979 Peter C. Woolsey examined crime in general in Los Angeles during the early 1850s, including that perpetrated by Indians. His claim that in those years the terms "Indian" and "crime" were synonymous is a valid one.[41] The following year, I published an article that covered the rise and fall of the Indian workers in Los Angeles under Spanish, Mexican, and American rule, placing blame squarely on the Mexican and American town governments for the Indians' social disintegration.[42] Making no reference to this work, William Mason published in 1984 an article that interpreted Indian-Hispanic relations in Los Angeles as essentially benign. According to Mason, that "Indians, settlers, and soldiers were on a more equal footing than is commonly supposed can be found in such factors as intermarriage between the groups, bilingualism among the *gente de razón*, and a generally amicable relationship with Indians who lived and worked in the pueblo."[43]

Supporting Mason's positive assessment over my negative one, historians Antonio Ríos-Bustamante and Pedro Castillo wrote that "the full extent of Mexican-Indian relations has never been adequately examined, and the information that does exist looks almost exclusively at the settlers' often exploitive use of Indian labor. Equally important aspects of the relationships, such as intermarriage and cultural exchange, have been virtually ignored. In large measure, this oversight is the result of an ethnocentric perspective that fails to acknowledge the intricate racial and cultural mixtures that characterized colonial society in Alta California."[44]

---

40. Robinson, *The Indians of Los Angeles*, 13–14.
41. Woolsey, "Crime and Punishment," 83.
42. Phillips, "Indians in Los Angeles."
43. Mason, "Indian-Mexican Cultural Exchange," 123–24. As historians continue to examine the early period, new perspectives have emerged that represent a different and not always positive picture of life in the pueblo. See, for example, Chávez-García, "'Pongo Mi Demanda'; and Chávez-García, *Negotiating Conquest*. See also González, *This Small City*.
44. Ríos-Bustamante and Castillo, *An Illustrated History of Mexican Los Angeles*, 45.

Another historian has accused those writing about intra-Indian violence and Indian drunkenness in the pueblo from suffering in part from "an unwitting tendency . . . to project the problems of contemporary urban Indians into the past."[45]

Certainly there were cases of amicable, even loving relationships between Indians and Mexicans, and Ríos-Bustamante and Castillo are correct to point out that this aspect of pueblo life has never been adequately examined. But the claim that relations between Mexicans and Indians were more harmonious than exploitive runs so counter to the documentary evidence that the accusation of ethnocentrism can easily be reversed. And so at odds with the historical data is the charge of projection that the countercharge of denial deserves consideration. Even though their brief statements do not seriously diminish the quality of their works, evidently these historians questioned the validity of a well-documented episode simply because it represented a negative picture of the peoples they were championing.

Historians, of course, are continually reassessing the past, as well they should, and the revising stems in part from the ever-changing perspective of what is historically important. But some of the revisionists claim a special relationship with the truth. As historian Edmund S. Morgan has explained, certitude eliminates surprise:

> If you have studied any part of history enough to be curious about it, enough to want to do some research, you already are aware of the generally accepted views, the orthodox views, the controversies among the experts in the field, what is taken for granted and what is in dispute. You want to learn a little more about some question, and you go to the source materials that are presumably the foundation of the orthodox views. You come across something that you had not known about, something that surprises you a little. Cultivate that surprise. . . . Ask yourself, Why did I not know that? Is it contrary to what I had been led to expect? Is it because I did not know enough? Or is it because the people who crafted the orthodox interpretations did not know enough? Or perhaps their angle of vision was limited by what came before.[46]

---

45. Hackel, "Land, Labor, and Production," 136.
46. Morgan, "Cultivating Surprise," 6.

Introduction   31

Maintaining curiosity and cultivating surprise are the hallmarks of a new breed of scholar. Whereas California history was once the domain of the historian and Californian Indians the preserve of the anthropologist and the pre-contact archaeologist, the historical archaeologist has entered the scene. Before the mid-twentieth century, historical archaeology tended to focus on buildings—military posts, ranch houses, and missions. But recently, archaeologists have broadened the scope of their investigations and have helped to make historical Indians increasingly visible.[47]

Because of urban sprawl, the Los Angeles region has lost much of its material history, and thus archaeological data are limited, although excavations have been conducted in the old section of the city and where some of the ranchos once existed.[48] Nevertheless, in 1992 Jay D. Frierman produced a monograph based primarily on archaeological evidence that dealt with both Indian and Hispanic life in the pueblo and on two ranchos. He bypassed the missions and concluded his study at the beginning of the American annexation of California, but he synthesized important archaeological data and thus provided a model for further study.[49]

The insights, analyses, and conclusions of archaeologists regarding the impact colonialism had on Native peoples have greatly expanded our understanding of this aspect of history. For example, artifacts sometimes reveal where Indians resided at the missions, in the pueblos, and on the ranchos; how they conducted their personal lives; and in some cases what they did in their spare time, even at night. What Kent G. Lightfoot has written about Indian life at the missions is also applicable to the pueblos and ranchos:

> [There] the celebration of "Indianness" tended to take place behind closed doors. In the underground "Indian" world of neophyte quarters, families and friends engaged in the manufacture of native tools and ornaments, the cooking and consumption of native foods, and the veneration of native ceremonies. During the day, neophyte workers and Indian officials accommodated themselves to the padres' rigid schedule

---

47. Thomas, "Columbian Consequences," 7
48. See, for example, Chace, "The Archaeology of 'Ciénaga' "; Sleeper, "The Many Mansions of José Sepúlveda"; and Wilson, "The Flores Adobe."
49. Frierman, "The Pastoral Period in Los Angeles."

of labor, church services, and communal meals. But at night and in spare moments during the work day, mundane native cultural practices—conducted out of sight of the padres and their spies—became vested with symbolic value as people connected to the world of their ancestors.[50]

Lightfoot's generalizations are supported by what a missionary said in 1801 about Indian behavior at Mission Santa Bárbara: "The neophytes know how to scheme their plots at night with such a secrecy and reserve so that the custody of the missions with a thousand neophytes altogether should not to be entrusted to two, three, or a few more soldiers who compose the guard."[51]

These insights have forced me to acknowledge that because my book relies almost exclusively on documentation produced by those who imposed the mission, pueblo, and rancho on the Indian peoples of the Los Angeles region, it is—strange as it may seem on first thought yet quite obvious on the second—a "daylight" history. Of course, most labor took place during the day, so the focus must be on what Indians did from sunrise to sunset. But recounting the activities of Indians (a people who left few written documents) from the descriptions of those interacting with them obviously presents an incomplete picture of what transpired. Silliman has written:

> We must plum the vast potential of historical archives, as ethnohistorians have done for decades, to illuminate indigenous experiences in post-Columbian North America, but we must be careful not to rely solely on colonial views inscribed by literate, elite, and frequently white men to create a picture of Native American life during historical periods. Native American experiences, opinions and lifeways are often hard to distinguish reliably in these kinds of historical documents, and we need information sources that speak to indigenous practices in colonial worlds. Basing historical interpretation completely on non-Native sources locks interpretation into the histories told by the colonizers . . . and, in effect, turns the history of colonization into the colonization of history.[52]

Although historians writing about California Indians probably would agree with most of Silliman's statement, they would no

---
50. Lightfoot, *Indians, Missionaries, and Merchants*, 198.
51. Heizer, ed., "A Californian Messianic Movement," 129.
52. Silliman, *Lost Laborers*, 5–6.

doubt disagree that exclusive reliance on documentary evidence "turns the history of colonization into the colonization of history." In some cases, the only evidence available comes from documentary sources. A historian of Latin America has pointed out that "the writings of outsiders, including foreigners, can provide excellent contemporary descriptions of ranch life. By reading a large number of travelers' books and memoirs, we can filter out the untrustworthy and corroborate better observations with other sources."[53] In fact, by studying the documentation of so-called primitive peoples, an anthropologist has written, historians "surround" themselves "with the testimony of amateur ethnographers."[54] Some of these "ethnographers" recorded more useful data than others, and some of their descriptions and opinions might shock our modern sensitivities, but Spaniards, Mexicans, Europeans, and Americans of the eighteenth and nineteenth centuries—not us—engaged the Indians. At any one time, the observers might express fear, compassion, disgust, pity, superiority, respect, disappointment, concern, hatred, or admiration. But few of the documents are so biased as to be useless. Some, in fact, serve dual purposes, simultaneously describing the behavior and activities of Indians and the values and attitudes of those writing them. Such documents are worth quoting at length.

Although the volume and availability of the documentation, of course, varies greatly from region to region, the claim by Julia G. Costello and David Hornbeck that after the breakup of the missions, "the native peoples of California virtually disappear from the documentary record" may have validity for the north but not for the south.[55] Because Los Angeles (and its harbor at San Pedro) was the terminus of oceanic and overland trade, into it came sailors, trappers, traders, and immigrants of several nationalities. Many left descriptions of the land, crops, animals, and people, including Indians working in the pueblo and on the ranchos. These documents, if not in abundance, are certainly in sufficient quantity

---

53. Slatta, *Comparing Cowboys and Frontiers*, 165.
54. Lévi-Strauss, *Structural Anthropology*, 18.
55. Costello and Hornbeck, "Alta California," 320.

to be culled and applied. Most can be found in archives, obscure publications, travel literature, and after the American takeover, in newspapers and government reports.

Drawing upon these documents and on a vast secondary literature produced by historians and anthropologists, I examine the origins and collapse of the missions, the emergence and expansion of the pueblo, and the creation and decline of the ranchos. But within each chapter, I cut across the grain in major ways. First, Indians are viewed more as workers than as victims. Those who dominated them are viewed more as managers than as oppressors. Second, the kind of work undertaken by the Indians in the three institutions is not just identified, as is often the case, but described.[56] Third, the dynamic nature of the institutions into which the Indians were incorporated is emphasized. Relations established by missionaries, settlers, and rancheros with the Indians they employed changed considerably from the early to the latter years of these institutions. This took place, in large part, because the nature, character, culture, and ethnicity of those managing the institutions often changed, as did the origins, tribal affiliation, and degree of acculturation of the Indian workers. Fourth, by taking a comprehensive approach, I move beyond the local, where most of the literature about Indian labor has been directed, to the regional, emphasizing the importance of Indian labor in shaping the economic history of an area extending from the Pacific Coast to the Colorado Desert in the east and from the Santa Ana River in the south to the San Gabriel and San Bernardino mountains in the north.[57] As will become apparent, Indian labor was the major factor in the first economic revolution of the Los Angeles region. Agricultural expansion changed the landscape in major ways and was a precursor of the area's more famous industrial development.

---

56. An exception is Webb, *Indian Life at the Old Missions*. A defender of the mission system, Webb nevertheless described the work undertaken by the Indians and by doing so acknowledged the economic contributions they made to sustain that system.

57. Richard L. Carrico, Florence Shipek, Albert Hurtado, James J. Rawls, Michael Magliari, William J. Bauer Jr., Randall T. Milliken, Laurence H. Shoup, and others have added much to our knowledge of Indian labor in the areas south and north of the Los Angeles region.

Finally, because residing *in, on,* and *at* foreign institutions based on stock raising and crop growing differed significantly from living *upon* a land abundant in natural resources, it follows that institutional and indigenous labor practices differed greatly as well. I contend, therefore, that knowledge of traditional Indian culture—especially its economic dimension—is crucial to comprehending the changes Indians underwent, willingly and unwillingly, after contact first with Spaniards and later with Mexicans and Americans. Put another way, an appreciation of who the Indians were allows for a better understanding of what they became.

CHAPTER I

Working the Land

Mukat and his twin brother created the universe. A power struggle between the two left Mukat dominant, but he turned into a tyrant who was finally bewitched by the Blue Frog. As he lay dying, Mukat instructed the first people to cremate the dead and to annually burn effigies in their memory. Coyote then came to power as the first ceremonial leader and followed Mukat's instructions. With the burning of Mukat's effigy, a new order of the world began in which primal innocence ended and sacral time ceased.

> Then in the place where Mukat was burned there began to grow all kinds of strange plants, but no one knew what they were. They were afraid to go near the place for a hot wind always blew there. One, Palmitcawut, a great shaman, said, "Why do you not go and ask our father what they are?" No one else would go so he followed the spirit of Mukat. By the aid of his ceremonial staff he followed the trail of Mukat's spirit although whirlwinds had hidden the trail. In one place were thickets of prickly cactus and clumps of interlaced thorny vines, but with the touch of his ceremonial staff they opened up for him to pass. Far away on the horizon he saw a bright glow where the spirit of Mukat was leaning against a rock. The creator's spirit spoke, "Who are you that follows me and makes me move on when I am lying still?" When the creator's spirit spoke Palmitcawut was dumb and could not answer, though Mukat asked him several

times. Finally, he was able to speak: "Yes, I am that one who disturbs you while you rest, but we, your creatures, do not know what strange things are that grow where your body was burned?" Mukat's spirit answered him, "Yes, that was the last thing I wanted to tell you, but you killed me before I could do so." Then he continued, "You need not be afraid of those things. They are from my body." He asked Palmitcawut to describe them and when he had finished the spirit of Mukat said, "That big tree is tobacco. It is my heart. It can be cleaned with white clay, and smoked in the big house to drive away evil spirits. The vines with the yellow squashes are from my stomach, watermelons are from the pupil of my eye, corn is from my teeth, wheat is my lice eggs, beans are from my semen, and all other vegetables are from other parts of my body."[1]

Thus, according to Cahuilla legend, the world was created and its strange plants diffused. The emphasis on domestic crops indicates that knowledge of agriculture had spread to the Desert Cahuilla, most likely from Indians residing to the east along the Colorado River.[2]

Corn, pumpkins, melons, and watermelons were planted in the desert in December. And to manage these crops, the Desert Cahuillas developed several techniques: ditch irrigation from wells, springs, streams and impoundment; water diversion of artesian flow to soak gardens before planting; runoff farming or the utilization of rainfall from catchments; and pot irrigation in which women and girls carried water in *ollas* often from wells to sprinkle on the vegetables. "Kitchen" farming, however, was a limited undertaking, its products supplementing the foods obtained by hunting and collecting. In short, the Desert Cahuilla practiced a mixed economy in which food production accompanied food procurement.[3] Although well aware that some Indians planted crops, the Mountain Cahuilla

---

1. Strong, *Aboriginal Society*, 130–43. Francisco Patencio, a Desert Cahuilla, told the myth to Strong in February 1925. Strong published it in *Aboriginal Society* in 1929. It was printed again in 1943 in Boynton, ed., *Stories and Legends of the Palm Springs Indians*, and again in 1971 in Collins, ed., *Desert Hours with Chief Patencio*.
2. For an analysis of the references to domestic crops in the myth, see Lawton, "Agricultural Motifs."
3. Lawton and Bean, "A Preliminary Reconstruction," 200–205. For a theoretical discussion of food procurement and food production, see Harris, "An evolutionary continuum of plant-people interaction."

of the San Jacinto and Santa Rosa Mountains and the Pass Cahuilla of the San Gorgonio Pass chose to rely on the natural resources of their respective ecological niches for subsistence.

Having long evolved from the band organization of their ancestors, members of the three Cahuilla divisions developed social systems based on kinship principles that linked members of their group but also allowed for village autonomy. In all the groups, the individual was born into lineage, clan, and either the Coyote or Wildcat Moiety. Each male had to take a wife from the other moiety. Within each moiety were several clans. Although a kinship group in which all members were related, some only distantly, by blood, a large and prominent clan also had political functions: defending its territory, organizing communal hunting expeditions, raising a large labor force, and settling intra-clan disputes. Each clan consisted of several lineages, one being the founding unit from which the others had segmented. Because wife and husband belonged to different lineages and because the wife usually relocated to her husband's village, members of different lineages resided in the same village. Thus, even though each village conducted its own economic and political affairs, each was linked by kinship to all the other villages.[4]

Although organized in basically the same kind of kinship system as the Cahuillas, the Serranos (as their name implies) were a mountain people. And given the environment in which they lived, small villages were situated in spots where water was available—in valleys fronting small canyons along the southern slopes of the San Bernardino range. Only at the extreme ends of the range—at Yucapia and Moronga that were well watered—were villages of significant size able to support several families. The Serranos remained a food-procuring people. They hunted and collected a variety of animal and plant life and to a limited extent fished.[5]

---

4. Bean, *Mukat's People*, 83–119. Depending on the typology, the Cahuillas, Serranos, and Tongva evolved from egalitarian societies to ranked ones or from bands to tribes. See respectively Fried, *The Evolution of Political Society*, 27–107; and Service, *Primitive Social Organization*, 59–109.

5. Benedict, "A Brief Sketch of Serrano Culture," 368.

What David Prescott Barrows wrote in the late nineteenth century about the environmental knowledge and subsistence patterns of the Cahuillas could also be applied to the Serranos:

> The problem of securing food for a tribe within the territory of the Coahuillas at first sight seems an impossible one. It is the ugly barrenness of the mountains and the arid sterility of the plains that impresses one. It is probably true that an untutored white man lost here would be likely to find hardly a single plant to yield him a mess of palatable food. Beauty of flower and foliage and splendor of fruition are alike sacrificed here to the necessities of the desert. There are no luscious fruits with juicy pulps awaiting the thirsty traveler, but at most only shriveled bags or rind filled with seeds, dangling from a dry and ghostly stalk, or small, bitter plums that are nothing but exaggerated pits, surrounded by a puckery skin. In all these mountains there is not an edible root that a white man's efforts would be likely to discover; there are no palatable nuts, except the piñones, high in the summits. The absence of food is, however, apparent rather than real. The desert is a kindlier mother than would be expected.[6]

From the mountain peaks to the desert floor grew the ponderosa, jeffrey, and the lambertiana pines, manzanita, scrub oak, and desert scrub.[7] Occupying the San Bernardino Valley and the San Gorgonio Pass were mule deer, mountain sheep, deer, rabbits, several species of rodents, and squirrels, snakes, tortoises, quail, eagles, ravens, some fish, bears, foxes, badgers, raccoons, skunks, coyotes, bobcats, and mountain lions. Flourishing in the valley and pass were different species of the oak, mesquite and screwbean, *piñón*, cacti, agave, yucca and nolina, seed pods, desert apricots, choke cherry, holy leaf cherry and a variety of berries, tubers and roots, greens and succulents, and seeds and mushrooms.[8]

Seasons and elevations determined substance activities. Because the Serranos and the Mountain Cahuillas lived in similar environments, their food quests were similar. In January and February, most gathering was limited to the agave. Hunting also took place. From March through May, women in the lower regions gathered

---

6. Barrows, *The Ethno-Botany of the Coahuilla Indians*, 51.
7. Altschul, Rose, and Lerch, "Man and Settlement," 6–7, 14–17.
8. Bean, *Mukat's People*, 36–67.

spring blossoms, greens, buds, and grasses. Men hunted small game and large browsing animals. In June and July in the lower elevations, collective undertakings obtained yucca and manzanita berries. In July and August, the Indians harvested wild grapes which were eaten raw, cooked in stews, or dried as raisins. July, August, and September saw large groups harvesting the piñón. Chia was also available. October and November was the acorn season, the harvest being perhaps the most important of all the subsistence activities. The family unit provided the labor to harvest its own crop. Men knocked the acorns from the trees; women collected and processed them. Some hunting, conducted by men, also took place. Hunting continued in December, but gathering largely ceased.[9]

As a mode of labor, hunting was only as successful as the quality of tools manufactured and the skill attained in using them. Cahuilla and Serrano men hunted rabbits and rodents with nets, snares, and throwing sticks, and deer and mountain sheep with bows and arrows. Individuals hunted most game, but large groups snared rabbits in nets spread in an arch into which the animals were driven. Men skinned the rabbits and women cooked them.[10] Collective rabbit hunts were designed to cull these animals before they devoured fresh greens and seed-producing plants.[11]

The processing of foods resulted from the labor expended by members of individual households. Because domestic needs determined productivity, marriage created an economic group. The adult members of the group were, in effect, skilled workers who manufactured the tools necessary to process grains, seeds, nuts, beans, and berries. In other words, household labor resulted in the family obtaining its necessary dietary requirements.[12] Francisco Patencio, a Desert Cahuilla who dictated his life story in 1943, recounted the processing of mesquite beans, which had remained unchanged from pre-contact times:

---

9. Ibid., 157. For more on the Cahuillas, see Bean and Sauble, *Temalpakh*; Bean, Vane, and Young, *The Cahuilla Landscape*; Hooper, "The Cahuilla Indians"; and Kroeber, "Ethnology of the Cahuilla Indians."
10. Bean, *Mukat's People*, 58–59.
11. Ibid., 146–47.
12. Sahlins, *Stone Age Economics*, 74–82.

The pods are often eight to ten inches long. When they are ripe, the pods split open and the beans fall out. Then they are gathered from the ground. If the mesquite beans are put away whole, they spoil at once. The Indian women crack them in several pieces. These dry hard, and are put away for winter food. The beans are easy food, they do not need to be cooked. These dry beans are pounded into a flour which is then wetted and patted into cakes. The cakes dry hard and have to be split to be eaten, but is good food. Sometimes the beans are pounded in a mortar, then made into a fine flour by grinding on a metate stone. This flour is made into soup.[13]

Spiritual assistance was part of the process. According to Patencio, "Some of the medicine men were not doctors for the sick—no. They were medicine men for other things. Some were medicine men for the flowers of the fruit and seed and grain, and the nuts and beans.... Other medicine men attended the fruit and seeds when they were green; others when the harvest was ripe." The Cahuillas also practiced fallowing. "Sometimes a certain place of seed was not gathered for a year, but this was only to let the ground have more seed for plants another year."[14]

Fallowing was possible because the Cahuillas resided in permanent villages, although seasonally some villagers would move to specific camp sites to hunt and gather. Storing also indicates a sedentary existence, as do the heavy stone *metates* on which acorns and other seeds were ground. Acorn meal, mesquite and screwbean cakes, dried fruits, and berries were stored, often to be consumed in January and February when collecting activities were limited. Large basket granaries were located near each household. A single granary might contain several bushels of acorns. Large ollas would often hold several quarts of seeds. Because the storage facilities of each household were in common view, everyone in the village knew what their neighbors were storing. This discouraged hoarding, which was a serious breach of social etiquette.[15]

Among the Cahuillas and Serranos, reciprocity was the mode by which goods were distributed between families and throughout

---

13. Boynton, ed., *Stories and Legends*, 59.
14. Ibid., 69.
15. Bean, *Mukat's People*, 53–55, 157.

the village. For example, the flow of goods between intermarried Cahuilla families continued as long as the couples remained together. At various rituals, such as those associated with the killing of large animals, items were also distributed. When a young man killed his first deer, a ritual was conducted in the ceremonial house, in which all villagers contributed food and feasted on the venison.[16]

What the Cahuillas could not grow, harvest, kill, and manufacture they could usually obtain through trade. As noted by Barrows, "their habitat occupies the dividing line between the desert and the coast valleys. The mountain Coahuillas can turn westward and meet the flora of the valleys reaching to the Pacific, or descend eastward into the desert and bring back its nourishing and remarkable supplies of food." When they and the Serranos turned westward it was often to exchange deer skins, seeds, obsidian, and salt with the Tongva for fish, sea otter skins, steatite, asphaltum, shell beads, and soapstone pots.[17]

According to Tongva legend, an invisible being called Nocuma created the world and all the animals, trees, plant, fishes, expanding a small stream into oceans so the fishes could survive. He also created the first Indians, Ejoni and Aé, but one of their descendants, Ouiot, became ambitious, haughty, and cruel and was assassinated at the village of Povuu'nga. Ages later the god Chinigchinich appeared at Povuu'nga where he taught the laws, rites, and ceremonies necessary for the preservation of life. One day, before a large congregation, he separated the chiefs and elders from the rest of the people, directing them to wear a particular kind of dress and teaching them how to dance. To these Indians, he gave the name of *puplem*, and they would know all things. In the event of scarcity of food or any infirmity, they were to supplicate him by dancing and

---
16. Ibid., 146–47.
17. Barrows, *The Ethno-Botany of the Coahuilla Indians*, 51; Bean, *Mukat's People*; 122–23; Davis, "Trade Routes and Economic exchange," 26.

the sick would be cured and the hungry fed. Chinigchinich also taught the puplem how to build the *vanquech* and how to conduct themselves therein. Only the chief and the puplem could enter its sanctuary where the laws and ceremonies were taught.[18]

One day the elders asked Chinigchinich to which village he wished to go when he died. To none, he replied, because they were inhabited by people. He intended to go where he would be alone and from where he could see the inhabitants of the villages. They offered to bury him, placing him under the earth, but he said no because they would walk upon him, and he would have to chastise them. Chinigchinich said that "when I die, I shall ascend above, to the stars, and from thence, I shall always see you. To those who have kept my commandments, I shall give all they ask of me, but those who obey not my teaching, nor believe them, I shall punish severely. I will send unto them bears to bite, and serpents to sting them; they shall be without food, and have diseases that they may die." Chinigchinich, at length, died.[19]

Thus the world was created, tyranny overcome, government established, and morality instilled, at least for the Acjachemem and the Tongva who lived near the sea. That Nocuma not only made the world but also expanded the sea so the fishes could survive suggests the importance of marine life in the lives of these peoples. The village of Povuu'nga, the site where Ouiot died and Chinigchinich taught, was located not far from San Pedro Bay.[20]

The two major rivers flowing into the coastal plain through their territory also shaped the economic life of the Tongva. Originating

---

18. Boscana, *Chinigchinich*, 31–34. Although Boscana recorded the legend between 1814 and 1826 while residing at Mission San Juan Capistrano, his informant apparently was a Tongva, not an Acagchemem. The manuscript came into the possession of Alfred Robinson who translated it into English and published it in 1846 as an appendix in his autobiography, *Life in California*. Since then it has been reprinted several times, most recently by the Malki Museum Press in 1978, which contains extensive notes by Harrington. For a brief history of the manuscript, consult Johnson, "The Various Chinigchinich Manuscripts of Father Gerónimo Boscana."
19. Boscana, *Chinigchinich*, 34.
20. Identifying the location of Povuu'nga has produced considerably controversy among anthropologists and archeologists. See Harrington's note 77, in Boscana, *Chinigchinich*, 148–50, but see also Boxt and Rabb, "Pavunga and Point Conception," 43–67 and following discussions, 67–91.

in the San Bernardino Mountains, the Santa Ana River began its southwesterly meandering until emptying into the Pacific Ocean near Newport Bay. A surface river, it usually flowed year-round. The Los Angeles River originated in the San Fernando Valley at Encino and was only a few feet wide. It flowed eastward mostly below the surface, along the base of the Santa Monica Mountains. Then the river turned southeast and followed the eastern terminus of the mountains. Debauching through two hills at the Glendale Narrows, the river entered the coastal plain. Here it rose to the surface and flowed year-round for part of its journey until it disappeared underground at Arroyo del Pueblo. On occasion, it turned west and south and emptied into the ocean at Ballona Creek on Santa Monica Bay, but for years the river failed to reach the bay. Numerous marshes, shallow ponds, and lakes covered a large area of the coastal plain. Tidal lagoons formed at the mouth at San Pedro Bay.[21]

Cottonwoods, several species of willows, and sycamores grew in abundance, and under them alder, hackberry, and shrubs. Roses, native grapes, briars, bramble, and California blackberries flourished. Oaks and walnuts grew where the river was relatively consistent. But the water-loving willows and cottonwood trees emerged where the floodwaters spread over the land. Cattail and bulrushes grew in the soggy soil where the river overflowed. Reedy plants such as pickleweed, cord grass, and leadwort spread out over the mud flats when the river reached the sea.[22]

A variety of wildlife benefited from the river and its vegetation. Deer, antelope, coyotes, gray fox, and mountain lions were prevalent. Grizzly bears left the mountains for the fish that spawned in the river and its streams. Hawks, condors, cuckoos, owls, vireos, and woodpeckers nested near the banks. Muskrats fed on the *tules*. Geese, ducks, and swans found sustenance on the river, as did at least seven species of fish, including the southern steelhead and pacific lamprey, both marine fish, and freshwater species,

---

21. Gumprecht, *The Los Angeles River*, 9–20. See also, Crandell, "Río Porciúncula," and Bowman, "The Names of the Los Angeles and San Gabriel Rivers."
22. Gumprecht, *Los Angeles River*, 8–20.

including the Pacific rook lamprey, arroyo chub, and three-spine stickleback.[23]

Clearly, the Tongva lived in a more diversified region than did the Cahuillas and Serranos, but they also resided directly in the path of Spanish intruders. Tongva traditional culture was immediately put under enormous stress, but ironically, those responsible for the stress left us much valuable information about that culture. Explorers, soldiers, and missionaries wrote extensively about Tongva economics, politics, ceremonies, and conflicts.

In the early 1770s Pedro Fages detected a distinction between Indians residing inland and those living along the Santa Ana River near the coast. The former, he found "rather dark, dirty, of bad figure, short of stature, and slovenly," but the latter were "fair, have light hair, and are good looking." The coastal Indians were "equipped for fishing; they have their rafts of reeds on which to go out to sea, and by means of these the Indians . . . communicate with the islanders of San Clemente and Santa Bárbara."[24] According to Father Gerónimo Boscana, the Indians who lived inland tended to relocate during different seasons, "on account of the temperature or want of food," but those living near the ocean "seldom moved because their maintenance was derived from the sea; and they were unlike the others who subsisted entirely upon the fruits and seeds of the fields."[25] Those residing along the rivers were equally as sedentary.

The government of the Indians also drew comments. According to Fages, each village was "subject to a despotic chief, who is the highest arbiter of peace and war; to him everyone contributes a part of what seeds and eatables he possesses."[26] Boscana, however, observed more complexity: "The form of government of these Indians was monarchical. They acknowledged but one head,

---

23. Ibid., 25–26.
24. Fages, *Description*, 21–23. For ethnographic information on the Tongva/Gabrielino, consult McCawley, *The First Angelinos*. An earlier study, dated but still useful, is Johnston, *California's Gabrielino Indians*.
25. Boscana, *Chinigchinich*, 65; See also Hudson, "Proto-Gabrielino Patterns of Territorial Organization," 52, 61–70.
26. Fages, *Description*, 21.

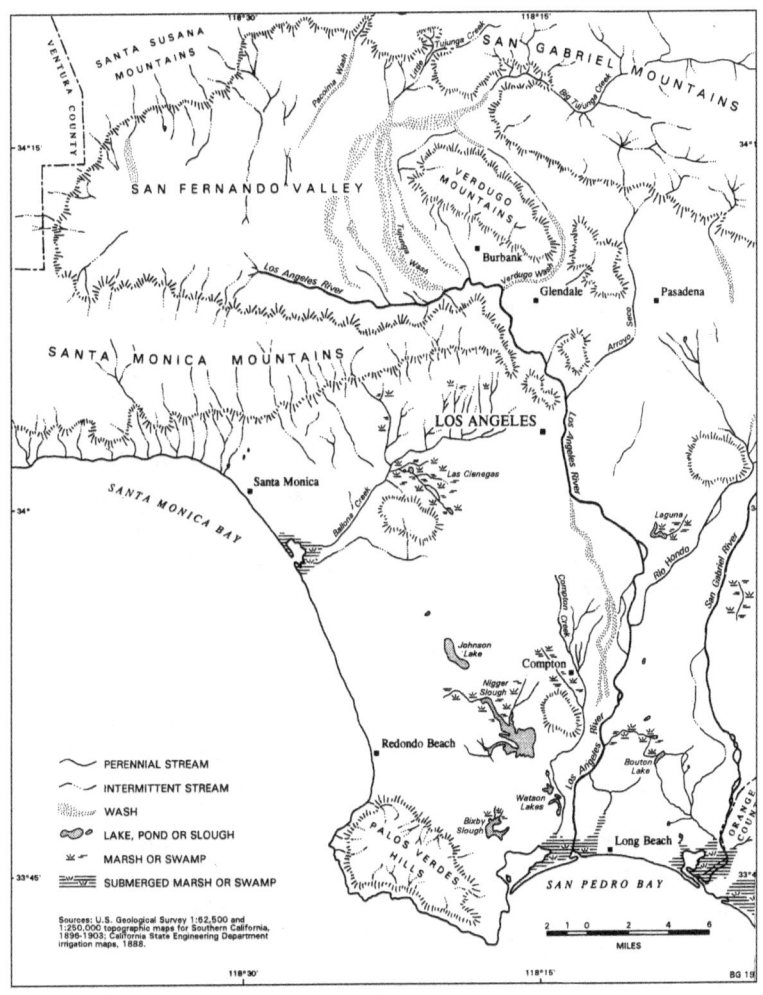

Los Angeles River Drainage Area As It Once Was.
Map by Blake Gumprecht; used with permission. *Reproduced from*
The Los Angeles River: Its Life, Death, and Possible Rebirth
(*Baltimore: Johns Hopkins University Press, 1999*).

and the puplem, or general council. This body served as a kind of check to the will of the captain, and without its sanction he could do nothing of importance."[27] Neither Spaniard observed a governmental structure that politically unified the Tongva. Instead, they correctly saw numerous village governments, each one led by a person they called a "captain" or "chief," but better identified as a headman (*tomyaar*) with limited powers.[28]

Domestic quarrels, noted Boscana, were infrequent, presumably because the Indians in each village were "all related to each other, and the fathers frequently exhorted their children to be good." Nevertheless, when a crime was committed, the puplem, not the tomyaar, ensured that justice was served:

> The case having been declared in the council, an elder was appointed to make public the crime, which he did by crying most bitterly throughout the *ranchería*, saying that "so and so has said or done this or that to our captain;" that "Chinigchinich is very angry and wished to chastise us by sending upon us a plague, of which we may all die. Arm yourselves, then, both old and young, to kill the offender, so that by presenting him dead to Chinigchinich he may be appeased and not kill us." This was repeated several times throughout the town. As the Indians were easily influenced, they immediately went out armed in search of the delinquent, and when they fell in with him they dispatched him, and together with the arrows with which they killed him he was borne to the presence of Chinigchinich. The parents of the deceased were permitted afterwards to take possession of the body, and perform the accustomed ceremony of burning it.

Although the puplem was predominant in the administration of justice, the tomyaar exerted considerable authority in determining when to hunt, collect, hold feasts, make war and peace, and settle differences with neighboring villages.[29]

As recounted by Hugo Reid, a Scot who recorded the oral traditions of the Tongva, "Animosity between persons or families was of long duration, particularly between those of different tribes.

---

27. Boscana, *Chinigchinich*, 41.
28. Regarding the government of these Indians, consult McCawley, *The First Angelinos*, 90–94. According to McCawley, in some areas the Tongva may have formed multi-village communities, although he admits that the evidence of such is limited. See also Gifford, "Clans and Moieties in Southern California."
29. Boscana, *Chinigchinich*, 42–43.

These feuds descended from father to son until it was impossible to tell how many generations. They were, however, harmless in themselves, being merely a war of songs, composed and sung against the conflicting party, and they were all of the most obscene and indecent language imaginable."[30] If, however, "a quarrel ensued between two parties, the chief of the Lodge took cognizance in the case, and decided according to the testimony produced. But, if a quarrel occurred between parties of distinct Lodges, each chief heard the witnesses produced by his own people; and then, associated with the chief of the opposite side, they passed sentence. In case they could not agree, an impartial chief was called in, who heard the statements made by both, and he alone decided. There was no appeal from his decision."[31]

Considerable discussion and diplomacy proceeded military action. Boscana wrote:

> Whenever a captain determined to make war upon another chief, he called together the puplem and revealed to them his desire to make war upon such a town for reasons which he explained, and it was discussed by the council whether they were sufficient of themselves to conquer. If sensible of their inferiority, some other friendly tribes were invited to join with them. To these they sent presents of as costly a kind as their treasury would admit and if aid was secured, then the day was fixed upon to assemble for battle. All this was conducted secretly but, nevertheless, the parties to be attacked were generally warned of their danger and, of course, prepared for the conflict.[32]

The men captured were immediately killed and the women and children taken prisoner were either sold or kept as slaves.[33] Reid

---

30. Reid, "Los Angeles County Indians," in *Los Angeles Star*, April 10, 1852; Heizer, ed., *The Indians of Los Angeles County*, 37–39. These letters were first published in the *Los Angeles Star* in 1852 and have been reprinted several times. Of particular importance is the 1885 publication because of the editor's explanatory notes and because the letters were copied directly from Reid's manuscript. The last ten letters are missing, however. See Hoffman, ed., "Hugo Ried's Account." Hoffman misspelled Reid's name. A brief history of the letters is in Heizer, ed., *Indians of Los Angeles County*, 1–5. I have used the original letters from the *Los Angeles Star*.
31. Reid, "Los Angeles County Indians," in *Los Angeles Star*, March 6, 1852; Heizer, ed., *Indians of Los Angeles County*, 15–16.
32. Boscana, *Chinigchinich*, 69–70.
33. Ibid., 70.

noted that "all prisoners of war, after being tormented in a most cruel manner, were invariably put to death. This was done in the presence of all the chiefs, for as war was declared and conducted by a council of the whole, so they in common had to attend to the execution of their enemies."[34] Boscana insisted that wars were never fought for territorial conquest, only for revenge, but Fages claimed that disputes arose over "the fruits of the earth and women."[35] Although war was largely undertaken by men, the efforts of women were crucial to its success. Preparation for war led to an increase in labor expended by women. They had to produce large amounts of *pinole* and prepare other provisions.[36]

Food procurement as a mode of labor was generally divided by gender. As Boscana explained, the women were "obliged to gather seeds in the fields, prepare them for cooking, and to perform all the meanest offices, as well as the most laborious."[37] Preparing the acorn was one of those tasks. Reid noted that the acorns,

> after being divested of their shell, were dried, and pounded in stone mortars, put into filters of willow twigs worked into a concave form, and raised on little mounds of sand, which were lined inside with a coating of two inches of sand; water added and mixed up—Then filled up again and again with more water, at first hot, then cold, until all the tannin and bitter principle was extracted. The residue was then collected and washed free of any sandy particles it might contain. On settling, the water was poured off. After being well boiled, it became a sort of mush, and was eaten when cold.

Reid also described the preparation of a favorite seed: "Chia, which is a small, gray, oblong seed, was procured from a plant apparently of the thistle kind, having a number of seed vessels on a straight stalk, one above the other, like wild sage. This, roasted and ground into meal, was eaten with cold water, being of a glutinous consistency, and very cooling. Pepper grass seed was also much used, the

---

34. Reid, "Los Angeles County Indians," in *Los Angeles Star*, March 6, 1852; Heizer, ed., *Indians of Los Angeles County*, 15.
35. Boscana, *Chinigchinich*, 69; Fages, *Description*, 12.
36. Boscana, *Chinigchinich*, 43.
37. Ibid., 56

tender stalks of wild sage, several kinds of berries and a number of roots. All their food was taken either cold or nearly so."[38]

Added to the women's labor of procuring and processing wild plants was that of manufacturing a variety of products. Women wove baskets of varying size in which to collect "seeds, pine nuts, madroña berries, acorns, etc," recalled Fages.[39] They "fashioned a kind of cloak out of the skins of rabbits," wrote Boscana. "These skins were twisted into a kind of rope that was sewed together so as to conform to the size of the person for whom it was intended, and the front was adorned with a fringe, composed of grass, which reached down to the knees." Beads and other ornaments adorned the collar of the garment.[40] Reid discussed traditional manufacturing:

> Hemp was made from nettles, and manufactured into nets, fishing lines, thread, &c. Needles, fish-hooks, awls and many other articles were made of either bone or shell, although for cutting up meat, a knife made of cane was invariably used. Mortars and pestles were made of granite, about sixteen inches wide at the top, ten at the bottom, ten inches high and two thick. Sharp stones and *perseverance* were the only things used in their manufacture, and so skillfully did they combine the two, that their work was always remarkably uniform....
>
> The pots to cook in were made of soapstone of about an inch in thickness, and procured from the Indians of Santa Catalina; the cover used was of the same material.... The vessels in use for liquid were roughly made of rushes and plastered outside and in with bitumen or pitch, called by them *sanot*.[41]

Boscana detected a division of labor based on age and wealth: "The old men and the poorer class devoted a portion of the day to constructing domestic utensils, their bows and arrows, and the several instruments used in making their baskets, likewise nets of various sizes, which were used for sundry purposes, such as for catching fish and wild fowl, and for carrying heavy burdens on

---

38. Reid, "Los Angeles County Indians," in *Los Angeles Star*, March 13, 1852; Heizer, ed., *Indians of Los Angeles County*, 22–23.
39. Fages, *Description*, 22.
40. Boscana, *Chinigchinich*, 56.
41. Reid, "Los Angeles County Indians," in *Los Angeles Star*, April 24, 1852; Heizer, ed., *Indians of Los Angeles County*, 44. The pestles and mortars are also called *manos* and *metates*.

their backs. The latter were fastened by a strap passed across the forehead. In like manner, the females used them for carrying their infants."[42] Fages noted that the men wove nets for carrying food and to bind about the body. They also made bows and arrows and "a kind of war club of tough wood in the shape of a well-balanced cutlass, which they use in war and in hunting conies, hares, deer, coyotes, and antelope, throwing it so far and with such certain aim, that they rarely fail to break the bones of such of these animals as come within range."[43] Most of the animals in the region were hunted, the exception being the rattlesnake. "A few eat the bear," wrote Reid, "but in general it is rejected, on superstitious grounds."[44]

Because of the abundance of game in the region and the hunting expertise of the Tongva, a priest acknowledged that they do not regulate their day by hours: "When they feel like it they go out and hunt and return towards evening, and if they do not, they spend the whole day in idleness."[45] That the men could spend time in "idleness" suggest a mode of food procurement that allowed them (the men, not the women) to work intermittently, to engage in activities associated with leisure time, and to be, at least temporarily, free of economic cares. Unlike the Desert Cahuillas who practiced mixed economy by both procuring and producing food, the Tongva had no need to plant, tend, and harvest domestic crops.[46] But like the Cahuillas, they burned swaths of land to maintain grasslands and thus to ensure the sprouting of wild seeds.[47]

---

42. Boscana, *Chinigchinich*, 56.
43. Fages, *Description*, 22. The weapon was probably the *makána*, or boomerang, used mainly to hunt rabbits and thrown near the ground. See Hoffman, ed., "Hugo Ried's Account," 29–30n7.
44. Reid, "Los Angeles County Indians," in *Los Angeles Star*, March 13, 1852; Heizer, ed., *Indians of Los Angeles County*, 22.
45. Geiger and Meighan, eds., *As The Padres Saw Them, 1813–1815*, 48. For a discussion of leisure time among hunting and gathering peoples consult Sahlins, *Stone Age Economics*, 13–14.
46. Social evolutionist Jared Diamond contends that factors other than an abundance of natural resources prevented hunting and gathering peoples from becoming agriculturalists. See his *Guns, Germs, and Steel*, 153–54.
47. McCawley, *The First Angelinos*, 115–16. For a study of Indian burning, consult Lewis, "Patterns of Indian Burning in California."

Of more interest to the Spaniards than Indians managing the land was how they managed their social relations, especially marriage and divorce. "We understand from these heathens that they each have only a single wife with the exception of two of their chiefs, who have two," wrote Juan Crespí.[48] The priests at Mission San Gabriel reported that "the Indians entered into no contracts regarding marriage. . . . At most, the pretendents gave . . . beads to the bride-to-be and . . . to her parents. If this gift was accepted, the groom and bride became man and wife, in fact, immediately. They remained as such only as long as they desired, that is, as long as both were satisfied and lived in harmony or until the man found another woman who pleased him more."[49] According to Reid, "If a woman proved unfaithful to her husband, and he caught her in the act, he had a right to kill or wound her without any intervention of chief or tribe. And any one hurting *him* made it a crime, for which he stood amenable to the captain. But more generally practiced was the injured husband informed the wife's paramour that *he was at liberty to keep her*. He then went and took possession of the lover's spouse and lived with her. The exchange was considered legal, and no resource was left to the offending party but submission."[50]

Males also married males, but as explained by Boscana the act was more about labor than love: "It was publicly done, but without the forms and ceremonies already described in their marriage contracts with the females. Whilst yet in infancy, they were selected and instructed as they increased in years in all the duties of the women—in their mode of dress, of walking, and dancing; so that in almost every particular, they resembled females. Being more robust than the women, they were better able to perform the arduous duties of the wife, and for this reason, they were often selected by the chiefs and others, and on the day of the wedding a grand feast was given."[51]

---

48. Brown, trans. and ed., *A Description of Distant Roads*, 355.
49. Geiger and Meighan, eds., *As The Padres Saw Them*, 65.
50. Reid, "Los Angeles County Indians," in *Los Angeles Star*, March 6, 1852; Heizer, ed., *Indians of Los Angeles County*, 16.
51. Boscana, *Chinigchinich*, 54.

Whether undertaken by males or females, considerable labor was expended in the production of medicines. The priests at Mission San Fernando recorded that,

> all observe the same customs with regard to curative methods. The best known are the following: *Pespibat* which is composed of wild tobacco, lime, and urine mixed together and fermented. This they take to relieve pains in the stomach and to heal wounds. *Chuchupate* in their idiom called *Cayat* is an herb, each stem or stalk of which has three round leaves with a spike in the middle. The flower is white. They chew the root and rub themselves where they feel pain. They use this also for headache. With the anise plant they purge themselves. With the herb called *Pasmo* they relieve pain of various toothaches. When boiled it is taken to sweat and when ground it is used like snuff tobacco. The *Chilicote* called *Yjaihix* in Indian, is toasted and mixed with the powder of crushed stone called *Bafa*, in Indian *Paheasa* and is then used to remove inflammation, to remove film from the eye, induce menstruation, to heal wounds, to cure urinary maladies; and when boiled it is used to bring about perspiration. Those... who are poisoned or crippled, cleanse themselves with powdered alum stone and copperas... mixed. When they feel oppressed they bleed themselves with a flint. When they are restless they refresh themselves with water derived from the bark of the ash tree. When they suffer pains in the side they put red ants in water and apply them alive externally at the same time striking themselves with nettles. They do not drink thermal waters but they bathe in them.[52]

The Indians extracted lime from sea shells and mixed it with wild tobacco that had been pounded into a substance. When consumed in this condition, it was nauseous and intoxicating, but when kneaded into thick cakes, it was less disagreeable. Its design was to clean the stomach and bladder.[53] Also, to ensure good health, the Indians, especially those residing near rivers and the ocean bathed daily, usually in the morning.[54]

When someone died, they placed a pot, a basket, an otter skin and beads in a deep hole. Then the corpse would be positioned on these items and covered with dirt. According to the missionaries

---

52. Geiger and Meighan, eds., *As The Padres Saw Them*, 73. For a discussion of how a neighboring people dealt with illness, see Timbrook, "Virtuous Herbs."
53. Reid, "Los Angeles County Indians," in *Los Angeles Star*, April 3, 1852; Heizer, ed., *Indians of Los Angeles County*, 33.
54. Boscana, *Chinigchinich*, 51.

at San Fernando, "Immediately they send notice to the rancherías of the district so that all, old, young, and children may paint themselves for the general feast during which they serve all kinds of pinole, meat, etc. Thereupon the chief earnestly commands all present never to mention the name of the deceased lest he come to haunt them. All must come weeping. Finally, they burn the hut and everything the deceased possessed."[55] Reid concurred: "If the deceased were the head of a family, or a favorite son, the hut in which he died was burned up, as likewise all of his personal effects, reserving only some article or another or a lock of hair." [56]

Some of the deceased were honored in a mourning ceremony. In fact, one of the principal functions of their calendar was to determine when to commemorate the death of an important person. As recorded by Boscana, "At the time of the death of a captain, or one of the *puplem*, . . . a *pul* observed the moon's aspect, also the month in which the death occurred. In the following year, in the same month, when the moon's aspect was the same, they celebrated the anniversary."[57]

Gambling and sporting events also engaged their time. Reid noted that the Indians loved to play and gamble at *peon*:

> It consists of guessing in which hand a small piece of stick was held concealed by another. Four persons on a side composed a set, who sat opposite each other. They had their singers who were paid so much a game, and an umpire who kept count, held the stakes, settled disputes, and prevented cheating. He was paid so much a night, and had to provide the firewood. He was provided with fifteen counters, which were of reed and eight or ten inches long. The guessers never spoke, but giving the palm of the left hand a sharp slap with the right pointed with the finger to the side they guessed contained the peon. Those who guessed right, won the peon, and the others took a counter each, and so on, until they possessed all the counters or lost all the peones, when the opposite side took the counting part.
>
> The peon was white, of an inch or so in length; but they had also a black one, which to prevent fraud, they had to remove to the other hand

---

55. Geiger and Meighan, eds., *As The Padres Saw Them*, 97.
56. Reid, "Los Angeles County Indians," in *Los Angeles Star*, March 27, 1852; Heizer, ed., *Indians of Los Angeles County*, 31.
57. Boscana, *Chinigchinich*, 67.

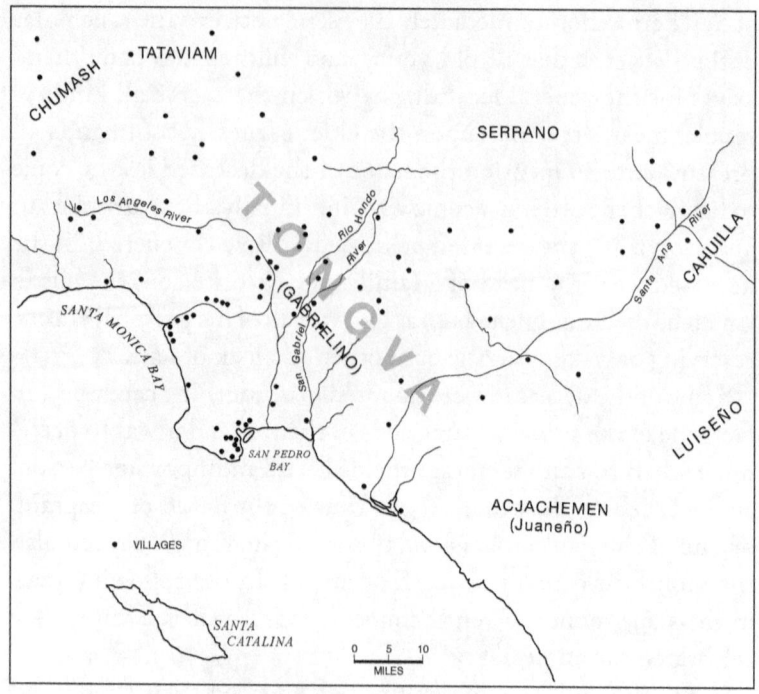

The Tongva and Their Neighbors, circa 1771.

on changing; so as always to retain one in each hand, to show when called upon.[58]

At one time or another, virtually all of the 14,500 Indians occupying the Los Angeles region attended or participated in games of peon.[59] As will become apparent, peon exhibited a remarkable persistence, outlasting many other aspects of the Indians' traditional culture destroyed or modified by waves of intruders.

58. Reid, "Los Angeles County Indians," in *Los Angeles Star*, May 1, 1852; Heizer, ed., *Indians of Los Angeles County*, 46–47. For an anthropologist's description of the game, see DuBois, "The Religion of the Luiseño Indians," 167–68.
59. The Tataviam numbered 1,000, the Tongva 5,000, the Serrano 1,500, and the Cahuilla 7,000. See O'Neil, "The Acjachemen in the Franciscan Mission System," M.A. thesis, California State University, Fullerton, 2002, 142–44. According to Hugo Reid, the Tongva resided in about forty villages. See Heizer, ed., *Indians of Los Angeles County*, 8. For the Tataviam, consult Johnson and Earle, "Tataviam Geography and Ethnohistory"; and King and Blackburn, "Tataviam."

CHAPTER 2

Missionary Intrusion

A month after establishing the first mission in Alta California at San Diego, Spaniards under the command of Gaspar de Portolá, on their way to Northern California, halted on July 28, 1769, at a river later called the Santa Ana. Because three earthquakes had struck the area, it was then appropriately named *El Dulcísimo Nombre de Jesús, del Río de los Temblores*. Father Juan Crespí noted in his journal that "along the edge of the river bed there are a great many grapevines and rose bushes; a great many catfish were seen in it, and there are a great many sand banks, showing what large floods it must carry. The bed is not deep, and the soldiers assured me it could be tapped farther up with no trouble, in order to irrigate all anyone could want of this handsome plain, whose soil is very good." In Crespí's estimation, the fertile soil and abundant water would produce enough grain "to supply, I will not say a city, but a province, with very excellent grazing all around."[1]

Crespí was also impressed with the local people, the Tongva. He described the fifty-four unarmed men who met his party as "well-behaved friendly heathens." The headman gave Portolá a string of shell beads and a net and received beads and a handkerchief in

---

1. Brown, trans. and ed., *A Description of Distant Roads*, 317, 321.

return. Evidently, the Indians saw in the Spaniards potential allies in their struggles against "mountain people" who wanted their land. The headman offered the Spaniards land from which they could harvest sage and procure bear meat and promised to build houses for them. Crespí promised to return "and build houses with them, and for God as well; and such tears of joy and happiness sprang to their chief's eyes as greatly touched the hearts of all of us present there, and I must sincerely admit that very gladly I would have remained with them."[2]

Once across the Santa Ana River, the Spaniards entered land overgrown with prickly pears and sage and then into an area covered with dry grass. They camped a short distance from a settlement, and that evening, noted Crespí, "the whole village came over, so that what with men and boys we counted about seventy souls of them, all very fine, well-behaved heathens like the ones at the river we last crossed, and we saw none of them carrying weapons." The following day the Spaniards continued to the northwest entering "a very wide-reaching, green, exceedingly spacious valley of dark, very level friable soil, all burnt off by the heathens." After about a league they came to a river running through a "green swamp very much clad in all sorts of plants and good grasses." Crespí also observed many "grapevines looking as though someone planted them here." More grapevines were found the next day "entwined in the trees and bearing very large clusters, cumin, and holythistles, all of it very tall, and many other kinds of weeds and plants that we did not recognize." Antelopes and rabbits were also observed and the scouts discovered large animal droppings.[3]

Continuing northwards, on July 31 the Spaniards came to a very large stream flowing through a swamp. The following day they sighted a few Indians who did not respond to their calls. But on August 2 at a river Crespí named *Nuestra Señora de los Angeles de la Porciúncula*, they encountered more friendly Indians. Crespí described the meeting:

---
2. Ibid., 317–19.
3. Ibid., 323–31.

At once on our reaching here, eight heathens came over from a good-sized village encamped at this pleasing spot among some trees. They came bringing two or three large bowls or baskets half full of very good sage, with other sorts of grass seeds that they consume; all brought their bows and arrows, but with the strings removed from the bows. In his hands their chief bore strings of shell beads of the sort that they use, and on reaching the camp they threw three handfuls of these beads at each of us. Some of the heathens came up smoking upon Indian pipes made of baked clay, and they blew three mouthfuls of smoke into the air toward each one of us. Then their chief made a speech, and they all sat down with us.

Indians and Spaniards exchanged presents—sage gruel for beads.[4]

When the Spanish returned to the area in August 1771 to establish a mission, they settled not among the friendly Indians on the Los Angeles River but among hostile ones some two leagues to the east on a river later called the Río Hondo.[5] The party consisted of ten soldiers who would serve as guards at the mission, four additional soldiers, four muleteers, and two priests.[6] Father Pedro Benito Cambón described the encounter with the Indians who,

> in full war-paint and brandishing their bows and arrows, with hostile gestures and blood-curdling yells, tried to prevent them from crossing the river. Our people finally fought their way to a chosen spot, dangerously pressed by the whole multitude of savages. And having dug themselves into fox-holes behind some bales and packing boxes as best they could (and as the exigency of the occasion demanded) the padres took out from one of the cases a canvas picture of Our Lady of Sorrows....
>
> At the sight of it they became as if transfixed in wonderment, and all of them threw their bows and arrows on the ground, as two "Tomeares" or Chiefs took from around their necks the necklaces they value so highly and are accustomed to wear in those distant lands, and placed them at the feet of the Sovereign Queen of the Angels.[7]

---

4. Ibid., 333–41.
5. Geiger, "The Building of Mission San Gabriel," 33. See also Bowman, "The Names of the Los Angeles and San Gabriel Rivers," 94–96.
6. Engelhardt, *San Gabriel Mission*, 3.
7. Quoted in Temple, "The Founding of San Gabriel Mission," 18–19. According to one interpretation, the Indians saw in the image of Our Lady of Sorrows visual similarities to their own spiritual beliefs. See Castillo, "Gender Status Decline" 69–70. See also Sandos, *Converting California*, 8–9.

Invitations were sent to neighboring villages. Soon to arrive were "increasing numbers of men, women, and children to view the painting of 'La Dolorosa,' bearing the little baskets of seeds which they proffered and laid at the feet of the Sovereign Lady."[8] On September 8, 1771, Fathers Cambón and Ángel Somera celebrated Mass and founded California's fourth mission—San Gabriel Arcángel. The Fathers hoped that "the pagans would not delay in embracing the sweet yoke of the law of the Gospel," as Father Francisco Palóu put it.[9] The next day the building of a palisade began, the local Indians cutting and carrying much of the timber used in its construction.

As at all the missions, the land officially granted by the government to the Church was extremely limited and extended no farther than the church buildings, cemetery, orchards, and vineyards. According to Spanish law, all lands beyond the immediate area, even where crops would be grown and stock raised, belonged to the Crown.[10] Moreover, Spanish military policy occasionally hindered religious strategy. Orders from Captain Pedro Fages reduced the number of soldiers at San Gabriel to ten and prohibited more than four or five Indians from entering the stockade at any one time, even though they always arrived without weapons. Cambón noted that once the corporal of the guard implemented the orders, the Indians grew restless and demanded "justice in the face of our apparent ingratitude. This should not have been their reward for helping us with our tasks, bringing us food and seeds during all this time, and entrusting their sons to us without any misgivings, for us to instruct them in the Holy Faith."[11]

After a soldier molested a wife of an important headman of a village on the Los Angeles River, Indians entered the compound,

---

8. Temple, "The Founding of San Gabriel Mission," 19. A scholar has suggested that the Indians use of wood, reeds, and mud helped shape the architecture of the first mission buildings. See Ettinger, "Hybrid Spaces."
9. Palóu, *Palóu's Life of Fray Junípero Serra*, 118–20.
10. Dwinelle, *The Colonial History of San Francisco*, 19–20. Despite its title, this important book contains in translation many of the documents of Spanish colonization throughout California.
11. Quoted in Temple, "The Founding of San Gabriel Mission," 21.

"wantonly plundering (something they had not dared up to this point)." Armed with clubs, they "threatened to attack us should we make any show of resistance." The guard quelled the demonstration, but fearing an outright attack, one of the priests journeyed south to the presidio at San Diego to plead their case to Captain Fages. Fages dismissed the priest by claiming that the Indians always acted this way and that they had nothing to fear.[12]

On October 9, 1771, a large number of Indians again entered the compound demanding food on threat of retaliation. They rounded up all the boys undergoing religious instruction, except five who concealed themselves in the Fathers' quarters. One of the boys, the oldest son of the headman, warned Cambón that they would return the next day and they would shoot him with arrows. And the following day Indians surrounded the compound, making offensive gestures. Some dispersed after the Spanish threatened to retaliate but others, recounted Cambón "made a tight knot at the very gates of the stockade." At that moment an Indian boy undergoing religious instruction dashed past the insurgents into the stockade, informing the Spaniards that in a nearby *cañada* a large number of armed Indians had assembled. They intended to attack the mission, stampede the horse herd, and kill the two soldiers guarding it. "With this report, muskets and other weapons were readied. All that remained to do was to warn the two with the horses and two other soldiers who were out in the brush looking for some stray cows."[13]

One of the soldiers searching for strays made it safely back to the stockade, but Indians fired on those guarding the horses. The soldiers returned fire, killing the headman and two other Indians. Corporal Aguilar and seven soldiers cut off the head of the dead leader and impaled it on the highest post of the stockade. That afternoon the corporal and seven men rode into a village to further intimidate the Indians. The few Indians with "the temerity of coming out of their huts to meet them, begged for peace,"

---
12. Ibid., 21–22.
13. Ibid., 22–23.

noted Cambón. "This was granted after the soldiers had taken away their bows and arrows and broken them to pieces."[14]

The following day the Spaniards awoke to plumes of smoke signals along the horizon. To present a united front to the Spaniards, Indians from several villages between the coast and the sierra, some ancient enemies, met to make peace. Others decided to ally themselves with the Spaniards. That day, recalled Cambón, "two chiefs came from the west to the mission to sue for peace, offering it on their own behalf. After several parleys and a good lecture which we gave them, along with gifts of beads and ribbons, they left, giving us many promises . . . of their future good conduct." Other Indians, however, assembled in a willow grove, a musket shot from the mission, and planned to attack on October 16. When a Spanish contingent from the south on its way to found another mission fortuitously arrived, the Indians dispersed. San Gabriel was saved. But according to Cambón, for months the Spaniards seldom saw an Indian except for "a boy hanging around and an adult of some 20 years, who from the start had become quite attached to us. The local rancheria moved away to another site far away from us."[15] According to Captain Fages, the Indians "learned a good lesson; they did not suffer themselves to be seen for a long time."[16]

More than twenty men of the Spanish contingent that had saved the mission remained at San Gabriel. Most were soldiers. They refused to work, disobeyed the corporal of the guard, and argued among themselves. They also damaged relations with the local Indians. As recounted by Father Junípero Serra,

> Six or more soldiers would usually head out on horseback in the morning, with or without the corporal's permission. They would go to the rancherías, even though they were many leagues away. When men and women would spot them, the Indians would break into a run. According to the Fathers, the gentiles had repeatedly complained to them that the soldiers were skillful in lassoing the necks of cows and mules and they would lasso Indian women in the same way for they were fodder for

---

14. Ibid., 23–25.
15. Ibid., 25–26.
16. Fages, *Description*, 18–19.

their unbridled lust. On occasions when the Indian men tried to defend the women, a number of them were shot dead.

When confronted by the priests about these incidents, the corporal would respond: "If the gentiles make such statements, let them prove them!"[17]

The ramifications of the conflict extended far beyond the Los Angeles region. In particular it postponed the founding of Mission San Buenaventura, which was the goal of the Spanish contingent. In May 1773 Serra acknowledged that "it had not been established to this day. I must confess that had I been present, even the San Gabriel Mission would have been abandoned, because I would have ordered the Fathers to return to San Diego. If we are not allowed to be in touch with the gentiles, what business have we, or what would hold us, in such a place?"[18] The founding of San Buenaventura was delayed for a decade.[19]

On October 2, 1773, an expedition arrived at San Gabriel. When it departed a few days later, six Cochimí families and six Cochimí unmarried young men (Indians from Baja California) remained behind. The missionaries placed them in charge of the recently baptized local Indians, and together they began digging irrigation ditches, erecting brush dams, and planting crops of corn, wheat, and beans. Difficulties emerged immediately. The Cochimíes could not communicate with the Tongva, refused to intermarry with them, and resented living next to them in tiny huts.[20]

Inside the stockade, the Cochimíes constructed a church, quarters for the Fathers and soldiers, offices, and granaries. All were made of poles with tule roofs.[21] In a letter to a colleague, Father Fermín Francisco de Lasuén acknowledged the importance of these Indians. It was the Cochimíes

> who put the mission on its way to prosperity; and to their toil is due if not all, at least the greater part, of what the mission produces and what

---

17. Junípero Serra to Antonio María de Bucareli y Ursúa, Mexico City, May 21, 1773, in Tibesar, trans. and ed., *Writings of Junípero Serra*, 1: 363. New translation by Rose Marie Beebe.
18. Ibid., 361.
19. Engelhardt, *San Gabriel Mission*, 8.
20. Street, *Beasts of the Field*, 16; See also, Street, "First Farmworkers, First *Braceros*."
21. Palóu, *Historical Memoirs*, 3: 219–20.

it needs for its sustenance. Despite all this, they are treated like stepchildren. Not only do they fail to receive the big returns they were promised when they were recruited, but they work much harder and receive less in return than in their own country. It becomes difficult, and some deem it impossible, to induce them to settle down, or to get the single to marry. And there are many of these, and many families, too, that have no place they can call home. They are awaiting the establishment of a mission to which they can belong. And consequently, far from improving their own lot as a result of their labors, they continue to bear the heaviest of burdens, that of giving a start to a new settlement.

Furthermore, if no remedy was found, "some day they may begin to complain about me and attribute their misfortunes to me."[22]

Pedro Fages mentioned in 1774 that gentiles and neophytes resided in one village, the Cochimíes in another, and both were located outside the stockade:

> At a short distance is the village in which the unconverted natives and the new Christians live; the latter attend regularly at Mass and the recital of the doctrine, and some of the former come so that the missionary fathers may catechise them. Close to the same stockade there have been constructed a few small houses for the five families of reduced Indians which the reverend father president brought from [Lower] California for the purpose of employing them in tilling the ground and sowing wheat. There is a quantity of that grain here sufficient not alone for support of the mission, but as well for supplying the new converts; for having, as they do, good fields and abundance of running water, they can sow all that they like, and, indeed, wheat, corn, and beans have given very satisfactory results in the tests which have been made.[23]

By this time, Father Palóu had concluded that the mission had enough seeds to grow more crops "with which to feed the new Christians and attract the heathen. This will be a great inducement, as the Indians are very poor, on account of the scarcity of wild seeds and game. And they lack fish because they are about

---

22. Fermín Francisco de Lasuén to Francisco Pangua, Monterey, August 3, 1775, in Kenneally, trans. and ed., *Writings of Fermín Francisco de Lasuén*, 1: 49–50.
23. Fages, *Description*, 19. To some, this passage refers to the mission after it was moved. But it must have written before the mission was relocated, because Fages's manuscript was not published until 1775. Moreover, had Fages visited the mission after relocation, it seems likely he would have mentioned this development.

eight leagues distant from the beach. This distance is all level country populated with many villages which maintain among themselves constant wars, making it impossible for them to go to fish."[24]

Palóu seems to have concluded that poor, isolated Indians were susceptible to conversion. But as Father Pedro Font explained, rules were to be followed:

> The method which the fathers observe in the conversion is not to oblige anyone to become a Christian, admitting only those who voluntarily offer themselves, and this they do in the following manner: Since these Indians are accustomed to live in the fields and the hills like beasts, the fathers require that if they wish to be Christians they shall no longer go to the forest, but must live in the mission; and if they leave, ... they [the soldiers] will go seek them and will punish them. With this they began to catechize the heathen who voluntarily come, teaching them to make the sign of the cross and other things necessary, and if they persevere in the catechism for two or three months and in the same frame of mind, when they are instructed they proceed to baptise them.[25]

Hugo Reid, who lived at the mission in the 1840s, painted a much darker picture of incorporation and conversion. Soldiers or neophytes often went on recruiting expeditions to villages where they either persuaded or forced individuals to return with them to the mission. There "the men were instructed to throw their bows and arrows at the feet of the Priest, and make due submission.— The infants were then baptized, as were also all children under eight years of age; the former were left with their mothers, but the latter kept apart from all communication with their parents. The consequence was, first the women consented to the rite and received it, for the love they bore their offspring; and finally the males gave way for the purpose of enjoying once more, the society of wife and family." Reid claimed that none understood the ritual and those who received it lost status with their people. "They had no more idea that they were worshiping God than an unborn child has of Astronomy." Their religious knowledge "consisted in being

---

24. Palóu, *Historical Memoirs*, 3: 221.
25. Font, *Font's Complete Diary*, 179.

able to cross themselves, under an impression it was something connected with hard work and still harder blows. Baptism was called by them *soyna*, 'being bathed', and strange to say, was looked upon, although such a simple ceremony, as being ignominious and degrading."[26]

After baptism the Fathers usually allowed adult neophytes to leave the mission for a specified number of days to hunt, gather, and visit relatives in their native villages. As a rule they did not fail to return and occasionally brought with them kin who remained because of the example set by the neophytes or because, as Father Font honestly admitted, they were "attracted by the *pozole*, which they like better than their herbs and the foods of the mountains; and so these Indians are usually caught by the mouth."[27]

By the end of 1774 nineteen Indians had died but the Fathers had baptized 116 souls, including children, and had married nineteen couples. Two of those marriages were between neophyte women and gentile men.[28] Mateo was baptized at the age of thirty-five or thirty-six on June 6, 1774. Selecting which of his several wives to wed in the Christian ceremony presented a problem that was overcome when he chose a woman later known as Francisca. Mateo was the headman of the village of 'Ahwiinga, located in the Puente Hills.[29] Probably because of his conversion, 21 men, 31 women, and 136 children from 'Ahwiinga received baptism between 1774 and 1802.[30]

During 1774 the mission's stock increased to 65 head of cattle, 66 sheep, 34 goats, 18 pigs, 4 breeding mares, 8 colts, 7 tame horses, and 16 saddle and pack mules. But that year the Indians sowed only 6 *fanegas* of wheat and harvested 90 fanegas. The 13 *almudes* of corn and 7 of beans they planted resulted in 240 and 30 fanegas respectively.[31] Construction projects also lagged, probably because

---

26. Reid, "Los Angeles County Indians," in *Los Angeles Star*, June 19, 1852; Heizer, ed., *Indians of Los Angeles County*, 74–77.
27. Font, *Font's Complete Diary*, 180–81.
28. Junípero Serra to Antonio María de Bucareli y Ursúa, Monterey February 5, 1775, in Tibesar, trans. and ed., *Writings of Junípero Serra*, 2: 231.
29. Johnston, *California's Gabrielino Indians*, 143; McCawley, *The First Angelinos*, 45–46.
30. Merriam, "Village Names," 104.
31. Serra to Bucareli, February 5, 1775, 229–31.

the missionaries intended to move the mission to the north where crops were already being grown. From December 1773 to December 1774, Indians constructed only two buildings and they were of poles. One housed a forge, the other stored corn.[32]

Relocation was achieved in May 1775, the abandoned area becoming known as *Misión Vieja*. The Fathers wrote that the new location had "an oak grove quite close which is very advantageous for obtaining timber and firewood, and is within sight of a great plain where the soil is not of the best quality for in part it is very sandy and rocky, but with the irrigation ditch which is very serviceable, the land will fructify."[33] Font arrived in January 1776 and was impressed with the ditch: "After dinner I went with Father Sánchez to see the creek from which they made the acequia for this mission of San Gabriel, and with which it has the best of conveniences. For, besides the fact that the acequia is adequate, and passes in front of the house of the fathers and of the little huts of the Christian Indians who compose this new mission . . . , it dominates all the plains of the immediate vicinity, which are suitable for planting or for crops." Font observed fat cows that "give much and rich milk," from which cheese was made and "very good butter."[34]

Although oaks and other trees suitable for construction and fire wood were in abundance, the area lacked limestone. Font hoped that "by careful search it will be found and will make possible the improvement of the buildings, which at present are partly adobe, but chiefly of logs and tule." One structure contained the quarters of the missionaries and a granary. "Somewhat apart from this building there is a rectangular shed which serves as a church, and near this another which is the guardhouse, as they call it, or the quarters of the soldiers, eight in number who serve the mission as guard; and finally, some little huts of tule which are the houses of the Indians, between which and the house of the fathers the acequia runs."[35]

The mission became agriculturally prosperous so rapidly that only two years after relocation it could export surplus products

---

32. Ibid., 229.
33. Quoted in Geiger, "The Building of Mission San Gabriel," 34.
34. Font, *Font's Complete Diary*, 177.
35. Ibid., 177–78.

to less productive missions. In 1777 it sent the following to Mission San Diego: 24 fanegas of wheat (12 for planting and 12 for consumption), ⅕ of a fanega of barley for sowing, 3 fanegas of beans, and a large quantity of onions, garlic, tomatoes, and chili. Forty fanegas of corn were designated specifically for the mission's neophytes.[36] This productivity was achieved by an Indian population that would not exceed 400 until 1779.[37]

Whether the Fathers yet possessed the "training manual," *Libro de los secretos de agricultura, casa de campo y pastores*, is not known, but in time it reached San Gabriel. Printed in Madrid in 1761 from a manuscript written over a century earlier, it contained instructions on how to establish agriculture and manufacturing and how to manage laborers. Another book on that topic, *Agricultura general*, published in Madrid in 1777, also reached California. It dealt with much of what the farmer needed to know, from selecting the soil to storing the products.[38] Although not designed specifically to change Indians economically, the manuals assisted the Fathers in their efforts to transform the Tongva from a food-procuring people to a food-producing people.

The Indians' vast knowledge of harvesting and processing wild foods probably allowed for a relatively easy transition to the planting and tending of domestic ones. And because the Indians continued to harvest wild foods, a certain amount of labor continuity was maintained between the pre- and post-contact periods. Food procurement, in other words, supported food production. Each season saw the Tongva engage in both traditional and imposed activities. During the winter they gathered acorns and planted wheat. During the summer they harvested the maguey plant and seeded corn. Pine nuts matured and the wheat was threshed that season as well. In autumn, when the peaches ripened, they collected the sweet resin they called the *guautta*.[39]

---

36. Webb, *Indian Life*, 85.
37. The Indian population of the mission in 1779 was 409. See Jackson, *Indian Population Decline*, 172.
38. Ibid., 54; Coronel, *Tales of Mexican California*, 104n2; Bancroft, *California Pastoral*, 237.
39. Geiger and Meighan, eds., *As The Padres Saw Them*, 81.

In December and January, but sometimes as early as November, the neophytes sowed wheat and barley. In March, April, and May, and sometimes in June, they planted corn, beans, peas, lentils, squash, cantaloupes, and watermelons. Barley was harvested in May and June, wheat in July and August. Indians separated corn, beans, peas, and lentils from their husks by thrashing them with sticks and stored them in dry, secure places. Corn, secured in granaries, was shelled by hand for making tamales, bread, and tortillas. Children were perpetually engaged in the capturing, trapping, and hunting of weevils, rats, mice, squirrels, and gophers, whose populations may have increased after the mission was established.[40]

Prior to incorporation the needs of the Tongva household largely determined where and when to hunt, fish, and gather and for how long. The products of their labor, moreover, were achieved by the tools they owned and manufactured themselves. Reciprocity was the mode of inter-family and intra-village distribution. But once they became members of the mission, they were subjected to a labor regime over which they had little control and the results of their labor went into a common pool to be distributed by those in charge. Those of a higher status taught the others new skills and the use of new tools they did not own. Enrolled in what amounted to an industrial training school, many neophytes nevertheless eagerly and often easily mastered new crafts.[41] The equipment with which they had to work included forges, anvils, carpenter's and cartwright's tools, coal-pit axes, large ironclad hoes for cultivating vines, shoemaker's awls, sheep-shearing scissors, wire and blades for cutting soap, scales, measures, funnels, pincers, compasses, hoes, axes, adzes, sickles, hammers, files, picks, plowshares, and plow points.[42]

---

40. Lugo, "Life of a Rancher," 228–29.
41. For more on food procurement and production, consult Sweet, "Ibero-American Frontier Mission," 15–16.
42. Perissinotto, Rudolph, and Miller, eds., *Documenting Everyday Life*, 32.

By 1786 Spanish artisans had trained enough Indians to allow the Fathers to send twelve of them to Santa Bárbara to assist in the construction of a presidio. By May they had helped in the manufacturing of twenty thousand adobe bricks.[43] The process consisted of tossing soil and straw into a trough built of boards. Water was then added to bring the mass to some consistency. Stripped of their clothing, except for a breechclout, Indians trod the mud and straw until the whole was thoroughly mixed. They carried the mixture in leather buckets to wooden molds, poured it in, then tapped and leveled it off. The frame was lifted and the adobe bricks were left to dry under the watchful eyes of Indian boys whose job was to protect the bricks from animals. After a number of days in the sun and after they had been turned frequently, the bricks were ready for use.[44]

Retired soldiers and blacksmiths Francisco Sinova and Santiago Moreno had settled at the mission in 1785 and 1791, respectively, and probably passed on their knowledge to at least four neophytes.[45] Felipe was from the village of Yakit; Juan Capistrano and Sabino Pomasaquimbot were from Tuyubit; and Pedro was from Guaspez.[46] Late the following year, Antonio Domingo Enríquez, one of twenty artisans the Spanish government sent to California, arrived at San Gabriel. He made looms, spinning wheels, warping frames, and combs. He taught the neophyte women how to card and spin and how to weave wool cloth, blankets, and cotton shirting.[47]

Neophyte men mastered other skills. As recalled by José del Carmen Lugo, "The plows were of wood and were made by the Indians themselves or by other persons in this country. At the tip there was a bit of iron. The plow had a long beam which was joined to the yoke which united the oxen. It was fastened to the yoke by a strip of braided leather or of twisted fiber commonly called *barzon*. To

---

43. Schuetz-Miller, *Building and Builders*, 15; Hackel, *Children of Coyote*, 302.
44. Webb, *Indian Life*, 105–6.
45. Schuetz-Miller, *Building and Builders*, 155–56.
46. Ibid., 117–18.
47. Fermín Francisco de Lasuén to José Joaquín de Arrillaga, San Carlos Mission, December 21, 1792, in Kenneally, trans. and ed., *Writings of Fermín Francisco de Lasuén*, 1: 263–64; Archibald, *Economic Aspects*, 147–48.

each plow was hitched a pair of oxen in charge of a driver." Neophytes also manufactured the *carreta*, the all purpose, two-wheeled contraption so important in the functioning of the mission. They cut blocks from oak, alder, or poplar trees which they fashioned into wheels. Through the holes bored in the centers of the wheels, they inserted as the axle any straight sapling about three *varas* long. A hub at each end held in place by pins secured the wheels. A tongue of about seven varas extended from the axle. The bed of the carreta was lashed to the top of the axle, the front of the bed resting on the tongue. A cow's horn filled with grease to service the wheels and an extra axle were lashed to the bed. No iron was used.[48]

The carreta was put to special use during the harvest. After cutting the wheat with sickles, neophytes would pile it in heaps to be loaded onto carretas. The grain was deposited in a circular area enclosed by a small wall called an *era*, into which Indians, mounted on stallions, would drive several mares. Chasing the mares one way, they would quickly force them to reverse directions. Seldom ridden and kept mainly for breeding purposes, mares were assigned the task, there being little concern if their legs were injured in the procedure. Once the threshing was completed, Indians winnowed the grain, first with rakes and then with shovels. The wheat was stored in a granary.[49] By the end of 1785, the neophytes had harvested 1,500 fanegas of wheat, 1,000 of corn. They tended to 1,200 head of cattle, 2,040 sheep, and 141 horses.[50]

The increasing number of animals called for workers trained in livestock management. Certainly from historical knowledge, if not from personal experience, the Spaniards knew the dangers inherent in allowing Indians to acquire equestrian skills. Thus from

---

48. Lugo "Life of a Rancher," 228–29, 232; Dawson, *California in '41, Texas in '51*, 48–49. According to an authority on the missions, by steadying the plow with one hand, while goading the team with a stick in the other hand, only one Indian managed the task. See Webb, *Indian life*, 55–56. But according to a firsthand observer of mission life in Northern California, one Indian guided the oxen while another operated the plow. See Carson, "Early Recollections of the Mines," 105.

49. Lugo, "Life of a Rancher," 228–29; Duhaut-Cilly, *A Voyage to California*, 129–30; Carvalho, *Incidents of Travel*, 313–34; Lawrence, "Caballos and Caballeros in Pastoral California," 15–16; Denhardt, "The Role of the Horse," 17.

50. Jackson and Castillo, *Indians, Franciscans and Spanish Colonization*, 117, 126.

the beginning of Spanish colonization in California, the need for herdsmen caused the civil authorities a great deal of consternation. They were fearful that once mounted, California Indians might become skilled warriors like the Apaches.[51] In August 1787 Governor Fages wrote to Father President Fermín Francisco de Lasuén forbidding Indians the use of horses. Lasuén replied that "no one is more concerned or more interested than the missionaries that the Indian should continue in his native ignorance of horsemanship. But Your Lordship is well aware of the cattle and horses which, with the King's pleasure, every one of the missions possesses, and that horsemen are needed to look after them. And these have to be Indians, for there are no others."[52] Because this dilemma was never resolved, a type of Indian worker emerged— the *vaquero*. As noted by Lasuén, the vaqueros were easily distinguishable by their clothing. They always received pantaloons and boots, "and where possible leather jackets, all made from buckskin in addition to a hat and shoes."[53]

The garb worn by most neophytes was produced from wool. The weavers manufactured large quantities of *jerga*, a coarse woolen cloth, from which the men made the *cotón*, a kind of tunic, and the *taparabo*, a breechclout wrapped around the waist and under the legs. The women fashioned the jerga into blouses, also called cotones, and petticoats. Both men and women received wool blankets.[54] And to keep up with demand, by the end of 1801 the number of sheep at the mission had increased to 12,500.[55]

The preparation and production of large quantities of woolen items called for a specialized workforce. Indians sheared where the sheep grazed, the wool being transported to the mission in carretas. Probably children removed the burrs, sticks, thorns, and whatever else from the wool. Indians washed the wool with

---

51. Bancroft, *History of California*, 1: 404.
52. Fermín Francisco de Lasuén to Pedro Fages, Mission San Carlos, August 21, 1787, in Kenneally, trans. and ed., *Writings of Fermín Francisco de Lasuén*, 1: 150–51.
53. Lasuén, "Refutation of Charges," Mission San Carlos, June 11, 1795, ibid., 2: 205.
54. Reid, "Los Angeles County Indians," in *Los Angeles Star*, July 3, 1852; Heizer, ed., *Indians of Los Angeles County*, 86; Geiger and Meighan, eds., *As The Padres Saw Them*, 147–48; Cole and Welcome, eds., *Don Pío Pico's Historical Narrative*, 160.
55. Jackson and Castillo, *Indians, Franciscans, and Spanish Colonization*, 126.

mission-made soap in large copper kettles and spread it out on bushes to dry. Then they carded the wool to make it easier to spin into yarn. Indians colored the products with imported dyes such as brazil-wood, long-wood, yellow wood, and indigo. Ultimately, the mission operated four looms and several spinning wheels. The wheels could be moved without difficulty, and probably much carding and spinning was done in the patios.[56]

Although the missionaries were economically free to develop any industry best suited to the needs of particular missions, they were nominally under the political control of the provincial government, and on occasion were profoundly affected by the policies of that government. Early in 1779, Governor Felipe de Neve issued a decree stating that the neophytes at each mission should elect from their own ranks two *alcaldes* (magistrates) and two *regidores* (councilmen). Following the plan of the Fathers to eventually turn the missions into Indian pueblos, his intent was to prepare Indians for self-government. The alcaldes were to possess limited authority over the other neophytes and were to be exempt from corporal punishment.[57]

Some alcaldes immediately took advantage of their recently obtained authority, demonstrating independence and initiative probably stemming as much from their traditional power base as from their newly acquired status. Nicolás José, for example, was from the village of Shevaanga which was located near the mission and where he may have held a political office. After being instructed in the faith of the Church, he was baptized on September 27, 1774, the third adult male to receive the sacraments. Nicolás José was elected alcalde sometime in 1779 and by late the following year he was providing the soldiers with as many women as they sought.[58]

The Fathers turned him over to the corporal of the guard for punishment, but when informed of the action, the governor notified the missionaries that only in cases of rebellion or murder could

---

56. Webb, *Indian Life*, 213–14.
57. Engelhardt, *San Gabriel Mission*, 43–44.
58. Hackel, "Sources of Rebellion," 652. Hackel uses "Sibapt," a variation of "Shevaanga," as the name of Nicolás José's village.

an Indian alcalde be arrested. When Father President Junípero Serra heard about the incident in January 1780, he complained to the governor that even if an alcalde "be scandalously living in concubinage, a thief, an autocrat who has his people flogged—even if he answers back to the Fathers insolently, and to the soldiers also, it will have to be endured, since the Fathers are no longer allowed to have him flogged, nor is the Corporal either."[59] But a few months later, Serra had resolved the problem to his satisfaction. In a letter to a priest, he noted that the governor had not issued instructions regarding the alcaldes and had not responded to his letters. Therefore, "according to the principle 'he who keeps silent consents,' I have already written to San Luis and San Gabriel and said to give them the punishment they deserve."[60]

Consequently, when the missionaries discovered that Nicolás José and at least six other Indians were plotting to kill the missionaries, the soldiers, and a Baja California Indian, they had the rebels arrested. Soon after, however, they pardoned Nicolás José, apparently having no choice in the matter given his considerable influence and status among the neophytes. Evidently, he retained the office of alcalde and continued to participate in ceremonies at the mission, serving as a marriage witness and godfather to Indians undergoing baptism.[61]

Nicolás José, however, had not been cured of his discontent. He was particularly disturbed that traditional ceremonies of his people had been prohibited. Perhaps he saw a connection between the prohibition and the large number of Indians mysteriously dying at the mission. After his wife and two-year-old son died, Nicolás José remarried only to witness his second wife's death eight months later. Moreover, by 1785, of the forty-seven baptized adults from his village of Shevaanga, sixteen had died. Of the fifty-four baptized children from the village, twenty seven were dead. Yet despite these

---

59. Junípero Serra to Felipe de Neve, Monterey, January 7, 1780, in Tibesar, trans. and ed., *Writings of Junípero Serra*, 3: 415.

60. Junípero Serra to Fermín Francisco Lasuén, Monterey, April 25, 26, 1780, in Tibesar, trans. and ed., *Writings of Junípero Serra*, 4: 5. New translation by Rose Marie Beebe.

61. Hackel, "Sources of Rebellion," 653. An anthropologist has identified the revolt as a revitalization movement with similarities to the Chinigchinich religion. See Lepowsky, "Indian Revolts and Cargo Cults" See also Sandos, "Toypurina's Revolt."

tragedies, Nicolás José remained at the mission, married for a third time in July and continued to serve as a marriage witness.⁶²

Discontent, however, seems to have been growing among both the neophytes and the remaining gentiles. In 1785 the neophyte population totaled 843 individuals, an increase that came not just from procreation but also from the incorporation of Indians from villages increasingly distant from the mission. The local neophytes may have had long-standing disputes with those arriving from beyond the area. Moreover, the mission's 1,200 head of cattle, 2,040 sheep, and 141 horses dispersed the game and destroyed plants on which the gentiles still depended. And the lands from which the neophytes harvested 1,500 fanegas of wheat and 1,000 of corn that year were lands taken from the gentiles' cycle of food procurement.⁶³

Although secure in his position at the mission, Nicolás José decided that the Spaniards should be eliminated. Sometime during the year he contacted Toypurina, a young woman who was supposed to have supernatural powers. Toypurina was born about 1760 into a prominent lineage and was raised in Japchivit, a village probably located north of the mission in the San Gabriel Mountains. Japchivit had remained largely beyond the reach of the missionaries. Some of those joining the rebels may have come from Asucsabit, Guinibit, Cucamobit, villages located to the east of the mission, where relatives of Toypurina resided.⁶⁴

Because of the devastating economic and social changes affecting the region, Nicolás José had little difficulty in convincing Toypurina and other gentiles to meet with him at Asucsabit to plan an attack on the mission. Several villages participated in the uprising. Four, including Asucsabit and Japchivit, provided all of

---

62. Hackel, "Sources of Rebellion," 655.
63. Jackson, *Indian Population Decline*, 172; Jackson and Castillo, *Indians, Franciscans, and Spanish Colonization*, 117, 126; Hackel, "Sources of Rebellion," 656.
64. Johnson and Williams, "Toypurina's Descendants," 34. As their title indicates, the authors examine Toypurina's life and her progeny after the rebellion. Regarding the location of Japchivit, consult King, *Ethnographic Overview of Angeles National Forest; Tataviam and San Gabriel Mountain Serrano Ethnohistory*, 74–75, 137–38. In the baptismal register of San Gabriel, there are 228 entries for Asucabit between 1774 and 1813 and 102 entries for Cucamobit between 1785 and 1813. See Heizer, ed., *Indians of Los Angeles County*, 108n8 and n9. Asucabit is identified as the meeting place in the trial of Temejasaquichí, in Beebe and Senkewicz, trans. and eds., "Revolt at Mission San Gabriel," 17.

their available men. During the night of October 25, 1785, gentiles, with the cooperation of a neophyte shepherd, stole mission sheep. But when Toypurina and several armed men arrived at the mission they were arrested. Somehow the missionaries got wind of the plot.[65]

Five Indians, who had been involved in the early plot, received twenty-five lashes and were released. Twelve more were released after being whipped fifteen or twenty times. Four Indians were brought to trial: Temejasaquichí, Ajiyivi, Toypurina, and Nicolás José. Temejasaquichí was found guilty of attempting to corrupt the neophytes with his powers, and Ajiyivi was convicted of being an accomplice in the rebellion and for having killed a soldier's cow. They were to serve out their sentences at the presidio at San Diego.[66]

When asked at her trial why she sought to kill the soldiers, priests, and Christian Indians, Toypurina replied that their presence did not sit well with her. She insisted that Nicolas José alone organized the revolt and she willingly agreed to use her influence with the other Indians. She admitted ordering Temejasaquichí to persuade the neophytes to trust her and not the priests. She reiterated that she was angry with the priests and the others at the mission for living on the Indians' lands.[67]

Found guilty, Toypurina was imprisoned at the mission, as much for her own protection as for punishment. Some of the Indians lashed for their involvement in the uprising threatened to kill her for tricking them into believing her. Perhaps to ingratiate herself with her captives, she soon asked to become a Christian. Impregnated by someone while under arrest, on May 12, 1786, she presented her two-day-old son for baptism, and on March 7, 1787, she received the sacraments and took the name Regina Josefa. Her son died in August. The following year she was sent to Mission

---

65. Hackel, "Sources of Rebellion," 648, 654–55.
66. Ibid., 655; the trials of Temejasaquichí and Ajiyivi, in Beebe and Senkewicz, trans. and eds., "Revolt at Mission San Gabriel," 16–18, 19–20. See also Fages, San Gabriel, January 4, 1786, in ibid., 22.
67. Trial of Toypurina, in Beebe and Senkewicz, trans. and eds., "Revolt at Mission San Gabriel," 18–19.

San Carlos Borromeo in northern California. There she married a soldier and bore him three children. She died in May 1799 at Mission San Juan Bautista.[68]

At his trial, Nicolás José was asked if he remembered that after his first attempt to kill the missionaries, soldiers, and a Baja California Indian, he had been warned that should he attempt a similar act, he would be severely punished. Yes, he remembered everything because he was one of the people imprisoned. Why, then, did he again attempt to harm the missionaries? Because "it was embedded in his heart to do this." Knowing that it was impossible to defeat the soldiers, why did he did he risk his life and those of his followers? Because he was angry at not being allowed "to perform his dances" and other activities. He admitted being the leader of the uprising. He had recruited neophytes to join with him and had given Toypurina beads so she would recruit gentiles. He insisted that Temejasaquichí had not advised him. He and Toypurina "were the cause of everything."[69] Convicted of leading the uprising, Nicolás José was sentenced to six years at the most distant presidio from the mission.[70]

It troubled the missionaries that the instigator of the rebellion had been an alcalde. Reflecting on the decree creating the office, Lasuén concluded that "the institution of alcaldes and regidores in the missions was untimely and unduly legalistic, for it makes such persons independent of the missionaries as regards punishment and dismissal from office when they deserve it, and it makes these officials lazy and haughty, connivers at wrongdoing and partners in it."[71] Between 1787 and 1796, elections for alcaldes

---

68. Hackel, "Sources of Rebellion," 658; Johnson and Williams, "Toypurina's Descendants," 36–39. Wrote a Catholic priest in 1969: "Probably in all of California annals there is no more outstanding Christian victory than the conversion of Toypurina, a native temptress brought forth from the darkness of evil, rebellion and paganism to the knowledge, love and service of the one true god." See Weber, "Toypurina the Temptress," 75–76.
69. Trial of Nicolás José, in Beebe and Senkewicz, trans. and eds., "Revolt at Mission San Gabriel," 20–21.
70. Pedro Fages to Jacobo Ugarte y Loyola, Arispe, December 14, 1787, in "Revolt at Mission San Gabriel," 26.
71. Fermín Francisco de Lasuén to Jacobo Ugarte y Loyola, Mission San Carlos, October 20, 1787, in Kenneally, ed., *Writings of Fermín Francisco de Lasuén*, 1: 168–69.

and regidores were held only intermittently, if at all, at most of the missions. During that period, the neophyte population of San Gabriel increased from 935 to 1,335.[72] That many people called for more managers, a situation probably replicated at most missions. Thus in 1796 the new governor encouraged the Franciscans to conform to the decree. In November, Lasuén sent a circular to the missionaries, instructing them to hold elections. Thereafter, on the first of January, two alcaldes and two regidores were elected at each mission for a one-year term.[73] At San Gabriel on January 1, 1799, Pedro Celestino and Eustaquio María were elected alcaldes and José Cupertino and Tranquilo José regidores.[74]

As political changes occurred, agricultural progress continued although not without setbacks. In 1795 the neophytes sowed 179 fanegas of wheat and 12 fanegas of corn and harvested 2,600 and 1,300 fanegas respectively.[75] Because the harvest was insufficient to feed the neophytes, the Fathers put half the population on half rations and sent the rest into the mountains to hunt and gather.[76] It seems that food production had yet to fully replace food procurement.

Construction projects continued. In 1795 work began on a new church of stone and mortar, but over a year later it had yet to be completed. By the beginning of 1799 the workers had completed the roof, except for a portion over the choir.[77] But construction must have slowed the following year when an epidemic of pneumonia hit the mission. Sixty-seven Indians died in November.[78] By December 20 the number of deaths had climbed to 120 individuals.[79] In January 1801 the *comandante* of the presidio at Santa

---

72. Jackson, *Indian Population Decline*, 172.
73. Engelhardt, *Missions and Missionaries*, 2: 367, 557–58.
74. Engelhardt, *San Gabriel Mission*, 73.
75. Jackson and Castillo, *Indians, Franciscans and Spanish Colonization*, 118.
76. Fermín Francisco de Lasuén, "Memorandum," Mission San Carlos, May 6, 1796, in Kenneally, trans. and ed., *Writings of Fermín Francisco de Lasuén*, 1: 378
77. Geiger, "The Building of Mission San Gabriel," 37; Webb, *Indian Life*, 130.
78. Fermín Francisco de Lasuén to José Gasol, San Carlos, December 9, 1800, in Kenneally, trans. and ed., *Writings of Fermín Francisco de Lasuén*, 2: 178.
79. Fermín Francisco de Lasuén to José Gasol, San Carlos, December 29, 1800, ibid., 178. Two letters were written on the same day.

Missionary Intrusion

Bárbara reported that the Indians at San Gabriel and San Juan Capistrano "hardly have time to complain that they are sick before they die."[80] The neophyte population declined from 1,136 in 1800 to 1,047 in 1802. By 1804, however, it had increased to 1,294.[81]

When 1804 ended the neophytes had built ten rooms to serve as a granary, weavery, carpenter shop, pantry, storeroom, and the Fathers' residence. They roofed the rooms with timber and tile. A year later they had completed nine more rooms, all of adobe with plastered walls and tile roofs.[82] Probably by this time, neophytes had also constructed a stone dam, called *La Presa*, near the village of Akuuronga, where there was a pool and much firewood.[83]

Whether the forty neophytes who had fled the mission by 1805 departed because of discontent with the work routine or for other reasons is not clear, but a priest claimed that he had the answer.[84] Commenting on this and other escapes, and fugitivism in general, he wrote: "Of those who voluntarily submit to the sweet yoke of the Gospel and of the moderate labor intended for their well-being, there are some in all the missions who shake off the yoke and flee to the mountains. And yet no reason for their flight can be discovered other than the inconstancy characteristic of Indians."[85] Even though the missionaries did not count fugitives as population loss, the number of Indians at San Gabriel dropped to 1,052 in 1806, only to begin another increase.[86]

---

80. Quoted in Mason, *Los Angeles Under the Spanish Flag—Spain's New World*, 36.
81. Jackson, *Indian Population Decline*, 172.
82. Geiger, "The Building of Mission San Gabriel," 38; Webb, *Indian Life*, 145.
83. McCawley, *The First Angelinos*, 42–43; Johnston, *California's Gabrielino Indians*, 166–67.
84. Cook, *Conflict*, 60.
85. Quoted in Guest, "Cultural Perspectives on California Indian Life," 41.
86. Jackson, *Indian Population Decline*, 172.

CHAPTER 3

Competing Institutions

Four years after the founding of Mission San Gabriel, Captain Pedro Fages wrote:

> One league to the westward from the mission there are great forests of oak, from which a supply of acorns is obtained. A great many Indians live there, hidden in their villages, which are found also on the seashore and on the plain throughout the eight leagues mentioned. The Río de Porciúncula, distant more than two long leagues, contains water sufficient to use for irrigation, as does also another copious stream which is farther on, some three leagues to the west. Nor are there lacking in the vicinity of the forest to which reference has been made, small streams from which water can be taken for the cultivation of the adjacent fields, so that the entire locality is most alluring, and offers facilities for the settlement of a few families of Spaniards. These might, without prejudice to the mission, have an assignment of fertile fields, with places adapted for all kinds of cattle. They would live in comfort, and with them we might begin to have hopes of a very important settlement.

Like the missionaries, with their particular reasons for establishing missions in California, Fages rationalized the founding of civilian settlements. In an oblique criticism of the soldiers and artisans assigned to the missions, he reasoned that if settlers were to come to California, "the Indians would soon cease to consider (as they now do) that we are exiles from our lands who have come here in quest of their women; for they would then see coming here to settle men who had their own wives.... They would then cease to feel the disquietude and misgiving in which they have lived from the first."[1]

In September 1778 Teodoro de Croix, the Governor General of the Northern Provinces of New Spain, approved the founding of a second pueblo in California, San José de Guadalupe being the first. The two towns would provide resources to found other pueblos and furnish supplies and recruits for soldiers at the presidios.[2] Croix instructed Captain Rivera y Moncada to recruit settlers and soldiers and escort them to Alta California. One body of soldiers and their families was to come up from Sonora, cross the Colorado River into California, and proceed on to Santa Bárbara to found a presidio. About half the members of the party, some thirty soldiers with families and five unmarried recruits, arrived at Mission San Gabriel on July 14. They soon learned how lucky they were. Shortly after crossing the Colorado River, Quechan Indians attacked the two settlements the Spanish had earlier founded there, killing and capturing all the residents and colonists.[3] The attack closed down an important route into California, which further isolated the region from the rest of New Spain. Henceforth, settlers and supplies had to come by ship or overland through rugged Baja California.

Awaiting the arrival of the second party, this one from Baja California, was Governor Felipe de Neve. At a village, perhaps Yaanga, he chose thirty-six boys and girls to be baptized into the Catholic faith. Who christened the Indians is not clear, but apparently the governor served as godfather to twelve of them. And shortly before the colonists arrived, he selected a young couple, whom he renamed Felipe de Neve and Felipa Teresa de Neve, sponsored their baptism, and saw them married in the Catholic faith. Evidently, the governor intended the pueblo to be an institution where Christian Indians could live outside the mission system.[4]

1. Fages, *Description*, 20, 43–44.
2. Harlow, *Maps and Surveys of the Pueblo Lands of Los Angeles*, 2–3.
3. Engelhardt, *San Gabriel Mission*, 44–46; Mason, *The Census of 1790*, 36–38.
4. Kelsey, "A New Look at the Founding of Old Los Angeles," 5.

While the Baja California contingent rested at San Gabriel, Felipe de Neve issued more instructions regarding the founding of the pueblo. It was to be built on the banks of the Los Angeles River. It was to be situated on elevated ground to be secure from flooding but connected to a main irrigation ditch called the *zanja madre*. The corners of the public plaza were to face the cardinal points so that the streets issuing from them would not be exposed to the four winds. Along the southwest side of the plaza, sites were designated for a church, public buildings, a jail, and a granary. The other side was to be divided among the settlers.[5]

On September 4, 1781, ten years to the month after the establishment of San Gabriel, a party of forty-four men, women, and children founded the Pueblo de Los Angeles near the village of Yaanga. The pobladores consisted of a few farmers, a hoe maker, a cowherd, a mason, and a tailor and included a mestizo, mulattos, two *negros*, Mexican Indians, and two Spaniards.[6] The land eventually set aside for the use of the pobladores, their offspring, and those who would come later was truly enormous—four square leagues, or a league in length from each corner of the plaza. Each poblador was to receive a house lot called a *solar*, which was to be twenty varas in width and forty in length, and two *suertes*, or farming lands. One suerte was supposed to produce a fanega of corn. In addition there were municipal lands called *propios*, to be leased or rented to raise revenue; *ejidos*, pasture lands near the pueblo; *dehesas*, distant pasture lands; and *realengas*, royal lands from which new settlers would be assigned their plots. Each poblador was also to receive livestock, implements, and seeds, the cost of which would be paid back in five years. During those years, he would also be provided with minimal rations and an annual stipend from the government and would be immune from paying taxes or the royal tithe. He would have use of the ejidos and dehesas for pasture, firewood, timber, and water. In return, the poblador was required to sell his surplus to the presidios and keep his horses and muskets ready for military service. He could not sell his lands which were

---

5. Harlow, *Maps and Surveys*, 5–6.
6. Ibid., 4–5.

to pass to his son and descendants. He had to build a house within three years, cultivate the land, and maintain a specified number of animals. He was to participate in public works projects, such as repairing dams, zanjas, roads, streets, the church, and public buildings, and maintaining the common lands.[7]

By the end of October, mules, mares, cows, calves, sheep, goats, and tools had been distributed, and the pobladores had completed work on a zanja and corrals.[8] But the yields of the wheat and corn were disappointing, at least to Governor Felipe de Neve. Concerned over the reliability of the pobladores, he notified his successor in 1782 that "the slight care they took in watching over the wheat harvest reduced the yield from a possible 400 fanegas to 260. Through the same neglect, they lost their first crop of corn. The plants, already sprouted, dried up because they failed to open up the irrigation ditch soon enough to water them. They then had to make a second sowing, which was in good shape but will produce a smaller yield."[9] By the end of 1784, houses and public buildings of adobe had replaced the palisade which consisted of poles stuck in the ground and plastered with mud.[10] From tar pits about two leagues from the town, the pobladores quarried sections of bitumen that had boiled up from the earth and solidified and spread them on the flat roofs which had been covered with dirt. The sun turned the tar again into liquid which oozed over the roofs.[11]

With the assistance of the local Tongva, that year the pobladores planted thirty-five fanegas of wheat and twelve of corn. But the gentiles consented to work only when it did not interfere with their food-procuring activities. Lieutenant José Francisco Ortega noted the dependence of the pueblo on Indian labor and the independence of the Indian laborers: "Only with the aid of the gentiles" were the settlers able to plant their crops, but because the Indians were "at present harvesting their abundant wild seeds,

---

7. Guinn, "The Plan of Old Los Angeles," 41; Harlow, *Maps and Surveys*, 2–8.
8. Harlow, *Maps and Surveys*, 6; Engelhardt, *San Gabriel Mission*, 58.
9. "Neve's Instructions to Fages, His Successor," quoted in Beilharz, *Felipe de Neve*, 165–66.
10. Schuetz-Miller, *Building and Builders*, 23; Bancroft, *History of California*, 1: 346.
11. Pattie, *The Personal Narrative of James O. Pattie*, 196.

they justly refuse with this good reason to lend a hand in digging and weeding."[12]

For several of the pobladores stock raising seems to have been emphasized over crop growing. By September 1786 nine pobladores owned 168 head of cattle, 119 ewes, 211 goats, 16 mules, and 69 horses.[13] At this early stage in the pueblo's history, it is unlikely that gentiles were employed in stock management. And few Indians probably participated in the pueblo's harvest of 1787, which failed to produce a crop that satisfied the needs of its eleven families and the soldiers at the presidios at Santa Bárbara and San Diego. The suertes of the town yielded 990 fanegas of maize, 77 of wheat, and 120 of kidney beans. The maize harvested was capable of supporting only seventy-six men with medium-size families.[14]

The pobladores were subject to the authority of the *ayuntamiento* (town council) that initially consisted of an alcalde (mayor) and two regidores (councilmen.) And over them was the *comisionado*, a non-commissioned officer who in emergencies could assume judiciary, legislative, and executive powers. His primary duties, however, were to maintain peace and harmony among the pobladores and to prevent or at least limit concubinage, incendiarism, drunkenness, and gambling.[15]

In 1787 the governor issued Comisionado Vicente Féliz a set of instructions. Most of them dealt with civil matters, but the governor ordered Féliz to pay particular attention to the pobladores' "pernicious familiarity" with the local Indians. Those from beyond the area who came for only a few days work were to reside near the soldiers' quarters where they could be easily observed. Indians apprehended in the act of stealing or killing stock were to be told the reason for the punishment and then lashed fifteen or twenty times in the presence of their leaders. Neophytes were prohibited from entering the pueblo without permission from their priests. Men caught illegally in the town would be warned and sent back

---
12. Quoted in Mason, "Fages' Code of Conduct Toward Indians, 1787," 94–95.
13. Mason, *Los Angeles Under the Spanish Flag*, 68.
14. Guest, "Municipal Institutions in Spanish California, 1769–1821," 263.
15. Ibid., 204; Guinn, "Muy Ilustre Ayuntamiento," 207.

to their mission; women would be counseled by a priest. Gentiles already residing near the pueblo were to be encouraged to move from the immediate area. And Indians from the mountains or from other distant regions were prohibited from establishing themselves in the vicinity of the pueblo. The comisionado was to make sure they resided in locations where their activities could be observed by day and at night when they congregated to dance. "By no means will it be permissible for them to enter [the pueblo] in large groups or gangs for their simple amusement, for the reason that, as much as possible, we must avoid their gaining knowledge of our exact movements and the hours when the women and children are left alone."[16]

Other rules defined labor relations: "When it is necessary to seek Indians in their rancherías so that they might be brought to work, it must be with the precise knowledge of the comisionado and the alcalde." If possible, permission from their leaders should be sought. And Indians should neither be forced to work "nor should they be promised that which there is no intention of giving them." Those Indians who chose to work were not to be left alone, "but have someone with them. In this way it will be easier to excuse reasonable shortcomings in their work, and they will work more usefully for those who employ them." Never were Indians to be allowed inside the settlers' houses, certainly not to sleep, and the women should grind the corn in the corridors or patios. An individual caught mistreating an Indian was to be punished in the presence of the victim, "so he may be satisfied and not feel obliged for him or his companions to take revenge."[17]

No doubt these instructions were often ignored, but they indicate that the pueblo, a tiny foreign enclave in a vast Indian territory, was both suspicious of and dependent upon its Indian neighbors. By ordering the return of neophytes caught in Los Angeles to their mission, the governor implied that some of them had indeed relocated to the pueblo. And by defining the type and degree of punishment, he also implied that crimes had been committed.

---

16. Mason, *Los Angeles Under the Spanish Flag*, 19–22; Mason, "Fages's Code of Conduct," 97; Guest, "Municipal Institutions," 340–41.
17. Mason, *Los Angeles Under the Spanish Flag*, 20–21.

Soon the Indians of the region would have other options regarding where and for whom to work. In late 1784 soldier José Manuel Nieto wrote to Governor Pedro Fages. Lacking grazing lands for his horses and cattle at the San Diego presidio, Nieto asked for "a place situated at three leagues distance from the Mission of San Gabriel along the road to the Royal Presidio of San Carlos de Monterey named La Sanja, contemplating Sir, not to harm neither a living soul, principally the Mission of San Gabriel, nor even less the Pueblo of the Queen of Angels. I humbly request of Your Worship's superior government that it see fit to decide as I have requested."[18]

On November 20 Fages submitted the petitions of Nieto and those of Juan José Domínguez and others to authorities in Mexico City, explaining that because the cattle were rapidly increasing "it is necessary in the case of several owners to give them additional lands; they have asked me for some *sitios* which I have granted provisionally, namely to Juan José Domínguez who was a soldier in the presidio of San Diego and who at this moment has four herds of mares and about 200 head of cattle on the river below San Gabriel, to Manuel Nieto for a similar reason that of la Zanja." The petitions were approved in 1786, with the stipulations that each individual receiving a land concession was to stock it with two thousand head of cattle and employ the necessary numbers of vaqueros and shepherds to manage the animals.[19] These retired soldiers, called *inválidos*, would become Southern California's first rancheros.[20]

Evidently the gentiles residing where the first ranchos were founded offered little or no resistance, probably because the rancheros and their families were few in number and thus not

---

18. Quoted in Robinson, *Land in California*, 48–49.
19. Cleland, *Cattle on a Thousand Hills*, 7–8.
20. In 1775 an individual in Northern California was the first to receive a land concession, but the rancho system truly began in Southern California. See Robinson, *Land in California*, 46.

perceived as a threat.[21] And even if the creation of a rancho resulted in the abandonment of nearby villages, population dispersal does not necessarily mean population decline. For some Indians, especially if the choice was theirs, moving their village on to a nearby rancho may not have been a terribly difficult or different experience. In pre-contact times, villages were often moved, especially in times of crisis.[22] And given the size and isolation of many of the ranchos, the Indian residents may have been spared the devastating diseases that contaminated those in the missions.[23]

Those gentiles seeking employment on the ranchos did so for the same reasons others sought work in the pueblo—to obtain the material items they themselves could not produce. But those Indians finding work on the first ranchos lost little of their traditional culture, because the rancheros sought only their labor. The gentiles learned to work with new tools, materials, animals, and equipment, but unlike those in the mission, they did not experience, at least initially, a disruption of their social relations and calendar of events.[24]

Ironically the gentiles, on whose lands the intrusion occurred, presented fewer obstacles to the founding, expanding, and improving of the ranchos than did Spanish officialdom.[25] Although the first distribution of land went relatively smoothly, obtaining land in California under Spanish rule was fraught with obstacles. Because the mission was the primary institution in the Spanish colonization of the region and because the missions soon appropriated most of the valuable land in their vicinities, few individuals petitioned the governor for land. Moreover, he lacked the

---

21. This interpretation is based on negative evidence. Had Indians attacked any of the first ranchos, it seems likely that someone, somewhere would have recorded it.
22. According to an archaeologist, Povuu'nga may have been moved several times, the term itself referring more to an area than a village. See Dixon, "Reviving Puvunga," 88.
23. That Indians working on the ranchos in time caught the same diseases that infected Indians in the pueblo and at the missions is not in doubt, but there is no record of population loss during the first two decades of the rancho system.
24. Indian cultural survival on the ranchos is discussed in greater detail in Chapter 13.
25. Elsewhere in California, gentiles not only resisted the creation of ranchos, but in some cases forced their abandonment. See Phillips, *Indians and Intruders*, 107–34.

authority to distribute land beyond the immediate boundaries of pueblos and presidios, and he could issue only temporary permits to those seeking land on which to graze animals. These permits were contingent upon the petitioners not infringing on pueblo, mission, and Indian lands. Title of the land remained with the Crown, the individual having only usufructuary rights.[26]

The concession that Juan José Domínguez received was called Rancho San Pedro. It totaled over sixteen square leagues. Domínguez left the management of the rancho to a *mayordomo* while he remained for several years at the presidio in San Diego.[27] Rancho San Pedro remained only partially developed, which resulted in the rapid rise in the number of feral horses. Late in his life, a neighbor remembered that Juan José Domínguez "did not look to his brood mares. They became wild and many horses of the San Gabriel mission joined them, so that when Juan José died, there were thousands of wild horses on the plains, to the great damage of the mission and other owners of stock."[28]

Unlike the native herbivores of the region such as antelope and deer, whose populations fluctuated from season to season depending on changing climate or other conditions, European horses and cattle tended to remain in the same locations. Native animals, moreover, did not graze in large herds and were selective in the plants they consumed. The stock of the rancheros grazed in large herds and were much less particular about what they ate. As a result, the introduced animals, especially as they replaced the native ones, caused considerable disruption to the environment.[29]

José María Verdugo, another inválido, chose land a league and a half west of San Gabriel and north of Los Angeles, creating Rancho San Rafael. But in granting grazing privileges, Fages told

---

26. The distribution of land in the form of concessions is discussed in Robinson, *Land in California*, 33–90; and in Cleland, *Cattle on a Thousand Hills*, 3–18. See also Hornbeck, "Land tenure and rancho expansion in Alta California, 1784–1846."
27. Cleland, *Cattle on a Thousand Hills*, 9.
28. Gillingham, *The Rancho San Pedro*, 82.
29. Schiffman, "The Los Angeles Prairie," 48.

Verdugo that he must not "prejudice" the mission, the pobladores, or the gentiles. Verdugo remained at the San Diego presidio and turned the management of the rancho over to his brother. Probably with the help of local gentiles, the brother built a house and planted a garden and a vineyard. A few years later, Verdugo retired from the army and moved on to Rancho San Rafael.[30] That gentiles took advantage of the opportunities the rancho offered is evident in the comments issued by a priest in 1795. Encountering Indians who had undergone considerable economic change, he told his superior about "a great field of water melons, sugar melons, and beans, with a patch of corn, belonging to an old gentile called Requi and to other gentiles of the same class, who live contiguous to the ranch of Verdugo."[31] Here food production seems to be as important, if not more so, than food procurement.

Nieto received the largest concession, but part of his rancho infringed on lands San Gabriel had put to use, in particular a tract called La Puente. Nieto's infringement prompted a strong response from missionary Miguel Sánchez. In March 1796 he told Father President Fermín Francisco de Lasuén that the mission pastured there 3,000 head of cattle, 4,000 sheep, and horses and needed the land: "The Indians are poor, indeed, while Nieto is not poor; he has more horses than the mission whose stock is exposed to thieves. His cattle must be sufficiently numerous. . . . This year it is said he harvested 1,000 fanegas of corn. . . . He harvested some wheat and a good quantity of beans, whereas we in the region harvested only 300 fanegas of grain."[32] When pressured by the missionaries to remove his animals, Nieto complained to the governor: "I find myself harassed in such a way on the part of the mission that being no longer able to endure it, I appeal to your Worship's powerful protection. . . . [T]he Reverend Father Missionaries of said mission . . . are continually warning me to abandon the place because it belongs to the Indians, and they do not

---

30. Cleland, *Cattle on a Thousand Hills*, 13–15.
31. Quoted in Engelhardt, *San Fernando Rey*, 6.
32. Quoted in Engelhardt, *San Gabriel Mission*, 66–68.

want me to stay under any title."³³ The governor ruled that Nieto could retain the land he had under cultivation, but the remainder could be used by the mission.³⁴

From the missionaries' point of view, consigning any land to private individuals was troubling. They had been given the responsibility of Christianizing and "civilizing" the Indians, so any land withdrawn from their potential use was of great concern. Fermín Francisco de Lasuén, in a memorandum written in May 1796, acknowledged that the missionaries had no power to deny or hinder anyone from taking possession of lands. Because it was their duty to congregate Indians into Christian communities, however, all lands should belong to the Indians. Besides, there was not enough land to be shared. Thus, the missionaries disputed Nieto's grant, not "because they have seen that he gets profit from it. They do it because they need these lands."³⁵

When Nieto moved on to that part of the concession known as Santa Gertrudis, he probably enlisted local gentiles in building an adobe house and corrals. His enormous herds of horses and black cattle thrived there. But disputes with the mission continued. In the fall of 1802, he complained to the governor that the mission was growing crops on lands close to his and that Indians were stealing and killing his cattle. He had brought up the issue with the missionaries but to no avail. He sought resolution from the governor: either give the tract to him or give it to the mission.³⁶ Apparently the issue was never resolved to his satisfaction, but when Nieto died in 1804 he was one of the richest men in California. His four children received undivided interest in the estate.³⁷ In 1806 one of his sons, Juan José Antonio Nieto, built an adobe house on the site of Povuu'nga, where Chinigchinich once appeared. The site apparently had been abandoned.³⁸

33. Quoted in Robinson, *Land in California*, 27.
34. Engelhardt, *San Gabriel Mission*, 70.
35. Fermín Francisco de Lasuén, "Memorandum," Mission San Carlos, May 6, 1796, in Kenneally, trans. and ed., *Writings of Fermín Francisco de Lasuén*, 1: 377–78.
36. Engelhardt, *San Gabriel Mission*, 70.
37. Cleland, *Cattle on a Thousand Hills*, 8.
38. Dixon, "Reviving Pavunga," 86–87. Merriam, "Village Names," 116.

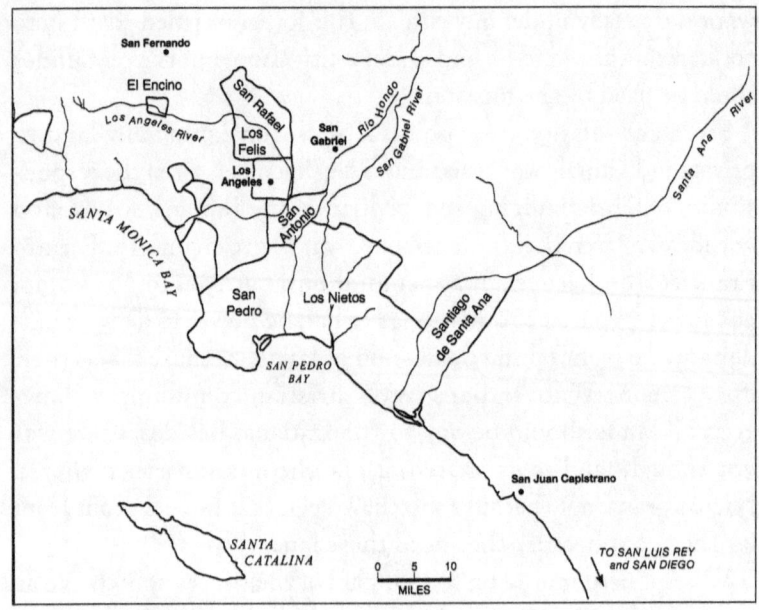

Missions, Pueblo Tract, and Spanish Concessions, 1771–1821

On land adjacent to the Nieto concession but south of the Santa Ana River, José Antonio Yorba and Juan Pablo Grijalva had been grazing cattle since about 1801. Grijalva petitioned Governor José Joaquín de Arrillaga for the land, but died before receiving the property. Yorba took up the issue, noting in his petition that since the death of Grijalva, "various people have been placed in charge of the affairs of the rancho but now Juan Peralta (my nephew) will represent my interests and we will stock the land with three hundred head of cattle and the same number of horses." Yorba asked the governor "to remember that I have a large family which at the advanced age of sixty, I cannot support by my own labor." On July 1, 1810, the governor granted Rancho Santiago de Santa Ana to Yorba and Peralta.[39] With the assistance of local gentiles,

---

39. Cleland, *The Irvine Ranch*, 12–13.

they built adobe houses adjacent to one another, introduced cattle, horses, and sheep, and planted orchards and a vineyard, the latter located near the Santa Ana River and enclosed with an adobe wall.[40]

When the missionaries at San Gabriel learned that the owners of the rancho had failed to notify them of the deaths of unbaptized Indians, they informed Father Vicente Francisco de Sarría, commissary prefect of the missions, about the situation. In September 1816 Sarría informed Governor Pablo Vicente de Solá that he had "met with retired Sergeant Antonio Yorba in an effort to assure the administering of the sacrament of baptism to these Indians. Yorba told me that of the Indians in his service, none had died in this fashion. He said that he did not meddle with those who belonged to Juan Peralta, who also has part ownership of the land." The departure of Peralta from the rancho soon after Sarría arrived prompted the priest to exclaim: "I was not able to see him to make my complaint to him regarding the negligence of having allowed deaths of this type, and of permitting the loss of these souls, who will cry out more for such misfortune than does that of the blood of Abel for the death by his brother Cain, begging the vengeance of God." Sarría implored the governor to "see his obligations in such things as these."[41]

What effect the inquiry had on the owners is not known, but on October 14, 1818, someone on the rancho baptized José María, age eight days, who was on the verge of death. His parents were from the Mountain Cahuilla village of Pasague. On December 2, 1818, Pedro, who was about ten years of age and also near death, received the sacraments. His parents were from the Mountain Cahuilla village of Nacuta.[42]

---

40. Gibson, *Tomás Yorba's Santa Ana Viejo*, 53–54.
41. Ibid., 49–50.
42. San Juan Capistrano Baptismal Registers, B#3678 and B#3684. Courtesy of Stephen O'Neil. For an explanation of mission register research, consult his "The Acjachemen in the Franciscan Mission System," 16–43.

CHAPTER 4

Missionary Expansion

To the priests at Mission San Gabriel, the founding of ranchos and a pueblo in a domain they considered spiritually theirs posed a double threat. An Indian lost to a poblador or ranchero was an Indian whose labor and perhaps soul were lost to the Church. And as Vicente Santa María lamented in 1795, in a letter to Father President Fermín Francisco de Lasuén, clearly the missionaries were losing: "The whole of pagandom . . . is fond of the Pueblo of Los Angeles, of the rancho of Mariano Verdugo, of the rancho of Reyes, and of the Zanja. Here we see nothing but pagans passing, clad in shoes, with sombreros and blankets, and serving as muleteers to the settlers and rancheros, so that if it were not for the gentiles there would be neither pueblo nor rancho. . . . Finally, these pagan Indians care neither for the Mission nor for the missionaries."[1]

Father Santa María was particularly concerned about a rancho in the San Fernando Valley that was employing Indians. At an unspecified time, Governor Pedro Fages had allowed Francisco Reyes to provisionally occupy land called Rancho El Encino, better known as Rancho Reyes. Reyes remained in Los Angeles but

---
1. Quoted in Engelhardt, *San Fernando Rey*, 5.

grazed his stock and that of Cornelio Ávila and others on the rancho.[2] Santa María, who visited the rancho in 1795, commented on the economic importance of the Indian workers: "We came upon a party of gentiles who were finishing a kiln for burning lime which they had already heaped up. Stone for the foundations of the buildings is near by." At an adjacent village, the priest observed Indians taking "care of the field of corn, beans, and melons belonging to ... Reyes.... These Indians are the cowherds, cattlemen, irrigators, bird-catchers, foremen, horsemen, etc." Reyes recruited his workers from the nearby villages of Taapu, Tacuyaman, Juyunga, Mapipinga, and Cahuenga.[3]

On the recommendation of Santa María, the governor authorized the establishment of a mission in the area. It had water, deposits of limestone, land to pasture cattle, and nearby pine trees.[4] Without protest, Reyes transferred his rancho to the Church and on September 8, 1797, Lasuén recorded the founding:

> It affords me great pleasure to inform Your Lordship that today, the solemn feast of the Nativity of Most Holy Mary, I blessed water, the grounds, and a large cross which we venerated and erected in a beautiful region known as *Achois Comihabit* by the natives, and located between the Missions of San Buenaventura and San Gabriel. I was assisted by Reverend Father Fray Francisco Dumetz who had been assigned to this mission, and by the troops assigned to guard it, in the presence of many pagans of both sexes and of all ages who showed themselves much pleased and satisfied. I immediately intoned the Litany of All Saints, and following this I sang the Mass, preached a sermon during it, and brought the function to an end by solemnly singing the *Te Deum*.
>
> When breakfast was over, the pagans offered ten of their children, five of each sex, to be baptized, and in the little *enramada*, in the very place where the holy sacrifice of Mass had been celebrated, I blessed the baptismal font and baptized them solemnly.[5]

---

2. Bancroft, *History of California, 1542–1800,* 1: 662–63; Cutter, "Report on Rancho El Encino," 202–3.
3. Quoted in Engelhardt, *San Fernando Rey,* 5.
4. Ibid., 5; Cutter, "Report on Rancho El Encino," 203–4.
5. Fermín Francisco de Lasuén to Diego de Borica, Incipient Mission of San Fernando, September 8, 1797, in Kenneally, trans. and ed., *Writings of Fermín Francisco de Lasuén,* 2: 44. For Reyes's later life as a ranchero, see Farris, "The Reyes Rancho."

The ten children, apparently the offspring of those working for Reyes, were from the village of Achoicomihabit.[6]

Missions Santa Bárbara, San Buenaventura, and San Gabriel donated to San Fernando 9 mules, 10 geldings, 12 mares, 1 stallion, 8 yokes of oxen, 120 cows, 3 bulls, 32 heifers, 200 lambs, 4 "service" rams, and 50 "altered" ones.[7] By the end of 1798, 40 fanegas of wheat had been planted and 300 fanegas harvested. Two and a half fanegas of corn seed had produced a crop of 40 fanegas. Smaller amounts of beans, peas, lentils, and garbanzos also had been grown.[8]

When Rancho El Encino became Mission San Fernando, Reyes' workers—gentiles—merely transferred their labor from one institution to another. The mission, therefore, began with some Indians already in possession of the skills crucial to its development. How many became neophytes is not known, but at the end of 1798, 135 Indians resided at the mission: 78 males and 57 females. Seven Indians had died and 147 had been baptized.[9] On April 7 of that year, José Antonio was laid to rest. Although the twenty-third Indian to receive baptism, he was the first neophyte to die at the mission.[10] In 1800 disease, probably pneumonia, may have struck some of the villages south of San Fernando but it did not spread to the mission.[11]

Initially the missionaries concentrated on incorporating Indians from the San Fernando Valley, especially those from the Tongva villages of Cahuenga, Siutcanga, Jajamonga, and Tujunga. Evidently, they were successful because in 1802–1803 they turned

---

6. Merriam, "Village Names," 93. John R. Johnson, personal communication, February 21, 2009.
7. Fermín Francisco de Lasuén to Fray Pedro Callejas, "The Mission-to-be of San Fernando," September 8, 1797, in Kenneally, trans. and ed., *Writings of Fermín Francisco de Lasuén*, 2: 45.
8. Engelhardt, *San Fernando Rey*, 97.
9. Felipe Goycoechea, Presidio of Santa Bárbara, December 31, 1798, in Neuerburg, trans., "An Early California Document," 113–15; Engelhardt, *San Fernando Rey*, 14.
10. Weber, ed., *The Mission in the Valley*, 5.
11. Merriam, "Village Names," 94. Engelhardt claimed that in 1800 a disease struck Cabuebet and that Father Xavier de la Concepción Uría baptized there thirty-three Indians near death. See Engelhardt, *San Fernando Rey*, 19.

TABLE 1. VILLAGE HEADMEN
BAPTIZED AT SAN FERNANDO, 1802–1804

Village	Age	Christian Name	Year Baptized	Group
Achoicominga	35	José Vicente	1802	Tongva
Apevit	55	Desiderio	1802	Tongva
Atamobit	60	Simón	1804	Serrano
Cacuycuyjavit	43	Juan José	1804	Tataviam
Coaybet	34	Pedro José	1804	Tataviam
Jotojonvit	29	Anastasio	1804	Tongva
Mapabit	60	Rogerio	1803	Tongva
Mojubit	60	Timoteo	1802	Tongva
Quissaubit	26	Benvenuto	1803	Serrano
Taapu	46	Salvador	1804	Chumash
Tochaborunga	45	Matías	1804	Tataviam
Vijabit	25	Candido	1802	Tongva

Source: Adapted, with the assistance of John R. Johnson, from C. Hart Merriam, "Village Names in twelve California Mission Records," *Reports of the University of California Archaeological Survey* (74) 1968: 85–102.

their attention to the Tataviam villages of the upper Santa Clara River and in 1803–1804 to the Ventureño Chumash from the Malibu Creek area and the Simi Valley. Some Serranos from the northeast also were recruited.[12] During these years the missionaries targeted village headmen from these groups, probably as a tactic to get villagers to enter the mission. The results were far from uniform, however. In some cases, headmen entered the mission only after the incorporation of several of their followers. Between 1802 and 1804, twelve headmen joined the mission, depriving the villagers who remained, at least temporarily, of leadership. The following year Toypurina's brother and headman of Japchivit was baptized as Tiburcio.[13] Intense recruiting resulted in the mission's population increasing to 985 in 1804.[14]

12. Johnson, "The Indians of Mission San Fernando," 255.
13. Merriam, "Village Names," 93–102; Johnson and Williams, "Toypurina's Descendants," 33.
14. Jackson, *Indian Population Decline*, 174.

Missionary Expansion

As the population increased, work routines became firmly established. In 1799 Indians began work on a new church, this one out of adobe, and built permanent quarters for the priests in a wing next to the church. Two years later they constructed an addition to the wing containing two granaries, two small rooms, a weaving room, and a dormitory for the girls and single women. Six houses, mainly for the use of the soldiers and official visitors were also built. Not until 1804 did the neophytes finish for their own use seventy houses of adobe. They roofed all the buildings with tiles.[15] Learning to manufacture tiles probably took little time and effort. Indians packed wet clay into a mold that was round like half a log. Once the clay had dried, which took days or sometimes a month, the workers removed the tile and fired it in a kiln. Indians stoked the kiln with alternate layers of fuel and lime rock.[16]

When the product was to be lime itself, from one to five days were required in the burning and cooling process. Lime was a crucial element in the protection of buildings. Mixing three or four parts lime to one of sand with water, the neophyte workers coated adobe walls with a plaster, and to insure it adhered to the adobe wall pressed pebbles or bits of broken tile into the exposed layer of mud mortar in which the brick had been laid. To achieve the same end, they sometimes cut furrows in the walls. Lime mortar also was used to seal stone foundations and buildings. Lime milk, which was a whitewash, served as a base for painting decorations on walls. As a hydraulic cement, lime was also crucial in the construction of dams and aqueducts.[17]

Indians built kilns on at least one of the mission's two major *estancias*, often called farms or ranchos. The most important, San

---

15. Engelhardt, *San Fernando Rey*, 15–16.
16. Webb, *Indian Life*, 106, 109. Once removed from the kiln, quicklime (pure calcium oxide) had to be used immediately or kept in air-tight containers to prevent a reaction with moisture. If the quicklime was to be used in construction, the calcium oxide had to be stabilized with the addition of water. Hydration was achieved by adding water directly to the quicklime (wet slaking) or by allowing it to react with the moisture in the air (dry slaking). Wet slaking reduced the burnt stone to powder in which additional quantities would be added to produce a paste (lime putty) or a solution (lime milk). Dry slaking entailed the spreading of the quicklime on the ground, stirring in small amounts of water, and allowing it to cure from several days to a month. See Costello, "Lime Processing in Spanish California."
17. Webb, *Indian Life*, 106.

Francisco Xavier, was located north of the mission at the head waters of the Santa Clara River on top of a mesa in the territory of the Tataviam. Important villages included Tochonanga, Pirú, Camulos, and Chaguayanga.[18] The area had already witnessed conflicts between Spaniards and gentiles. In 1797, Francisco Xavier Ávila lost his life participating in an inter-village fight. Three years later, Indians killed Melchor López in the area. He may have been seeking Indians to employ.[19]

Nevertheless, between 1797 and 1804 thirty-two Indians from Chaguayanga received baptism.[20] And it was probably these neophytes who during 1804 constructed an adobe building measuring thirty-eight by six varas and containing five rooms with tile flooring. One of the rooms served as a granary. The estancia became a stopover for those traveling between southern and central California. It also attracted gentiles from surrounding villages to plant, tend, harvest, manage stock, and keep the buildings and equipment in repair.[21]

Although the missionaries employed gentiles on their estancias, they complained when rancheros hired them on their estates. In 1804, when an individual attempted to found a rancho near San Fernando, the priests objected on moral grounds:

> It is known that the rancheros leave their wives alone with only a few gentiles as company for two or more weeks at a time. On other occasions the reverse is true; they are alone with only a few Indian women, who prepare food for them. At other times the rancho is left alone, in the care of only a few gentiles, which is to say that it is like the water-jar which goes from time to time to the fountain; sooner or later it will break. Do they attend mass once in awhile? Some go once a year, but they seldom miss a fiesta or fandango. We are told of a neophyte who was once punished for not often going to mass, who said to the priests why didn't they whip the rancheros, who never or very seldom go to mass.[22]

---

18. Johnson, *The Indians of Mission San Fernando*, 255; Johnson and Earle, "Tataviam Geography and Ethnohistory," 191–93; Perkins, "Rancho San Francisco," 102–3, 123n10.
19. Mason, *Los Angeles Under the Spanish Flag*, 36.
20. Merriam, "Village Names," 95.
21. Engelhardt, *San Fernando Rey*, 16; Perkins, "Rancho San Francisco," 102–3.
22. Quoted in Mason, "Indian-Mexican Cultural Exchange," 130.

Most of the neophytes at San Fernando, however, attended Mass on a regular basis and did so within a mission bright in colors and designs, combining both traditional and Catholic motifs and themes. From azurite, malachite, ocher, diatomite, and oxide of manganese imported from Mexico, the neophytes manufactured blue, gray, purple, yellow, red, and black pigments. Over doorways and windows they painted vines, flowers, double and zigzag lines, and rows of triangles.[23] A neophyte (or neophytes) also produced a remarkable set of paintings, the *Via Crucis*, or Stations of the Cross, depicting Christ's tragic journey from Pilate's judgment hall to Mount Calvary. Unmistakable is the artist's love of the Savior and his hatred of Christ's persecutors, but he painted some of the persecutors not as Romans but as Spaniards. It was common practice for European painters to adorn their Biblical subjects in contemporary costumes. Evidently, the artist used woodcut illustrations from a religious book as his model. But the facial characteristics of his subjects may have emanated from his own experiences and imagination. In the huge, unintelligent eyes and sinister, grotesque, almost moronic expression of many of the soldiers, the artist may have been demonstrating an anti-Spanish or anti-soldier bias.[24]

In several paintings, apparently the artist went further than just turning Romans into Spaniards. He also metamorphosed some of the citizens of Jerusalem into Indians. In Station Four, an individual assisting Christ is dressed in what looks like a cotón and thus may be a neophyte. In Station Six, the bare-chested men with the fleshy bodies lifting the cross from Christ seem to be wearing the taparabo and may also represent neophytes. The woman wiping the face of Christ has been identified as the biblical figure Veronica but she looks Indian, especially when compared to the heavily-robed, European women identified as Mary and Mary Magdalene to her right. Whereas the Indian woman is actively

---

23. Webb, "Pigments Used by the Mission Indians," 137–50.
24. Phillips, "Indian Paintings from Mission San Fernando"; For an updated version of this article, see his "The Stations."

Stations of the Cross, no. 4.
Author's collection.

assisting Christ, the European women look on as passive, sobbing witnesses.[25] That the artist (or artists) could get away with such audacity under the observation and even guidance of his superiors probably stemmed from the priests' inability to realize that neophyte discontent could be manifested with such cleverness.

---

25. Phillips, "The Stations," 79. In dress and physical appearance Veronica shares much with the Indian women in Ferdinand Deppe's painting of Mission San Gabriel. Both are wearing red petticoats and white blouses. Both have long black hair. The painting is reproduced in Chapter 6.

Stations of the Cross, no. 6. *Author's collection.*

The Fathers saw in the paintings what they wanted to see—visual proof of the success of their missionary endeavors. The neophytes probably had no difficulty in comprehending the artist's "true" intentions.[26]

Because the Stations of the Cross apparently were painted about the time a new church was completed, the Fathers may have commissioned them especially for that purpose.[27] In 1804 the neophytes had begun construction of the mission's third church. Many of them had come under the tutelage of the Spanish-born carpenter Manuel Gutiérrez, probably the architect of the church. Gutiérrez resided at the mission in 1805 and 1806. The neophyte mason Tomás may have also been active in the construction.[28] Built of adobe with a tile roof, it was completed in 1806.[29] On December 6 Father Pedro Muñoz performed the blessing and dedication and Father José Señán delivered the sermon. Neophyte musicians from Missions Santa Bárbara and La Purísima Concepción added to the ceremony. Two days later, a little girl received the sacraments in the new church.[30]

Building projects also took place on the mission's other major estancia, San Joaquín de Cahuenga, located in Tongva territory at the southern end of the San Fernando Valley. Between 1798 and 1806, sixty-two Indians from Cahuenga had received baptism.[31] By the end of 1808 the Indians at the estancia had built a stone masonry dam fed by a ditch which tapped into a small stream.

---

26. Ibid. Advocating the position that the paintings represent artistic defiance of Spanish colonialism is Christ, *Los Angeles Times Sunday Magazine*, October 1, 1936. Other sources on the paintings include Weber, "The Stations at Mission San Fernando"; Mills, "Old Indian Paintings at Los Angeles"; Pelzel, "The San Gabriel Stations of the Cross from an Art-Historical Perspective," 115–19. In a counter argument, one scholar has suggested that the only Indian in all the paintings is the one in the *cotón* in Station Four who may be the painter himself. See Neuerburg, "The Indian Via Crucis." Although Neuerburg lacked comparative knowledge regarding how colonized peoples sometime mocked their rulers in art, song, and sculpture, his identification of the religious figures in the paintings and his explanation of their place in Catholic art make the article well worth reading.
27. According to one authority, the stations were painted about 1805–1807. See Weber, ed., *The Mission in the Valley*, 10.
28. Schuetz-Miller, *Building and Builders*, 74, 115, 198.
29. Bancroft, *History of California, 1801–1824*, 2: 115.
30. Engelhardt, *San Fernando Rey*, 16–18. The significance of music in the missions is discussed in Sandos, *Converting California*, 128–53.
31. Merriam, "Village Names," 94. The number sixty-two is based on the assumption that the villages of Cabuebet, Cabuenga, Caguenga, and Cahuenga were one and the same.

Once enough water had been impounded in the dam, it was released by a floodgate to irrigate the fields.³² But the construction of the dam brought the Fathers into conflict with the Pueblo de Los Angeles. Claiming the dam diverted water needed by the *vecinos* for irrigation, the ayuntamiento appointed a committee to inquire into the matter. It recommended that the Fathers be allowed use of a sufficient quantity of water from the reservoir to irrigate a small tract of land. If the diversion reduced the water supply to the pueblo, it would have to cease. The agreement was reached in late March 1810.³³ But the reservoir never met the needs of the mission.³⁴ In 1811 the neophytes completed a pipe aqueduct made of clay and half a league in length, which directed water from the reservoir to a fountain at the mission.³⁵

No doubt playing a major role in the construction projects such as this one were neophyte carpenters Juan Francisco Taotao and Fortunato. The former was from the village of Momonga, the latter from Cahuenga. Also from Momonga was the mason Tomás.³⁶ In 1813 the neophyte workers repaired the building damaged in the earthquake of December 1812, finished a new fountain to receive the water from the reservoir, and constructed a new village for themselves.³⁷ Because San Fernando became famous for its iron grill work, by this time a few neophytes probably had become expert blacksmiths.³⁸

To the priests, however, the neophytes had yet to undergo the cultural transformation the mission was designed to achieve. Their answers to a questionnaire sent to all the missionaries in 1813 clearly acknowledge neophyte defiance. Adult Indians did little to encourage their children to learn agricultural and mechanical arts and held "a supreme indifference" to Europeans and those from Latin America.³⁹ They demonstrated no inclination to learn to

---

32. Weber, ed., *The Mission in the Valley*, 14.
33. Mason, *Los Angeles Under the Spanish Flag*, 45–46; Dorland, "The Los Angeles River—Its History and Ownership," 32–33. Dorland's date of 1801 should be 1810.
34. Engelhardt, *San Fernando Rey*, 47.
35. Weber, ed., *The Mission in the Valley*, 14.
36. Schuetz-Miller, *Building and Builders*, 114–15.
37. Engelhardt, *San Fernando Rey*, 22–24.
38. Weber, ed., *The Mission in the Valley*, 22.
39. Geiger and Meighan, eds., *As The Padres Saw Them*, 29.

read and write in their own languages or in Spanish.[40] Those who undertook speaking Spanish, spoke it imperfectly.[41] They never ceased procuring food, consuming "pinole and seeds which they are accustomed to use in their pagan state and may even prefer them." They made meal from acorns and hunted deer, coyote, antelope, rabbits, squirrel, birds, and snakes.[42]

Although the Franciscans saw progress "in those who were born of Christian parents," they were disappointed in the morality of the neophytes. As a whole, the Indians were "not true to their agreements nor do they keep their promises." Moreover, they were "very much inclined to lying. Many even glory in knowing better than the other how to deceive and not be detected. Some lie in the face of every evidence." But their dominant vices were "drunkenness, stealing and fornication." The neophytes were generous with their material possessions, readily sharing beads, seeds, and other things, but they "will likewise loan their own wives to one another."[43]

As to whether the Indians retained any superstitions and traditions, the missionaries admitted that they still made "large circles in the center of which they raise a pole covered with bundles of feathers from the crow and which is adorned with beads. As many as pass the pole pay homage to it and returning round about blow to the four winds thus asking relief of their necessities." The five gods and one goddess they worshiped were "*Veat, Jaimar, Chuhuit, Pichurut* and *Quichepet*. The last mentioned is the husband of the goddess *Manisar* who gives the Indians corn or seeds."[44]

The ability to retain aspects of their traditional culture may account, in part, for most neophytes remaining at the mission. In 1813 the neophyte population increased to 1,043, remaining slightly above 1,000 for the next several years before beginning to decline.[45] Disease kept the population from further increase.

---

40. Ibid., 35.
41. Ibid., 19.
42. Ibid., 85.
43. Ibid., 101, 103, 105, 107, 125.
44. Ibid., 58. For an analysis of these deities, consult Hudson and Blackburn, "The Integration of Myth and Ritual," 225–30.
45. Jackson, *Indian Population Decline*, 175.

The missionaries acknowledged in 1814 that "among the more prominent diseases is syphilis from which a considerable number die. Spring is the time when they often take sick. The number of deaths exceeds that of births."[46]

Whether disease or other factors drove some Indians from the mission is not known, but those caught were flogged. In 1816 one neophyte received four lashes a day for ten days; three got six lashes a day for ten days, and four received nine lashes a day for ten days.[47] In 1818 forty-seven remained at large, their average age being thirty-seven. Thirteen men and women were over the age of fifty. Because most had been baptized as adults, they were more likely to flee than those converted when young or born at the mission.[48] Evidently some neophytes preferred to return to a food-procurement mode of subsistence in a landscape of diminishing wild animal and plant life than remain in an food-producing institution that more or less guaranteed ample sustenance.

The relatively small labor force probably accounts for the fact that the number of fanegas of wheat harvested by the Indian workers never surpassed the 6,400 fanegas attained in 1806, although 5,008 fanegas were harvested in 1810. The fields yielded only 3,000 fanegas in 1817. Corn production fluctuated greatly as well. Seven hundred fanegas were harvested in 1810, dropping to 200 in 1815, but increasing to 1,000 in 1817.[49] That year the mission was growing sugar, but a priest admitted that the *panocha* was not "as good as that which comes from San Blas and other places. The winters here are too cold and water is too scarce."[50] The size of the grape harvests is not known, but a grape brandy called *aguardiente* probably was being manufactured by the 1820s. According to a Spanish soldier, it was "appreciated above any other."[51] The largest number of cattle and sheep belonging to the mission, 12,800 and 7,800 respectively, was attained in 1819. The number of horses peaked at 1,320 in 1822.[52]

---

46. Geiger and Meighan, eds., *As The Padres Saw Them*, 73.
47. Cook, *Conflict*, 120.
48. Hackel, *Children of Coyote*, 95–96.
49. Engelhardt, *San Fernando Rey*, 97.
50. Quoted in Archibald, *Economic Aspects*, 175.
51. Cole and Welcome, eds., *Don Pío Pico's Historical Narrative*, 150.
52. Engelhardt, *San Fernando Rey*, 102.

Mural depicting Indians picking grapes.
Courtesy of the Santa Bárbara Museum Archive-Library.

Evidently, from 1813 to 1818 few building projects were undertaken, but during the latter year, neophytes finished a soap factory, or *jabonería*, and were building another village for themselves. This village ultimately contained forty houses.[53] By the end of 1822 they had completed the *convento*. A two-story structure, it contained rooms for the two priests and guests, a chapel, kitchen, storeroom, winery, refectory, and a reception room called a *sala*. The building

---

53. Ibid., 24.

Missionary Expansion 109

Wall design depicting an Indian hunting a deer. *Courtesy of the Santa Bárbara Museum Archive-Library.*

was unique. The sloping tile roof was supported on its front side by twenty-one Roman arches, but piers rather than columns supported the arches. Neophytes painted its exterior in bright colors and Indian blacksmiths forged wrought-iron grillwork.[54] Over a doorway in the sala, a neophyte created a mural consisting of seven Indians picking grapes from two monstrous trees. On a wall in another room, an artist depicted a hunter, disguised in a pelt and stalking a deer. An arrow has hit its mark. Food procurement and food production are nicely captured in the two decorations.[55]

---

54. Weber, ed., *The Mission in the Valley*, 15.
55. Photographs of the mural of Indians picking grapes can be found in Pauley and Pauley, *San Fernando, Rey de España*, 180. A photograph of a reproduction of the wall decoration painted by Geoffrey Holt in 1937 can be found in Christensen, *The Index of American Design*, 35.

The products produced at San Fernando did not always benefit the producers. During the ten years prior to Mexican independence in 1821, the mission had been obligated to supply the presidio at Santa Bárbara with much of its surplus. The soldiers, evidently, felt they had the right to take from the mission and its estancias whatever they wanted. In March 1821 they carried away fifty two *arrobas* of tallow and some cattle. "Will the Mission at this rate ever be able to emerge from penury?" an irate Father Francisco Ibarra asked Captain José de la Guerra y Noriega of the presidio. He sought from the captain a list regarding what rations the mission must furnish. He also wanted to know how many shoes would be needed and how much soap to produce. Ibarra concluded by insisting that "not even by treating the Indians as slaves will it be possible to meet so many expenses."[56]

Ibarra also had to deal with unruly soldiers stationed at the mission. Paying no attention to the law forbidding soldiers from intimate contact with the neophytes, the soldiers entered the Indians' quarters and workshops at will. The soldier that Ibarra confronted in the smithy in July 1821 explained that he was there to get some work done. Ibarra wrote to José de la Guerra y Noriega about this incident, also noting that "not many days ago I discovered the Indians slaughtering cattle. When I asked by whose permission they were doing so, they replied that the soldiers had so directed. I did not care to examine further, for there was no need of it, since everything could be inferred from what had happened before. Many of the Indians wear fineries, and they are given to drink."[57] Apparently, some of the neophytes were "moonlighting," manufacturing on their own time handkerchiefs and shirts for the soldiers.[58] On September 17 Ibarra informed José de la Guerra y Noriega that the mission could not supply the presidio with the seventy or eighty fanegas of corn demanded, because the harvest probably would yield only one hundred. A few days later he told the captain that rabbits and worms had caused serious damage to the crops at the mission's

---

56. Quoted in Engelhardt, *San Fernando Rey*, 36–37.
57. Ibid., 37–38.
58. Duggan, *The Chumash and the Presidio*, 76n114.

estancia of San Francisco Xavier, but fifteen pack mules laden with thirty fanegas of corn would soon depart for the presidio.[59]

Land claims brought the mission into conflict with both the presidio at Santa Bárbara and the Pueblo de Los Angeles. The missionaries pastured stock on a tract called Pirú, north of the mission. In 1821, José de la Guerra y Noriega sought the land for a rancho and petitioned the government for such. But protests from the missionaries at San Fernando and San Buenaventura prevented the land transfer.[60] Sometime in 1822 neophytes constructed a fence on the Cahuenga estancia that encroached upon pueblo land. Inside the fence were springs and branded and unbranded cattle. Some of the cattle belonged to Antonio Reyes, Aniceto Zúñiga, Francisco Ávila, José Polanco, and Nicolás Elizalde, who were all residents of the pueblo. The protest these individuals issued to the comisionado resulted in the appointment of *jueces de campo* to monitor future brandings of mission cattle and to ensure that fences were properly placed.[61]

Difficulties with the presidio mounted especially after Mexico achieved its independence from Spain. In mid-1825 Ibarra told José de la Guerra y Noriega that he could provide only thirty or forty *pesos* worth of soap, not the three hundred requested. Of the one hundred fanegas of beans, twenty-five or thirty would go to the soldiers stationed at the mission and ten to the government as a tithe, so he could send only sixteen to the presidio. The remaining forty-four or forty-nine were for the Indian laborers who picked them. That year the priest also wrote to the storekeeper at the presidio, asking what benefits the mission had received from the presidio. He knew full well that the answer was none. He emphasized that the soldiers should raise grain themselves and should not rely on the work of the neophytes.[62]

To Ibarra the army had failed the mission and emboldened the neophytes:

---

59. Engelhardt, *San Fernando Rey*, 38–40.
60. Bancroft, *History of California*, 2: 566, 569.
61. Mason, *Los Angeles Under the Spanish Flag*, 62–63.
62. Engelhardt, *San Fernando Rey*, 40–41.

> Now, consider what your presidio has contributed to the welfare of this Mission ... and you will be able to infer that this Mission is under no obligation to your presidio. The government, you say, demands aid for the presidio from the pueblo and the Mission. This is a sacred duty, as you call it. Well, from this obligation of the Mission to support the presidio follows the duty of the presidio to aid the Mission, so that it can advance spiritually and temporally; but the very opposite obtains, so much so that the Mission is now in a worse condition than at the beginning, because at that time the troops would follow runaway Indians and bring them back. The soldiers do this no more, nor do they allow it; but with the greater apparent liberty, and the better opportunity for gratifying themselves at the presidio or in the mountains, the Indians go away whenever they please, so that we have come to such a pass that we have not the necessary men to do the work at the Mission. The holy virtue of justice, I thought, consisted in punishing the guilty and rewarding the innocent. I see that such is not the case, but that it consists in self-interest and harassing the innocent the more.[63]

From 1822 to April 1827 the mission provided the presidio with supplies worth over 21,000 pesos. Payment was a draft on the Mexican government—which meant no payment.[64]

José de la Guerra y Noriega was not the only Mexican official causing Ibarra problems. The recently appointed governor, José María de Echeandía, a liberal hostile to the missionaries, sought from them pledges of loyalty to the Mexican Republic. He and the territorial assembly also wanted to know the extent of mission lands. Ibarra agreed to obey the laws of Mexico and in 1827 he sent the governor a concise description of the lands belonging to San Fernando, its landmarks, fields under irrigation, and the numbers of livestock. Although it produced enough wheat to feed its residents, neither corn nor beans could be planted on more than one fanega because of the lack of water. And the threat of grasshoppers forced the Indians to plant them at the wrong time of year. Normally these crops would have been raised on the estancias of Cahuenga and San Francisco Xavier, but the floods

---

63. Ibid., 42.
64. Ibid., 36.

of the previous two years had inundated the soil with sand.[65] In 1828 the neophytes harvested only 700 fanegas of wheat and 200 of corn. Grazing on mission lands, however, were 8,000 head of cattle, 7,500 sheep, 1,200 horses, and 90 mules.[66]

Because commerce with the outside world had opened up after Mexican independence, the products of these animals and those at San Gabriel began to attract traders and supercargoes. Alfred Robinson arrived at San Fernando in April 1829, but was not impressed with Ibarra, "a short, thick, ugly-looking old man, whose looks did not belie his character." He was even less taken with the priest's reluctance to part with the mission's products. "The niggardly administration of this place," he claimed, compared badly with the "liberality and profusion of other missions" visited. Ibarra distrusted any one who sought to purchase his tallow and hides, yet "he had accumulated an immense amount in his storehouses, where many of the latter had been destroyed by the length of time they had remained deposited. The tallow he had laid down in large, arched, stone vats of sufficient capacity to contain several cargoes."[67] During his visit, however, Robinson purchased from the "old man" items worth three thousand pesos.[68] Ibarra may have been hoarding the hides and tallow for the difficult days he perceived lay ahead.

By the end of 1829, the mission's cattle had declined to 6,000 head, sheep to 3,000. Horses and mules had dropped to 400 and 60 animals respectively. And even though the neophyte population remained a respectable 831 individuals (428 males and 403 females), within a few years it too would plummet.[69]

---

65. Ibid., 47. See also "Mission Inventory, 1827," in Weber, ed., *The Mission in the Valley*, 26–27.
66. Guzmán, "Guzmán's 'Breve noticia,'" 215; see also Engelhardt, *San Fernando Rey*, 98, 102.
67. Robinson, *Life in California*, 24.
68. Robinson, "Journal off the Coast of California," April 30, 1829, in Ogden, ed., "Alfred Robinson," 208.
69. Engelhardt, *San Fernando Rey*, 93, 102.

CHAPTER 5

Urban Magnet

Nine years after the founding of the Pueblo de Los Angeles, the population of the pobladores had increased by about 100 persons. The Los Angeles Census of 1790 counted 140 individuals. Twenty-seven men were identified by their occupations: 11 farm workers, 6 vaqueros, 3 muleteers, 2 shoemakers, 1 weaver, 1 blacksmith, 1 mason, 1 tailor, and 1 servant. Livestock numbered 953 cows, 222 bulls, 243 bull calves, 254 heifers, 171 oxen, 416 sheep, 22 goats, 89 gelded horses, 599 mares, 33 stallions, 186 colts, 145 fillies, 133 broken horses, 29 mules, and 10 young mules. At the beginning of the year, 1,848 fanegas of corn, 340 of beans, and 9 of wheat were in storage.[1]

To manage the animals and tend to the crops, the pobladores increasingly relied on Indian labor, a development not to the liking of at least two priests. In 1796 José Senán voiced his concerns in a letter to the viceroy: "The Indian plows, the Indian sows, the Indian reaps—in a word, he does almost everything," he declared. "Yes, Your Excellency, this is what goes on. And, what is more regrettable, these same pagan Indians, because of their close

---

1. Mason, *The Census of 1790*, 82–86; Mason, *Los Angeles Under the Spanish Flag*, 25–26; Ríos-Bustamante, *Mexican Los Ángeles*, 56.

TABLE 2. LOS ANGELES HARVESTS, 1790S (IN FANEGAS)

	Maize	Kidney Beans	Wheat
1790	1,848	340	9
1792	1,021	114	124
1793	2,169	268	101
1794	2,032	413	60
1795	4,720	528	90
1796	4,382	395	508

Source: Adapted from Francis F. Guest, "Municipal Institutions in Spanish California, 1769-1821" (Ph.D. dissertation, University of Southern California, August 1961).

relationship with the settlers, or the *gente de razón*, should be the first to receive baptism. But, influenced by their bad example, or by their private interests, they still remain in the darkness of heathenism, while Indians from the more distant *rancherías* are to be found, in great part, with the body of the Church."[2]

Father Isidro Alonso Salazar, writing to the Viceroy the same year, postulated a link between Indian labor and poblador immorality. The towns of Los Angeles and San José "have made little progress. The residents are a group of laggards." The employment of gentiles freed the young men to visit Indian villages to solicit the women. "The Indian is errand boy, cowboy, and manual laborer for them—in fact, general factotum." Rewarded with blankets and cotones, they fared better than the neophytes and thus had no incentive to enter the missions.[3]

By the beginning of the nineteenth century, most of the gentiles who initially worked for the pobladores had been replaced by Indians from beyond the immediate area. In 1803 the comisionado informed a priest at San Gabriel that 150 of the 200 gentiles residing in the pueblo were from outside the area.[4] That these

---

2. Quoted in Guest, "Municipal Government in Spanish California," 326.
3. Archibald, *Economic Aspects*, 94–95; Guest, "Municipal Institutions," 240–41.
4. Mason, "Indian-Mexican Cultural Exchange," 128–29.

newcomers could find work probably resulted in large part from the population decline of Yaanga. Between 1781 and 1805, 132 members of the village received baptism and evidently were incorporated into San Gabriel.[5]

Seaman William Shaler failed to mention Indians when he visited Los Angeles in mid-1804, but he did note that it was "composed of about 100 families, many of whom are in easy circumstances, and some possess from 3,000 to 5,000 head of cattle. This part of the country is fertile, and produces large quantities of grain and pulse; they are rapidly advancing in the culture of the vine and the wine produced there is of a good quality."[6] Suggesting that the gente de razón were "in easy circumstances" probably meant that others did much of the work. But opportunities for the Indian workers may have declined significantly from 1805 to 1806, when locusts caused severe damage to the pueblo's crops of corn and beans. If unemployment increased, it may have affected the crime rate, not just for Indians but for the pobladores as well. In 1809 the comisionado reported that gambling, drunkenness, and other excesses were on the increase, that the people were becoming increasingly vicious, scandalous, and intolerable, and that his stocks were seldom without occupants.[7]

The growing of hemp, a project encouraged by Governor José Joaquín Arrillaga, had begun in 1807 and kept some people employed. That year he raised the price of hemp from 3½ pesos per arroba to 4 pesos. But evidently the local authorities could not or would not employ enough gentiles to do the labor, so they turned to Mission San Juan Capistrano for assistance. Father Francisco Suñer sent one hundred neophytes to the pueblo but withdrew them in 1810. Perhaps the recall was in accordance with a royal decree stating that recently converted Indians were not to labor for private individuals except voluntarily, and if choosing to do so could not work more than ten leagues from their mission. Only the governor, not the president of the missions, could permit

---

5. Merriam, "Village Names," 120.
6. Bynum, ed., *Journal of a Voyage*, 64.
7. Bancroft, *History of California*, 2: 111.

Indians to work in a pueblo and only if they were provided with spiritual care.⁸

The incident prompted Father President Estevan Tapis to write to Governor Arrillaga. He acknowledged the hardship the withdrawal had had on the pueblo but insisted that he possessed no power to counter Father Suñer's decision. Tapis concluded by suggesting that each poblador "ought to proportion his field to the strength of his own arms rather than to that of strangers. If he cannot successfully plant and cultivate more than twelve or thirteen fanegas, let him plant less, in which case it will be easy for him to work it with the aid of his family." On occasion he might hire a day laborer.⁹

Father Tapis was not alone in complaining about the pobladores' dependence on others. In 1814 the missionaries at San Gabriel claimed that the economic relationship established between gentiles and the gente de razón hindered the spiritual development of the former and sapped the initiative of the latter:

> In the town and on the ranchos of the people of the other classes both men and women who are pagans assist in the work of the fields. Also they are employed as cooks, water carriers and in other domestic occupations. This is one of the most potent causes why the people who are called *gente de razón* are given to so much idleness. Since the pagan Indians are paid for their labor by half or a third of the crops they remain constant in the service of their masters during the season of planting and harvesting. The latter, with few exceptions, never put their hands to the plow or the sickle. As a result of this another drawback arises, namely, that the [Indian] adults delay having themselves baptized. In the service of their masters they live according to their pagan notions and practices.¹⁰

Administering to gentiles in the pueblo was probably beyond the religious reach of the missionaries but they still had hope for the pobladores. By mid-July 1815, work had begun on a church but was stopped, apparently because the pobladores offered little assistance. Moreover, the Indian carpenter and mason José Antonio

---

8. Ibid., 90–91; Mason, *Los Angeles Under the Spanish Flag*, 43.
9. Engelhardt, *San Juan Capistrano Mission*, 50–53.
10. Geiger and Meighan, eds., *As The Padres Saw Them*, 129.

Ramírez had departed, mainly because the pobladores considered his demands—six *reales* per day, a barrel of wine every three months, and board—excessive. Father Joaquín Pascual Nuez had opposed the hiring. As explained in a letter to Lieutenant José de la Guerra y Noriega he did not "think an Indian capable of being master builder of such a work as a church." Needed was a man capable of preparing lumber for doors, windows, and other items. Laborers were also needed. In October 1815, the comisionado requested that the San Gabriel missionaries release fifty neophytes to work in Los Angeles, apparently on the church.[11] But the church remained unfinished due in large part to the flood of 1815 which inundated the plaza and destroyed several houses of the pobladores. What remained of the village of Yaanga may have been swept away.[12]

In October 1816, Mariano Payeras, who was now the Father President of the missions, informed the governor that the missionaries at San Gabriel had requested several times to be relieved from providing spiritual care and assistance to the pobladores: "Among the many reasons which they give, the most cogent seems to be that it is not humanly possible to take care of both the mission and the pueblo because of the great Indian population of the former and the many residents of the latter, which are daily increasing prodigiously."[13]

In November, Payeras again contacted the governor. Again he noted that the "priests of San Gabriel have asked to be relieved of the spiritual care of the Pueblo of Los Angeles. Both I and the Reverend Father Prefect [Sarría] believe that their request is reasonable. The townspeople anxiously desire that a permanent priest be assigned to them." The pueblo continued "to grow greatly, and, together with its ranchos, is too much of a burden for the Reverend Fathers of San Gabriel."[14] By the end of 1816 the population had increased to 560.[15]

---

11. Engelhardt, *San Gabriel Mission*, 94–95, 123–24.
12. Gumprecht, *Los Angeles River*, 139–40; Crandell, "Río Porciúncula," 309–10.
13. Mariano Payeras to Pablo Vicente de Solá, Mission La Purísima, October 22, 1816, in Cutter, trans. and ed., *Writings of Mariano Payeras*, 111–12.
14. Mariano Payeras to Pablo Vicente de Solá, Mission La Purísima, November 21, 1816, ibid., 114.
15. Mason, *Los Angeles Under the Spanish Flag*, 52.

The church had to be rebuilt on higher ground before a priest could be assigned.[16] And for a time, financing the project presented a problem. But in 1819, Payeras received from Missions San Fernando, San Gabriel, San Juan Capistrano, San Luis Rey, and San Diego seven barrels of aguardiente as pure alms. He sold the aguardiente to the presidios with other minor gifts for 575 pesos, 6½ reales. Among the neophytes Mission San Luis Rey sent to the pueblo were master carpenters and masons. Their wages were set at one real per person a day, which were paid in cattle at a comparable price. This assistance resulted in the walls of the church rising as high as the arches of the windows.[17]

On November 5, 1821, Payeras sent a circular to all the missionaries, requesting money, cattle, tallow, cloth, pack mules, and aguardiente. He began by pointing out that in the pueblo "Catholic souls are without a pastor close to them, and that the one they must call upon is 3½ leagues away with a river in-between, and with responsibility for another distinct and numerous congregation. Thus, even though its inhabitants may confess yearly, life being uncertain, many die without the sacraments, and hardly one of them, especially the women, can go to San Gabriel to hear Mass, and in it the Divine word. What a pity!" Payeras estimated the debt incurred for construction to be at 2,000 pesos, but the pueblo had only 50 in its treasury. He requested two carpenters each from Missions San Fernando, San Gabriel, San Juan Capistrano, and San Luis Rey, and six sawyers from San Diego.[18]

Several missions promised assistance. Santa Bárbara would contribute one barrel of aguardiente; San Buenaventura would help cover the debt and would also send a generous supply of church items for the interior and the sacristy; San Diego offered two barrels of good white wine; San Fernando promised one barrel of aguardiente; San Gabriel doubled the amount.[19] Because San Luis

---

16. Gumprecht, *Los Angeles River*, 139–41.
17. Mariano Payeras, "circular," Mission La Purísima, November 5, 1821, in Cutter, trans. and ed., *Writings of Mariano Payeras*, 311–12.
18. Ibid.
19. Engelhardt, *San Gabriel Mission*, 132–33.

Rey had provided neophyte labor, it probably sent no supplies. Evidently, the gente de razón contributed nothing.

As of May 1822, the church had yet to be completed. This prompted Payeras to inform José de la Guerra y Noriega that the "church should have been finished last year, but almost no work was done on it. I agreed with everybody that we would dedicate it this year during the Pueblo's fiesta in September, or perhaps it is in October, after it has been roofed, whitewashed, and painted; but I fear that we will suffer further delays."[20] Evidently, the church was completed in December, but not until early 1826 was a priest in residence. Until then, the Fathers from San Gabriel celebrated Mass in the church on Sundays and holy days of obligation.[21]

The church served not just the pobladores but *Isleños* as well. On November 29, 1826, the resident priest baptized an Indian from San Clemente Island as Francisco Andrés. He was one of 163 Indians from San Clemente, Santa Catalina, and another island who would receive the sacraments in Los Angeles by the end of 1836. Many Isleños, however, never underwent baptism and those who did received the sacraments on their death beds. Not inclined to join a mission, the Isleños remained in the pueblo where they formed a community separate from the gentiles already there and became known as the Pipimares.[22] A Mexican recalled late in her life a mourning ceremony conducted by the Pipimares. It was held in an open plain outside the pueblo. After a few days of horse racing, gambling, and drinking, the Pipimares concluded the ceremony by dancing and throwing seeds and the possessions of the dead Indians into a bonfire.[23]

As residents of the pueblo, the Pipimares and the gentiles would be subjected to the social and political turbulence soon to rack California. An incident occurred in August 1826 which portended

---

20. Mariano Payeras to José de la Guerra y Noriega, Mission Soledad, May 26, 1822, in Cutter, trans. and ed., *Writings of Mariano Payeras*, 319.
21. Engelhardt, *San Gabriel Mission*, 136–37.
22. Johnson, "The People of *Quinquina*," 9, 21–22.
23. Cesarea Valenzuela de Lawrenzana [Lorenzana,] Los Angeles, November 30, 1913, Victor Prudhomme Collection, No. 439, Los Angeles County Museum.

that period. Buenaventura, a neophyte from San Luis Rey (perhaps one of the laborers on the church), having consumed too much liquor, went into a tirade and declared that the government no longer existed, that the officials were louts, and that next year it would be proper to kill all Spaniards. To the pueblo's officials, the outburst was justification to throw the Indian in jail and put him through a long trial.[24] Buenaventura's claims probably resulted from his knowing that Mexico had gained its independence from Spain in 1821.

Initially, independence had little effect on the pobladores. More mundane activities occupied their time, such as dealing with the thousands of wild horses grazing near the pueblo. Because these animals competed with cattle and domesticated horses for the herbage, about 1824 the ayuntamiento authorized a *matanza*. First, corrals had to be constructed. This was probably done by Indian laborers who dug holes into which were placed large posts and smaller poles, all being linked with leather ropes. The corrals were round, with a diameter of about one hundred varas. José del Carmen Lugo, who was about ten at the time, remembered that the vaqueros

> drove whole herds of wild and tame animals into these enclosures and closed the great gates. There were some small gates, through which only one horse could pass at a time. Two or three lancers were stationed at each of these gates to spear the wild horses as they emerged, this being done after the ranchers had indicated the animals they were claiming. The slaughter of wild horses continued until none but the animals that had been claimed were left in the corrals. Many thousands of horses were slaughtered in these times.

The vaqueros skinned animals and staked their hides to the ground to prevent shrinking. With no more treatment than this, they were either sold or put to other uses.[25]

Lugo also witnessed the great flood of 1825: "At twelve o'clock in the night, my father heard a great noise. He was sleeping at the time in a house here in the *pueblo*. He spoke to me—I was sleeping

---

24. Hittell, *History of California*, 1: 739; Engelhardt, *Missions and Missionaries of California*, 3: 241.
25. Lugo, "Life of a Rancher," 231.

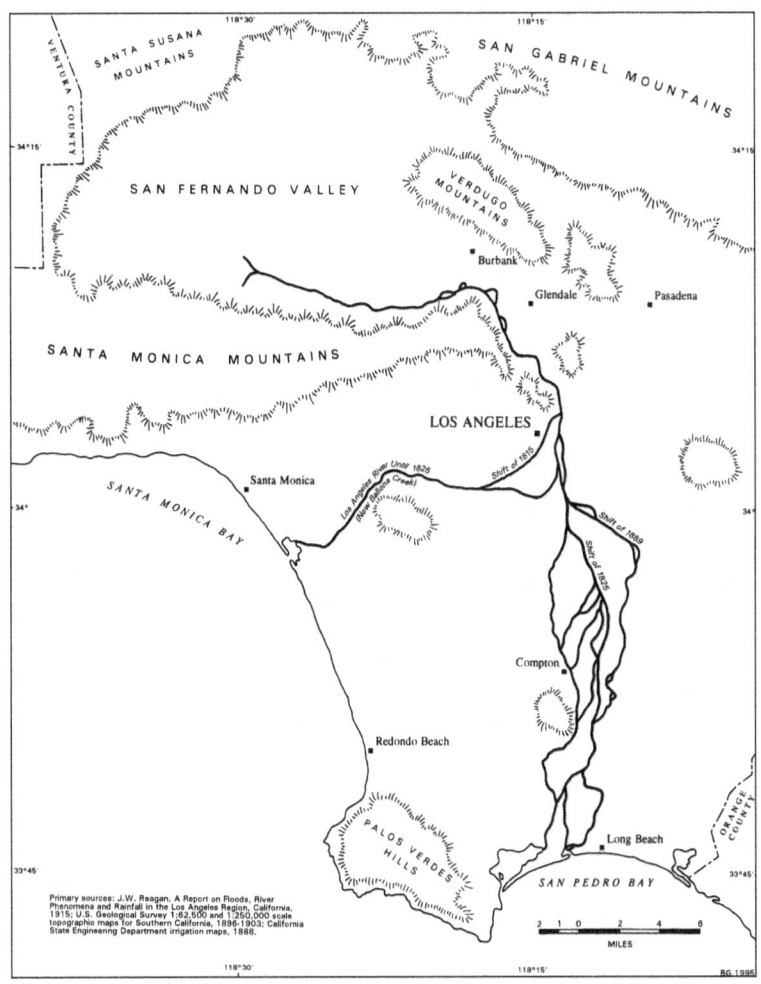

Changing Courses of the Los Angeles River.
Map by Blake Gumprecht; used with permission. *Reproduced from*
The Los Angeles River: Its Life, Death, and Possible Rebirth
(*Baltimore: Johns Hopkins University Press, 1999*).

outside—and asked what the dreadful noise was. I responded that I did not know. He then said we should investigate." Young Lugo went to the river bank which was about one hundred varas from his house, and discovered a rush of water "overflowing vegetable gardens, fences, trees, and whatever was before it. The water was running with great violence, making enormous waves." Most of the pueblo, however, was not aware of the pending catastrophe until young Lugo notified the authorities while his brothers and their servants dashed through the streets sounding the alarm. Many of the pobladores fled to high ground in carretas loaded with their belongings. Some escaped with their animals, but large numbers of horses and cattle perished in the flood.[26]

Prior to the deluge, the river flowed west to Santa Monica Bay and south towards San Pedro Bay which it seldom reached, sinking instead into depressions which formed lakes, ponds, and marshes. The flood drastically altered the local landscape. It cut a channel directly south to the sea, which drained the marsh land and destroyed the local forests.[27] It was after the flood, recalled Lugo, that "the entire country was covered with mustard and also with mallows. The stems of all the plants were very coarse."[28] The Santa Ana River also changed course before reaching the ocean where it formed the Balboa peninsula.[29]

About this time, political change swept away the old order. With Mexican independence, the office of the comisionado was abolished and the ayuntamiento became the governing body. The first alcalde served as mayor and president of the council, the second alcalde would take his place on needed occasions. Two regidores, a secretary, a treasurer and a *síndico* made up the rest of the ayuntamiento.[30] Auguste Duhaut-Cilly, a French naval officer, arrived

---

26. Ibid., 190–91.
27. Warner, Hayes, and Widney, *An Historical Sketch*, 17–18; Gumprecht, *Los Angeles River*, 141–42; Bancroft, *California Pastoral*, 346. Environmental disruption resulting from Spanish and Mexican occupation of California is discussed in Preston, "Serpent in the Garden," 260–98.
28. Lugo, "Life of a Rancher," 190–91.
29. Guinn, "Exceptional Years," 34; Crandell, "Río Porciúncula," 310–11.
30. Guinn, "Muy Ilustre Ayuntamiento," 207.

in 1827 and was impressed with the pueblo's "air of liveliness, ease, and neatness," but thought the authority of the alcalde, combing the functions of mayor and justice of the peace, insufficient to "assure the security of property." There were too many disputes to his liking. Counting eighty-two houses, the officer figured that the pueblo "might contain one thousand inhabitants, including two hundred Indian domestics and laborers."[31]

Being French, perhaps he was compelled to evaluate the quality of the wine and brandy: "The land around the village and the low ground separating the two channels of the river appeared to me to be cultivated with some care, the principal crops being corn and grapes. The vines grow well here, but the wine and brandy that come from them are quite inferior in taste to the exquisite fruit from which they are made, and I believe that this inferiority must derive from the making rather than from the vintage."[32]

According to the 1830 census, 764 vecinos and 198 Indians resided in the pueblo. That year they harvested 221 fanegas of wheat, 2,085 of corn, and 114 of beans, and manufactured 83 barrels of wine and 166 of aguardiente. Under their management were 24,394 head of cattle, 692 oxen, 2,014 horses, and 187 mules. The census-taker divided the Indians into two categories—Domesticated Indians (neophytes) and Domesticated Heathens (gentiles)—and noted the amicable relations established between the gentiles and the vecinos: "The heathens of the neighborhood, who come here and work with the whites, are treated well and live a civilized and quiet life." The gentiles outnumbered the neophytes, 127 to 71 and consisted of 67 males, 41 females, and 19 children. The neophytes consisted of 50 males, 13 females, and 18 children.[33] Given the high ratio of males to females, the gentiles probably had a much more stable family life than did the neophytes, most of whom were males from Missions San Luis Rey and San Diego and probably fugitives.

It was probably the actions of these fugitives that prompted the ayuntamiento to expand its authority over the Indian residents.

---

31. Duhaut-Cilly, *A Voyage to California*, 145.
32. Ibid.
33. Charles, ed., "Transcription and Translation," 84.

TABLE 3. INDIANS RESIDING IN LOS ANGELES, 1830

	Neophytes	Gentiles
Male adults	40	67
Female adults	13	41
Male children	9	11
Female children	9	8
Total	71	127

Source: Adapted from W. N. Charles, "Transcription and Translation of the Old Mexican Documents of the Los Angeles County Archives," *Historical Society of Southern California Quarterly* 20 (2), June 1938: 84–88.

On January 22, 1833, reacting to Indian drunkenness, it adopted a resolution appointing a citizen to "exercise a watchful supervision over the conduct of the aborigines."[34] On February 12, it discussed the possibility of establishing a night patrol governed by one of the regidores "owing to the present state of the aborigines."[35] The issue was deferred until the following day when it was decided to give such authority to the alcalde. The ayuntamiento also considered a proposition to print and post in customary places the act prohibiting the sale of liquors in taverns after eight o'clock in the evening. Those violating the law would be subjected to a fine of two pesos for the first offense, double that for the second, and they would be treated as a flagrant law breaker for the third offense. The proposition passed by a majority. The act applied to all the residents of the pueblo.[36]

Later in the same year the ayuntamiento discussed limiting the sale of liquor to Indians on holidays from eight to eleven o'clock in the mornings and from four to eight o'clock in the evenings. For the first offense a four-peso fine would be imposed, for the second offense eight pesos, and for the third offense fifteen days in

---

34. Minutes of the Ayuntamiento, January 22, 1833, Los Angeles City Archives, 2:16.
35. Minutes of the Ayuntamiento, February 12, 1833, ibid., 25.
36. Minutes of the Ayuntamiento, February 13, 1833, ibid., 25–26.

jail.³⁷ If implemented, the law had little effect in curtailing liquor sales which had become an important part of the local economy. During 1834 the ayuntamiento collected 337 pesos in taxes from tavern keepers.³⁸

In January 1835 the ayuntamiento appointed Tiburcio Tapia to the position of judge of the Indians although his duties remain unclear.³⁹ A year later it passed several articles designed to preserve order in the town and to keep its unruly inhabitants occupied.⁴⁰ On January 28 it ordered the regidor, Bacilio Valdez, and a few vecinos to patrol the streets the following Sunday, arrest all drunken Indians, and assign them to work on the zanja madre. The volume of water was insufficient to supply the needs of the pueblo.⁴¹

---
37. Session of August 20, 1833, in Robinson, ed., "The Indians of Los Angeles," 157.
38. González, *This Small City*, 206n8.
39. Session of January 8, 1835, in Robinson, ed., "The Indians of Los Angeles," 158.
40. Minutes of the Ayuntamiento, January ___, 1836, Los Angeles City Archives, 3: 148–49.
41. Session of January 28, 1836, in Robinson, ed., "The Indians of Los Angeles," 158.

CHAPTER 6

New Management

By 1806 at least fifteen priests had served at Mission San Gabriel.¹ Such high turnover prevented the formulation of long-range plans regarding the economic development of the mission and the management of the neophytes. But arriving that year was a missionary who would impose order and initiate continuity. To many of his contemporaries, Father José María Zalvidea was an exemplary missionary. Father Vicente Francisco de Sarría insisted that he was "one of the best missionaries in this land and his merit is shown by his untiring tenacity in his teaching, instructing and in the spiritual formation of his neophytes."² Father Mariano Payeras maintained that "his value is distinguished because of his activity and close attention to all of the concerns that comprise the ministry in California."³ Michael White recalled "a tall, jawboned, stout man, very industrious and intelligent, constantly at his work, spiritual, but also in developing the resources of San Gabriel mission."⁴ Zalvidea

1. A list of the missionaries and where they served is in Geiger, *Franciscan Missionaries*, 282–93.
2. Quoted in Geiger, *Franciscan Missionaries*, 267.
3. Mariano Payeras, Mission La Soledad, December 31, 1820, "Report on the Current Status of the Nineteen Missions of New California," in Cutter, trans. and ed., *Writings of Mariano Payeras*, 281.
4. White, *California All the Way Back*, 92.

"loved his 'mission children' very much," claimed Eulalia Pérez. "This is what he called the Indians whom he personally had converted to Christianity."[5] To some, however, the priest was not as saintly as his reputation indicated. Agustín Janssens concluded that the many attributes credited to him were "incomprehensible, and for them to be true one must believe he had second sight or was inspired. I was inclined to think that many of these reports were exaggerated, or never happened."[6] According to Hugo Reid, Zalvidea, "a man of talent," possessed a mind "as ambitious as it was powerful, and as cruel as it was ambitious."[7]

Reid acknowledged, however, that Zalvidea "remodeled the general system of government, putting everything in order and to its proper use, and placing every person in his proper station. Everything under him was organized and that organization kept up with the lash!" Indeed, if the line between management and labor had not yet been firmly drawn, it certainly was after his arrival. Zalvidea divided the neophytes "into various classes and stations. There were baqueros, soap-makers, tanners, shoemakers, carpenters, blacksmiths, bakers, cooks, general servants, pages, fishermen, agriculturists, horticulturists, brick and tile makers, musicians, singers, tallowmelters, vignerons, carters, cart-makers, shepherds, poultry keepers, pidgeon tenders, weavers, spinners, saddle makers, store and key keepers, deer hunters, deer and sheep skin dress makers, people of all work, and in fact every thing but coopers, who were foreign; all the balance, masons, plasterers, &c., were natives."[8]

Zalvidea's managerial skills are reflected in the mission's grain production. The year before his arrival, the neophytes had planted 130 fanegas of wheat and 12 of corn, resulting in harvests of 1,600 and 500 fanegas respectively. The 300 fanegas of wheat and 16 of corn they planted the year he arrived produced harvests of 4,800

---

5. Pérez, "An Old Woman," 102.
6. Janssens, *The Life and Adventures*, 22.
7. Reid, "Los Angeles County Indians," in *Los Angeles Star*, June 19, 1852; Heizer, ed., *Indians of Los Angeles County*, 76–77.
8. Reid, "Los Angeles County Indians," in *Los Angeles Star*, July 3, 1852; Heizer, ed., *Indians of Los Angeles County*, 82–83.

and 2,400 fanegas.[9] Building projects also increased. Master carpenter Salvador Carabantes was kept busy manufacturing doors, windows, and their frames. Performing important labor as well was the neophyte mason Remigio.[10] In 1807 the neophytes began constructing rooms for themselves. Built of adobe and roofed with tile, the doors and windows were framed with pine. The following year they completed forty-seven more rooms.[11] Initially, the neophytes disliked living in their new quarters. They could not burn them and their contents when the occupants died, as was their custom.[12]

Burning would have curtailed the spread of contagious diseases, which were, according to Hugo Reid, inadvertently spread by a policy introduced by Zalvidea. The jerga, a coarse woolen cloth distributed to the neophytes, "kept the poor wretches all the time diseased with the itch."[13] In May 1810, Zalvidea and a fellow priest informed the Father President of the missions that the hospital was crowded with from three to four-hundred "habitually infirm" Indians.[14]

Disease probably contributed to the neophyte discontent that exploded into rebellion in 1810. Late in the year, neophytes looted the storehouse and attempted to release prisoners from the guard house. About the same time, a large force of Indians, mainly Serranos in league with Mohaves, raided some of the mission's estancias on their way west, stealing property and animals. Evidently, they intended to attack San Gabriel and then San Fernando. Within two leagues of their destination they called off the attack having learned that militia from Los Angeles had arrived.[15] Led

---

9. Jackson and Castillo, *Indians, Franciscans, and Spanish Colonization*, 118.
10. Schuetz-Miller, *Building and Builders*, 155.
11. Geiger, "The Building of Mission San Gabriel," 37–38.
12. Reid, "Los Angeles County Indians," in *Los Angeles Star*, June 26, 1852; Heizer, ed., *Indians of Los Angeles County*, 78.
13. Reid, "Los Angeles County Indians," in *Los Angeles Star*, July 3, 1852; Heizer, ed., *Indians of Los Angeles County*, 86–87. That wool garments were breeding grounds for vermin was suggested by a priest in 1817. See Archibald, *Economic Aspects*, 157.
14. Engelhardt, *San Gabriel Mission*, 86.
15. Beattie and Beattie, *Heritage of the Valley*, 8–10; Mason, *Los Angeles Under the Spanish Flag*, 46–47.

by Bartolomé Tapia, the militia consisted of five corporals and twenty-seven soldiers.[16] For participating in the revolt, twenty-four neophytes and sixteen gentiles were sent to the presidio at Santa Bárbara where they were lashed nine days in a row and assigned to public works projects.[17]

Ironically, there seems to be a correlation between the rebellion and a rise in the Indian population at San Gabriel. Spanish retaliatory military campaigns resulted in the abandonment of villages and the dispersing of populations to the mission. In 1811 Zalvidea baptized Indians from Guachama, Jurupa, Muascupiabit, Yucapia, and other villages in the area that became known as San Bernardino. The Indians, mostly Serranos, traveled to the mission for the ceremony.[18] The population of the mission increased from 1,199 in 1810 to 1,678 in 1813.[19]

By this time the missionaries throughout California had received questionnaires from the Department of Oversees Colonies. The thirty-six questions sought information about the Indians' traditional culture and the progress they had made at their respective missions.[20] Because his companion had only recently arrived, Zalvidea was probably the sole respondent at San Gabriel. He noted that the neophytes suffered from "venereal disease, consumption and dysentery of blood. This last mentioned ailment is seasonal for this enemy of Indian nature recurs at the approach of winter and lasts until the beginning of summer. The number of deaths is double the number of births."[21] But venereal disease was probably the most deadly of all the ailments, it having permeated them "to such an extent that many of the children at birth give evidence immediately of the only inheritance their parents give them. As a result of every four children born, three die in their first or second year, while of those who survive the majority do not reach the age of twenty-five."[22]

---

16. Mason, *Los Angeles Under the Spanish Flag*, 47–48.
17. Engelhardt, *San Gabriel Mission*, 92.
18. Beattie and Beattie, *Heritage of the Valley*, 5n7; Bancroft, *History of California*, 2: 323n2.
19. Jackson, *Indian Population Decline*, 172.
20. See Meighan, "An Anthropological Commentary," 3–9.
21. Geiger and Meighan, eds., *As The Padres Saw Them*, 73.
22. Ibid., 105.

Regarding social and spiritual matters, Zalvidea was equally as explicit: "The Indian husband loves his wife in so far as she serves his convenience." but husbands often left their wives for other women. "It is a different matter, however, when it concerns the children for the parents love them to such an extent that we might say they are their little idols." Although the adults lacked "any inclination toward work," the missionaries were "educating them in the arts and agriculture. So little by little the diligence exerted to this end bears fruit."[23]

Because few Indians exhibited an inclination to read and write, the government should "send male teachers in primary education for the boys and female teachers for the girls. Their utmost solicitude should be exerted so that not a single word be uttered in school except in the Spanish tongue not sparing any means to obtain that goal." Some Indians still practiced idolatry, but it was being eliminated "by dint of effort. It would disappear all the faster if the old people and young ones did not live together for the former are the ones who mislead the young." Gains had been achieved "in moral and political matters," but even they "came about by the intervention of God." Their vices consisted of gambling, theft, and lack of chastity.[24]

Lack of economic progress, however, can be blamed in part on the missionaries themselves. They maintained the ancient practice of grinding grain on metates, an undertaking that was time consuming and labor intensive. Why more mills were not built in California baffled foreign visitors. French naval captain Jean F. G. de la Pérouse claimed that the small mill he presented to Mission San Carlos in 1786 would allow four women to do the work of one hundred.[25] When another naval officer, Georg Heinrich Von Langsdorff, arrived at the mission in the early 1800s, he noticed that the mill was no longer in use. Labor considerations, he concluded, contributed to the lack of mills in California. Because the Fathers "have more men and women under their care than they could keep constantly employed the whole year, if labor were

---

23. Ibid., 23.
24. Ibid., 39, 57, 61, 105.
25. La Pérouse, *Voyage Round the World*, 1: 450.

too much facilitated, they are afraid of making them idle by the introduction of mills."[26]

If Zalvidea had such concerns, he overcame them in 1816 when neophytes under his supervision began construction of a grist mill at the junction of two *arroyos* at the foot of the Pasadena table land. Working with crude adzes, some of the neophyte workers cut pine and sycamore logs into timbers. Others fashioned the massive foundations on which the walls would rest. Claudio López supervised the workers.[27] The two-story building with a roof of red tiles was completed at the end of the year. The three rooms of the lower story contained the horizontal wheel chambers into which flowed water from a cistern outside through a horizontal spout-flume. Water from the two arroyos fed the cistern. After turning the water wheel, the water flowed through a channel into a pond, later known as Lake Vineyard. A vertical shaft extended into the second story, turning a heavy millstone over one that was fixed. An Indian fed a hopper, situated above the stones, with grain that spilled through a spout into a hole in the top millstone. Ground meal was expelled from the side of the millstones into a box, which Indians then scooped out and stored. Because El Molino Viejo, as it was called, ground all the grain the mission residents consumed, it freed Indian women for other tasks.[28]

At each mission, grain was sown on estancias in varying degrees of development. Antonio Francisco Coronel noted that each estancia "had a foreman, white or Indian. Some of them were large horse and cattle ranches; others raised sheep, others field crops only. Some ranches had both crops and livestock, in which case there was a foreman for each department. The Indian laborers lived in villages on the ranches, very much as in the mission itself."[29] Beginning in 1822, when he was named San Gabriel's mayordomo, Claudio López managed the estancias. "Ask anyone

---

26. Von Langsdorff, *Voyages and Travels*, 2: 169.
27. Cleland, *El Molino Viejo*, 6–12.
28. Ibid. The building housing the mill has been restored and contains a model of El Molino, demonstrating how it functioned.
29. Coronel, *Tales of Mexican California*, 76.

who made this, or who did not," recalled Reid, "and the answer on all sides is the same: El difunto Claudio! And great credit is due him for carrying out, without flogging, the numerous works set before him." Claudio López supervised several officers "for all kinds of work, from tending of horses down to those superintending crops, and in charge of vineyards and gardens."[30]

José del Carmen Lugo recalled that each estancia was governed by a mayordomo who was a gente de razón. Assisting him were *caporales*, "intelligent Indians who understood a goodly part of the Spanish language." An important duty of the caporal was to translate orders from the mayordomo to the Indian workers. And "under the eye" of the mayordomos and caporales were the Indian vaqueros who broke horses and mules and managed the rodeos.[31] Another duty of the caporal was to record every animal branded. He did this with a notched stick called a *bali*. On each of the four sides of the stick was carved a symbol of a bull, cow, heifer, and ox. Symbols of a stallion, mare, colt, and gelding were carved on another stick. When an animal was branded, a notch was cut into the sharp edge of the stick.[32]

According to the French naval officer Eugène Duflot de Mofras, the mission ultimately created seventeen estancias for large animals such as horses and cattle and fifteen for smaller animals such as sheep, goats, and pigs.[33] Neophytes raised turkeys on San Francisquito which was situated near the mission. Their cages were located next to the soap works in an upper story. Turkey dung was used in the curing of leather. Hogs were raised on another estancia, primarily to make soap, but this may have been disagreeable work. Reid noted that "the Indians, with some few exceptions, refused to eat hogs, alleging the whole family to be transformed Spaniards!"[34]

---

30. Reid, "Los Angeles County Indians," in *Los Angeles Star*, July 3, 1852; Heizer, ed., *Indians of Los Angeles County*, 84; Bancroft, *History of California*, 2: 568n26.
31. Lugo, "Life of a Rancher," 225–26.
32. Hoffman, ed., "Hugo Ried's Account," 27n2. A drawing of the stick is at the end of Hoffman's notes. The original is on display in the California History Gallery at the Natural History Museum of Los Angeles County.
33. Duflot de Mofras, *Travels*, 1: 183.
34. Reid, "Los Angeles County Indians," in *Los Angeles Star*, July 3, 1852; Heizer, ed., *Indians of Los Angeles County*, 86.

One of the estancias may have served as a refuge for a mission unable to feed all of its neophytes. By mid-May 1816, the fields near the mission had become so exhausted that some six hundred neophytes were planting crops on La Puente which was about three leagues distant.[35] When traveling to the mission on Saturdays and returning to the estancia on Sundays after Mass, these workers often became so disorderly that Zalvidea sought permission from Governor Pablo Vicente de Solá to erect a chapel at La Puente, where on certain days the Indians would be collected for Mass and where they could go for devotions.[36] Evidently, a chapel was never built, but within a decade neophytes had constructed two buildings, each one 33 × 6½ varas and 4 varas high arranged so as to form two sides of a square. The adobe walls were nearly a vara thick with loopholes every five varas.[37] The buildings reminded an American visitor of British barracks.[38]

It was on the estancias, especially the most isolated ones, where Indian culture was best preserved. A northern California ranchero mentioned that "the Indian vaqueros, who lived much of the time on the more distant cattle ranges, were a wild set of men." The "hill vaqueros" were different from those living near the missions.[39] How different obviously varied from mission to mission, but on the estancias, hunting and gathering restrictions were probably fewer than at the mission, allowing for a blending of traditional and mission work routines. Living in *jacales* with their wives and families away from the daily observation of the Fathers, the vaqueros better retained their language, social customs, and traditional spiritual beliefs than did those residing at the mission.[40] Although produced much later in time, the drawing "California Vaqueros Returned from the Chase" seems to capture this kind of life. All but one of the men appear to be Indians who

---

35. Bancroft, *History of California*, 2: 356.
36. Beattie and Beattie, *Heritage of the Valley*, 11.
37. Smith, "The Journal," in Brooks, ed., *The Southwest Expeditions*, 98–99.
38. Rogers, "Daybook," November 27, 1826, ibid., 215.
39. Vallejo, "Ranch and Mission Days in Alta California," 85.
40. See Mora, *Californios*, 39, 89.

"California Vaqueros Returned from the Chase,"
by Harrison Eastman, 1854. *Courtesy of the Bancroft Library,
University of California, Berkeley.*

have assembled at a jacal. An Indian woman looks on as a young girl prepares a meal.

Had such a drawing been available to him, Governor Solá would have been troubled by the two mounted Indians. In January 1818 he reminded Father President Vicente Francisco de Sarría about the royal laws and regulations regarding neophytes and their use of horses. Sarría was to inform the missionaries that the corporal of the guard at each mission was to produce a list of the vaqueros who managed the cattle and horses. Those not on the list were to relinquish their bridles and saddles, and any neophyte found illegally mounted was to be arrested. In a circular, Sarría instructed the missionaries to comply with the governor's orders.[41]

Posing a far more serious threat to the missions than mounted neophytes were mounted gentiles. Sometime in May 1819 a small party of Mohaves on a trading expedition arrived at Mission San Buenaventura. Nervous soldiers fired on the visitors. In the ensuing fight, two soldiers, a neophyte, and ten Mohaves lost their lives. Apparently, the incident led to the Mohaves attacking Indian villages near San Gabriel on their return to the Colorado River.[42] Later, rumors spread among the Spanish that the Mohaves intended to attack Missions San Buenaventura, San Fernando, and San Gabriel. The expedition that Lieutenant Gabriel Moraga organized to punish the Mohaves confronted no Indians but gained important information. As noted by Father José Señán of San Buenaventura, "Moraga himself has told me ... that the reports of many murders committed in the rancherías of the region not far from San Gabriel are true. Some of the dead were gentiles, several others, neophytes who had run away from San Gabriel, and three from San Fernando."[43] As a result of the crisis, the number of gente de razón residing temporarily or permanently at or near San Gabriel increased to 175 of whom 51 or more were soldiers.[44]

Whereas the Mohaves remained confrontational, the Serranos sought accommodation. After being dispersed during the 1810 rebellion, the Serranos apparently had reorganized under a chief called Solano. In 1819 they sent word to San Gabriel, requesting to be instructed in agriculture and stock raising. The missionaries sent Pedro Alvarez to Guachama. He was to guide the Indians in constructing a zanja, four leagues in length, from a creek to where the crops were to be planted. By using the shoulder blades of slain cattle as digging sticks, they completed the task in time for

---
41. Engelhardt, *Missions and Missionaries of California*, 3: 29.
42. Bancroft, *History of California*, 2: 332–35; Beattie and Beattie, *Heritage of the Valley*, 139. The incident is fully described in Engelhardt, *San Buenaventura*, 47–48.
43. José Señán to Juan Cortés, Mission San Buenaventura, February 26, 1820, in Simpson, ed., *The Letters of José Señán, O.F.M.*, 136–37.
44. Bancroft, *History of California*, 2: 357.

the growing season of 1820. Invitations were sent to neighboring villages to witness the planting, and a thousand Indians eventually arrived.[45] Writing on June 2, 1820, Father Mariano Payeras mentioned that "San Gabriel had formed a rancho named San Bernardino 20 leagues away in an easterly direction and that the site is suitable for a mission and that according to the Father Ministers of the said mission, all the conditions are present there for a good establishment."[46]

When Fathers Payeras and José Bernardo Sánchez passed through the area a year later, crops had been planted and a zanja constructed. Sánchez wrote in his diary that "beyond a rockstrewn plain toward the east there is a large water ditch which has been made for the missionaries of San Gabriel by a certain Pedro Alvarez in order to irrigate the lands which they now have under cultivation, all kinds of seeds being sown." Cattle had been introduced, and most of the two hundred Indians there had "been made Christians at San Gabriel."[47] But a report issued in 1822 stated that the area was also "a place of refuge" occupied "by fugitive Christians who hide cattle there and dig out bears."[48]

The Indians who maintained the Mill Creek Zanja, as the ditch became known, were kept busy. Francisco Alvarado, testifying in a water-rights case many years later, recalled seeing Indians repairing the ditch. They would "throw rocks and sand out of this ditch so the waters could run down again." He also noted that "some years there was not much water and those years the ditch did not break. Some winters there were very high waters and then it would break the ditch."[49] In his testimony, Daniel Sexton explained that "the Indians cultivated twice as much land as there is cultivated now. The soil was the best and they cultivated grain, vines, pumpkins and squashes." They built "their village on the southwest side

---

45. Beattie and Beattie, *Heritage of the Valley*, 12–14.
46. Mariano Payeras to missionaries, Mission La Purísima, June 2, 1820, in Cutter, trans. and ed. *Writings of Mariano Payeras*, 264.
47. Beattie, "San Bernardino Valley in the Spanish Period," 15–18.
48. Report at Mission San Gabriel for the Year 1822, in ibid., 18.
49. Francisco Alvarado testimony in "History: The Mill Creek Zanja," compiled by Rumble, Works Project Administration Project, no. 3428, 55.

of the ditch and they cultivated on the north side."⁵⁰ The Indians constructed their lodges in the traditional style of brush and reed and for mayordomo Carlos García they built a house and a granary in adobe. In January 1821, García baptized a dying child at Jumuba and Zalvidea recorded the baptism the following month.⁵¹

At least one Indian not from the area resided on the estancia. When Captain José Romero and a contingent of soldiers arrived in late December 1823, they were met by Salvador, a neophyte who had fled Mission San Juan Capistrano eleven years before. He and another Indian, Pedro Celestino, joined the expedition on its way to the Colorado River. Once through the San Gorgonio Pass, the soldiers encountered an Indian, his wife, another woman, and a child. The Indian told them that most of his companions had withdrawn into the mountains, having known of the expedition for several days, and that he was a Cahuilla on his way to San Gabriel. The soldiers proceeded to a village they called Agua Caliente because of its hot springs. There they met two Cahuillas, José and Vicente, who had once worked on some ranchos.⁵²

Whether residing on or beyond Rancho San Bernardino and whether practicing some or no agriculture, the Cahuillas and Serranos remained politically independent, culturally intact, and economically self-sufficient. This was not the case of Indians incorporated into Mission San Gabriel. Individuals from widely dispersed villages, some with long-standing disputes and speaking different languages, were force to interact in a foreign social environment. Even though they had been "reduced by the Spanish missionaries to the same religion and labor," noted Reid, the Tongva never "mixed their blood" with the Serranos who they "considered much inferior."⁵³

---

50. Daniel Sexton testimony in "History: the Mill Creek Zanja," 63.
51. Beattie and Beattie, *Heritage of the Valley*, 12–14.
52. Bean and Mason, trans. and eds., *Diaries and Accounts of the Romero Expeditions*, 35–38.
53. Reid, "Los Angeles County Indians," in *Los Angeles Star*, February 21, 1852; Heizer, ed., *Indians of Los Angeles County*, 8–9.

To maintain order among the disparate groups, Father Zalvidea and the other missionary divided the Indians into distinct categories based on age, gender, and marital status, all of which ran counter to traditional culture, especially the practice of housing young unmarried men and women in different quarters called *monjeríos* and *dormitorios*. José del Carmen Lugo recalled that "the single men at the mission lived in a separate building, and at night when they retired to their quarters the door was locked and the key delivered to the *padre*." The unmarried women lived in a building managed by a matron. "When they were rounded up at night they also were locked in, and the key was taken to the *padre*." In the morning, an alcalde freed the young men and the matron freed the young women.[54]

When Eulalia Pérez, the widow of a soldier, arrived at the mission in 1821, the system was well in place: "The young girls between the ages of seven and nine were brought to the monjerío. They would be raised there and would leave when they were to be married. An Indian mother would care for them in the monjerío. When I was at the mission, that mother's name was Polonia. They would call her *Madre Abadesa*." A blind Indian named Andresillo would stand at the door and call out the name of each girl as she entered. Once the girls were locked inside the dormitory, the keys were turned over to Pérez. If a girl failed to show up, she and her mother, if she had one, were punished.[55] Pérez became especially attached to a neophyte named Victoria, who until the age of six had lived in the prominent village of Comicrabit. Upon reaching the age of thirteen, at the insistence of Pérez, Victoria married Pablo María, a man twenty-eight years her senior. One of the elders of the equally important village of Yutucubit, he treated his young wife with kindness. She bore him three children, the first when she was fourteen.[56]

Happy marriages such as this one were perhaps common but so were sexual encounters outside of marriage, especially between

---

54. Lugo, "Life of a Rancher," 224.
55. Pérez, "An Old Woman," 107.
56. Dakin, *A Scotch Paisano*, 33–34.

Indian women and the gente de razón. For many years, children born from mixed parents were secretly strangled and buried. Indian men considered women engaging in such unions contaminated and to induce miscarriages put them through a regimen of sweating and drinking herbs. When Zalvidea discovered this practice, he concluded that all miscarriages were self-induced and "when a woman had the misfortune to bring forth a still-born child, she was punished," recalled Reid. "The penalty inflicted was shaving the head, flogging for fifteen subsequent days, irons on the feet for three months, and having to appear every Sunday in church, on the steps leading to the altar, with a hideous painted wooden child in her arms!"[57]

Boys and men breaking the law were locked in the stocks or confined to a cell. According to Eulalia Pérez, "when the crime was serious, they would take the delinquent to the guardhouse. There, they would tie him to a canon or to a post and whip him twenty-five times or more, depending on the crime. Sometimes they would put them in the stocks head first. Other times they would put a shotgun behind their knees and tie their hands to the gun. This punishment was called Ley de Bayona. It was very painful."[58] Reid noted that Zalvidea combined flogging with the stocks: "He was an inveterate enemy to drunkenness, and did all in his power to prevent it, but to no purpose." Rather than flog Indians while drunk, he put them in the stocks until sober. Flogging followed and if this was deemed insufficient punishment, he poured into their mouths a dose of warm water and salt. "It was of no use, the disease was as incurable as consumption."[59]

Although punishment was often remembered and recorded, most of the activities at the mission were so mundane as to be overlooked by residents and visitors alike. An exception is Eulalia Pérez who had much to say about her supervisory duties and the mission's work routine:

---

57. Reid, "Los Angeles County Indians," in *Los Angeles Star*, May 29 and July 3, 1852; Heizer, ed., *Indians of Los Angeles County*, 70, 87.
58. Pérez, "An Old Woman," 109.
59. Reid, "Los Angeles County Indians," in *Los Angeles Star*, July 3, 1852; Heizer, ed., *Indians of Los Angeles County*, 87.

The girls would be let out of the *monjerío* in the morning. First they would go to the Mass said by Father Zalvidea. He spoke the Indian language. Then they would go to the *pozolera* to eat breakfast. Sometimes the breakfast would be *champurrado* (chocolate mixed with *atole* made from corn). On feast days they would have bread and something sweet. On other days they would normally have *pozole* and meat. After breakfast, each girl would go to her assigned task, which might be weaving, unloading items from *carretas*, sewing, or something else.

When they were assigned to unload *carretas*, at eleven o'clock they would have to put one or two aside. These *carretas* were used to take drinks to the Indians who were working the fields. The drinks were usually a mixture of water, vinegar, and sugar, but sometimes they were water, lemon, and sugar. I was the person who prepared and sent out those drinks so the Indians would not get sick. That is what the Fathers ordered done.

All work stopped at eleven. At noon, they would go to the *pozolera* for their meal of meat and vegetables. At one o'clock they would return to their jobs. The workday ended at sunset. Then they all would go to the *pozolera* to eat their dinner, which was *atole* with meat. Sometimes it was plain *atole*.[60]

By teaching two Indians, Tomás and "El Gentil," how to prepare meals and eventually turning them into the "the best cooks in this whole part of the country," Pérez endeared herself to the missionaries who appointed her the *llavera*, the keeper of the keys of the mission. Her duties were manifold. To apportion the daily rations to the Indians at the pozolera, she had to know the number of single women and men, laborers and vaqueros, who would be there on any day. From the clothing storehouse, she distributed the materials to make dresses for the children and the single and married women. And she supervised the cutting of clothes for the men. Apparently, Indian women were excluded from this activity because "all the work having to do with clothing was done by my daughters under my supervision. I would cut and arrange the pieces of material and my five daughters would do the sewing. When they could not keep up with the workload, I would let the Father know. He would then hire women from the pueblo of Los Angeles and pay them." Pérez also supervised the manufacturing

---

60. Pérez, "An Old Woman," 107–8.

of soap and oversaw the crushing of olives to make olive oil. She saw to the distribution of everything related to the making of saddles and shoes—leather, calfskin, chamois, sheepskin, red cloth, tacks, thread, and silk. Every eight days, she provided rations and provisions for the soldiers and the gente de razón working at the mission. Assisting her was Lucio, an Indian "whom the Fathers trusted completely."[61]

The difficulty of the work, rather than the gender of the workers, seems to have determined who did what, where and when. "The heavy work of the field was done by the men," recounted Lugo. "Women who were not employed in the weaving or in the houses were put to work on the lighter tasks that were near the mission. Nevertheless, it was not uncommon to employ women in field labor, because there were nearly always more of them than there were of men." Under the guidance of a director, the strongest women labored at the looms. Women also sewed and cleaned the buildings.[62]

Regarding the male labor pool, the vaqueros occupied the top rung in the hierarchy. But they were divided into two categories—bareback riders and saddle riders. Pérez recalled that "those who rode bareback received nothing more than their shirt, blanket, and loincloth. Those who rode with saddles received the same clothing as the gente de razón. They were given a shirt, a vest, pants, a hat, boots, shoes, and spurs. And they were given a saddle, a bridle, and a *reata* for their horse."[63] Lugo recalled much the same thing. To the saddle rider "the mission gave the saddle and trappings, the bridle, spurs, boots and shoes. To the others, nothing more than was given the other Indians—a spear, a coarse shirt, breech clout, and a blanket. No Indian who was not a cow-herder was permitted to ride a horse."[64]

Other neophytes also occupied privileged positions. Lugo mentioned that "a few of the Indian boys received a slight education.

---

61. Ibid., 104–6.
62. Lugo, "Life of a Rancher," 226.
63. Pérez, "An Old Woman," 104.
64. Lugo, "Life of a Rancher," 226.

They were taught to read, to sing, and play musical instruments.... Some of them learned how to assist at the mass, and generally these were servants of the padres and were better clothed and treated."[65] Pablo Tac, a literate neophyte from Mission San Luis Rey, described the hierarchical system in a manuscript he prepared in Rome while studying for the priesthood. Although writing about his own mission, what Tac said about its social structure was duplicated to varying degrees at San Gabriel, San Fernando, and all the missions. The Father had his "pages, alcaldes, majordomos, musicians, soldiers.... The pages are for him and for the Spanish and Mexican, English and Anglo-American travelers.... The musicians of the Mission for the holy days and all the Sundays and holidays of the year, with them the singers, all Indian neophytes."[66]

By the time Tac wrote his manuscript, the office of alcalde was no longer occupied by independent and sometimes defiant individuals. Now it was held by those selected by and thus in the service of the missionaries. Writing in late 1826, a British naval officer noted that "the Padre selects one or more of those amongst his Indians he considers the most trustworthy and places him over the others as Alcalde with an increased quantity of Rations and some few privileges by way of distinction."[67] Hugo Reid claimed that a Father at San Gabriel was complicit in ensuring that the alcaldes were chosen "from among the very laziest of the community; he being of the opinion that they took more pleasure in making others work, than would industrious ones! ... They carried a wand to denote their authority, and what was more terrible, an immense scourge of raw hide, about ten feet in length, plaited to the thickness of an ordinary man's wrist!—They did a great deal of chastisement, both by and without orders. One of them always acted as overseer on work done in gangs."[68]

---

65. Ibid.
66. Tac, "Indian Life and Customs at Mission San Luis Rey," 99–100.
67. Beechey, *Narrative of a Voyage*, 1: 356.
68. Reid, "Los Angeles County Indians," in *Los Angeles Star*, July 3, 1852; Heizer, ed., *Indians of Los Angeles County*, 85.

The alcaldes also undermined the status of those traditional political and religious leaders still at the mission. As recounted by Reid, Zalvidea "had no predilection for wizards, and generally (as some one or another was always reporting evil of them), kept them chained together in couples and well flogged. There were, at that period, no small number of old men rejoicing in the fame of witchcraft, so he made sawyers of them all, keeping them like hounds in couples, and so they worked, two above and two below in the pit."[69]

Commenting on the alcaldes were trappers Jedediah Smith and Harrison Rogers who along with several companions arrived at the mission on November 28, 1826. Smith noted that "the immediate supervision of the different kinds of business is confided to Overseers . . . raised in a manner somewhat better than the common mass under the eye of the father from whom they sometimes receive a limited education."[70] On December 10, Rogers observed two alcaldes lashing five neophytes, men between the ages of fifty and sixty, twelve to fourteen times on the buttocks for not reporting to work. The commandant stood by with his sword to ensure that the Indian charged with the flogging carried out his duty. On January 3, 1827, Rogers witnessed four or five Indians brought to the mission. A "stubborn" Indian who "did not like to submit to the lash was knocked down by the commandant, tied, and severely shiped [whipped], then chained by the leg to another Ind. who had been guilty of a similar offense." Eleven days later on a Sunday, he saw someone whipping four Indians who had been gambling and fighting. Each received thirty to forty lashes.[71] So serious was the theft of oranges that one of the priests asked Rogers to have his blacksmith fashion a trap large enough to snare Indians. On a Tuesday he noticed eight or ten boys gathering oranges under the watchful eye of the mayordomo.[72]

---

69. Reid, "Los Angeles County Indians," in *Los Angeles Star*, July 3, 1852; Heizer, ed., *Indians of Los Angeles County*, 87.
70. Smith, "The Journal," in Brooks, ed., *Southwest Expeditions*, 130.
71. Rogers, "Daybook," December, 10, 1826, January 3, 14, 1827, ibid., 223, 233, 238.
72. Rogers, "Daybook, December 14, 1826, January 7, 8, 1827, ibid., 225, 235–36.

Economically, Rogers saw an institution running smoothly, with an Indian workforce of one thousand persons. The mission manufactured brandy, ground its corn at a water mill "of tolerable quality," possessed upwards of thirty thousand head of cattle, as well as horses, sheep, hogs, and other animals. While strolling through the shops, he observed Indian men constructing plows and spinning wheels and sixty Indian women weaving and spinning yarn. Indian carpenters and blacksmiths also were at work. The soap factory greatly impressed him; it was far more extensive than he imagined. Rogers also witnessed the arrival of the captain of a schooner that had dropped anchor at San Pedro. The captain had come to buy tallow, soap, and hides.[73]

Neophytes first scraped the hides and then soaked them in vats of water. That accomplished, the workers put the hides in other vats containing water into which had been poured the proper amount of liquid lime. Remaining in the solution for three or four days, the hides were removed and the hair scraped off, which the liming process had loosened. Once washed to remove the lime, the hides were ready for the tanning vat. Indians sprinkled crushed oak bark at the bottom of the vat onto which was placed a hide. Another layer of bark was sprinkled over the hide and another hide was placed in the vat, and so on until it was full. An Indian worker then poured water over the pack. The hides remained in the solution from three to six months or longer, during which time they were repacked several times with bark and fresh water. Once that process was completed, Indians removed the pack from the vat and again washed the individual hides to remove all sediment and bark. They rubbed oil, grease, or tallow into the hides to replace the natural oil lost in the tanning process and then hung the hides in a drying room. When thoroughly dry, they were ready for the leather shop where Indians turned them into saddles, shoes, bridles, reins, and other practical items.[74]

---

73. Rogers, "Daybook," November 29, December 1, 13, 16,1826, January 6, 7, 1827, ibid., 217, 220, 225, 226, 235–36.
74. Webb, *Indian Life*, 193.

To make soap and tallow, the neophytes at San Gabriel tossed the fats of the cattle into vats. Fires under the vats separated the fats. The suet, that portion deposited around the kidneys and loins, was converted into tallow. The tallow from an average steer amounted to about 4 arrobas, the lard to about 2½ arrobas. The tallow was placed in casks or hide bags which had been whitewashed to keep insects out and then secured in storerooms. The greasier fats were used in the making of soap. Indians removed the wood ashes from the fires under the soap or tallow vats and leached them to produce a liquid containing sodium and potassium carbonates. They poured this liquid and the melted fats into a vat or kettle to boil. Allowed to cool, the soft soap flowing on top of the water was skimmed off and poured into molds. When solid, Indians cut the product into bars of various sizes. Placed on shelves, and turned occasionally, the bars were allowed to dry until ready for use or to sell.[75]

Hides and tallow became important export items in 1821 when Mexico opened up its ports to foreign shipping. At San Pedro they were exchanged for manufactured and luxury goods that arrived in increasing volume. Immigrants William Hartnell and Hugh McCulloch, who were granted a trading permit by the governor, erected an adobe warehouse at San Pedro in 1821 from where hides and tallow were traded to the first ship that put in. A few years later the permit was transferred to Mission San Gabriel. Under the direction of Father José Bernardo Sánchez, the warehouse was used both as a storehouse and as an office to conduct business with the supercargoes.[76] As a boy, José de Carmen Lugo remembered seeing "carretas loaded with hides and tallow headed for the ships at San Pedro."[77]

---

75. Ibid., 201–3.
76. Burger, "Furs, Hides, and a Little Larceny," 395.
77. Lugo, "Life of a Rancher," 230.

Much of this economic change would not be witnessed by Father Zalvidea, at least not at San Gabriel. In 1826, mentally and physically ill, he was transferred to San Juan Capistrano.[78] To Reid the priest's temporal accomplishments were truly impressive. Under his management, neophytes planted the large vineyards "intersected with fine walks, shaded by fruit trees of every description, and rendered still more lovely by shrubs interspersed between." It was Zalvidea "who laid out the orange garden, fruit and olive orchards" and supervised the neophytes in the building of the mill and the construction of "fences of tunas" that encircled the fields. Regarding Zalvidea's spiritual achievements, however, Reid was less impressed: "In a short time he mastered the language and reduced it to grammatical rules. He translated the prayers of the church, and preached every Sunday a sermon in their own tongue. His translation of the Lord's prayer, commencing with Ayoinac (our Father) is a grand specimen of his eloquence and ability." But whatever insight the neophytes gained into the Catholic religion "did not one iota alter their own."[79]

Having served with Zalvidea, Father José Bernardo Sánchez became the senior missionary. Reid recalled a man "of cheerful disposition, frank and generous in his nature, although at times he lost his temper with the strange, unruly set around him." Whereas Zalvidea had a "certain restraint in his presence, arising from his austerity and pensiveness," Sánchez was different: "His temper was governed according to circumstances. In Ecclesiastical affairs, his deportment was solemn; in trade he was formal; in the government of the Mission, active, lively and strict." Sánchez resumed the sermons in Spanish. A neophyte named Benito translated each sentence into the Tongva language.[80]

Reid claimed that Sánchez improved the moral condition of the neophytes: "The same regulations which had been observed

---

78. Engelhardt, *San Gabriel Mission*, 143–44.
79. Reid, "Los Angeles County Indians," in *Los Angeles Star*, July 3, 1852; Heizer, ed., *Indians of Los Angeles County*, 77, 82.
80. Reid, "Los Angeles County Indians," in *Los Angeles Star*, June 19 and July 20, 1852; Heizer, ed., *Indians of Los Angeles County*, 77, 90.

by his predecessor, were still in force under him, but more lenity was shown to the failing of the Neophites. Although the lash was ever ready, yet many other modes of chastising were adopted in its stead for minor offenses." Moreover, "a more healthy state prevailed even in their morals. Many an Indian who had previously stolen and committed other acts of insubordination, from a vindictive spirit, now refrained from such deeds, through the love and good will held to their spiritual and temporal ruler."[81]

Even the personal habits and material lives of the neophytes improved under Sánchez's administration. The women's jergas were

> converted into sweat-cloths, and more suitable garments provided them. This measure effected a great change, for now of a Sunday might be seen coming out of church, women dressed in petticoats of all patterns and colors, with their clean chemise protruding from the bosom, with a 'kerchief round the neck and rebosa [sic] round the shoulders; while the men had their pants, jacket, trousers, hat and fancy silk sash. Even the children sported in a white or fancy shirt, with a handkerchief tied round the head.
>
> This was, indeed, a transformation, and one for which they felt grateful. It elevated them to better thoughts and principles, and made them esteem themselves more than anything else would have done. Nor did the reformation stop here. The married people had not only sheets provided for their beds, but even curtains. It was the duty of the Mayordomo to visit each room weekly, and see that every article was kept clean and report accordingly. The Priest paid a monthly visit for the same end.[82]

Alfred Robinson met Sánchez in 1829 and maintained that he had advanced the mission "to its present flourishing condition. Possessing a kind, generous, and lively disposition, he had acquired, in consequence, a multitude of friends, who constantly flocked around him; whilst through his liberality the needy wanderer, of whatever nation or creed, found a home and protection

---

81. Reid, "Los Angeles County Indians," in *Los Angeles Star*, July 10, 1852; Heizer, ed., *Indians of Los Angeles County*, 92.
82. Reid, "Los Angeles County Indians," in *Los Angeles Star*, July 10, 1852; Heizer, ed., *Indians of Los Angeles County*, 92–93.

in the Mission."⁸³ One of the fur trappers arriving at the mission in February 1831 also was impressed with the priest. George C. Yount dictated his experiences years later but remembered Sánchez as "a man of the highest order of talents, and withal so bland, so gentle, so affectionate and paternal, he gave dignity to everything, with which he came in contact—All looked up to him as to a parent, dutiful and affectionate children, look up & bow with entire reverence—His wishes were the all prevailing law, which no one would violate.... Every department of the establishment bore the impress of his very enlarged & comprehensive mind—Order, method and regularity were perfectly maintained."⁸⁴

Whereas the social order of the mission impressed Yount, the Mass fascinated Robinson:

> The imposing ceremony, glittering ornaments, and illuminated walls, were well adapted to captivate the simple mind of the Indian, and I could not but admire the apparent devotion of the multitude, who seemed absorbed, heart and soul, in the scene before them. The solemn music of the mass was well selected, and the Indian voices accorded harmoniously with the flutes and violins that accompanied them. On retiring from the church, the musicians stationed themselves at a private door of the building, whence issued the reverend father, whom they escorted with music to his quarters; there they remained for a half hour, performing waltzes and marches, until some trifling present was distributed among them, when they returned to their homes.⁸⁵

Robinson was less taken with what followed: "The remaining part of the Sabbath is devoted to amusements, and the Indian generally resorts to gambling, in which he indulges to the most criminal excess, frequently losing all he possesses in the world—his clothes—beads, baubles of all kinds, and even his wife and children! We saw them thus engaged, scattered in groups about the Mission, while at a little distance quite an exciting horse race was going on; the Indians betting as wildly on their favorite animals as upon the games of chance, which found so many

---

83. Robinson, *Life in California*, 22–23.
84. Camp, ed., "The Chronicles of George C. Yount," 43.
85. Robinson, *Life in California*, 22–23.

devotees."[86] Reid recorded a similar picture: "After Sunday Mass, provisions were distributed for the ensuing week, including a half a pint of aguardiente to the men and a pint of wine to the women. A football game and races followed, the day culminating in a type of field hockey, pitting men against women. People flocked in from all parts to see the sport, and heavy bets were made. The Priest took a great interest in the game, and as the women seldom had less than half a dozen quarrels, in which hair flew by the handful, it pleased him very much. The game being concluded, all went to prayers, and so ended the Sabbath."[87]

Yount recounted another contest, one that demonstrated the mutual respect trappers and neophytes accorded one another:

> The hunters, in their leather apparel, mockasins [sic] and strange accouterments, were of course a great curiosity there, and the Indians, so civilized, were hardly less a wonder to the trappers, than the trappers were to them—Many feats of skill were mutually exhibited—Wild Redmen of the woods the trappers had known full well enough; but these same human beings, brought under salutary rules of living well, educated and civilized, they had never known, nor had they even supposed it possible thus to tame such wild and wayward beings—Their feats with the lasso or Riata astonished the Americans hardly less than did the latter excite in the former amazement by their skillful use of the Rifle.[88]

The mission's economic affairs also impressed Yount: "It was common for this Priest to purchase whole cargoes of Groceries & Provisions, and to freight the Ship with Hides and Tallow for its return voyage." When a vessel arrived the priest "would order out his vaqueros for a Rodeo, and the herds were gathered in for the slaughter—and many hundreds were slain in a day. Here might be seen thousand of hides drying and being packed for the Market and there the numerous cauldrons trying out the Tallow." Regarding the meat, Indians received the first choice followed by "hogs and many dogs, and then Vultures and Buzzards." Coyotes and

---

86. Ibid., 13.
87. Reid, "Los Angeles County Indians," in *Los Angeles Star*, July 10, 1852; Heizer, ed., *Indians of Los Angeles County*, 94–95.
88. Camp, ed., "Chronicles," 44.

wolves got their turn at night. But if the Grizzly came near, the "Indians, with their lariat, on fleetest horses, would soon lasso the monster and drag him to a cruel death—His mangled body soon paid the forfeiture for his insolence, to increase the immense heaps of carcasses, on which the other abovenamed animals were daily fed."[89]

Intending to extend his operations literally into the Pacific Ocean, William Wolfskill, another fur trapper, convinced Father Sánchez to join with him in building a schooner that would ply the California coast in search of the sea otter. The Father gave the task to Joseph Chapman, a sailor and jack-of-all-trades residing at the mission.[90] Chapman spoke a mongrel language, intermingling English, Spanish, and Indian words in ways that made him difficult to understand, but according to Robinson, "Father Sánchez... used to say that Chapman could get more work out of the Indians in his unintelligible tongue than all the mayordomos put together." The result was a schooner "of about sixty tons that had been entirely framed at S. Gabriel and fitted for subsequent completion at St. Pedro. Every piece of timber had been hewn and fitted thirty miles from the place, and brought down to the beach upon carts."[91] Perhaps the neophyte José de los Santos Juncos had this project in mind when late in his life he recalled that "the pines were carried in the carretas, but the Indians being so numerous some Indians were employed to bring them on foot, such a bringer being required to make two trips from San Gabriel to the mountains and back in one day, each trip returning with a pine timber (of small size such as he could carry) on his shoulder. They gave azotes [lashes] to the bringers who did not complete their two trips in one day."[92] Christened the *Guadalupe* in honor of the patroness of Mexico, the schooner evidently sailed from San Pedro in January 1832. It proceeded as far south as the island

---

89. Ibid., 43.
90. Polley, "Ship Building," 39.
91. Robinson, *Life in California*, 71.
92. Quoted in McCawley, *The First Angelinos*, 192.

*Mission San Gabriel in 1833, by Ferdinand Deppe.
Courtesy of the Santa Bárbara Mission Archive-Library.*

of Cerros but otter hunting failed to live up to expectations and Wolfskill abandoned the enterprise the following year.[93]

To Robinson the agricultural wealth of the mission was much more impressive than its ship building accomplishments:

> There are several extensive gardens attached to this Mission, where may be found oranges, citrons, limes, apples, pears, peaches, pomegranates, figs, and grapes in abundance. From the latter they make yearly from four to six hundred barrels of wine, and two hundred of brandy; the sale of which produces an income of more than twelve thousand dollars. The storehouses and granaries are kept well supplied, and the corridor in the square is usually heaped up with piles of hides and tallow. Besides the resources of the vineyard, the Mission derives considerable revenue from the sale of grain; and the weekly slaughter of cattle produces a sufficient sum for clothing and supporting the Indians.[94]

---

93. Warner, "Reminiscences of Early California," 15; Polley, "Ship Building," 39; Wilson, *William Wolfskill*, 84–85. Another vessel may have also exported products of the mission. Michael White claimed to have sailed it to Mazatlán and San Blas with dry tongues, olives, wine, dried beef, soap, and aguardiente. See White, *California All the Way Back*, 32. The possibility of two vessels was advanced by Warner, Hayes, and Widney, *An Historical Sketch*, 13; and by Ogden, *The California Sea Otter Trade, 1784–1848*, 110–11.

94. Robinson, *Life in California*, 23.

New Management

The mission dominated the trade in the Los Angeles region. It possessed far more cattle, sheep, and horses, employed far more Indian workers, and claimed far more land than any of the ranchos. According to a report issued in 1828, on its numerous estancias were 24,300 head of cattle, 2,035 horses, 135 mules, 4 burros, 13,500 sheep, 50 goats, and 125 swine.[95] The resources of the two most prosperous ranchos in the area failed to measure up. That year Rancho San Pedro could claim 9,621 head of cattle, 200 horses, and 12 mules and Rancho Santa Gertrudis, 3,620, 201, and 8 respectively. Neither rancho raised sheep.[96] Moreover, none of the ranchos could match the one hundred Indian vaqueros working at the mission and on its estancias.[97]

During the early 1830s the vessels owned by Henry Virmond, a German merchant of Acapulco, frequently put into San Pedro Bay. Ferdinand Deppe, also German, served as supercargo, and on at least one occasion visited San Gabriel, where he made a sketch of the mission. He later produced a painting from the sketch which is remarkable not just for the background view of the mission itself but for the foreground details as well.[98] To the left, the white man speaking with the priest probably is a supercargo. Two Indian pages stand nearby. To the right, an Indian family is relaxing in front of a jacal, the traditional lodge that many neophytes favored over their adobe apartments. The Indian women are well dressed in blouses and petticoats, a result of the trade with the outside world. Of the two men, one has on the garb of a gente de razón, the other is in a taparabo. Behind them another Indian (perhaps a bareback vaquero) is holding a horse without a saddle. He seems to be talking with a woman and her child.

This idyllic scene, however, was soon to change. In 1832 matanzas began at Missions San Luis Rey and La Purísima, but the one at San Gabriel was especially significant. Apparently the Fathers,

---

95. Guzmán, "Guzmán's 'Breve Noticia,'" 217. See also Jackson and Castillo, *Indians, Franciscans and Spanish Colonization*, 127.
96. Charles, "Transcription and Translation," 84–88.
97. Barrows, "Michael White, the Pioneer," 20.
98. Bancroft, *History of California*, 2: 779; 3: 644n10. According to one scholar, the priest is José Sánchez, the Californio is mayordomo Claudio López, and the white man is supercargo James Scott from Boston. See Temple, "The Founding of San Gabriel Mission," 27–28.

fearing that the missions would soon be dissolved, sought to obtain as much wealth as they could in the limited time they had left. Their goal, however, was not self-enrichment; the money was to assist the neophytes, in particular to buy them clothes.[99]

Shortly before the death of Father José Sánchez in January 1833, an incident may have occurred that hastened his demise. As remembered by Eulalia Pérez, neophytes from San Luis Rey, San Juan Capistrano, and other missions, evidently aware that the break-up of the missions was imminent, demonstrated their freedom by temporarily occupying San Gabriel and confining Sánchez to his room. There he remained for eight days: "He was filled with sorrow because of what the Indians had done.... He became ill and never was the same again. His eardrums burst and he bled from his ears. His headache lasted until he died."[100] This version of his death is not corroborated by anyone else, but the passing of Father Sánchez, recalled Reid, left "everyone who knew him sad at his loss."[101] Long-time mayordomo and trusted aid Claudio López died the same month.[102]

Under the new management of Father Tomás Eleuterio Esténaga, the matanza continued. Robinson claimed that at San Gabriel "the ruin was more perceptible than at other places, owing to the superiority of its possessions." Lacking sufficient numbers of vaqueros to slaughter the cattle, the missionaries turned to the gente de razón, a development that Robinson found troubling.[103] According to Angustias de la Guerra Ord, someone at San Gabriel contacted some residents of Los Angeles and perhaps San Diego to kill a large number of cattle. "The men who killed the cattle were

---

99. Bancroft, *History of California*, 3: 348–49; de la Guerra, "Occurrences in California," 234.
100. Pérez, "An Old Woman," 106–7. Historian Hubert Howe Bancroft noted that Pérez's story may be factual but wondered why there was no other record of the incident. See *History of California*, 3: 642n8.
101. Reid, "Los Angeles County Indians," in *Los Angeles Star*, July 10, 1852; Heizer, ed., *Indians of Los Angeles County*, 95.
102. Pérez, "An Old Woman," 107. According to Hubert Howe Bancroft, López was mayordomo from 1821 to 1830. See Bancroft, *History of California*, 4: 717.
103. Robinson, *Life in California*, 111. The recounting of this matanza by secular historians produced sharp response by a Franciscan historian, who argued that because the number of animals slaughtered was exaggerated, a wholesale slaughter did not take place. See Engelhardt, *Missions and Missionaries of California*, 3: 557–58 and Appendix K, 654–63.

Mission San Gabriel in 1833 (details).

157

supposed to keep half of the hides from the cattle they slaughtered and turn over the other half to the mission. I do not know if these contracts were made before the death of Father José Sánchez or if the slaughter began before he died, but the destruction happened after his death."[104]

One of those receiving a contract was Pío Pico. He mentioned in his memoirs that he could "slaughter as many as I wanted as long as I gave them half the skins." He recruited ten vaqueros and thirty pedestrian Indians from Missions San Luis Rey and San Diego, and they slaughtered 2,500 head of cattle at the estancia of San José and about the same number at Los Coyotes.[105] "During these horrible slaughters," recalled Antonio María Osio, "the animal fat had to be strewn along the ground and the meat left to rot in the fields."[106] In November 1833, the Los Angeles ayuntamiento instructed the rancheros to burn the carcasses of the slaughtered cattle.[107]

The number of cattle destroyed is not known, but it may have been extremely large. According to Osio, "because Esténaga gave away the possessions of the Fathers, after a short time he was obliged to accept meat and lard as charity. Don Tomás Yorba would send him these items from his Santa Ana Ranch. Yorba also loaned him a cow so that he would have milk."[108]

---

104. De la Guerra Ord, "Occurrences in California," 235.
105. Cole and Welcome, eds., *Don Pío Pico's Historical Narrative*, 136–37. In 1834 the *Lagoda* sailed from San Pedro with 25,000 hides. See Nunis, ed., *Faxon Dean Atherton*, 24.
106. Osio, *The History of Alta California*, 118–19.
107. Quoted in Frierman, "The Ontiveros Adobe, *History of California*, 3: 637n5.
108. Osio, *The History of Alta California*, 119.

CHAPTER 7

Emancipation and Secularization

Following independence, achieved in 1821, the Mexican government initiated legislation designed to expand agricultural production and land distribution in its northern regions. The Colonization Act of 1824 proclaimed that "those national lands which are neither private property nor belonging to any corporation or pueblo ... can therefore be colonized." Fearing that foreigners might take advantage of the law, the act clearly stated that Mexican citizens were to be given preferential treatment. No grantee was allowed ownership of more than one square league of irrigable land, four square leagues of crop lands dependent on the seasons, and six square leagues to pasture cattle.[1]

Because the act failed to spell out guidelines for its implementation, in 1828 the government added supplemental regulations. In particular, territorial governors were authorized to grant vacant lands to contractors, families, or privates persons "whether Mexicans or foreigners, who may ask for them, for the purpose of cultivating and inhabiting them." If the settler failed to comply with the regulations, he could lose his land. Moreover, "in those territories where there are missions, the lands occupied by them

---
1. Dwinelle, ed., *The Colonial History of San Francisco,* "Addenda No. XII," 23–24.

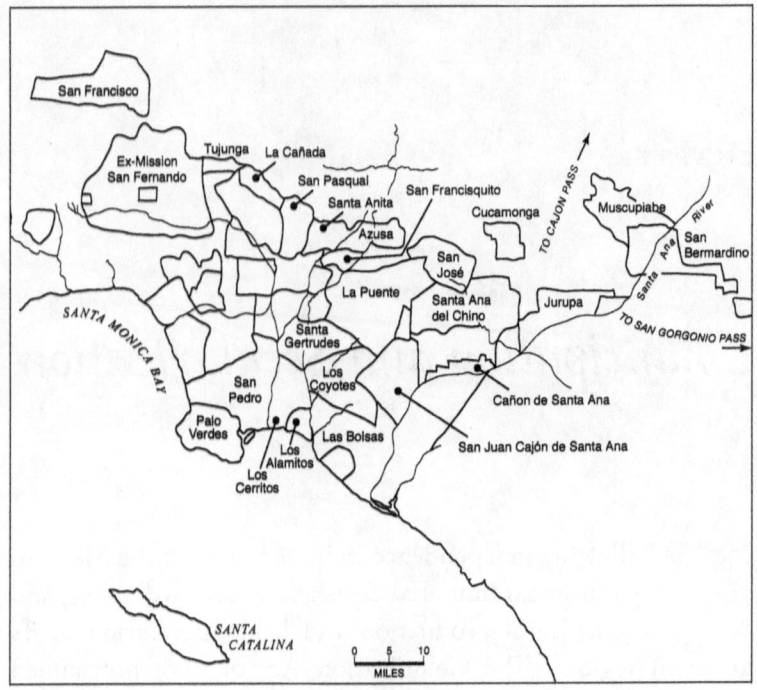

Mexican Land Grants, 1822–1846

cannot be colonized at present, nor until it be determined whether they are to be considered as the property of the establishments of the neophytes, catechumens, and Mexican colonists." This act became the legal foundation for granting land in Alta California. No longer would land be consigned provisionally to relatively few individuals. Instead, title would be granted on a much more permanent basis to numerous petitioners.[2]

By 1830 Ranchos Tajuata, Boca de Santa Mónica, La Brea, La Ballona, Las Ciénegas, Las Vírgenes, San Vicente y Santa Mónica, and Sausal Redondo had been established in the Los Angeles region, but they remained largely undeveloped.[3] And the six ranchos with

---

2. Ibid., "Addenda No. XIV," 25–26. See also Hornbeck, "Land tenure," 371–90.
3. Ríos-Bustamante and Castillo, *An Illustrated History of Mexican Los Angeles*, 18; Beck and Haase, *Historical Atlas of California*, 37–38.

Emancipation and Secularization 161

enough wealth to be identified in the census of that year—San Pedro, Santa Gertrudis, San Rafael, San José, Simi, and Santiago de Santa Ana—had evolved from early Spanish concessions. All emphasized stock raising over crop growing. Rancho Santiago de Santa Ana raised only 160 fanegas of corn, but grazing on the estate in 1830 were 3,348 head of cattle (including 58 oxen), 178 horses (96 mares and 82 stallions), and 22 mules. Eighteen Mexicans—seven adults males, six adult women, and five children—resided on the rancho. Fifteen adult Indians also lived there—three neophytes and twelve gentiles, along with four children.[4]

Rancho Santa Gertrudis was the only other rancho identified as employing Indians, but on it neophytes outnumbered gentiles by thirty to fifteen. Twenty-two neophytes were adult males, most coming from Missions San Diego and San Luis Rey. In comparison, the Mexicans residing on the rancho totaled twenty-two males, twenty-three females, and twenty-five children. Obviously, the Mexicans had established families on the rancho whereas the neophytes formed a community of males. Some of the Indians must have been entrusted with managing the rancho's 3,620 head of cattle, 260 horses (160 mares and 110 stallions), and 8 mules. Rancho Santa Gertrudis paid little attention to agriculture, harvesting only 20 fanegas of wheat and 74 of corn in 1830.[5]

In 1834 Bernardo Yorba, son of José Antonio Yorba, received title to Rancho Cañón de Santa Ana, located adjacent to Santiago de Santa Ana but north of the Santa Ana River. Two years later the rancho's population included Bernardo, his wife and seven children, seven Mexicans, two non-Indian servants, and eighteen Indians. The Indians constructed a two-story building with thirty rooms, a school, harness shop, and about twenty rooms for themselves.[6] José Dolores Sepúlveda and J. J. Warner (an early American settler) visited the rancho several times during the mid-1830s. The emphasis on crop growing impressed both of them. According to Warner, Yorba "cultivated more extensively than any person

---
4. Charles, ed., "Transcription and Translation," 84–88.
5. Ibid.
6. Bakken, "Rancho Cañón de Santa Ana," 207–8; Haas, *Conquest and Historical Identities*, 48–49.

upon the river. He did this mainly for his own consumption, and for that of his employees and servants, of whom he had a large number." Sepúlveda recalled that "during these years, he had a vineyard and corn and beans and wheat, and had a great many servants engaged in cultivation. They worked Indians in those days—a great many of them."⁷

On twelve of the seventeen ranchos identified in the census of 1836 resided 286 Indians. The increase is most evident on two ranchos. In 1830 eighteen Indians resided on Santiago de Santa Ana, forty-five on Santa Gertrudis.⁸ In 1836 the numbers had risen to sixty-eight and sixty-nine respectively. The vast majority of Indians (including children) identified in the census were labeled servants, although Rancho San Pedro employed six vaqueros and six cooks in addition to six servants.⁹

Neophytes were also to receive land. In April 1826, Governor José María Echeandía had met with several missionaries in San Diego. After a prolonged discussion they agreed that some neophytes might be emancipated. But the Fathers agreed to surrender their temporal authority only over those neophytes of good conduct and long service residing in selected areas. In July Echeandía issued a decree emancipating qualified neophytes in the military districts of Monterey, Santa Bárbara, and San Diego. An adult male who had been a Christian from childhood or for fifteen years and who had some means of making a living could apply to a presidial comandante for his freedom. Once the comandante received a favorable report from the neophyte's priest, he could issue a permit entitling the Indian and his family to live where they pleased. The name of the neophyte would be erased from his mission's register and he would become a Mexican citizen.¹⁰

---

7. Quoted in Stephenson, *Don Bernardo Yorba*, 32–33. Testimony of José Dolores Sepúlveda, The Anaheim Water Company, et al., Plaintiffs and Respondents vs. The Semi-Tropic Water Company, et al., Defendants and Appellants. Transcript on Appeal in the Superior Court of Los Angeles County, State of California.
8. Charles, ed., "Transcription and Translation," 84–88.
9. Layne, ed., "The First Census of the Los Angeles District," 157–61.
10. Bancroft, *History of California*, 3: 102–3; Engelhardt, *Missions and Missionaries of California*, 2: 239–40. For more recent studies of emancipation, consult Haas, "Emancipation and the Meaning of Freedom in Mexican California" and Ivey "Secularization in California and Texas."

TABLE 4. RANCHOS AND INDIAN RESIDENTS, 1836

	Number of Rancho Indians
San Antonio (Lugo in census)	11
Los Alamitos	33
Santiago de Santa Ana	68
Cañon de Santa Ana (San Antonio in census)	18
Las Bolsas	23
Los Coyotes	14
Santa Gertrudis	69
San Juan Cajón de Santa Ana (Pacifico in census)	10
San Pedro	23
San José	6
Rodeo de las Aguas	8
San Rafael (Verdugo in census)	3
Total	286

Source: Adapted from J. Gregg Layne, "The First Census of the Los Angeles District," *Historical Society of Southern California Quarterly* 18 (3), June 1936:157–66.

Although a few Indians took advantage of the law to secure their freedom, the legal status of most neophytes did not change until 1834 when Governor José Figueroa issued a proclamation implementing the secularization act passed the previous year by the Mexican legislature designed to breakup the missions. Of the act's twenty-three articles, the first four dealt with general matters: the missions would be converted into Indian pueblos; until replaced by parish priests, the missionaries would attend only to the spiritualities of the neophytes; and the territorial government would assume the administration of temporalities.[11]

Specificity began with article five. To every individual head of a family and to all single males over twenty-one years of age, "a lot of land, whether irrigable or otherwise, of not exceeding

---

11. The act is published in translation in Dwinelle, *The Colonial History*, "Addenda No. XIX," 31–34, and in Bancroft, *History of California*, 3: 342–44n. It was also published in the *Los Angeles Star* of January 19, 1856.

four hundred varas square, nor less than one hundred, shall be given out of the common lands of the Missions." Common and when possible municipal lands were to be assigned to each Indian pueblo. According to articles six and seven, one half of each mission's cattle, seeds, and equipment for cultivation would be distributed to the neophytes. But article eight emphasized that all lands and animals not distributed would remain under the care and responsibility of mayordomos or other officers whom the governor would name. Articles nine through thirteen covered issues such as the subsistence of the missionaries and their responsibilities, which included maintaining the libraries, holy vestments, and the furniture of the church.[12]

Articles fourteen through seventeen dealt with the government of the Indian pueblos. Number sixteen was of special significance: "The emancipated Indians will be obliged to assist at the indispensable common labor which, in the opinion of the Governor, may be judged necessary for the cultivation of vineyards, orchards, and corn-fields, which for the present remain undisposed of." Article seventeen obligated the neophytes to render personal service to the priests. Articles eighteen and nineteen placed further restrictions on them. They could neither sell, burden, nor alienate the lands granted them nor sell their cattle. If an individual were caught engaging in such activities, his property could be confiscated. Moreover, when an Indian land proprietor died without an heir, his property would revert to the government. Articles twenty through twenty-three stated that the governor would name commissioners of the missions, that the missionaries could slaughter cattle only for the subsistence of the neophytes but not in large numbers, and that the debts of the missions would be paid out of "the common mass of the property."[13]

The governor also issued orders to each commissioner or *administrador* as he was usually called. Upon arriving at his respective mission, he was to present his credentials to the priests who would immediately hand over to him the accounts and other documents

---

12. Dwinelle, *The Colonial History*, "Addenda No. XIX," 31.
13. Ibid., 32.

relating to the property, liquidated and not liquidated. He would conduct inventories of the houses, workshops, and the implements and utensils in each. Crops would be identified and the number of horses and cattle estimated. Most importantly, the administrador was to inform the neophytes that the mission would be turned into a village. The land upon which an individual labored and the house in which he lived belonged to him. But the land granted to the individual would be decided by the administrador, the priests, and the mayordomo (called steward in the proclamation). The administrador would select one or more mayordomos and fix their pay. He could also grant to neophytes living in villages distant from the mission and consisting of twenty-five or more persons the lands on which they resided. Communities with fewer than twenty-five residents would form a sub-branch of the nearest village.[14]

As the articles clearly state, the secularization of the missions did not free the neophytes but placed them under different management. Title to land was denied them. True ownership of the animals and equipment placed in their care also was denied. In effect, property was to be collectively, not individually, transferred. Moreover, the land to be granted was limited to a mission's buildings, orchards, and vineyards. Its estancias were not eligible for distribution, being located on lands belonging to the government.[15]

To implement the act, José María Híjar, the newly appointed governor of California, arrived in 1834. He was also to oversee a colonization plan whereby lands once used by the missions and not needed by the Indians would be distributed to the colonists who accompanied him to California. Before Híjar could assume his duties, however, Mexican President Antonio López de Santa Anna canceled his appointment as governor. But Híjar and his followers remained in California and may have encouraged Indians to revolt against Governor Figueroa.[16]

---

14. Ibid., 32–33.
15. Haas, "Emancipation"; Garr, "Planning, Politics, and Plunder," 299. The fate of the few Indian "pueblos" founded beyond the missions is discussed by Garr.
16. Beattie and Beattie, *Heritage of the Valley*, 29–30.

One of Híjar's subordinates, Lieutenant Buenaventura Araujo, invited the non-Christian Cahuillas to meet with him at San Gabriel. In October two hundred armed gentiles on their way to the mission raided the estancia at San Bernardino, seizing ornaments and sacred vessels of the chapel and grain belonging to the neophytes residing there. Intending to persuade the Indians to turn back, Father Tomás Eleuterio Esténaga, Lieutenant Araujo, the mayordomo of the mission, and a vaquero met them at La Puente. The Cahuillas promptly seized the priest and carried him off to the mountains apparently to kill him. Somehow Araujo negotiated his release and they returned to San Gabriel. A short time later, Lieutenant Colonel Nicolás Gutiérrez arrived and spoke with four leaders of the Cahuillas He ordered them to return the cart, horses, and religious objects they had taken from the priest and the horses they had stolen from San Bernardino. The leaders rejoined their followers, but instead of returning with the stolen items, they headed east. Gutiérrez called for reinforcements from Los Angeles which arrived quickly and twenty *paisanos* set out to punish the Indians. The rear guard of the Cahuillas that attacked the pursuers lost four men before retreating. When confronting the main body of Cahuillas, however, the paisanos turned back and the Indians returned to their villages in the mountains. But on December 30 Indians again raided San Bernardino killing thirteen or fourteen neophytes, capturing others, and burning a portion of a village. Upon receiving word of the attack, a military party of fifty-eight men departed the mission for the estancia, where they found that most of the neophytes had remained loyal to the church. Renegade neophytes, however, may have directed the attack.[17]

Many of the paisanos joining this and other expeditions lived at or near Mission San Gabriel. Seventy-two men, women, and children resided there in 1836.[18] They and others sought and sometimes competed for the lands the Indians had improved. For

---

17. Hutchinson, *Frontier Settlement in Mexican California*, 278–80; Bancroft, *History of California*, 3: 359–60, 630–31; Beattie and Beattie, *Heritage of the Valley*, 29–31.
18. Layne, ed., "The First Census," 149–53.

example, retired soldier Juan Mariné found what he was looking for at the mission's estancia of San Pasqual. In 1833 he had petitioned the governor for the property, claiming that Father José Bernardo Sánchez had agreed to release the land but only with permission from the Indian alcaldes. Sánchez told the alcaldes that the transfer was permanent, to which they supposedly agreed. On February 18, 1835, the governor declared that Mariné was owner of the land. As with all petitioners, neither he nor his heirs had the right to divide or alienate the land and he could not subject it to rent, mortgage, or other encumbrances. He could enclose the land and plant whatever he wanted, but he was to build and occupy a house within one year. When ownership was confirmed, he was to contact a proper magistrate who would mark its boundaries and authorize juridical possession. Any contravention of these conditions could forfeit the title.[19]

Shortly before petitioning for San Pasqual, Mariné married Eulalia Pérez, who thought that the land had been given to her. In her memoirs, she wrote:

> In addition to supporting me and all my daughters until they married, Father Sánchez gave me two ranchos, that is, land for one rancho and land for an orchard. Before he gave them to me, he first had all the Indians gather together in the teaching room. Then Father Zalvidea, who spoke their language, asked them if they wanted to give me that land for an orchard and for a rancho, since I had always taken care of them and helped them. He said that those who agreed should raise their hand. All the Indians raised their hands and said they wanted me to have the land. When Father Sánchez turned over the land to me, I was already married to Juan Mariné. Later, Juan gave me half the land and kept the other half for himself.[20]

Francisco Villa, however, already had settled at San Pasqual. Married to a "daughter of the mission" he claimed that the mayordomo of the mission, José Pérez, had granted him a tract where he planted crops and built a house. Villa was convinced that the land was his so he was naturally upset when he was informed

---
19. Robinson, *Land In California*, 80–81.
20. Pérez, "An Old Woman," 112.

that Mariné had title to San Pasqual. In October 1837 he sought justice from the Los Angeles ayuntamiento which created a special committee to investigate the dispute. At San Gabriel, Mariné provided the committee members with the document from the governor granting him the land. They also spoke with José Pérez who insisted he had not given Villa permission to occupy the land. The committee ruled in favor of Mariné and recommended that Villa vacate the property. The ayuntamiento accepted the recommendations, and evidently Villa abandoned the land he had improved.[21] Mariné failed to live up to the stipulations in the grant, namely that he occupy and cultivate the land, but he died in 1838 before losing the property. Mariné's son by a previous marriage sold his interest in the rancho which exchanged hands several times during the next few years. Eulalia Pérez, now age sixty-two, retained a house and garden at San Gabriel.[22]

Scotsman Hugo Reid also sought mission land. To acquire property, he, like many foreigners in California, had converted to Catholicism and had become a naturalized Mexican citizen. Eulalia Pérez introduced him to Victoria, a neophyte long under her care. For a time Reid was stymied because Victoria was married. But after her husband died from smallpox, Reid married Victoria at San Gabriel in September 1837. He took responsibility for Victoria's children and became a land owner.[23]

By the time of the marriage, Victoria had received title to two estancias—Santa Anita and La Huerta Cuatín, also called La Huerta de Peras. Because the two ranchos were Victoria's dowry, they came into Reid's possession. Reid, however, preferred to live near San Gabriel on a parcel of mission land he obtained called Uva Espina. He employed Indian workers to build a two-story adobe house, strengthened with beams hauled most likely by Indians from the San Bernardino Mountains. At their new home

---

21. Minutes of the Ayuntamiento, October 7, November 4, 11, 1837, Los Angeles Archives, 3: 452–53.
22. Robinson, *Land in California*, 81–82; Robinson, *Ranchos Become Cities*, 175–76; Layne, ed., "The First Census," 97. Eulalia Pérez's age has long been debated, but the census of 1836, (p. 150) under the name Helena Guillén, puts her age at sixty.
23. See Dakin, *A Scotch Paisano*, 1–50.

the Reids entertained and Victoria sewed fine linens. On some dresses and on the edges of table covers she depicted Indian symbols with fine bead work. Victoria also supervised the numerous Indian servants who worked without wages. Instead, they received food, clothes, and assistance for their services. The Indian servants resided at a village on the banks of the San Gabriel River.[24]

Juan Bandini moved in with the Reids in the fall of 1838, after Indians had sacked his rancho near San Diego. In September the governor granted him Rancho Jurupa and selected him as administrador of Mission San Gabriel. Bandini replaced José Pérez, who had succeeded Juan José Rocha.[25] In March the following year, Bandini told the governor that he had restored the property of the mission which he had found in very bad condition. He sought to resign and asked that the five hundred pesos owed him for his salary be paid in mares and other mission property. He admitted taking forty young bulls from the mission's herd but agreed to return them if ordered to do so. Although the government may have accepted his resignation, Bandini reconsidered and served out the year.[26]

The formal duties of Bandini and his counterparts were undefined until January 1839 when Governor Juan Alvarado issued a set of regulations. Each administrador was to present an exact account of the debts owed by and to his mission, but he had no authority to make sales to foreign merchants or to private persons or to pay debts accrued by the mission without governmental permission. Nor could he order the slaughter of cattle except for the subsistence of the Indians and the Mexican residents. Because the looms were to be put back into operation, trafficking in mules and horses for woolen goods was prohibited. The administradores were to vacate the premises they occupied for areas where they would construct houses for themselves. They were to prevent any person from settling on mission lands while the Indians remained in the area. They were to present a census of all the inhabitants,

---
24. Ibid., 51–56;
25. Ibid., 61; Engelhardt, *San Gabriel Mission*, 185–86.
26. Bancroft, *History of California*, 3: 644n10

distinguish their classes and ages, and identify those who were emancipated and those established on mission lands.[27]

The governor was especially concerned about the high salaries of the administradores, so in March 1839 he replaced them with mayordomos with increased responsibilities. Mayordomos were to furnish the missionaries with every necessity for their existence. They could compel the Indians to work at their respective tasks and to chastise them moderately for any misdemeanors they might commit. They were to see that the neophytes attended church on the customary days and hours. They could enlist as many servants as necessary as long as they were from the mission being administered. After one year the mayordomos could employ Indians for their own private undertakings, but permission from the workers was to be obtained.[28] Evidently, the title "administrador" continued to be applied to those who were in fact mayordomos.

To determine if the mayordomos were enforcing the regulations, the governor of California appointed William Hartnell (originally from England) *Visitador General*. His job was to inspect the missions and report on their conditions. Hartnell arrived at Mission San Gabriel on June 7, 1839, and two days later assembled the neophytes. He inquired if they had enough to eat, if they understood that the amount of clothing issued depended on the mission's income, and if they had any complaints to lodge against Bandini. Hartnell noted that "they all appeared very happy and there was not a single complaint." Bandini provided Hartnell with statistics regarding neophytes, crops, and animals. Only 369 Indians remained at the mission: 174 men, 121 women, 41 boys, 12 girls, and 21 infants. Horses at the mission and adjacent estancias numbered 1,701. Other animals included 981 cattle, 81 oxen, 13 mules, 2 burros, and 1,045 lambs. Indians had planted 22 fanegas of wheat, 2 of barley, and 4 of corn, 3½ of beans, 1½ of peas, and ½ in lentils. "The vineyards also promise a much greater yield than last year," he noted. "They have worked hard to enclose them with palisades; they are now all already so fenced except the large one which is being

---

27. Dwinelle, *The Colonial History*, "Addenda No. XXXVII," 56.
28. Ibid., 58–59.

enclosed with ordinary sticks. The cultivated fields likewise have their palisades." In mid-June, Hartnell granted Bandini permission to kill up to 100 head of cattle for the purpose of making soap.[29]

Bandini informed Hartnell that on various occasions he had been told by the Indian alcaldes that "some Indian men and also some Indian women do not participate in work on account of the lack of clothing to cover themselves. Knowing this to be the case, I was compelled to dissimulate when the Indians failed to appear at their tasks and who excused themselves from work." Bandini sought permission to negotiate a loan of two or three thousand pesos for clothing, to be paid in brandy, wine, or other goods.[30] Whether the neophytes used the lack of clothing as an excuse to cease working or whether it was a result of their Christian upbringing is not known, but Hartnell allowed Bandini to sell the produce from the year's grape harvest to purchase clothing. Bandini was to make every effort to sell to a supercargo, "for there is no advantage in expending the Mission harvest in the stores of Los Angeles, it being well known that merchants on land must necessarily add charges to their sales prices."[31] On the last day of the year, Bandini distributed to 233 Indian men and women various articles of woolen and cloth clothing, handkerchiefs, and other items valued at 1,615 pesos.[32]

At the time of the distribution, some of the neophytes had received emancipation based on the decree issued in 1826 by then Governor José María Echeandía. But emancipation did not always proceed as expected. In late 1839, when Father Tomás Eleuterio Esténaga ordered the emancipated Indian Juan Pablo to make stirrups and saddle trees for the vaqueros, the Indian not only failed to comply but appropriated the tools of two dead carpenters. Juan Pablo and Francisco de Asís were the last of the carpenters. This episode prompted the priest to write to Hartnell:

---

29. Hartnell, Diary, Mission San Gabriel, June 7–19, 1839, in Farris, ed., *The Diary and Copybook of William E. P. Hartnell*, 34–40.
30. Quoted in Engelhardt, *San Gabriel Mission*, 188.
31. Hartnell to Juan Bandini, Mission San Gabriel, June 15, 1839, in Farris, ed., *Diary and Copybook*, 39–41.
32. Engelhardt, *San Gabriel Mission*, 189.

These conditional liberation papers are truly illusory and are an injury to the other neophytes, since they all have an equal right to be emancipated and all can make a living for themselves, and live by themselves by carting firewood and water, or by making adobes, which is work that all understand. If only the most useful are emancipated, who and how will one-half of the community maintain itself, composed as it is of aged, infirm, children, etc.? This is an anomaly which has been perpetrated in these missions for many years, since they should have emancipated either all or none.[33]

As Indians departed the mission, paisanos entered it. In January 1840, Father Esténaga complained to Father Francisco Durán about this development:

> Thank Heaven, at this Mission there is still some bread, though not every day; a little meat, but only for the noon meal; and some wine and brandy; but there is nothing else; and just now the holy family of Santiago Argüello and that of the Estudillos are arriving. That will make the provision still more scarce. During the last two months, the mother of the three Picos, with her daughter, cousin, niece, grandchildren, male and female servants, have occupied the Mission in grand style. In addition came Señora Luisa, the wife of Agustín Zamorano, with her six or seven children.

In a postscript he noted that "two more carts with Indian male and female servants have arrived, and the dying Mission is expected to feed them all! This truly is a fine way of proceeding."[34] Three weeks later Esténaga reported that "thirty-eight white people must be maintained and are at home at this Mission, not counting the male and female servants of the Mission nor those of the Argüellos, Estudillos and the whole brood."[35] Manuel González resided at the Indians' village where he established a tavern selling aguardiente.[36]

When Hartnell returned to the mission in July 1840, the Indians told him that Bandini had sold aguardiente to all the Indians who could afford it and then punished most severely those who got drunk. He also had taken to his rancho the mission's best

---
33. Ibid., 194–95.
34. Ibid., 189–91.
35. Ibid., 191.
36. Ibid., 195.

horses and twelve new carretas, had traded mission horses for several chamois skins, and had given boots to a chief and two vaqueros. After Mass on July 26, Hartnell assembled the Indians to announce that he and Esténaga had selected Juan Crespín Pérez as mayordomo. The Indians accepted the selection on the condition that Pérez take no action without the approval of the priest and that no other mayordomo be selected.[37] It was not long, however, before the appointment of Pérez was regretted. Early the following year, Esténaga complained to the prefect (a district officer appointed by the governor) in Los Angeles that Pérez was wasting mission property and recommended that he be removed. The prefect concluded that Pérez had taken 250 more pesos than his salary called for. Pérez remained mayordomo.[38]

The specifics of what transpired at Mission San Gabriel support the generalizations of seaman Richard Henry Dana who was in California during this period:

> Ever since the independence of Mexico, the missions have been going down; until, at last, a law was passed, stripping them of all their possessions, and confining the priests to their spiritual duties; and at the same time declaring all the Indians free and independent *Rancheros*. The change in the condition of the Indians was, as may be supposed, only nominal: they are virtually slaves, as much as they ever were. But in the missions, the change was complete. The priests have now no power, except in their religious character, and the great possessions of the missions are given over to be preyed upon by the harpies of the civil power, who are sent there in the capacity of *administradores*, to settle up the concerns; and who usually end, in a few years, by making themselves fortunes, and leaving their stewardships worse than they found them.[39]

Dana understood that secularization harmed commerce: "The dynasty of the priests was much more acceptable to the people of

---

37. Hartnell, Diary, Mission San Gabriel, July 26, 31, August 1, 1840, in Farris, ed., *Diary and Copybook*, 123–26.
38. Bancroft, *History of California*, 4: 637n14; Engelhardt, *San Gabriel Mission*, 196. In early 1837 Baja and Alta California were joined into one department that was divided into three districts, Los Angeles being the capital of one district. Each district was governed by a prefect who acted as a kind of petty governor, his functions being executive rather than judicial. See Bancroft, *History of California*, 3: 585–86.
39. Dana, *Two Years Before the Mast and Twenty-Four Years After*, 166.

the country, and indeed, to every one concerned with the country, by trade or otherwise, than that of the administradores." To maintain their credit, the priests paid their debts. But most of the administradores were "men of desperate fortunes—broken down politicians and soldiers—whose only object is to retrieve their condition in as short a time as possible. The change had been made but a few years before our arrival upon the coast, yet, in that short time, the trade was much diminished, credit impaired, and the venerable missions going rapidly to decay."[40]

Not all change at San Gabriel was negative, however. By the beginning of the 1840s, some of the neophytes may have returned to living in their traditional dwellings. According to Hugo Reid, Father Tomás Eleuterio Esténaga allowed the neophytes to vacate their adobe houses for those made of tules, where "they could now breathe freely again." Reid considered Esténaga

> a truly good man, a sincere Christian and despiser of hypocrisy. He had a kind, unsophisticated heart, so that he believed every word told him. There was never a purer Priest in California. Reduced in circumstance, annoyed on many occasions by the petulancy of administrators, he fulfilled his duties according to his conscience, with benevolence and good humor. . . . Everything he got was spent in charity upon those of the *ranchería* whom he considered as worthy of it and they remembered him with gratitude and affection.[41]

In September 1840 Esténaga received his allotment of nine hundred pesos provided by the territorial assembly. He spent it and another one thousand pesos of his allowance on clothing for the neophytes.[42]

Secularization, at least initially, had little impact on the mission's wine production. In 1834, San Gabriel's vines totaled 163,579, far larger than any other mission.[43] Wine growing also was maintained to a large degree on the private ranchos carved

---

40. Ibid.
41. Reid, "Los Angeles County Indians" in *Los Angeles Star*, July 17, 1852; Heizer, ed., *Indians of Los Angeles County*, 97–98.
42. Engelhardt, *San Gabriel Mission*, 192.
43. McKee, "The Beginnings of California Winegrowing," 60.

from the mission's estancias. This was certainly the case at Uva Espina, Hugo Reid's property located near the mission. Thriving on the rancho in the early 1840s were 20,500 vines of dark grapes, 2,070 of white, and 160 of maroon. There was, moreover, enough land for an additional 40,000 vines. Reid's orchards consisted of 21 fig, 7 plum, 25 pear, 5 apple, 32 orange, 40 pomegranate, 2 *albérchigo*, 240 peach, 8 Mexican cherry, 3 walnut, 7 olive, and 40 lemon trees.[44]

Indians maintained his vineyards and orchards, but Reid had to spend considerable time and energy keeping them in line. Assisting him was a fellow Scot, Jim McKinley, who also had problems with the workers. In May 1843, Reid informed his friend Abel Stearns that "nothing new or strange merely Jim & the Indians can't agree, so I must settle affairs in my double capacity of Master & Magistrate."[45] Early the following year he notified authorities in Los Angeles that the Indians were addicted to gambling and were losing their blankets to one another.[46] In 1844 approximately three hundred Indians remained at the mission.[47]

During this time Indians were continually running away. A few of them returned to the village of Akuuronga where neophytes had built the dam called La Presa.[48] "Scantily clothed and still more scantily supplied with food," recalled Reid, "it was not to be wondered at. Nearly all of the Gabrielinos went north, while those of San Diego, San Luis and San Juan overran this county, filling the Angeles and surrounding ranchos with more servants than were required. Labor in consequence was very cheap." Moreover, recently arrived Sonorans gambled with the Indian men and "taught them to steal; they taught the women to be worse than they were." Reid acknowledged that the neophytes already were

---

44. Reid to Abel Stearns, Uva Espina, June 1, 1844, Able Stearns Collection, SG Box 53, The Huntington Library; Dakin, *A Scotch Paisano*, 113–14.
45. Reid to Abel Stearns, May __1843, Stearns Collection, SG Box 53; Dakin, *A Scotch Paisano*, 119. By "magistrate" Reid meant justice of the peace. Evidently he served as such during 1843. See Langum, *Law and Community of the Mexican California Frontier*, 47.
46. Engelhardt, *San Gabriel Mission*, 214.
47. Jackson, *Indian Population Decline*, 173.
48. McCawley, *The First Angelinos*, 42–43; Johnston, *California's Gabrielino Indians*, 165–66.

"addicted both to drinking and gaming, with an inclination to steal while under the domination of the church; but the Sonoreños most certainly brought them to a pitch of licentiousness before unparalleled in their history."[49] From 1843 to 1845, several Mexicans and naturalized Mexicans received lots near the mission, including Próspero Valenzuela, Serafín de Jesús, J. Alvitre, Antonio Valenzuela, Ramón Valencia, Francisco Sales, Manuel Sales Tasion, Michael White (English), Manuel D'Oliveira (Portuguese), and Arno Maube (French).[50]

Some neophytes also got land. Emilio Joaquín explained to the prefect of Los Angeles that he was well past fifty years of age and was tired of working at the mission. He asked for three hundred varas of land where he could "work exclusively for my family's benefit." With the support of Father Esténaga, the prefect recommended to Governor Manuel Micheltorena that he issue the grant because it would "serve as an example to his peers ... so that they will also dedicate themselves to the industry of agriculture and work." The governor agreed but in 1843 granted only two hundred varas.[51]

One of the few female neophytes to get land was Rufina. In 1844 Father Tomás Eleuterio Esténaga allowed Rufina and her family to occupy a house and plant crops on land near the mission. The following year, her husband, Manuel D'Oliveira petitioned for the land and an additional fifteen varas. In an appended statement, Esténaga wrote that he had granted Rufina use of the land "to compensate in a just and equitable manner the considerable and frequent services that Rufina has given to the mission." Pico honored the request, including the additional varas.[52]

He also honored the petition of Manuel Antonio who occupied land later called Rancho Potrero Grande. There he built a house and corrals and managed livestock. In 1845 he wrote to Governor

---

49. Reid, "Los Angeles County Indians" in *Los Angeles Star*, July 17, 1852; Heizer, ed., *Indians of Los Angeles County*, 98–99.
50. Bancroft, *History of California*, 4: 637n14.
51. Chávez-García, *Negotiating Conquest*, 61–62.
52. Ibid., 76–77.

Pío Pico: "For eleven years, I have been living on the lands of the old mission with the consent of the mission [administrators] . . . . Despite my right [to the property] . . . and my repeated requests, they have not given me a piece of land on which to put my meager possessions or to support my family. Instead, they have taken the land that I requested in order to give it to others who do not enjoy the same rights or have sufficient livestock. Please give me title to the land that I occupy." Father Esténaga supported the request, noting that the Indian "should be conceded the land as an award for his service . . . which he has provided from infancy to the present." Once the Los Angeles ayuntamiento supported the Indian, Pico granted him the land.[53]

Because Mission San Fernando had a history twenty-five years shorter and far less turbulent than San Gabriel's and because it had been created from a rancho, its breakup followed a different path. As early as 1827, Governor Echeandía contemplated turning San Fernando into an Indian pueblo and the missionaries into parish priests but the plan never materialized. When the secularization process began in 1834, Father Francisco Ibarra concluded that the mission was doomed. He was overcome with grief and left for Sonora in July 1835 in the company of Father Esténaga of San Gabriel. Departing their posts without permission was close to apostasy but the Father President defended their actions, and the two priests returned to their respective missions after about a year in exile. Ibarra arrived in time to bury his replacement, Father Pedro Cabot.[54]

When Ibarra returned, the breakup of the mission was well underway. An individual had been sent to secularize the mission in 1834 but the Indians refused to recognize him. In mid-1835 Lieutenant Antonio del Valle became its administrador at a salary

---

53. Ibid., 60–61.
54. Engelhardt, *San Fernando Rey*, 48–49, 52–57.

of eight hundred pesos per annum.[55] He took over a mission with a neophyte population at 792.[56] The inventory he drew up estimated the buildings to be worth 15,511 pesos. The 32,000 grapevines were valued at 16,000 pesos, the fruit trees at 2,400, the tools, implements, and looms at 1,650, and the 191 volumes in the library at 417. Creditors owed the mission 5,736 pesos. A short time later Antonio del Valle was replaced by Anastasio Carrillo as administrador. In mid-1838 Carrillo was succeeded by Captain José María Villavicencio. Because he was frequently called away for military duties, Villavicencio often left the mission under the management of Carrillo and others. Antonio del Valle remained in the area and in 1839 obtained possession of the estancia San Francisco Xavier which was valued at 1,925 pesos.[57]

In late June, William Hartnell arrived at the mission. He noted in his diary that the neophytes were terribly upset at losing the estancia:

> They say the site is very sorely missed because the mission used to plant there every year and in ordinary years it is the only place where there is some assurance of reaping a harvest. They say they are afraid of being very hungry from now on if their beloved San Francisco is not returned to them. . . . The Indians put forth this complaint with great circumspection through their *alcaldes* but I am convinced that if they are not heeded in this their most just request, they will be extremely disgusted and the very least they will do, many of them, will be to flee from the mission.

Hartnell was concerned that one man could cause such "incalculable damage to an entire working community" and was not pleased when Antonio del Valle asked him to intervene with the governor on his behalf. Fearing to move to Rancho San Francisco, because of Indian hostility, the Californio sought permission for himself and his family to occupy two rooms near the church which Cornelio López and his family were occupying until he could secure his house on the rancho. Hartnell noted in his diary that

---

55. Bancroft, *History of California*, 3: 353n16; Engelhardt, *San Fernando Rey*, 50.
56. Jackson, *Indian Population Decline*, 175.
57. Engelhardt, *San Fernando Rey*, 59; Bancroft, *History of California*, 3: 646–47, 648n13.

he would inform the governor "to act as he sees fit in this particular."⁵⁸ Although Antonio del Valle returned to the rancho, it was only for a short stay because he died in 1841.⁵⁹

In 1839, 503 neophytes remained at the mission, but they had to contend with increasing numbers of paisanos moving onto mission lands.⁶⁰ On September 7, Father President Durán pleaded with the government to intervene on behalf of the neophytes whose labor he claimed was being exploited:

> Why cannot these colonists in the vicinity of San Fernando do the same as those of the pueblo of Los Angeles with respect to San Gabriel; or, at least, alternate the burden with the Mission Indians? Why must the labor be done by the Indians alone without the least co-operation of the surrounding white people? I ask Your Honor for some relief in behalf of these unhappy Indians who for the last five years have been molested to extremes without mercy, whereas their character and their suffering might move the very stones to pity. I hope that something will be done, for I ask nothing more than what appears to be quite just.⁶¹

In July 1838 Odón Chihuya had requested his freedom in a memorial he presented to the administrador to forward to the acting governor. Although the administrador failed to comply, Hartnell sent the memorial to the governor.⁶² A year later he signed a document freeing the neophyte: "Whereas, José Odón, a neophyte of the Mission of San Fernando, has asked to be segregated from the community, knowing his good character, and that he is able to take care of himself, I have determined by these counts to emancipate him from said establishment, to this end that he may support himself, and live in such a manner as may suit himself."⁶³

Other neophytes petitioned for land. Urbano Chari, caretaker of the mission for thirteen years, had been in charge of the

---

58. Hartnell, Diary, Mission San Fernando, June 23, 1839, in Ferris, ed., *Diary and Copybook*, 45–46.
59. Perkins, "Rancho San Francisco," 107.
60. Jackson, *Indian Population Decline*, 175.
61. Quoted in Engelhardt, *San Fernando Rey*, 60.
62. Hartnell, Diary, Mission San Fernando, June 23, 1839, in Farris, ed., *Diary and Copybook*, 47.
63. Johnson, "Indians of Mission San Fernando," 258; Cohen, *El Escorpión*, 2–3.

warehouse, storeroom, and pantry. In June 1839, he informed Hartnell that the governor had promised him cattle and horses to pasture at El Escorpión where his son had built a corral. Intending to relocate there, Urbano Chari agreed to remain at the mission because he was needed, but he insisted to "be heeded in other matters." Hartnell relayed his request and sent a favorable report to the governor.[64] It was not until 1845 that Urbano Chari, along with Manuel and Odón Chihuya, received a half square league at El Escorpión.[65]

Samuel, who had been emancipated in 1838, petitioned Governor Manuel Micheltorena for land northwest of the mission where he was already residing. He told the governor that he had provided the mission with part of what he had raised. Samuel received a grant of one thousand square varas in 1843. He put in an orchard, built a house, and planted wheat, corn, and beans, and vegetables. About the same time thirty nine neophytes, including Alcalde Pedro Joaquín, sent a petition to the governor requesting that their cultivation rights be recognized. The governor recognized their rights.[66]

In mid-1843 Micheltorena also granted to Tiburcio Cayo, Román, and Francisco Papabubaba a square league of land at Encino.[67] After Tiburcio Cayo died in 1845, Francisco Papabubaba and Román, along with Roque, again petitioned for Encino. Governor Pío Pico responded favorably. He emphasized that the Indians and their families had occupied for some time "the place called Encino by virtue of a grant made by my predecessor." By the authority conferred in him and "in the name of the Mexican nation," Pico granted them property rights to one square league of grazing land.[68]

José Miguel Triunfo received in 1843 a tiny tract at Cahuenga where the old estancia of the mission was once located. It was

---

64. Hartnell, Diary, June 23, 1839, in Farris, ed., *Diary and Copybook.* 46–47.
65. Johnson, "Indians of Mission San Fernando," 260.
66. Ibid., 259–61.
67. Ibid., 260.
68. Cutter, "Report on Rancho El Encino," 206.

situated within Rancho Providencia, which was granted the same year to Vicente de la Osa.[69] Evidently, a land dispute forced Triunfo to relocate, because the 1850 census of Los Angeles has him, his wife Rafaela, and their five children residing on Rancho Encino. Five Indian adults, a Mexican tailor, and an American carpenter also lived there.[70] After one of his sons died and the other was apparently imprisoned, Triunfo went crazy and died. His wife remarried an Apache Indian.[71]

A less tragic but equally poignant biography is that of Rogerio Rocha. He never received property rights but remained on land near the mission far longer than most who did. Rocha was born in 1824 and somehow survived childhood while five of his siblings did not. His father was from the Chumash village of Quimisac. His mother was from Tujunga. Rocha became a blacksmith and violinist and may have attained some status or perhaps authority in the mission. In 1841 he married a girl of fourteen whose parents were from the villages of Taapu and Piiru. His only child, a daughter, was born in 1843 but soon died. That year he occupied a tract of land on Pacoima Creek where he raised crops and tended an orchard watered by a spring. Unlike most of the Indians who soon sold or were cheated out of their lands, Rogerio Rocha, although eventually evicted, maintained his residence for over forty years.[72]

---

69. Robinson, "The Spanish and Mexican Ranchos," 8.
70. Newmark and Newmark, eds., *Census of the City and County of Los Angeles*, 73.
71. Johnson, "Indians of Mission San Fernando," 276. Johnson has Triunfo residing near Tujunga but the 1850 Los Angeles census places him at Encino.
72. Ibid., 270–74; For the eviction of Rogerio Rocha, see Rust, "Rogerio's Theological School." See also McCawley, *The First Angelinos*, 213.

CHAPTER 8

Urban Unrest

In 1836 Los Angeles was designated the capital of the territory and elevated from pueblo to *ciudad*, the latter being more symbolic than substantive.[1] Still, the ciudad deserved a census and in 1836 the census-taker divided the population into two groups—gente de razón and Indians. Of the 553 Indians living in the Los Angeles district, 252 resided in the ciudad itself and they were about evenly divided between gentiles and neophytes. The one hundred who claimed that they were from the Los Angeles area probably had lived in the ciudad for some time. The seventy-five identified by the missions from where they came obviously were neophytes and most may have recently arrived. In addition, nineteen Indians were from Baja California. Ten were identified as Yumas (Quechans). Three Cahuillas, one Isleño (Islander), one Yaque (Yaqui), and four Cayegos(?) were also listed, but thirty-one Indians were simply identified as gentiles. One Indian was from the village of San Felipe, another from Agua Caliente. The six Indians labeled "Tulares" were probably Yokuts from the southern San Joaquín Valley. Because only five

---

1. Bancroft, *California Pastoral*, 259; Garr, "Los Angeles and the Challenge of Growth," 148–49. One historian has postulated an early shift in the economic orientation of the pueblo, claiming that after 1822 it took on characteristics of an urban settlement with increasing numbers of shopkeepers, merchants, and artisans. See Nelson, "The Two Pueblos."

TABLE 5. MISSION ORIGINS OF INDIANS
IN LOS ANGELES, 1836

Mission	Number
San Fernando	0
San Gabriel	13
San Juan Capistrano	9
San Luis Rey	23
San Diego	30
Total	75

Source: Adapted from J. Gregg Layne, "The First Census of the Los Angeles District," *Historical Society of Southern California Quarterly* 18 (3) June 1936: 81–99.

Indians were identified as vagrants or individuals having no occupation, full employment seems to have been achieved. Except for a shoemaker and a few laborers, all were listed as servants.[2]

In the section of the census devoted to the gente de razón, fifteen women, most with young children, were listed as prostitutes. No Indians were identified as such, but it is difficult not to conclude that some had entered the workforce in this capacity. Whether the women chose this profession on their own or whether husbands or other men forced them to enter it is not known. But given what is known about Indian prostitution elsewhere in California, the latter seems more likely.[3]

Although Mexicans from several states, especially Sonora, were represented in the census, Californios dominated the crafts and trades such as tailor, hatter, shoemaker, silversmith, carpenter,

---

2. Layne, ed., "The First Census," 83; Mason, "Indian-Mexican Cultural Exchange," 139.
3. Layne, ed., "The First Census," 82–83. In his *Two Years Before the Mast*, Richard Henry Dana wrote that at San Diego he had "frequently known an Indian to bring his wife, to whom he was lawfully married in the church, down to the beach, and carry her back again, dividing with her the money which she had got from the sailors," 169–70. Regarding one scholar's interpretations of the temptations that the gente de razón faced in the Indian village, see González, *This Small City*, 89–117.

cooper, baker, blacksmith, cigar maker, and mason. Most laborers, merchants, vendors, and store keepers were from Los Angeles. Eleven individuals listed their profession as tavern keepers. One each was from Chile, Ireland, and Portugal. Another was from the Mexican state of Veracruz. Five were from California and two from Sonora. Of the thirty-two individuals identifying themselves as vaqueros, one was a Sonoran but all the rest were natives of Los Angeles and probably Californios.[4] Perhaps Californio vaqueros monopolized this profession in the Los Angeles District as did Indian vaqueros on the outlying ranchos.

Sometime in 1836 the Los Angeles ayuntamiento consigned to the Indians a plot of city land for their exclusive occupancy and allowed the residents to elect their own alcaldes.[5] Called *Ranchería de Poblanos* (village of laborers) it was located between the vineyards of Tomás Sánchez and Juan Domingo, near Aliso and Alameda Streets and close to the zanja madre.[6] The Indians, adhering to a custom dating to pre-contact times, bathed to ensure good health, but now they bathed not in rivers but in zanjas. Because they also washed clothes in the ditch, complaints were issued. Addressing the issue at mid-year, the committee on zanjas decided to inform the Indians that they must build a bathing place away from the zanja, where they would not dirty the water. If in violation, they would be reprimanded.[7] But preventing women from washing clothes in the zanja proved to be so difficult that the ayuntamiento ordered the *zanjero* to patrol the area daily and report any violations weekly.[8]

Of less concern to the authorities were the Indians removed from San Nicolás Island in 1835. They were the remnants of a population nearly wiped out by otter-hunting Indians from Kodiak Island, Alaska in the employ of the Russian-American Trading

---

4. Layne, ed., "The First Census," 82.
5. The legislation designating the plot of land given the Indians in 1836 was mentioned in the Session of June 1, 1838. See ibid., 159.
6. Session of May 12, 1845, in Layne, ed., "The First Census," 162. See also Robinson, *The Indians of Los Angeles*, 17–18.
7. Session of June 9, 1836, in Robinson, ed., "The Indians of Los Angeles," 158.
8. Session of June 30, 1836, ibid., 159.

Company.⁹ The operation rounded-up from six to eighteen men, women, and children, (except for a mother and child accidentally left behind) and put them ashore at San Pedro. From there, all but one were taken to Los Angeles where some remained; others were sent to Mission San Gabriel. A prominent citizen, evidently Isaac Williams, obtained a middle-age woman who worked for him for many years.[10]

An Indian the sailors called Black Hawk remained at San Pedro and performed valuable labor for John Forster, who ran the depot where the hides and tallow were stored.[11] George Nidever recalled that Black Hawk

> lived on the beach among the hunters, where I saw him several times. I think he was one of the most muscular men, white or Indian, I ever saw. He was but a little above the medium height, heavy set and full and broad shoulders and chest. He was partly foolish, from a fracture of the skull received in a fight with the N. W. Indians, but he was perfectly harmless and invariably good humored. He was always willing to work, cheerfully performing the most fatiguing tasks, ofttimes without being solicited. If a boat was to be hauled ashore he would frequently rush into the water, catch hold of the boat and run it high and dry on the beach, a feat that usually required from 3 to 4 ordinary men to perform. I also saw him take under his arm and bring a considerable distance to the shore a spotted seal that had been shot from shore. The seal would weigh not less that 300 to 400 lbs., besides being very awkward to handle. It would have required 3 men at least to bring it ashore. I never heard what became of him.[12]

What became of Black Hawk is that one day he fell from a cliff into the ocean and drowned.[13]

Lacking the freedom of Black Hawk, Indians working in the ciudad were subjected to the laws of the ayuntamiento and occasionally were punished severely for breaking them. In early 1837 two Indians, Julián and Timoteo, confessed to murdering Ignacio Ortega. On March 6 Second Alcalde José Sepúlveda sought from

---

9. McCawley, *The First Angelinos*, 208–9.
10. Ellison, ed., *Life and Adventures of George Nidever*, 37–38; *Los Angeles Star*, December 13, 1856.
11. Busch, ed., *Alta California*, 172–73.
12. Ellison, ed., *Life and Adventures of George Nidever*, 38.
13. *Los Angeles Star*, December 13, 1856.

officers of the ayuntamiento their opinion regarding his intention to execute the prisoners by firing squad. They unanimously supported the decision, but a short time later the governor ordered Sepúlveda to send the prisoners to him where they would be tried by a council of war.[14]

Evidently, the Indian alcaldes had no say in this case.[15] But occasionally they pressed for Indian rights, as on April 27, 1838, when they complained to the ayuntamiento about the actions of Juan Domingo. He had appropriated thirty-six varas of land belonging to the Ranchería de Poblanos. In their petition the alcaldes succinctly presented their case:

> The Alcaldes for the Indians of this city, Gabriel, Juan José and Gandiel, in the name of all the Indians herein appear before your authority with due submission and respect and say that in the year 1836 a piece of land was granted to said Indians, to build their homes thereon, the piece of land which they occupied prior to possessing this, was taken away from them.
>
> The land now occupied by them has been taken possession of by Señor Juan Domingo and we supplicate you to act in accord with justice and order said Domingo to vacate said lands, so that the Indians can proceed to build their homes. We do not address the Illus. Ayun. knowing that at present the members of the same are scattered, and we beg of you to refer this matter to them, when opportunity presents itself. We reiterate our supplication swearing it is not through malice.[16]

The special committee reviewing the petition concluded that Domingo had indeed taken thirty-six varas of land from the Indians and thus had "failed to comply with the duties of a honest man." The ayuntamiento ruled in favor of the Indians, fined Domingo twelve pesos, and ordered him off the property.[17]

A more pressing issue came to occupy the time of the ayuntamiento, namely the anti-social behavior of both Mexicans and

---

14. Guinn, "Muy Ilustre Ayuntamiento," 210–11.
15. Session of March 11, 1837, in Robinson, ed., "The Indians of Los Angeles," 159; Newmark, *Sixty Years, 1853–1913*, 238.
16. "Petition of the Indians, in Robinson, ed., "The Indians of Los Angeles," 159–60.
17. Report of Special Committee on Indians' Petition, June 2, 1838, ibid., 160–61. The Mexican peso was equivalent in value to the American dollar. And the terms "peso" and "dollar" were used interchangeably.

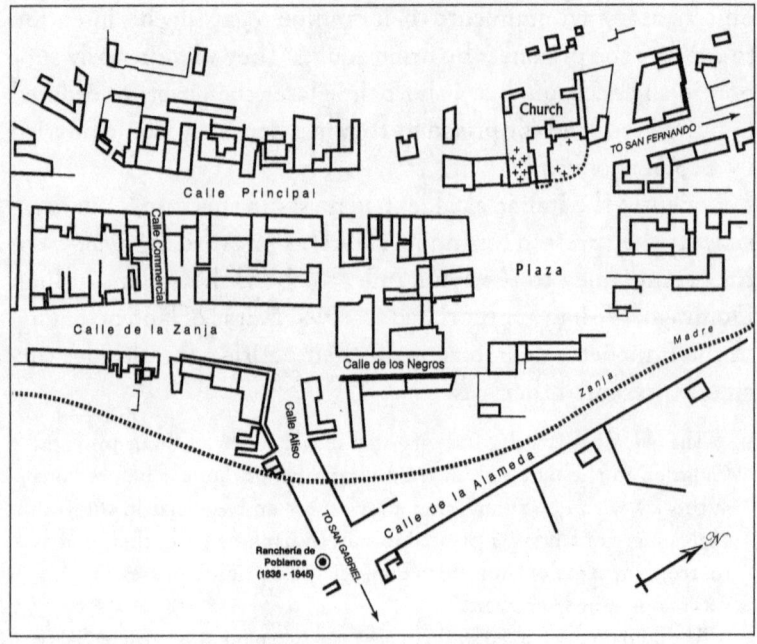

Los Angeles, circa 1836.

Indians stemming in large part from the rapidly expanding retail liquor business. Although grapes had been grown since 1803, Joseph Chapman, an American, planted four thousand grapevines between 1824 and 1826. Other growers followed. By 1831 Los Angeles could claim 100,000 vines. Jean-Louis Vignes, originally from Bordeaux, is generally credited with establishing California's commercial wine industry. He settled in the ciudad that year, imported cuttings from France, and soon had a large vineyard under cultivation. Evidently his first harvest was in 1837 and two years later wine was aging in his cellars.[18] But when Vignes petitioned in mid-1839 for more land, in particular the property

---

18. Kindall, "Southern Vineyards," 28–31; McKee, "The Beginnings of California Winegrowing," 63–66.

occupied by the Indians, the ayuntamiento ruled that the "lot belongs to the Indians, and is scarcely sufficient for their huts." Should the Indians ever be removed, however, Vignes would have the preferential claim.[19]

The ayuntamiento required that all tavern keepers pay a monthly license fee of four pesos. The number of those paying the fees fluctuated monthly throughout 1837 but the average was about ten per month. Some of those paying the fees were owners of vineyards, indicating that they had a retail outlet for some of their products.[20] Early in 1838 the ayuntamiento passed an ordinance prohibiting any individual from selling liquors without first notifying the síndico or one of the alcaldes. Failure to do so would result in a ten-peso fine for the first offense, twenty for the second, and punishment to the full extent of the law for the third. Another ordinance required those marketing liquors to notify the síndico of the number of barrels sold to individuals. Once a barrel was tapped, a duty was charged.[21] In November, nine citizens, who were most likely tavern operators, signed a petition protesting a recent prohibition of selling liquors on Sundays and sent it to the ayuntamiento. They argued that business was bad because during the week "scarcely a quart of anything is sold; in view of the above we beg that you allow us to carry on the liquor business on Sundays, from the time that mass is concluded to the hour of the ringing of the bells to pray for the souls in purgatory."[22]

Called into session on January 3, 1839, the ayuntamiento kept in force those ordinances that prohibited individuals from holding games of chance on their premises, that punished those causing disturbances on the streets, and that required persons performing dances in the city to pay license fees. It also introduced a new ordinance requiring any one taking valuables from an Indian as

---

19. Session of July 6, 1839, in Robinson, ed., "The Indians of Los Angeles," 161.
20. Minutes of Ayuntamiento, Receipts, 1837, Los Angeles Archives, 3: 71–81.
21. Minutes of the Ayuntamiento, January 20, 1838, ibid., 2: 402–6.
22. Petition to the Ayuntamiento, November 9, 1838, ibid., 1: 609. See also Wilson, *William Wolfskill*, 101–2.

security for aguardiente, or for any other reason, would forfeit the brandy and would be required to return the valuables to the Indian.[23] But on January 19 the ayuntamiento ordered all Indians with no employer rounded up. They were to be assigned to those responsible for repairing the roof of the church's baptistery.[24] The ayuntamiento expected to be paid for providing the workers. An Indian's labor was valued at 12½ reales per day. At the end of the construction, the ayuntamiento billed the contractor for 126 pesos.[25]

More than likely some of those assigned to the church were recently arrived neophytes, whose numbers by this time were rapidly increasing. Losing neophytes to Los Angeles obviously affected the missions from which they fled, especially if the neophytes were skilled workers. The mayordomos of some missions made special efforts bring back the most needed. But the local authorities did not always comply with their requests. In April 1839 the prefect prohibited the mayordomos from removing fugitive neophytes without his consent.[26] While inspecting Mission San Fernando in June, Visitador General William Hartnell wrote to the secretary of the prefect, asking that Zapatero be returned to the mission because he was "sorely missed."[27] By this time Zapatero probably had departed for the southern San Joaquín Valley where he participated in the formation of a post-contact Indian society.[28]

From Mission San Gabriel, Hartnell again wrote to the prefect, seeking his assistance in rounding up neophytes from Missions San Diego, San Luis Rey, and San Juan Capistrano who had taken refuge in the pueblo. The prefect promised to comply with his wishes.[29] On June 14, Hartnell received a letter from

---

23. Minutes of Ayuntamiento, January 3, 1839, Los Angeles Archives, 2: 453–55.
24. Session of January 19, 1839, in Robinson, ed., "The Indians of Los Angeles," 161. For an account of the construction of the church see Owen, "The Church by the Plaza," 22.
25. McGroarty, ed., *History of Angeles County*, 1: 323.
26. Bancroft, *History of California*, 3: 640n6.
27. Hartnell to Francisco del Castillo, Mission San Fernando, June 20, 1839, in Farris, ed., *Diary and Copybook*, 44.
28. Johnson, "Indians of Mission San Fernando," 62–63. The formation of a post-contact society at Tejón is discussed in Phillips, "Bringing Them under Subjection," 1–19.
29. Hartnell, Diary, June 11, 1839, in Farris, ed., *Diary and Copybook*, 36.

the mayordomo of San Luis Rey about neophytes fleeing his mission. Hartnell asked the prefect to assist the two alcaldes, Samuel and Pablo, that the mayordomo had sent to escort the Indians back to the mission. The prefect replied that he had given orders appropriate to the matter.[30] Another neophyte fleeing San Luis Rey appealed directly to the prefect for protection. In a petition written for her, María Jacinta insisted that she was not able to support her family of two unmarried daughters, her husband having died at the mission. Age thirty-plus years, she sought to live out the "few remaining days" of her life outside the mission, where she had worked and suffered and where for the past five or six years had not received one "piece of cotton" for her family. She signed the petition with a cross on May 12, 1839. Two days later the prefect forwarded her petition to the territorial government.[31] In 1840 Agustín Janssens, the mayordomo at Mission San Juan Capistrano, sent two Indian alcaldes to Los Angeles to round up neophytes. Janssens recounted in his memoirs that the neophytes had fled because there was "no means of livelihood at the mission."[32]

If livelihood were found in Los Angeles, it was probably in the vineyards whose size and products impressed foreign visitors. American naval officer William Dane Phelps arrived in September 1840 and wrote: "There are many good vineyards here among others we visited that of Don Luis Vigne containing about 17,000 vines all in good bearing this year and nearly ripe. Mr. Vigne is a Frenchman & understands the culture of the vine. He says that were it not for the vermin this would be a first rate wine growing country, but they are so much troubled by the Wolves, Foxes, and a species of ground squirrel that destroys the Grape, that it is difficult to protect their vineyards from being stripped by them."[33]

---

30. Hartnell, Diary, June 14, 1839, ibid., 38.
31. Minutes of the Ayuntamiento, May 12, 1839, Los Angeles Archives, 2: 324.
32. Janssens, *The Life and Adventures*, 107; Hartnell, Diary, August 17, 1840, in Farris, ed., *Diary and Copybook*, 131n23. Beginning in December 1840, Janssens served as acting mayordomo. The governor officially appointed him to that office in February 1841. See Engelhardt, *San Juan Capistrano*, 129.
33. Phelps, *Alta California, 1840–1842*, 70–71.

Because the vineyards, orchards, and crops of the pueblo depended on irrigation, it was essential that the zanjas be maintained and repaired. Thus, in March 1841 the ayuntamiento announced that the time had come to repair the zanja madre. The ditch was under the charge of a commissioner who kept a list of the owners of vineyards and other cultivated lands who employed laborers. When notified, the cultivator was to send one or two Indians to the ditch. Each one was to be provided with a day's ration and the proper implements. And the cultivators were to select two of their own to assist the commissioner in managing the Indians. They were to be mounted and would be exempt from providing workers. The commissioner was to see that the main ditch and the minor ones remained repaired and that each cultivator had a good stop gate which did not leak. If the main ditch leaked at any point, the cultivator nearest the break was responsible for its repair. Those ignoring the rules would be fined four pesos for the first offense, eight for the second, and some form of punishment for the third. An Indian who deposited filth into the ditches or who washed clothes there would be fined one peso.[34]

Visitors to the ciudad commented on Indian labor. Eugène Duflot de Mofras, who arrived in California in 1841, noted that "all labor in El Pueblo is done by Indians recruited from the small ranchería on the banks of the river on the outskirts of the village. These poor wretches are often mistreated, and do not always receive in full their daily pay, which is fixed at one real in money and one real in merchandise."[35] "The number of half-civilized Indian laborers is much larger here than in the North," maintained Edward Vischer the following year. "Hence it is much easier to get agricultural workers and make farming much more remunerative."[36]

Not mentioned by the visitors was the ciudad's increasing social unrest. In January 1844 the ayuntamiento passed a resolution stating that all persons without occupation or some manner of making

---

34. Bancroft, *California Pastoral*, 355–56.
35. Duflot de Mofras, *Travels*, 1: 186.
36. Gudde, ed. and trans., "Edward Vischer's First Visit to California," 203.

a living were liable to a fine or incarceration. Upon discharging his servant or day laborer, the employer was to issue a document indicating the circumstances of the release and whether the person was at liberty to work for someone else. No servant or worker was to be hired without this document. Those seeking employment for the first time had to secure a certificate from the authorities. Persons failing to present their documents were to be arrested and tried immediately; if found guilty they were to be jailed as prisoners of the city. And "any person found in an inebriated condition on the streets or becoming scandalous in word or action shall perform eight days of public labor or pay a fine imposed by the Judges."[37]

Indian drinking may have been cause for alarm, but so was any potential disruption of the labor force. Thus in 1844, when smallpox threatened the ciudad, the ayuntamiento issued a proclamation which rhetorically asked what would become of the ciudad if it did not take action to counteract the disease: "It would bereave the town of the arms dedicated to agriculture (the only industry of the country) which would cease to be useful, and in consequence misery would prevail among the rest." The proclamation established rules of hygiene. Stimulating peppers and spices and unripe fruit were not to be eaten; all salted meats were to be washed before eaten; houses were to be fumigated by the burning of sulfur; travelers were to remain in quarantine for three days before entering the city; vaccination was to be enforced; and all saloon keepers were to be notified that allowing the gathering of inebriates would result in a five peso fine for the first offense and closure for the second.[38] Although the precautions probably limited the spread of the disease, so did its type. Hugo Reid wrote to a friend in May that "the number of smallpox cases is three and I think the smallpox is of the type *variola vacinae* which is relatively milder and less contagious."[39]

The ciudad may have been spared an epidemic, but its social problems remained. In an effort to curtail Indian liquor consumption,

---

37. Minutes of the Ayuntamiento, January 12, 1844, Los Angeles Archives, 2: 545.
38. Guinn, "Muy Ilustre Ayuntamiento," 9–10.
39. Cook, "Smallpox," 189–90; Guinn, "Muy Ilustre Ayuntamiento," 9–10.

on November 11, 1844, the síndico offered a proposal to the ayuntamiento that it approved without discussion: "Touching upon scandalous inebriety of the Indians on holidays which necessarily demoralizes them and injures their respective employers, it becomes indispensable to take some steps towards preventing the same." Taverns were not to open. Neither were other houses that sold grape brandy. Failure to comply with the law would result in the judge imposing the fine.[40]

Because they now outnumbered the gentiles, most of those frequenting the taverns probably were neophytes. Over 1,000 neophytes may have resided in the Los Angeles district, although the census of 1844 puts the figure at 650. Of those located in the ciudad itself, 258 came from eight missions. In addition, 39 Indians were from Los Angeles, 14 from Baja California, and 1 from Sonora. Also in the pueblo were 21 Cahuillas, 13 Paiutes, 4 Utes, 11 Quechans, 4 Isleños, and others from different locations.[41] Given the increase in the numbers of those seeking work, many must have remained unemployed or only seasonally employed.

Moreover, they entered a town whose government was intent on determining where they prayed and where they were buried. In December 1844, the ayuntamiento divided the cemetery into two squares of twenty five varas each. One was for the ministers, the other for vaults and monuments. The remaining land was for the Indians.[42] Early the following year, the ayuntamiento approved a recommendation from the síndico to establish a separate place in the church for the Indians who "are a dirty class and on mixing prevent the white people from hearing mass."[43] Segregation was not limited to the church. When in April 1845 neophytes Merced (from San Juan Capistrano), Josefa (from Baja California), and Romualda (from San Luis Rey) came down with "the sickness of Saint Lazarus," the ayuntamiento requested that the

---

40. Minutes of the Ayuntamiento, November 11, 1844, Los Angeles Archives, 2: 642–43.
41. "Register of the City of Los Angeles," ibid., 3:784–97; González, *This Small City*, 226n49. According to González, some of the gentiles may have been captives.
42. Session of December 30, 1839, in Robinson, ed., "The Indians of Los Angeles," 161–62.
43. Session of January 11, 1845, ibid., 162.

TABLE 6. MISSION ORIGINS OF INDIANS
IN LOS ANGELES, 1844

Mission	Number
San Antonio	1
San Miguel	3
San Buenaventura	1
San Fernando	1
San Gabriel	13
San Juan Capistrano	25
San Luis Rey	138
San Diego	76
Total	258

Source: Adapted from *Register of the City of Los Angeles and Its Jurisdiction for the Year 1844*, Los Angeles City Archives, vol. 3.

surgeon examine the women. If he determined their sickness was incurable, they would be compelled to leave the pueblo for some uninhabited place.[44]

Most of the Indian residents soon would be forced to relocate. Because of the thefts and disorders committed by the Indians, in May 1845 several vecinos asked the ayuntamiento to consider removing them from Ranchería de Poblanos. Their request was referred to the police commission.[45] But the report produced by the commission was ambiguous regarding the merits of removal. It noted that members of the commission had reconnoitered the village and the area to where the Indians would be relocated, but admitted that "both places represent obstacles which must be overcome." If the Indians were removed, "worst evils" might occur to owners of cattle or employers of Indians. If they remained, the waters of the zanja would continue to be polluted. Nevertheless, the police commission recommended removal. The village should be relocated "on the heights across the river, at the most convenient

---
44. Session of April 5, 1845, ibid., 162. The term refers to leprosy, but there is no evidence that the disease ever took hold in the region.
45. Session of May 12, 1845, ibid., 162.

place." But removal "shall be prudently made, allowing the necessary time to the Indian families that they may not be injured." Members of the ayuntamiento approved the report and sent it to the territorial government for consideration.[46]

After the government approved the report, on June 21 the ayuntamiento formed a commission consisting of Juan Sepúlveda, Luis Jordán, Juan Bandini, and Juan Manso, to expedite the removal of the Indians.[47] As of early December, however, the commission had yet to issue its report, prompting the ayuntamiento to demand action. Juan Sepúlveda accepted responsibility for the delay.[48] At the next meeting, Sepúlveda resigned as president of the commission and Luis Jordán took his place.[49] On December 22 Jordán reported to the ayuntamiento that he had transferred the Indians across the river.[50] Their new site was called Pueblito. In 1838 this land had been granted to Antonio Albitre who had promised to build a house and a corral for his milk cows.[51] Evidently, the land had been vacated by the time of the removal. In February 1846 Juan Domingo and Raymundo Féliz petitioned the ayuntamiento for the land the Indians had vacated. Their request was rejected on the grounds that the area had been designated a place for parks and for washing.[52] But Domingo persisted, and on down payment of 186 pesos of the 200 he offered for the property, he received judicial possession on June 16.[53]

The new settlement became as crime-ridden as the old. In February 1846, Jean-Louis Vignes, Francisco Figueroa, and other vecinos petitioned directly to Governor Pío Pico, noting that "when the 'Indian Ranchería' was removed to the 'Pueblito' we thought that the isolation of these aborigines would prevent the committing of excesses and thefts, and also believing that this unfortunate generation would find the means to prolong their existence, but we

---

46. Session of June 7, 1845, ibid., 163.
47. Session of June 21, 1845, ibid., 164.
48. Session of December 6, 1845 ibid., 164.
49. Session of December 13, 1845, ibid., 165.
50. Session of December 22, 1845, ibid, 165.
51. Minutes of the Ayuntamiento, October 13, 1838, Los Angeles Archives, 3: 527–28.
52. Session of February 14, 1846, in Robinson, ed., "The Indians of Los Angeles," 165.
53. Session of June 16, 1846, ibid., 167.

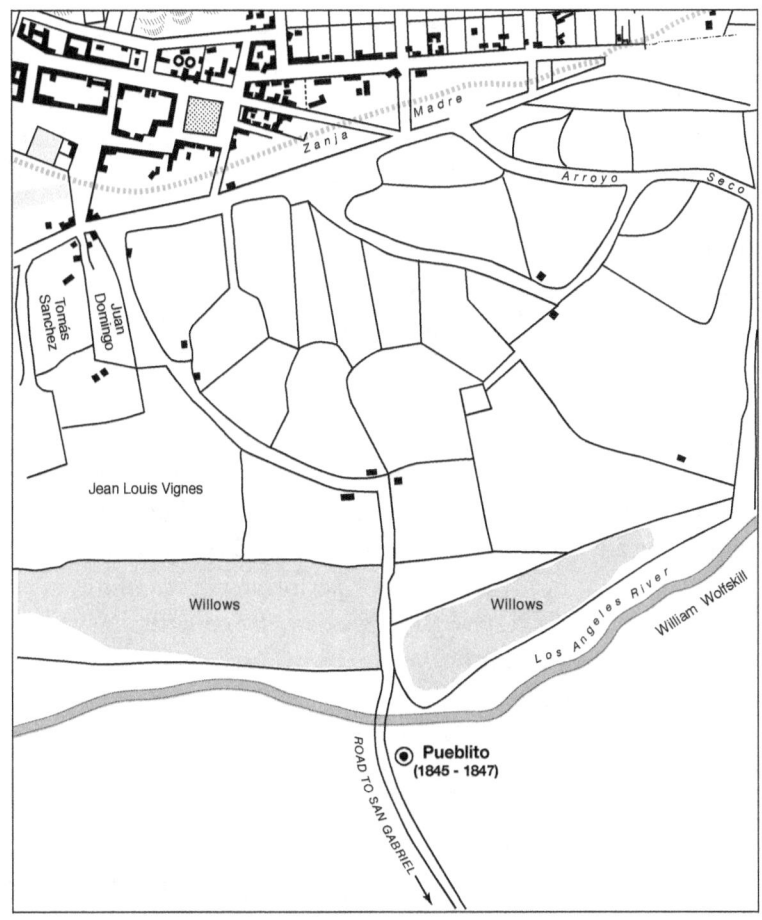

Los Angeles circa 1847 Vineyards and Indian Village

are sorry to say it has proved to the contrary. Taking advantage of their isolation they steal all neighboring fences and on Saturdays celebrate and become intoxicated to an unbearable degree." The petitioners were also concerned about the spread of venereal disease among the Indians, blaming it on the "vice" of polygamy. If corrective measures were not taken, the Indian population would soon disappear. The Indians should either be placed in an area where they could be strictly policed or provided with living quarters by their employers. "This would tend to stop the excesses of prostitution and the white people would therefore not be so apt to encourage same."[54]

Pico turned the petition over to the ayuntamiento, which in turn sent it to the police commission which had much to say about the Indian village. It "consists of a few mean Indians who work in the neighborhood, and also of a few others of the same class who sleep there, are bachelors, and are attracted there through their natural instinct of associating with their own race. The result of this congregation in this certain place, is that whenever help is desired by any of the white people they go directly to this place for the same, as nearly all the labor performed in the community is done by them." Despite the disorders the commissioners did not think there was "any harm in permitting them to enjoy themselves in their own style." Debauchery should be prevented and thefts eliminated, but the perpetrators "should be punished by the respective authorities and according to law." The commission recommended that the Indians be allowed to remain but they should come under the jurisdiction of the municipality and until then, the alcaldes should take the necessary action to end the disorders. The ayuntamiento, however, rejected the commission's recommendations, insisting that the ranchería should be moved to another place and come under the supervision of "an honest warden."[55]

Also under pressure to relocate were the Pipimares. In April 1846 four vecinos petitioned the ayuntamiento to remove them from their small village, evidently because they were holding

---
54. Session of February 19, 1846, ibid., 167–68.
55. Minutes of the Ayuntamiento, February 19, 1846, 2: 413–18.

ceremonies there.⁵⁶ The following month the commission investigating the case presented its report, noting that "this Indian village has been located there for years and no complaint having ever been made against those Indians." Therefore, it "did not find it just to remove this town from one place to another, as these offenses may result from one or two individuals, and it is not just that the others should suffer the penalty merited only by the delinquents."⁵⁷ On May 16 other vecinos presented another petition to the ayuntamiento, also calling for the removal of the Pipimares. Another commission was formed.⁵⁸ A week later it reported that because only a few Pipimares remained, their employers should be asked if they wanted to "domicile them on their lands." If not, the Indians should be congregated in the main village. The ayuntamiento approved the petition but what happened to the Pipimares remains a mystery.⁵⁹

These legal actions had little effect in curbing Indian crime or crimes committed against Indians. In early May 1846 the síndico complained that because Indians engaged in all kinds of "excesses and robberies," they do not prepare for work.⁶⁰ The city government and individual vecinos, however, found a way to keep Indians "employed." In late May four Indians each received sentences of fifteen days on public works projects for being drunk and disorderly. The same punishment was applied to five Indians in early June. At mid-month Antonio María Lugo exchanged a cow for an Indian prisoner whom he put to work.⁶¹ On July 8, it was reported that an Indian named Francisco had fled from the project to which he had been assigned. Apprehended, he had his term increased by two months.⁶²

---

56. Session of April 18, 1846, in Robinson, ed. "The Indians of Los Angeles," 169.
57. Session of May 9, 1846, ibid., 169–70.
58. Session of May 16, 1846, ibid., 170.
59. Session of May 23, 1846, ibid., 170. Only four Indians were identified in this report, a number which seems too small.
60. González, *This Small City*, 48, 206n76.
61. "1846 Verbal Transactions of the Second Justice's Court," May 25, 1846; June 8, 15, 22, 1846, in Copy Book of Legal Cases in Los Angeles, 1840–1850, 1: 9–26, HM 38278, The Huntington Library.
62. Ibid., July 6, 8, 10, and 13, 1846, 27–31.

CHAPTER 9

Land of Opportunity

On January 31, 1830, a sixty-man caravan from New Mexico arrived at Mission San Gabriel.[1] The goal of the expedition was to obtain stock, and according to William Garner, who had settled in California a few years earlier, the New Mexicans purchased many animals at a low price "and among them were some very splendid animals."[2] Another expedition, this one commanded by William Wolfskill, arrived at the mission in February 1831. The party consisted mainly of American trappers, but accompanying them were several New Mexicans. J. J. Warner noted that they brought "*serapes* and *fresadas* (woolen blankets) with them for the purposes of trading them to the Indians in exchange for beaver skins." But on their arrival in California, "they advantageously disposed of their blankets to the rancheros in exchange for mules." The New Mexicans returned to Santa Fe in the summer of 1831 with mules "of very fine form." The profit margin "caused quite a sensation in New Mexico."[3]

The road that the traders and trappers followed (called the

---
1. Antonio Armijo, "Diary," in Hafen and Hafen, *Old Spanish Trail: Santa Fe to Los Angeles*, 159–65.
2. William Robert Garner to editors of the *North American and United States Gazette*, Monterey, November 6, 1846, in Craig, ed., *Letters from California, 1846–1847*, 103.
3. Warner, et al., *An Historical Sketch*, 33.

Old Spanish Trail) terminated at Los Angeles, but subbranches eventually extended over a wide area. Warner recalled that, "Los Angeles was the central point in California of this New Mexican trade.... From thence they scattered themselves over the country from San Diego to San Jose, and across the Bay to Sonoma and San Rafael. Having bartered and disposed of the goods brought, and procured such as they wished to carry back, and what mules they could drive, they concentrated at Los Angeles for their yearly return."[4]

The New Mexicans also participated in a slave trade that extended throughout the Southwest. Antonio Francisco Coronel recalled that in a Los Angeles household there was a Paiute girl who had been exchanged for animals from some New Mexicans. Although buying Indians was forbidden by law, it was tolerated "in view of the great benefits to the Indians: they were educated and treated as members of the family."[5] In January 1833 Ignacio del Valle notified the alcalde of Los Angeles that a New Mexican, Francisco Vigil, had offered to sell him an Indian boy. He rejected the offer. Late that month the authorities in Los Angeles arrested Antonio José Rocha for attempting to purchase an Indian from Juan Sánchez, a trader from New Mexico. Rocha insisted that he intended to raise the boy to be a good Catholic and then release him at adulthood.[6] Although a few Indian slaves ended up in Los Angeles, the pueblo never became a market in the slave trade. Local Indians provided all the necessary labor.[7]

The arrival of the traders troubled Mexican officials and missionaries for other reasons. As early as March 1831, Governor Manuel Victoria had informed his presidio commanders at Santa Bárbara and San Diego that those from New Mexico had established trade relations with "the wild Indians, Christian fugitives and actually some of the mission neophytes." The Indians robbed

---

4. Ibid., 34.
5. Coronel, *Tales of Mexican California*, 26.
6. Hafen and Hafen, *Old Spanish Trail*, 269–70.
7. The possibilities of numerous captives in Los Angeles are discussed in González, *This Small City*, 119–44.

the missions of horses and sold them to the traders "who take the animals to their own country by various routes."⁸ William Garner noted that following the arrival of the first caravan from New Mexico "the wild Indians began to steal from the settlements."⁹ In February 1833 Father Vicente Pascual Oliva alerted Governor José Figueroa to what he perceived to be a deteriorating situation: "The introduction of articles of commerce to this territory by natives of New Mexico has caused extensive robberies, both open and concealed. They sell, they trade, they induce the Indians to steal animals to sell."¹⁰

Although the herds of the vecinos were relatively safe from Indian stock raiders because the ciudad was protected by the ocean and mountains, those belonging to many rancheros were not.¹¹ In early 1833 the Los Angeles ayuntamiento debated a request from Pedro Féliz, owner of Rancho San José, that he and four vecinos be allowed to follow the Indians who had stolen a large number of his horses. Because the raiders had headed north toward the southern San Joaquín Valley, the ayuntamiento allowed the party to go only as far as the estancia of San Francisco Xavier. To venture beyond that point was simply too dangerous.¹²

Sonorans also found the horses and mules of the rancheros tempting and rather easy targets. Many arrived after Mexican independence in 1821 and were particularly active in stealing stock from the ranchos along the Santa Ana River. Tomás Yorba told José de la Guerra y Noriega in November 1834 that he was "disgusted to see my country so much under the influence of these devils. Here it is so ruined by banditry that one doesn't know what to do."¹³ In mid-July of the following year, he again complained

---

8. Governor Manuel Victoria to Commanders at Santa Bárbara and San Diego, Monterey, March 10, 1831, in Cook, trans. and ed., "Expeditions," 162.
9. William Robert Garner to editors of the *North American and United States Gazette*, Monterey, November 6, 1846, in Craig, ed., *Letters from California*, 103.
10. Vicente Pascual Oliva to José Figueroa, San Gabriel, February 17, 1833, in Cook, ed., "Expeditions," 162–63.
11. Gudde, trans., ed., "Edward Vischer's First Visit to California," 203.
12. Minutes of the Ayuntamiento, February 27, 1833, Los Angeles City Archives, 2, 29.
13. Tomás A. Yorba to Captain Don José Noriega, Lomas [Santa Ana], November 22 and 29, 1834 in Gibson, *Tomás Yorba's Santa Ana Viejo*, 199–201.

to his friend: "Every day it is getting worse here with so many Sonoran thieves as well as local ones."[14] That the "local ones" were neophytes seems obvious. Christian Indians were so successful in stealing horses from the estancia of San Francisco Xavier that on July 26, 1835, Antonio del Valle asked the governor to station a corporal there.[15] Early in 1837, Indians drove off one hundred horses probably from the same estancia. Antonio del Valle sent six vaqueros after the raiders. In a prolonged engagement they killed two Indians but suffered three casualties and were forced to retreat. Another party followed the Indians, who evidently escaped with sixty animals. During the pursuit, however, the paisanos encountered other stock raiders and managed to recover the animals they had stolen.[16]

Stock raiding became so serious throughout much of California that in August 1839 Juan Bandini predicted an impending economic disaster. He told the Los Angeles ayuntamiento that the past eight years had brought the country to "a state almost of ruin. Stockraising was and is the principal occupation of the Californians, but in the time mentioned it has fallen off inevitably, due to ... the raids of Indians and others." Deploring the corresponding decline in agriculture, he pondered, "What is going to become of the country?"[17]

On May 14, 1840, the mayordomo of Mission San Gabriel notified the alcalde in Los Angeles that *Chaguanosos* had raided the mission of three herds of mares. A term of uncertain origin or meaning, "Chaguanosos" may refer to Indians, American trappers, or New Mexicans, or members of all three groups operating in concert. But a caravan of New Mexicans arrived in Southern California in November of that year, so they were not the Chaguanosos. If, as is more likely, the raiders (including perhaps some trappers) were Utes under the command of Walkara, their

---

14. Tomás A. Yorba to Señor Capitán Don José Noriega, Santa Ana, July 15, 1835, ibid., 219.
15. Engelhardt, *San Fernando Rey*, 52.
16. Ibid., 57–58; Bancroft, *History of California*, 4:77.
17. Quoted in Francis, *An Economic and Social History*, 651–62. For a discussion of Indian stock raiders north of the Los Angeles region, see Phillips, *Indians and Intruders*, 107–16.

incursion was the first of what would be several into the region. Whoever they were, the raiders divided into several parties and struck at Ranchos La Puente and Chino while proceeding eastward.[18]

Agustín Janssens was working on Rancho Jurupa at the time and recorded what he witnessed. While Juan Bandini and his family hid in the brush, "two of us remained at the house to watch the movement of the strangers. At sunset, dust could be seen on the plain as though they were coming from Rancho de la Puente toward our ranch. They were driving many horses. We had driven our own horses down the river in the direction of Santa Ana de los Yorba. As soon as it began to be dark, an order was given to find out what direction they were taking. At about ten, the *vaqueros* returned, saying they had taken the cañón, as though they were going to the valley. With that good news the family returned to the house."[19]

A party of paisanos and Indians caught up with the Chaguanosos on the Mohave Desert, but in the ensuing fight an Indian and a Mexican lost their lives and another man was wounded. The robbers also killed or stole their mounts which forced the pursuers to retreat on foot. Two other armed parties also went in pursuit. Although they failed to overtake the robbers, they did force them to abandon equipment and more than half their animals. The raid became widely known throughout the region and in time gained the mythic status as the greatest robbery of California stock ever.[20]

---

18. Beattie and Beattie, *Heritage of the Valley*, 140; Lawrence, "Mexican Trade between Santa Fe and Los Angeles, 1830–1848," 33. One historian claimed the raiders were Indians from New Mexico, under Canadian chiefs, in league with roving bands of trappers. See Bancroft, *History of California*, 4: 76–77. In a detailed analysis of the Chaguanosos and the raid, the Beatties have suggested that Walkara could well have been involved in the raid. See Anonymous, "Chaguanosos and Horse Stealing," in George William and Helen Pruitt Beattie Collection B 15, The Huntington Library. Another scholar reported that Narciso Botello used the term "Chanquanosos" in describing the New Mexicans. See González, *This Small City*, 113. "Chaguanosos," however, could be a corruption of "Chaquetones," the name of Walkara's band of Utes.
19. Janssens, *The Life and Adventures*, 104–5; Bailey, *Indian Slave Trade*, 150.
20. Beattie and Beattie, *Heritage of the Valley*, 140–41.

Events that occurred the following year, however, would have longer-term ramifications. In January 1841, Antonio María Lugo petitioned Governor Juan Bautista Alvarado for the estancia at San Bernardino. He noted that three of his sons and their families already resided there along with about two hundred Indians who had been baptized by Father José María Zalvidea when he was stationed at San Gabriel. But to Lugo, they were living "in a state of greatest abandonment," having reverted to "all their customs on account of not having anyone to venerate, or a priest to aid them with their spiritual nourishment." If Father Zalvidea, then at Mission San Juan Capistrano, were sent to the rancho to administer to the Indians, Lugo would "maintain him in the manner which his character demands." He also promised to construct a chapel in the vicinity of where the gentiles lived, and "I hope that many of them may be converted and agree to receive the water of baptism." Moreover, reasoned Lugo, "this religious step will have good results, as much in the service of Christianity as for the interests of the stock industry of the greater part of the Department. The reason is sufficiently clear. In order that the inhabitants who are in the vicinity of San Bernardino may be instructed in the Christian faith, a regular village will be formed, and its police will check those who through that route (which is one the robbers usually take) drive out mules and horses which they steal with such frequency."[21] Zalvidea remained at San Juan Capistrano.

In 1842 the Lugo family obtained title to eight square leagues in the San Bernardino Valley encompassing four of the mission's estancias—Guachama, Jumuba, Agua Caliente, and Yucaipa.[22] By 1844 the Lugo family had invited Juan Antonio, who was then living in the San Jacinto Mountains, to move onto the rancho. Juan Antonio had brought under his rule five or six lineages, numbering between 250 and 300 individuals, and had emerged as a paramount chief of the Mountain Cahuilla. He accepted the invitation and settled near the headquarters of Vicente Lugo at

---

21. Ibid., 48–49.
22. Ibid., 51–52.

a place called Politana.[23] Felipe Lugo recalled that "as there were so many Indians, my father selected men to go who could protect the stock which my father was sending out there." On the rancho was Juan Antonio, "who had much influence with the Indians in keeping them quiet. This Juan Antonio controlled the Indians living around in different villages, and he aided in protecting the property of my father and sons."[24] The Cahuillas and the Lugos became so interdependent that their relationship constituted more an alliance of equals than a simple employer-employee arrangement. In February 1844, Antonio María Lugo notified a friend in Los Angeles that Cahuillas were then battling Indians near San Bernardino who apparently had come to run off livestock. Juan Antonio operated under written instructions from Mexican officials to kill Indian stock raiders and confiscate their property.[25]

Some rancheros, such as Michael White, had to defend their estates on their own. White petitioned for a grant at the mouth of the Cajon Pass, explaining that "this land which I ask . . . is the road by which the Indians enter and go out with stolen horses, as they have been doing for some time. If Your Excellency thinks proper to grant it to me, it will create an obstacle to the Indians making incursions with the freedom which till now they have enjoyed—I having on two occasions taken from them the horses they had stolen." In 1843, with the recommendations of local rancheros, the governor granted him Rancho Muscupiabe. White built a house of logs and earth and corrals for his stock. A man

---

23. Strong, *Aboriginal Society*, 150; Harvey, "Population of the Cahuilla Indians: Decline and its Causes," 189–90; Wilson, "A GIS Based Analysis of Prehistoric and Post-contact Mountain Cahuilla Settlement and Subsistence Patterns," 114–15. All three scholars claim that Juan Antonio brought clans to Rancho San Bernardino. However, by dividing the three hundred Cahuilla by the number of "clans" (five) each unit totals sixty members. This number is more in keeping with the size of lineages than of clans.

24. Quoted in Raup, *San Bernardino, California*, 16–17. According to an anthropologist, because some Wanakik (Pass) Cahuillas had already settled in the San Bernardino area and because Juan Antonio was married to a Wanakik, the Mountain Cahuilla were allowed to move to the area. See Bean, "The Wanakik Cahuilla," 116–17.

25. Hayes, "Concerning Warner's Rancho," Notes on California Indian Affairs, 120–23, C-E 81, The Bancroft Library; Beattie and Beattie, *Heritage of the Valley*, 61–62; Beattie "San Bernardino Valley before the Americans Came," 118; Shinn, *Shoshonean Days*, 96. *Los Angeles Star*, June 7, 1851; Phillips, *Chiefs and Challengers*, 48–51.

of limited resources, he employed few if any Indians to maintain and protect his property. Indian stock raiders robbed him of all his animals and he abandoned the rancho after nine months.[26]

Indians raided Rancho Azusa in early May 1845 and made off with a *caballada* of horses. The four men that Henry Dalton sent out after the raiders found the horses on a mountaintop, but the Indians had fled. The following month Dalton and several other rancheros received circulars from Benjamin Wilson requesting that each ranchero provide a man, mounts, money, and corn for a campaign against the raiders. Governor Pío Pico had persuaded Wilson to undertake the task.[27] Wilson divided the eighty men, most of whom were paisanos who rendezvoused at Rancho San Bernardino, into two companies. The pack train proceeded over the Cajon Pass, while Wilson led the other company up the San Bernardino River to Bear Lake and down the Mohave River. On the desert Wilson encountered four Indians. One was a notorious raider named Joaquín, who was raised as a page at Mission San Gabriel. Apparently, he had become difficult to control and was sent to the estancia at Chino to work. The mayordomo had punished him for some kind of disobedience by cutting off one of his ears and searing his lip with the cattle brand of the mission. Wilson acknowledged that this was "the only instance I ever saw or heard of this kind" of punishment.[28]

Wilson sought to interrogate the Indians about the stock raiders but was unable to convince Joaquín that he and his people would not be harmed. Wilson and Joaquín fired simultaneously. The white man took an arrow in the shoulder and lived. The Indian took a bullet in the chest and died. Wilson recalled that before Joaquín died, he uttered "a tirade of abuse in the Spanish language, such as I had never heard surpassed." The paisanos killed the other three Indians in a fight in an open field. Wilson, unable to continue,

---

26. Quoted in Beattie, "San Bernardino Valley," 111–12. Most of the ranchos in Southern California abandoned because of Indian raids were located east of San Diego. See Bancroft, *History of California*, 3: 611–12.
27. Jackson, *A British Ranchero in Old California*, 80.
28. Wilson, "The Narrative of Benjamin D. Wilson," 385–86.

Land of Opportunity 209

turned over the company to Enrique Avila, a Californio from Los Angeles, who returned to camp two days later with unfavorable news. As Wilson recounted, "About ten leagues below the camp they had struck a fresh trail of Indians, pursuing it up a rocky mountain, found the Indians fortified in the rocks, attacked them a whole day and finally were obliged to leave the Indians in their position, and come away with several men badly wounded."[29]

Wilson procured fresh horses and provisions at Rancho Jurupa but because of wounds or other reasons, twenty of his men quit. His next campaign was designed to capture two neophytes from Mission San Gabriel who supposedly had convinced some young Cahuilla men to raid the ranchos. At the village of Agua Caliente, Wilson spoke with Cabezón, now Chief of the Desert Cahuilla. Cabezón attempted to dissuade Wilson from continuing. Wilson took Cabezón prisoner and warned him that unless the two men were delivered, he would treat all the Cahuilla as enemies. Cabezón was convinced that the threat was not an idle one, so he sent some of his men after the neophytes. The following night the Indians delivered to Wilson two severed heads of the neophytes. Wilson left the heads at Agua Caliente and returned to Rancho Jurupa.[30]

A short time later, twenty-one men, including Wilson, Avila, several paisanos, and twelve American trappers who were eager to join, surrounded the village that had withstood Avila's assault on the first campaign. While Wilson was attempting to persuade the Indians to surrender, one of them shot an American in the back. Wilson ordered his men to fire, and they kept firing "until every Indian man was slain." The women and children were taken prisoner. Wilson was startled to learn "that these women could speak Spanish very well . . . and that the men we had killed had been the same who had defeated my command the first time, and were likewise Mission Indians." Wilson left the prisoners at Mission San Gabriel.[31] In recording these campaigns, not once did Wilson mention that stolen stock had been recovered.

---
29. Ibid., 387.
30. Ibid., 387–89.
31. Ibid., 389–90.

In October 1845 Wilson notified Isaac Williams of Rancho Chino that four Utes had told him that their chief, Walkara, with 180 armed men would soon arrive at Rancho San Bernardino. Williams alerted Governor Pío Pico about the situation, and word was sent to all the rancheros in the area to stand in readiness. The crisis was somewhat diffused when Antonio María Lugo informed Pico that relatively few Utes had arrived and that they had come to trade, not to raid.[32] Nevertheless, Pico and six civilians, armed with muskets and lances, departed Los Angeles to contact the Utes. On their way they met an individual from New Mexico named Moya. He knew the language of the Utes and agreed to accompany the paisanos to the rancho. Pico recalled that "there were about thirty men and women, all of them well mounted and armed with rifles and arrows. Our interpreter told them who I was and that I had come to greet them, etc. They seemed very friendly and we all marched together to the ranch of San José." At sunset, Utes and Mexicans held a conference, passing around a large tobacco pipe. They told Pico that the purpose of their trip was to sell some buffalo hides and the four children they had taken from their enemies along the way. Three were girls, the oldest not more than thirteen years old. Pico told the Utes that "in California such traffic was not tolerated, referring, of course, to the Indian children, but for them to give them to me as a gift and I would reward them. They agreed to this and I ordered them at the same time not to go beyond that place, where they could sell their hides, and to let me know four or five days before they left so I could reciprocate their gift--that is, the four little Indians." The following day Pico returned to Los Angeles and placed the children in the care of respectable families. A few days later he sent the Indians horses, glass beads, and other objects.[33] Evidently the Utes remained in the area for three months before departing with large numbers of horses. Vicente Lugo and his companions overtook the Indians on the Mohave River but they were too powerful an opponent to be

---

32. Beattie and Beattie, *Heritage of the Valley*, 65–66.
33. Cole and Welcome, eds., *Don Pío Pico Historical Narrative*, 154–44.

engaged so the pursuers turned back for reinforcements. Apparently, the Utes easily escaped.[34]

Isaac Williams offered to build a fort in the Cajon Pass if the government would allow him to import duty free goods worth 25,000 pesos.[35] In mid-July 1846, he predicted that if the Cajon Pass was not secured, the Utes would strike again.[36] Nothing came of his proposal. In April the following year, he complained to Abel Stearns that the valley was full of Indians and that the government had failed to provide him with protection. His vaqueros were forced to spend valuable time guarding his herds of horses instead of attending to other matters.[37]

By this time the U.S. military forces had occupied most of coastal California during the Mexican-American war. To protect the eastern section of the Los Angeles region, on February 6, 1848, Colonel Jonathan D. Stevenson ordered Kit Carson (a second lieutenant in the Regiment of Mounted Riflemen) to Rancho San Bernardino. According to the order, Carson was to proceed at once to José María Lugo's house near the Cajon Pass. There he would take command of a party of dragoons and then take up "a position, as will best protect the surrounding country from the 'Utah Indians' or others who may commit any depravations." In "case of necessity," he was authorized to impress local civilians into his command. If the soldiers took up a position in the Cajon Pass, it was not for long, because by the end of February they were already back in Los Angeles. But on March 1 Carson led another detachment to the pass. This one consisted of eighteen privates and an officer. He remained at the pass until the end of the month when he was replaced by Lieutenant George Stoneman. Evidently, the presence of soldiers in the pass discouraged its use by stock raiders until May when the post was abandoned.[38]

---

34. Beattie and Beattie, *Heritage of the Valley*, 66.
35. Ibid., 66–67; Bancroft, *History of California*, 5: 37n1.
36. Julian [Isaac] Williams to Abel Stearns, n. p., July 15, 1846, Abel Stearns Collection, Box 69.
37. Julian [Isaac] Williams to Abel Stearns, Rancho del Chino, April 7, 1847, ibid.
38. Hussey, "Kit Carson at Cajón," 32–34, 38n31; Quaife, ed., *Kit Carson's Autobiography*, 122–23. Carson mistakenly called the Cajón Pass the Tejón Pass.

In mid-February 1848, Stevenson had placed Andrés Pico, brother of the former governor, in charge of defending the region against Indian stock raiders. He was to identify all individuals capable of bearing arms who would be on call to defend the ranchos against Indian incursions. Those failing to answer the call would be fined not less than ten dollars and not more than twenty-five.[39] Shortly after receiving his commission, Pico and several men pursued Indians who had stolen forty horses from his rancho. They overtook the robbers and recovered the animals. A short time later, Indians robbed José Sepúlveda of one hundred horses. Ramón Carrillo and fifteen men caught up with the stock raiders, but in the ensuing fight Sepúlveda's son was wounded and a servant killed. The Mexicans regained possession of the stock except for the animals that the Indians had killed.[40]

Recruiting Mexicans in the struggle against the stock raiders was perhaps the only way to curtail the raids. Writing in May to the American military governor of California, Colonel Stevenson admitted that the army could not by itself protect the people from the stock raiders: "The Indians must be sought for by the people of the Country who know every foot of ground as well as the passes through which the Indians enter and depart." More than likely the success of Andrés Pico was "communicated by the Christian Indians to their associate wild Indian thieves which has undoubtedly the effect to restrain them especially in the lower part of this District."[41] The strategy may have worked at least temporarily because the next raid apparently did not occur until May 1849 when Utes struck at Rancho Azusa. The following month Abel Stearns led a party after the Utes who had stolen horses from the outskirts of the pueblo. Stearns and his men caught the Utes in the Cajon Pass, killing ten and recovering the horses. But two of his men lost their lives.[42]

---

39. Colonel J. D. Stevenson to Andrés Pico, Los Angeles, February 14, 1848, Pacific Division, Records of the 10th Military Department, Letters Received, RG 98, Microcopy 210, Roll 3, United States National Archives.
40. Stephen Foster to Colonel R.B. Mason, Santa Bárbara, April 20, 1848, ibid.
41. Colonel J. D. Stevenson to Colonel R. B. Mason, Los Angeles, May 1848, ibid.
42. Cleland, *Cattle on a Thousand Hills*, 65.

Isaac Williams informed the commander of U.S. military forces in California in August that his rancho and several others were exposed to "the constant depredations of wild Indians who descend from the valley and steal our cattle and commit other hostilities upon our people." The two passes (Cajon and San Gorgonio) through which the Indians descended could easily be defended by twenty-five soldiers in each, but he understood the difficulty of stationing soldiers in such remote areas. He recommended, therefore, that the army provide arms and equipment (or reimburse him for doing so) to the fifty "Christianized Indians" living in the immediate vicinity "whose character and capability are well known to me and my neighbours." The fifty Indians would be sufficient to protect the property of the rancheros.[43]

Arming Indians was probably not considered, even though the rancheros were clearly on the defensive. In January 1850 Walkara and about fifty Utes arrived in the vicinity of Rancho San Francisco, the former estancia of Mission San Fernando. They stole oxen from some immigrants passing through the area and captured one of the immigrants, an acquaintance of Walkara's from Utah. The chief freed him on the condition that he not reveal his location. The following day, the immigrant and a companion contacted the Utes, seeking the return of their oxen. Walkara refused their request and ordered them to leave by a different route. Forty-seven Mexican and American volunteers proceeded to the rancho, scoured the area, and followed a trail for a distance before turning back.[44] The Utes easily located the stock of José María Lugo and Francisco Alvarado and departed California with large numbers of horses.[45]

Except for providing weapons to the volunteers, Company A of the 2nd Infantry that was bivouacked at Rancho Chino, was

---

43. Isaac Williams to General Bennett Riley, Rancho del Chino, August 10, 1849, Pacific Division, Records of the 10 Military Department, Letters Received, 1846–1851, RG 98, Microcopy 210, Roll 4, U.S. National Archives.
44. Immigrant to B. D. Wilson, San Francisco Rancho, January 15, 1851, Benjamin Hayes Diary, n.d., in Benjamin Hayes Scrapbooks, vol. 39, The Bancroft Library; Benjamin Hayes to Abel Stearns, Los Angeles, January 25, 1850, Abel Stearns Collection RG, Box 34.
45. H. M. Nimmo to Abel Stearns, San José, February 10, 1850, Abel Stearns Collection, SG, Box 45.

virtually useless against the mounted and mobile Indian raiders. Regarding the company commander, Captain C. S. Lovell, a local resident quipped: "For all the good he does, he might as well be in San Francisco."[46] Local rancheros had no choice but to take action against the raiders. Thus when the Utes stole seventy-five horses from Rancho San Bernardino in January 1851, Mexicans and Indians (probably Cahuillas) gave chase. In a letter to Abel Stearns, Lewis Granger described the campaign: "Fifteen men (paisanos and Sonorans) started in pursuit, came upon the Utahs 100 miles from the Cahon pass, attacked them, but were repulsed with the loss of one man, a Sonoran, who fell at the first fire, pierced with five balls. Had it not been for the darkness of the night, the party in pursuit would have been all killed, as the Utahs were 50 strong, armed with rifles and revolvers. They were on guard and under arms, being no doubt appraised of the approach of the party in pursuit. Cannot a post of U.S. troops be established at the pass!"[47]

Although the Utes were better armed, the Paiutes caused more damage. Reporting from Rancho Chino in late March 1851, James Wall Schureman held that the former were "a brave tribe, well armed in part with rifles, pistols & lances.... Their excursions into these valleys take place but once a year. The latter is a more annoying tribe to the Rancheros ... as their depredations are committed every month. They are but poorly armed with the bow and arrow, and are easily cowed if they can be found."[48] An individual warned in early June that "the moon has come again—and with her, it is said, the dread Pay-u-tahs. But this time they will find few horses, (unless they go far into the center of the county, and thus expose themselves to almost certain capture,) as the rancheros of the frontier, generally, have sent away their stock.... None are kept on the

---

46. T. F. to editors, Los Angeles, November 5, 1850, *Daily Alta California*, November 27, 1850; Beattie and Beattie, *Heritage of the Valley*, 134; Woodward, ed., *Journal of Lt. Thomas W. Sweeny, 1849–1853*, 262–63n111.

47. Lewis Granger to Abel Stearns, Los Angeles, February 4, 1851, in Hafen, ed., *Letters of Lewis Granger*, 30; *San Francisco Herald*, February 14, 1851.

48. James Wall Schuerman to Sister, Rancho del Chino, March 31, 1851, James Wall Schuerman, Letters, 1842–1851, 84/73c, The Bancroft Library.

ranchos of the vast extent of territory from Chino to the Cajón and San Gorgonea [sic], except for indispensable use." The writer reminded his readers of the "robbery in January last, which the Lugos and Alvarados tried to retrieve, but which ended to them only in a painful march, a shameful defeat."[49] A well-armed party of thirty-six Utes clashed with Cahuillas in August, wounding an important leader, Manuel Largo. The *Los Angeles Star* reported that Captain Lovell at Chino lacked "sufficient force at his disposal to pursue them, and he has requested [that] the County attorney . . . raise a company of men in the city to co-operate with the military at Chino. It is supposed that Walker [Walkara] is at the head of the Utahs. Our citizens should act with promptness."[50] Evidently, the citizens failed to act.

In May 1852 two white men arrived in Los Angeles from the Great Salt Lake claiming that they had been captured and released by Walkara. The Ute chief told them that he had stolen three hundred horses from California the previous year and intended to take another one thousand this year.[51] In June an unidentified party of Indians stole sixty mares from Diego Lorato, near Rancho Yucaipa and fled towards the Mohave River. Twenty six men and some local Indians gave chase. They recovered three or four animals.[52] The *Star* reported in December that Utes led by Walkara was "lurking about the Cajon Pass, undoubtedly waiting an opportunity to steal horses. Whether this report is true or false, rancheros should be on their guard, for the experience of former years proves that the Utahs are very expert horse-thieves."[53]

So were the Paiutes. In February 1853 they stole two bands of horses from Rancho San José, which was owned by Ignacio Palomares. A party recovered all the animals except five that had been killed for food. Regarding this raid, the *Star* noted that "the Pah-

---

49. B. to editors, Chino, June 4, 1851, *Los Angeles Star*, June 7, 1851, in Benjamin Hayes Scrapbook, vol. 94.
50. *Los Angeles Star*, August 16, 1851.
51. *Los Angeles Star*, May 22, 1852.
52. Unidentified newspaper, probably the *Los Angeles Star*, June 5, 1852, in Benjamin Hayes Scrapbooks, vol. 39.
53. *Los Angeles Star*, December 25, 1852.

Utahs are wild Indians of the Desert. They are expert thieves, and are under no control of our government. This band of Indians are said to be at present in the San Fernando Valley."[54] The following month, Indians, evidently Paiutes, stole eight horses, killed one, and injured another near Rancho Santa Ana.[55] A short time later Indians stole six horses belonging to Juan Ávila tied near Isaac Williams' ranch house. The Indians mounted the six horses and ran off 150 animals. Ávila also lost fifty saddle horses. Thirty men recruited from the local ranchos and led by John Foster followed the raiders north and joined up with a party led by Ávila and José Sepúlveda also searching for the raiders. Now numbering fifty men, the pursuers searched for six more days before turning back. The raid and pursuit prompted a strong response from those producing the Spanish-language section of the *Star*: "After this time lost, the neglect of their affairs, the leaving of their families exposed to the rise of another attack by the savages, and having lost hope of getting revenge, they returned home to wait until the Indians should come back for a few horses they had left and perhaps kill them and their families." Emphasized, however, was the fact that the "Indians who despoil this country are distant tribes, not the peaceful Indians who are in our vicinity."[56]

To remedy this state of affairs, in August the county formed the Los Angeles Rangers, consisting of one hundred men of which only twenty-five were active members. Each member was to furnish his own arms, but local rancheros would provide the horses. The county and private subscription would pay for forage, herding, and equipment. The horses would be kept in the city and in a state ready for the first emergency.[57] Evidently the Rangers were not prepared for the Indian raid in April 1854. Rancho Chino was hit again, this time for 130 horses. Isaac Williams immediately sent a party of Mexicans in pursuit. The Mexicans attacked a village near Owens Lake on the east side of the Sierra Nevada, killing

---

54. *Los Angeles Star*, February 26, 1853.
55. *Los Angeles Star*, March 19, 1853; See also the *Daily Alta California*, March 31, 1853.
56. "La Estrella," in *Los Angeles Star*, April 2, 1853. "La Estrella" was a section of the *Star* written in Spanish.
57. *Los Angeles Star*, August 6, 1853.

several Indians and taking a few prisoners. But they attacked the wrong village and recovered no horses.[58] In July, Paiutes raided several ranchos between San Gabriel and San José. Ignacio Alvarado lost forty-three horses. Henry Dalton lost a large number as well. When about to be caught in the Cajon Pass, the raiders killed several of the horses and escaped with as many as they could. The rancheros recovered about forty mares.[59] The same month a local newspaper queried: "How long have our ranchers and farmers got to submit to this state of things, and groan under the shameful and vexing evil, when a few well mounted men stationed in the Cajon Pass or vicinity, would put an end to these frequent incursions and depredations?"[60]

The economic impact the raids had on the local economy was discussed by the editors of the *Star*: "The depredations of the Indians are a great annoyance to our farmers; that they are fast draining the wealth of the county in more respects than one, not only in the amount of stock stolen, but the insecurity which is felt by all is a great hindrance to successful farming and grazing operations, and occasions an additional expense in the care of the animals."[61] The *Santa Bárbara Gazette* summarized and assessed the repercussions resulting from the loss of stock in the counties of San Bernardino, Los Angeles, Tulare, San Diego, San Luis Obispo, and especially Santa Bárbara: "We learn from good authority that in '50, '51 and '52, over three thousand horses were stolen from this county alone by the Indians, and it would be a moderate estimate to say that the loss in this county was only one-fourth of the aggregate loss in the above named six counties, this making a total loss of twelve thousand horses in three years, or an annual drain of four thousand head.... Regarding all these facts and considerations, we believe we do not exaggerate when we estimate that the annual loss of the six Southern counties from Indian depredations, at two hundred thousand dollars for the three years preceding 1853."[62]

---

58. *Los Angeles Star*, July 1, 1854, in Benjamin Hayes Scrapbooks, vol. 39.
59. *Southern Californian*, July 20, 1854, ibid.
60. *Los Angeles Star*, July 25, 1854, ibid.
61. *Los Angeles Star*, April 2, 1853.
62. *Santa Bárbara Gazette*, November 15, 1855.

For San Diego and Los Angeles counties alone, the *Star* came up with a much higher figure:

> How many thousands of horses were stolen in the years '50 '51 '52 '53 from the Ranches of San Ysabel, Santa Margarita, Las Flores, El Tamuel, San Jacinto, Agua Caliente and numerous other ranches in San Diego County? Who that has lived in this county, for the past five years, does not recollect the magnificent droves of horses stolen from San Bernardino, San Jose, El Chino, El Rincon, Santa Ana, El Neguil, the Verdugos, Tajunga, San Fernando, Cahuenga and every other exposed Rancho in this country? . . . We are confident we are under the mark, when we estimate the loss of . . . horses alone at 300,000 dollars and when we add the loss of horned cattle, the insecurity of person and property, and the abandonment of the frontier settlements, this estimate is insignificant.[63]

In late March 1855 when the *Star* reported that Walkara had been poisoned, the rancheros probably issued a collective sigh of relief.[64] Walkara had died of pneumonia on January 29.[65] The raids would continue, some now conducted by Americans, but they occurred less frequently and mainly in the eastern part of the region.[66]

---

63. *Los Angeles Star*, October 20 1855.
64. *Los Angeles Star*, March 31, 1855.
65. L. R. Bailey, *Indian Slave Trade*, 170.
66. For Americans engaged in stock raiding, see the *Southern Californian*, May 23 and 30, 1855.

CHAPTER 10

Skilled Labor

The horseman who suddenly appeared out of the darkness one night in April 1844 clearly stunned the members of an American exploring party camped in the southern San Joaquín Valley. He was a "Christian Indian," wrote John C. Frémont, "well dressed, with long spurs and a *sombrero*, and speaking Spanish fluently. It was an unexpected apparition and a strange and pleasant sight in this desolate gorge of a mountain—an Indian face, Spanish costume, jingling spurs, and a horse equipped after the Spanish manner."[1] What Frémont observed was a highly skilled laborer whose expertise resulted from years of training, practice, and experience and whose ostentatious accoutrements belied their utility.

His saddle had evolved from the one Spanish soldiers brought to California and was designed for work, not war. Craftsmen fashioned the saddle tree with a high pommel and cantle from a light wood—often willow—and padded it underneath with part of a hide. They added thick wooden stirrups and stout iron rings to which was fastened the single cinch. Instead of being placed just behind the forelegs as with the Spanish saddle, the cinch was moved back to the front of the belly of the animal. This allowed

---

1. Frémont, *Memoirs of My Life*, 1: 362.

for an equal distribution of the pull on the horse when the rider roped an animal. Covering the saddle was the *mochila*, a leather blanket, sometimes decorated, containing two openings for the projection of the pommel and cantle. With a pair of heavy holsters added, the saddle weighed nearly two arrobas.[2]

A vaquero usually herded a caballada of eight horses when accompanying a ranchero over a great distance. If the two men maintained a constant rate, at the end of about eight leagues, they would replace the two horses they had ridden for two fresh ones from the caballada. If a horse gave out, it was left on the road.[3] "No stabling, no grooming, no farriery, no shoeing, no docking, no clipping, no jockeying, are connected with the care of the California horse," wrote Joseph Warren Revere, an American naval officer. "After a hard day's journey he is unbridled and unsaddled, and suffered to roam at large until he is again wanted by his master."[4]

Longtime California resident William Heath Davis noted that "a large number of horses were needed on each rancho for herding stock, as they were used up very fast. They were numerous and cheap, and the owners placed no restraint upon the vaqueros, who rode without a particle of regard for the horses, till they soon became unfit for further use in this way. The vaqueros were continually breaking in young colts three years old and upwards, to replace those already beyond service."[5]

If treatment of their mounts generated some criticism, no one, Baldwin Möllhausen in particular, disputed their equestrian abilities:

> The skill of these men in riding and throwing the lasso is quite wonderful; and two of them will capture the wildest horse, or the most furious bull. They are well-mounted on horses specially trained for this service,

---

2. William Robert Garner to editors of the *North American and United States Gazette*, November 8, 1846, in Craig, *Letters from California*, 110–12; Wierzicki, *California As It Is & As It May be*, 81–82; Rojas, *The Vaquero*, 29–33; Denhardt, "The Role of the Horse," 15–17; Frederick, "The California Montadura," 179–86. A photograph of the California saddle can be found in Forbis, *The Cowboys*, 106.
3. Bryant, *What I Saw in California*, 319–20.
4. Revere, *Tour of Duty in California*, 108.
5. Davis, *Seventy-five Years in California*, 36.

"Californians Throwing the Lasso," by William Smyth.
From F. W. Beechey, *Narrative of a Voyage
to the Pacific and Beering's Strait in the Years 1825–1828.*

and one of them rides forward on the right side of the animal, about twenty or thirty feet off, while the other keeps a little behind, at about the same distance on the left side, and at the moment when the right hand horseman flings his lasso over the head of the beast to be captured, the one on the left casts his round the left hind foot, so that the victim is soon brought down. The lassos are then fastened to the saddle-bow, the saddles being so constructed that they cannot be dragged on one side, and the horse, who knows well what he is about, stands like a wall, throwing himself with his whole strength to one side, so that the line remains tightly stretched, and the riders can dismount, and go to the fettered animal, and do what they please with him. I have often been astonished at the confidence and exactness with which these men will lasso a wild horse in full career.[6]

Edwin Bryant was equally impressed:

The men are almost constantly on horseback, and as horsemen excel any I have seen in other parts of the world. From the nature of their pursuits and amusements, they have brought horsemanship to a perfection

---

6. Möllhausen, *Diary of a Journey from the Mississippi,* 329–30.

"Grizzly Bear Hunt."
From *Frank Leslie's Illustrated Newspaper*, April 21, 1858.

challenging admiration and exciting astonishment. They are trained to the horse and the use of the lasso, (*riata,* as it is here called,) from their infancy. The first act of a child, when he is able to stand alone, is to throw his toy-lasso around the neck of a kitten; his next feat is performed on the dog; his next upon a goat or calf; and so on, until he mounts the horse, and demonstrates his skill upon horses and cattle. The crowning feat of dexterity with the *riata,* and of horsemanship, combined with daring courage, is the lassoing of the grisly [sic] bear. This feat is performed frequently upon this large and ferocious animal, but it is sometimes fatal to the performer and his horse.[7]

Mariano Guadalupe Vallejo also mentioned that herdsmen and hunters in different parts of the country were often killed by grizzlies.[8] Revere recounted that sometimes a single vaquero would hunt a bear "without other aid than his horse, his inseparable friend the riata, and the accustomed knife worn in his garter. Thus equipped, he will lasso the largest and most ferocious bear; and,

---

7. Bryant, *What I Saw in California,* 447.
8. Vallejo, "Ranch and Mission Days," 91.

drawing the brute to a tree, and taking a turn or two around him, will dispatch him with his knife, while the sagacious horse keeps the riata fastened to the saddle at its fullest tension."[9]

Vaqueros also lassoed bears to pit them against bulls in a uniquely California spectacle, in which Indians were some of the most ardent spectators. Vaqueros would bait a bear with a cow or horse they had killed while hiding nearby, sometimes a day or longer, until their prey appeared. If everything went according to plan, three or four vaqueros would surround the bear. Two of them would toss their reatas over the bear's head, while a third roped a hind leg. By pulling in opposite directions, the vaqueros would choke the bear until it nearly suffocated, loosening the tension in time for it to catch its breath. This was repeated until the bear lost much of its energy. Vaqueros then muzzled the bear, bound its claws together, and extended it on a cow hide stretched over tree branches which was hitched to a yoke of oxen. If possible, while on their way to the plaza the vaqueros would douse the bear with water to somewhat reduce its rage.[10]

If the bear survived the journey to the plaza, which was not always the case, vaqueros would attach the end of a long rope to one of its paws and the other end to a foreleg of the bull.[11] Antonio Francisco Coronel commented that "sometimes the bear won, sometimes the bull; I saw both cases. It was a pretty brutal spectacle, but people were used to it and didn't see anything wrong with such fights."[12] Revere was more vivid: "The bear sometimes climbs upon the fence of the corral, but is pulled back again by the bull, and they never abandon the conflict until one or the other is killed. It would seem incredible that the largest and most savage bull could be a match for crushing force, the terrible scythe-like claws, and the dreadful jaws of a full-grown grizzly bear; but the knowing ones of the California fancy say that it is about an even

---

9. Revere, *Tour of Duty*, 107.
10. Vallejo, "Ranch and Mission Days," 91; Von Langsdorff, *Voyages and Travels*, 2: 181. See also Mora, *The Californios*, 130–35; Denhardt, "The Role of the Horse," 20.
11. Beechey, *Narrative of a Voyage*, 1: 389–90.
12. Coronel, *Tales of Mexican California*, 82

thing between them, the victory inclining as often to one side as the other."¹³

José del Carmen Lugo failed to mention bull and bear fights in his memoirs, but he did recall bullfights, not the formal *corrida de toros* in a *plaza de toros* with professional *matadores*, *picadores* and *banderilleros*, that had evolved in Spain and Portugal and were brought to New Spain, but a sporting event at a local *feria* or a fiesta. On the day of the fiesta, a bull would be released in the plaza which had been enclosed, and a youth with a cape, shawl, or bright cloth would entice the bull to charge and would execute a few passes. In turn, several young men would follow until the bull grew tired and was turned out. He would be replaced by "another until all were exhausted. Sometimes the bull was killed in the plaza, this being done on horseback with a *rejón* or stick, a vara or less in length with a knife inserted in the end. The bull was steered into the desired position, and the blow was given between the *llaves* (shoulder-blades). Some hit the vital spot, but some did not. The killing, like that of exciting the animal, was always done on horseback. I have seen the exciting done on foot on rare occasions, but never a killing."¹⁴

Who steered the bull into the "desired position" was not addressed by Lugo. But at a bull fight in Northern California an American immigrant, Nicholas Dawson, commented that "Spaniards also fight bulls on horseback, with Indians on foot, who toss a small blanket to enrage the bull. The bull makes at them, and they avoid him by springing to one side. The shouts are given when an Indian is knocked down or killed, favor appearing to be on the side of the bull."¹⁵ Coronel mentioned that men and horses were often injured in this sport.¹⁶

The written accounts of Lugo, Dawson, and Coronel are supported by the visual evidence presented by Edward Vischer. His painting of a bullfight at Mission Dolores in 1842, although produced from memory many years later, captures the essence of the

---

13. Revere, *Tour of Duty*, 146.
14. Lugo, "Life of a Rancher," 232–33.
15. Dawson, *California in '41, Texas in '51*, 109.
16. Coronel, *Tales of Mexican California*, 82.

"Bullfight (after High Mass) . . . at Mission Dolores
[San Francisco Asisi]," by Edward Vischer.
Courtesy of the Bancroft Library, University of California, Berkeley.

event. The small figure with a red cloth on a stick, the *muleta* of the official bullfight, may be an Indian engaging in the *quite*— the drawing away of the bull from the prostrate rider and the horse it has knocked down. Although the mounted man with the pole under his arm resembles a picador, more than likely he is not preparing to pick the bull but to stab it with a rejón. Perhaps the nearby vaquero with the reata was intent on lassoing the bull if the killing did not succeed. Seated in the bleachers in the background must be the local paisanos, while Indian spectators are standing on the building to the right. And in the foreground, another Indian with a muleta and several vaqueros seem to be ready to participate in the spectacle.[17]

Those fighting the bulls probably were Californios, but most of those transforming wild horses into the ones that performed

---

17. Van Nostrand, ed., *Edward Vischer's Drawings, 1861–1878*, Plate 14, no page number. In an introduction to the book, Thomas Albright discusses the accuracy achieved and liberties taken by Vischer.

such remarkable feats probably were Indian vaqueros. Foreign visitors, such as Solomon Nunes Carvalho, found the breaking of wild horses a fascinating undertaking. After selecting the animal to break, the vaquero would tie one end of the lasso "around the nose of the horse; a blanket is strapped on his back by a strong surcingle; he then jumps on him, and introducing his knees under the surcingle, he is now firmly seated. On his feet are immense spurs; he touches the horse with them, and off he bounds with the speed of the wind, his rider guiding him with perfect ease." After an hour, the vaquero would picket the animal to a post.[18]

Once they had trained the horses, vaqueros utilized them in a variety of ways, but separating cattle belonging to several rancheros was the most obvious. José de Carmen Lugo wrote:

> The *rodeo*, or roundup, was presided over by a *juez de campo*, or field judge. The owners who had stock in the region began, each man picking out what he considered his and driving it to one of the separating places that had been selected. He had only to steer the animals gradually to the edge of the place and keep them there. If an animal resisted it was lassoed.
>
> After each individual had pointed out which were his, he requested the organizer of the roundup and the field judge to pass upon the matter. If he was found to be in the right, he drove his stock home. No documents were given. None were necessary; and furthermore, in those days there were very few who could write.[19]

The rodeo was not just a labor-intensive undertaking but also a social gathering. Once the work was completed, the rancheros and vaqueros often remained to partake of the host's hospitality and to catch up on local affairs. Young men vied with one another in feats of horsemanship and roping.[20]

Whereas the rodeo was designed to collect cattle, the matanza was designed to slaughter them. According to William Heath Davis, "the cattle were driven from the rodeo ground to a particular spot on the rancho, near a brook and forest. It was usual

---

18. Carvalho, *Incidents of Travel*, 313–14.
19. Lugo, "Life of a Rancher," 230–31.
20. Bell, *Reminiscences of a Ranger*, 301–2.

to slaughter from fifty to one hundred at a time, generally steers three years old and upward; the cows being kept for breeding purposes. The fattest would be selected for slaughter, and about two days would be occupied in killing fifty cattle, trying out the tallow, stretching the hides and curing a small portion of meat that was preserved."[21]

As to the processing of the tallow, Davis wrote: "The *manteca*, or fat lying nearest the hide of the bullock, was taken off carefully, and tried out apart from the interior fat, or *sebo*. The latter constituted the tallow for shipment about seventy-five to one hundred pounds being obtained from each creature. The former, of which forty to fifty pounds were obtained, was more carefully and nicely prepared, and was saved for domestic use; in cooking being preferred to hog's lard." Being more likely to burn than the sebo, the manteca was intently watched. "When the fat of either kind was sufficiently melted and cooked it was allowed to cool partly, and while still liquid was transferred to hide bags, which were prepared to receive it by fastening at four points on the edge of four upright stakes set in the ground, the mouth of the bag being thus held open."[22]

Most rancheros sold their products, especially hides and tallow, to supercargoes at San Pedro. Seaman Richard Henry Dana, who arrived in 1835, claimed that it was "the best place on the whole coast for hides" and remembered "large ox-carts, and droves of mules loaded with hides . . . coming over the flat country." Once the sailors had landed their long-boat, loaded "with goods of all kinds, light and heavy," the real work began:

> The hill was low, but steep, and the earth, being clayey and wet with the recent rains, was but bad holding-ground for our feet. The heavy barrels and casks we rolled up with some difficulty, getting behind and putting our shoulders to them; now and then our feet slipping, added to the danger of the casks rolling back upon us. But the greatest trouble was with the large boxes of sugar. These, we had to place upon oars, and lifting them up rest the oars upon our shoulders, and creep slowly up

---

21. Davis, *Seventy-five Years in California*, 40.
22. Ibid., 35–36.

the hill with the gait of a funeral procession. After and hour or two of hard work, we got them all up, and found the carts standing full of hides, which we had to unload, and also to load again with our own goods.

Dana was clearly perturbed at the "lazy" Indian cart drivers, "squatting down on their hams, looking on, doing nothing," especially after responding to the sailors request for help by "only shaking their heads, or drawling out 'no quiero.'" He added that "having loaded the carts we started up the Indians, who went off, one on each side of the oxen, with long sticks, sharpened at the end, to punch them with. This is one of the means of saving labor in California—two Indians to two oxen."[23]

Despite his repeated demonstrations of Anglo superiority, Dana recorded much valuable information about various aspects of Mexican culture and Indian behavior in California. He also left us an important manifest of the cargo he and his sailors unloaded at San Pedro and other harbors. For the hides and tallow, the paisanos got tea, coffee, sugar, spices, raisins, molasses, hardware, crockery, tinware, cutlery, dry goods, liquors, cigars, silks, hardware, boots, shoes, calicoes, stockings, pins, combs, shawls, awls, necklaces, jewelry, and furniture. Dana thought the maritime merchants clearly got the better of the exchange noting that the hides "which they value at two dollars in money, they give for something which costs seventy-five cents in Boston.... Things sell, on an average, at an advance of nearly three hundred per cent upon the Boston prices."[24] Tallow sold for eight pesos per hundred weight.[25] Nevertheless, because the cattle cost virtually nothing to raise and slaughter and because the hides were sold uncured (eliminating much time and labor), the exchange was perhaps not as uneven as Dana suggested.

Davis commented on the economic trust established between the supercargoes and the rancheros: "The merchants sold to the rancheros and other Californians whatever goods they wanted,

---

23. Dana, *Two Years before the Mast*, 96–97.
24. Ibid., 77–78.
25. Phelps, *Alta California, 1840–1842*, 64.

to any reasonable amount, and gave them credit from one killing season to another. I have never known of a single instance in which a note or other written obligation was required of them." The rancheros "always kept their business engagements, paid their bills promptly at the proper time in hides and tallow, which were the currency of the country, and sometimes, though seldom, in money. They regarded their verbal promise as binding and sacred, relied upon their honor, and were always faithful."[26]

The volume of trade the trust ensured perpetuated an economic system based on stock raising that resulted in dramatic changes in the landscape. By the time William Dane Phelps arrived in August 1840, cattle and other domestic animals had largely denuded the region from San Pedro Bay to close to Los Angeles, an area once densely covered with a variety of vegetation. "The country in the near neighbourhood of the port is dry & sterile without wood or vegetation," wrote Phelps. "The ground is covered as far as the eye extends with a kind of wild mustard which grows as high as a mans [sic] head. It is now dead and dry."[27] Three years later, another visitor observed "Black Mustard, then in a dry state. This plant, which when cultivated in the best gardens in Virginia, seldom attains three feet, on the plains of San Pedro reaches to eight or nine! Verily, not only do the birds of the air take shelter under its branches, but the cattle of a thousand hills get fat on it."[28] Because cattle also found protection in the mustard, prior to a rodeo, vaqueros from different ranchos would spread out in a line and run their horses through the growth, trampling the stalks, flushing out the cattle, and scattering jack rabbits that infested the area. They speared them with lances or knocked them over with the weighted ends of their whips.[29]

Managing cattle, of course, was only one aspect of life on a rancho. Although José del Carmen Lugo described a typical labor routine, his knowledge came from living on Rancho San Antonio:

---

26. Davis, *Seventy-five Years in California*, 83.
27. Phelps, *Alta California*, 63.
28. Anonymous, *Visit to Los Angeles in 1843*, 12.
29. Gillingham, *The Rancho San Pedro*, 216.

At three o'clock in the morning the entire family was summoned to their prayers. After this, the women betook themselves to the kitchen and domestic tasks, such as sweeping, cleaning, dusting, and so on. The men went to their labor in the field—some to herd cattle, others to look after the horses. The milking of the cows was done by the men or the Indian servants. Ordinarily some women had charge of the milking, to see that the milk was clean and strained. The women and the Indian servants under them made the small, hard, flat cheeses, the cheese proper, butter, curds, and a mixture made to use with beans.

The women's labors lasted till seven or eight in the morning. After that they were busy cooking, sewing, or washing.[30]

Residing on Rancho San Antonio in 1836 were ten neophytes from Mission San Luis Rey.[31]

By the 1840s most of the Indians employed on the ranchos in the Los Angeles region were neophytes. The census of 1844 identified 254 neophytes from four missions working on the ranchos. Twelve ranchos employed 257 Indians. All forty-nine neophytes from Mission San Gabriel found work on Rancho Santa Anita, now the property of Hugo Reid. Of the forty-one neophytes laboring on Rancho La Puente, thirty came from Mission San Juan Capistrano.[32] Formerly an estancia of Mission San Gabriel, in 1845 the rancho came into the possession of John Rowland, a naturalized Mexican citizen originally from the United States. Evidently, the Indians were not terribly disrupted by the change of ownership.[33]

A few rancheros hired gentiles. The eleven Indians employed on Rancho San José were Serranos. Of the twenty-six residing on Rancho Jurupa, nine were Cahuillas.[34] Rancho Jurupa had been assigned to Juan Bandini in 1838 while he was serving as administrador. The following year Bandini sent Agustín Janssens and

---

30. Lugo, "Life of a Rancher," 215–16.
31. Layne, ed., "The First Census," 159.
32. "Register of the City of Los Angeles and its Jurisdiction for the Year 1844," Los Angeles Archives, 3: 784–97. This list of the Indians residing in the Los Angeles region was excluded from Northrop, ed., "The Los Angeles Padrón of 1844," because Indians had no surnames and thus were difficult to distinguish one from another. John R. Johnson kindly provided the document along with a database of the 1844 census prepared by Lorraine Escobar, which has also been most useful.
33. "Petition of John Rowland," in Beebe and Senkewicz, eds., *Lands of Promise and Despair*, 430. See also, Engelhardt, *San Gabriel Mission*, 201–2.
34. "Register of the City of Los Angeles."

TABLE 7. MISSION ORIGINS OF RANCHO RESIDENTS, 1844

Mission	Number
San Buenaventura	2
San Gabriel	49
San Juan Capistrano	115
San Luis Rey	88
Total	254

Source: Adapted from *Register of the City of Los Angeles and Its Jurisdiction for the Year 1844*, Los Angeles City Archives, vol. 3.

some Mexicans to the rancho. As described Janssens, "it was level, valuable, and prosperous.... There was a *ranchería* of Cahuillas, who worked on the ranch and who were always having dances."[35] Rancho Azusa also employed Cahuillas but its owner, Henry Dalton, had to walk a fine line between discipline and diplomacy. On April 3, 1845, when his workers sought permission to search for mescal for three days, permission was granted.[36] Dalton also had to deal with intra-Indian violence on the rancho. In late July, Juan Bautista killed another Indian in a drunken brawl.[37] He was arrested the following month but his fate is unknown.[38]

Some of the rancheros sold wine and brandy at the stores which most operated on their estates. Alcohol, luxury goods, and necessities were often purchased on credit, thus forcing many Indians to work off what they owed. Allowing or encouraging Indians to accumulate debts clearly served the interests of the rancheros. According to an American settler, the store was designed not just to turn a profit but also to keep the workers from venturing to Los Angeles to purchase supplies where "they generally got drunk and stayed away from work longer than the allotted time."[39]

---

35. Ellison and Price, eds., *Don Agustín Janssens, 1834–1856*, 104–5.
36. Daily Occurrences at Azusa, 1: April 3, 1845 Henry Dalton Collection, DL 1138, The Huntington Library.
37. Ibid., 1: July 26, 1845.
38. Ibid., 1: August 2, 1845.
39. Newmark, *Sixty Years*, 175.

TABLE 8. MISSION ORIGINS OF RANCHO RESIDENTS, 1844

Mission	Number
San José	11
Santa Ana del Chino	67
Alamito	10
Santa Anita	49
La Puente	41
Santiago de Santa Ana	36
Jurupa	26
Ranchos not identified	48
Total	288

Source: Adapted from *Register of the City of Los Angeles and Its Jurisdiction for the Year 1844*, Los Angeles City Archives, vol. 3.

Of the thirty-six Indians residing on Rancho Santiago de Santa Ana in 1844, it is assumed that most of the adults purchased items from its store. In late March 1845, for example, José, a sheepherder, bought 19½ *cuartillos* of brandy for 14 *pesos*, 2 *reales*. He also purchased 3 varas of *manta* for 6 reales and winter pants for 6 pesos. A San Gabriel neophyte bought 22 pesos' worth of *indianilla*, pants, and a blanket but no brandy.[40]

Debts were incurred. Brígido, a shoemaker, owed 3 pesos for a pair of shoes, 1 peso and a real for a cut of sole leather and thread, 12 pesos for 6 varas of strips of linen, 3 pesos and 4 reales for 3 silk kerchiefs, 4 pesos and 2 reales for 2 bottles and 1 pint of brandy. Of the 25 pesos the weaver Timoteo once owed, mainly for purchasing brandy, he had worked off 22 of them, but he still owed 1 peso for 3 measures of corn. Nicolás worked off his debts by the month. Nicasio owed nine months of work and 13 pesos for 13 cuartillos of brandy. Domingo and another Indian named Nicolás each owed three months of work.[41]

---

40. Stephenson, "Tomás Yorba, his wife Vicenta and his Account Book," 147–48; "Register of the City of Los Angeles," vol. 3.
41. Stephenson, "Tomás Yorba," 147–48. See also Haas, *Conquests and Historical Identities*, 51–52.

CHAPTER 11

Aftermath

In October 1845 Governor Pío Pico, implementing an act passed by the Mexican government in May, issued a proclamation for the selling and leasing of the missions. Each lease would include "all the lands, out-door property, implements of agriculture, vineyards, orchards, workshops, and whatever according to the inventories made, belongs to the respective Missions with the mere exceptions of those small portions of land which have always been occupied by some of the Indians of the Missions." Excluded from the contract were churches and the curates' houses. At the end of nine years, the renters would return to the government all the equipment and cattle that came with the transaction. *Jueces de paz* were "to see that no one be hindered in the free use of his property; they will quiet the little disturbances that may occur, and if necessary impose light and moderate correction." Serious crimes would be dealt with by higher authorities.[1]

The neophytes were free to "establish themselves in their Missions or wherever they choose. They are not obliged to serve the renters, but they may engage themselves to them, on being paid

---

1. "Proclamation for the Sale of the Missions, October 28, 1845," in Dwinelle, *The Colonial History*, "Addenda No. LXIII," 90–92.

for their labor, and they will be subject to the authorities and to the local police." Indians occupying "portions of land, in which they have their gardens and houses, will apply to this government for the respective title, in order that the ownership thereof may be adjudicated to them, it being understood that they cannot alienate said lands, but they shall be hereditary among their relatives, according to the order established by law." On January 1 of each year, the Indians were to select four overseers, "who will watch and take care of the preservation of public order." They were subject to the juez de paz and they could be replaced if they did not perform up to expectations. Furthermore, the overseers were to select "every month, from among the best of the Indians, a sacristan, a cook, a tortilla-maker, a vaquero, and two washerwomen for the service of the Padre Minister, and no one shall be hindered from remaining in this service as long as he chooses."[2]

Accepting the inevitable, Father Narciso Durán, commissary prefect of the missions, recommended to the governor that he form a commission consisting of Pico's brother Andrés and Juan Manso. This commission would take inventories at the missions with the view of implementing the act.[3] As recalled by Pío Pico, "This being done, with the approval of the assembly I made an announcement to the public, offering to lease what remained of the establishments. This method did not achieve good results because no proposals for rental were made to the government excepting in the case of San Fernando."[4] In December 1845, Pico leased the mission to his brother and Juan Manso who were obligated to pay 1,120 pesos per annum for the nine-year contract.[5] An inventory taken on January 1, 1846, valued the animals and equipment at 2,170 pesos.[6] Three years later, a priest noted that the church had been neglected. The choir loft had a railing of painted wood, a bench for singers, but no instruments. The pulpit was dilapidated.

---

2. Ibid.
3. Bancroft, *History of California*, 4: 550, 637n14.
4. Cole and Welcome, eds., *Don Pío Pico's Historical Narrative*, 121–22.
5. Engelhardt, *San Fernando Rey*, 64–65; Robinson, "The Spanish and Mexican Ranchos," 10–11.
6. Engelhardt, *San Fernando Rey*, 65.

TABLE 9. LIVESTOCK AND IMPLEMENTS AT
RANCHO EX-MISSION SAN FERNANDO, JANUARY 1, 1846

	Number	Value (pesos)
Livestock		
Horses (unbroken)	710	1,065.00
Horses (tame)	16	128.00
Cattle	74	185.00
Sheep	375	562.50
Oxen (Yoke)	9	108.00
Implements		
Tables	4	6.00
Benches	4	4.00
Copper kettles	2	4.00
Copper ladles	3	3.75
Tools in smithy	—	20.00
Tools in carpentry shop	—	30.00

Source: Adapted from Zephyrin Engelhardt, *Mission San Fernando Rey: The Mission in the Valley*, 64–65.

Statues of Saint Joseph with the Infant, La Purísima Concepción, and San Fernando remained, as did paintings of Saint Francis, the Assumption of Our Lady, and Nuestra Señora del Pilar. And on the walls of the church was "a most unspectacular set" of the Stations of the Cross.[7]

On June 17, 1846, Pío Pico sold the mission to Eulogio de Célis. Because it was a sale, Pico was not bound by any limitations regarding the size of the land, but Célis was to maintain the mission, provide food and clothing to the priest, care for old Indians, and respect their right to plant crops.[8] In his memoirs, Pico insisted that the mission was transferred as a mortgage security for the amount of money Célis had made available to the government.[9] That may or may not be true, but it is doubtful that any money

---

7. "Last Inventory, 1849," in Weber, ed., *The Mission in the Valley*, 40–41.
8. Engelhardt, *San Fernando Rey*, 65–67; Robinson, *The Story of San Fernando Valley*, 10.
9. Cole and Welcome, eds., *Don Pío Pico's Historical Narrative*, 145.

changed hands. Moreover, there may have been a stipulation in the contract that conveyed one half of the property to Andrés Pico.[10] Whatever the truth, Andrés Pico remained on the property, and he and Célis turned the mission into a successful enterprise. The property became known as Rancho Ex-mission San Fernando.[11]

Pico allowed and probably encouraged the neophytes who remained to engage in activities of both pre- and post-contact origins. Isabela Villegas heard stories about the fiestas from her grandmother and parents who had moved to the mission in 1837. On May 30, the feast day of San Fernando, Indians and Mexicans would attend Mass, feast at long rows of tables in the orchard at the rear of the church, and engage in or observe horse racing, a rodeo, and a bullfight. In the evening there were songs and dancing. And the Indians continued to practice their ancient mourning ceremony:

> The Indians had special fiestas of their own; the greatest of these was the anniversary of the death of an Indian chief. Indians came to San Fernando from what at that time were great distances. Whole tribes would make the yearly pilgrimage, some coming from Tehachapi, and others as far as San Jacinto. Those tribes known as the Mission Indians were the Tijungas [Tujungas], El Encino, and El Escorpión, and, of course, those who lived in the mission proper. The feature of the fiesta was a dance in which all the members of the different tribes joined. A large image of the Indian chief was erected, around which a fire was built. As the dancers moved in a circle about the image, they cast into the fire some personal belongings of their dead. The music to the dance was the wailing and weeping of the dancers themselves.[12]

Rancho El Escorpión, under the leadership of the Indian Urbano Chari, may have been heavily represented at the fiestas. According to the Los Angeles Census of 1850, thirty-nine Indian resided on the rancho. Age fifty-five, Urbano Chari was a farmer

---

10. The sale is discussed in the *Los Angeles Star*, June 24, 1854.
11. Robinson, "The Spanish and Mexican Ranchos," 10–11.
12. Villegas, "San Fernando Mission, 1797–1825," 8–9. Also published in Weber, ed., *The Mission in the Valley*, 31–32. For accounts of post-contact Indian communities forming at other missions, consult Johnson, "The Chumash Indians After Secularization," 1–33; Haas, *Conquests and Historical Identities*, 45–137; and Hackel, *Children of Coyote*, 421–39.

with property valued at five hundred dollars. Moreover, at one time or another, most of the twelve Indians residing on Rancho El Encino probably attended as well. One of the three Indians who had received the grant, Román, age fifty-five, was listed as a farmer with property worth one thousand dollars. Evidently he and his followers were allowed to reside on the rancho which had become the property of Vicente de la Osa.[13]

The fifty-three Indians listed in the census as residing at the mission also would have attended the fiestas. Except for the six who were age fifteen and younger, all were adults including the twenty males identified as laborers. Ten were age fifty-five or older. Alfonso, Gaspar, Luicillo, and Polinario were ninety-five, ninety-four, seventy-five, and seventy respectively and apparently were too old to work. Although the twenty-three adult women residing at the mission received no designation regarding their work, it is assumed they continued to labor in the kitchen, patio, and fields. Ten were fifty-six years or older. Limpia was ninety, Agassita eighty-five, Romualda eighty, and Mamerta seventy-five.[14]

Aged Indians probably enhanced the image then forming of Mission San Fernando as an institution with a distant and romantic past. While camped north of the mission in 1853, William P. Blake, a member of a U.S. surveying team, observed an Indian harvesting a *tuna*, the gigantic prickly pear. At the mission he found gardens "enclosed by walls, but the graceful palms rose above them, and groves of olive, lemon, and orange trees could be seen within." The only industry Blake mentioned was the making of aguardiente: "Several men were employed in filling a large still with the fermented pulp and skins of grapes, from which the juice had been pressed." The building presented "an imposing appearance, having a long portico formed by a colonnade, with twenty arches, built of brick, or adobe, and plastered and whitewashed. The floor is paved with tiles, and a pleasant promenade in front of

---

13. Newmark and Newmark, eds., *Census of the City and County of Los Angeles*, 70–73; Robinson, "The Spanish and Mexican Ranchos," 8. According to John R. Johnson, José Miguel Triunfo resided northeast of the mission. See "Indians of Mission San Fernando," 260.
14. Newmark and Newmark, eds., *Census of the City and County of Los Angeles*, 70–71.

Picking prickly pears near San Fernando.
From *Reports of Explorations and Surveys*.

the edifice is thus afforded. The remains of a large fountain, with a circular basin ten feet or more in diameter, were directly in front of the main entrance, and gave an indication of the splendor of the establishment in former days."[15]

In June the following year the editors of the *Los Angeles Star* noted that the "church and other buildings remain generally in excellent preservation, and its vineyard and olive orchards are superior to any in the State." Regarding the mission's future, they insisted it was too close to Los Angeles for an Indian reservation, "but it might be appropriated for a General Superintendency, if two other Reserves are made in the South."[16] In July 1855 the *Star* praised its location which was "beautiful and romantic, with an abundance of water and fine timbers. The Church and other

---

15. Blake, *Report of a Geological Reconnaissance*, 74–75.
16. *Los Angeles Star*, June 24, 1854.

buildings are still in a good state of preservation, and its beautiful vineyards and orchards of Olive and other fruit trees, are laid out with a magnificence and taste which has few, if any equals."[17] High praise also came from Captain E. D. Townsend who in October observed "two gardens belonging to this Mission. In both of them are vineyards, olive-trees, pomegranates, figs, etc. The gardens are not kept in good order, but naturally they are the handsomest I have seen. There is plenty of water for irrigation, and the remains of a fountain are still left in front of the main building."[18] That year the artist Henry Miller found the church and the building in which Pico lived "in good condition, built of adobe and white washed. The proprietor and his family being absent, I went to a Frenchman who attends to one of the large orchards and vineyards, for which he shares the profits of the sales of fruit, wine and brandy, with the proprietor."[19]

What J. E. Pleasants recollected late in his life may have been a romantic exaggeration, but his description of the social life at Rancho Ex-mission San Fernando in 1856 reveals much about its proprietor. Although the mission and its orchards, vineyards, and cemetery had been provisionally returned to the Catholic Church in late 1855, Andrés Pico continued to reside at the mission itself and

> maintained a large stock ranch on what had been mission lands before secularization. He lived in a luxurious style and had a large household of trained servants, chiefly Indians. Like the grandee that he was, he entertained lavishly. His silver and china table-service made a brilliant display. His household furnishings were plain but massive and luxurious. The plain old mission furniture was retained but many an expensive and more ornate piece had been added. His table afforded an ample style of living; the dinners consisted of five to six courses—all of the far-famed California-Spanish cookery, which no nation—not even the French, has ever excelled. Two young Indian boys served as waiters. They were clad in the simple tunic of the day. Before the meal, one of them stood by the host, Don Andres, at the head of the table and said grace, and at the close of the meal, the other took his place and returned thanks.

---

17. Ibid., July 21, 1855.
18. Edwards, ed., *The California Diary*, 112.
19. Miller, *Account of a Tour*, 41–43.

At the mid-day and evening meals, and on the veranda in the evening, we were delightfully entertained by native musicians who played on three stringed instruments then mostly in vogue—the harp, violin and guitar. They played the dreamy old Spanish airs which were, to me, the most enjoyable feature of the day.[20]

Pico obviously needed a large labor force to manage his property and maintain his lifestyle. How many Indians he employed is not known, but they preserved in limited ways aspects of the old mission economy. Five members of the California State Agricultural Society visited the mission in 1855 and observed two plots of thirty and thirty-three acres. Each plot contained seventeen thousand vines. In addition, there were five hundred old olive trees, from which eight hundred gallons of oil was produced each year. "The work on and about this place is done by Indians, numbers of whom were in the orchard pearing, and spreading pears, on plats made of cornstalks, weeds, etc., to dry."[21] A member of the delegation offered his personal reflections: "After visiting the wine cellars, which are cool, capacious, and well stored with that beverage which the gods, in the plenitude of their mercy bestowed on man, we returned to the dwelling, where was spread a sumptuous dinner which both from the place, as well as, the dishes with which our appetite was destroyed, brought vividly to our recollection, those days of old, when the priests, seated at the head of their tables, dispensed with the hand of true libertality, a profusion of that abundance which a gentile clime and their own administrative talent that surrounded them."[22]

Not only were those "days of old" long gone, the modern world had intruded, literally, onto Pico's property. In 1857, Congress passed the Overland California Mail Bill, authorizing the postmaster general to select routes and offer contracts. The contract to John Butterfield led to mail and passenger service opening up between Missouri and California. On September 8, 1858, the first

---

20. Pleasants, "A Fourth of July at San Fernando in 1856," 49, 52. For a discussion of Indian dependence on haciendas, consult Wolf, *Sons of the Shaking Earth*, 207–10.
21. *Transactions of the California Sate Agricultural Society*, 294,
22. *Southern Vineyards*, August 1, 1858.

Aftermath 241

stage left San Francisco for St. Louis.[23] In October it stopped at the rancho which had become a station on the route. A passenger noted that the main structure "was once a fine adobe building, with large pillars in front and a fine belfry and fountain. A niche in the centre of the building contains a fine piece of old statuary. Part of the building is now used as a stable for the company's horses; and the only inhabitants we saw were a few Indian women, washing in a little brook which gurgles by, who giggled in high glee as we passed."[24]

Despite its idyllic setting, the rancho and stage station were located in a still volatile area. In early January 1859, Paiutes stole fifty horses from Rancho San Francisco. The men who had immediately set out to recover the animals turned back when they realized that the Indians had erased their tracks. "Those persons owning ranchos in the vicinity of the mountains would do well to attend more closely to the security of their stock," warned the editors of Star, "as the Indians are likely to come back again to take their usual provision of horse meat."[25] And come back they did. "We have been informed by a friend who has been out in the mountains," wrote the editors in March, "that a band of Indians, numbering over twenty, supposed to be Pah-Utes, had been committing depredations on the ranches in the vicinity of San Fernando. They ran off a band of horses belonging to Salazar's ranch; also, three horses belonging to the Overland Mail Company, and shot arrows into five or six others belonging to the same company."[26]

Still, visitors saw in the ruins not a dangerous place but romantic one. Waxed a stage passenger in October 1860:

> The buildings all belong to the time of the old missions; no signs of modern enterprise, save the wooden stable of the Overland Mail company, break the harmony of the scene. Half a dozen tile-covered, crumbling, clumsy adobe buildings—the old church, high, large and

---

23. Cleland, *From Wilderness to Empire*, 308.
24. Ormbsy, *The Butterfield Overland Mail*, 115–16.
25 *Los Angeles Star*, February 12, 1859.
26. Ibid., March 19, 1859.

prominent among them—are the houses of the town. In front of the old church building are the remains of a fountain which once spouted up water joyously on festival days, but it has dried up long ago, and now serves only to tell that the place was once better cared for than at present.

Three or four old orchards, planted before the secularization of the Church property, are in sight. The ancient vines, and pear, fig, and olive trees, unexhausted by more than a quarter of a century of fruitfulness, are still in full bearing, notwithstanding their neglected condition. The stage did not stop more than fifteen minutes, so we could only look at the adobe walls, which serve as fences, from a distance, and so much of the trees as was perceptible over them.[27]

As it turned out, this description may have been the final one to be written by a passenger. The Civil War forced the company to abandon the route for one passing through Salt lake City.[28]

In 1862 the federal government officially returned the mission buildings and grounds to the Catholic Church. Andrés Pico remained on the premises.[29] He was clearly in residence when visited by the artist Edward Vischer in 1865. Vischer visually recorded a functioning rancho. In the background of the first painting is the convento of the former mission; in the middle ground, vaqueros are training recently broken horses; and in the foreground Andrés Pico is speaking with some of his Indian workers, two of whom Vischer erroneously claimed to be 130 and 115 years old. In the second painting, Vischer seems to have captured leisure time. Pico is holding the hand of a child in the corridor of the convento and behind him two persons are relaxing at the fountain. Beyond them is an orchard. To the left of Pico, three men are engaged in a conversation; to the right, framed in the arch, are a Mexican saddle, a guitarist, and a carreta. In the background, vaqueros are lassoing a cow.[30]

By this time, Andrés Pico had conveyed his interest in the rancho

---

27. "Notes of a Trip to Los Angeles—No. 2," *Daily Alta California*, October 7, 1860.
28. Cleland, *From Wilderness to Empire*, 310n6.
29. Robinson, *Ranchos Become Cities*, 88; Engelhardt, *San Fernando Rey*, 81; Robinson, "The Spanish and Mexican Ranchos," 13–14.
30. Van Nostrand, ed., *Edward Vischer's Drawings*, Plates 32 and 33.

Aftermath

Andres Pico and Indians at Rancho San Fernando, by Edward Vischer.
Courtesy of the Bancroft Library, University of California, Berkeley.

to his brother, Pío, the former governor who, in turn, sold the rancho in 1869 to the San Fernando Farm Homestead Association.[31] Andrés remained on the property, as did a few Indians who continued to practice an ancient but modified tradition. Writing to the *Star* in 1874, an individual recounted:

> Last Saturday evening I witnessed a strange sight. Within a hundred yards of the house of General Pico and Mr. Maclay is an old adobe building inhabited by a number of Indians. In front of the house they had dug a pit, in which they placed a quantity of fuel and set the same on fire. The Indians, both men and women, then gathered around in a semi-circle and commenced a wild, weird song, while one of them, who, I presume, had been appointed Head Devil, took charge of the fire, and together with his imps would stir it up occasionally, and from time to time throw in some old rag to be consumed. On making inquiry of Gen. Pico what the meaning of this was, he informed me that it was an old religious custom of the Indians; that their ancestors had practiced it for many generations, and that they were merely burning the clothing of those who had died during the past year. In the meantime there was a

---
31. Robinson, *Ranchos Become Cities*, 88.

Andres Pico at Rancho Ex-mission San Fernando, by Edward Vischer. *Courtesy of the Bancroft Library, University of California, Berkeley.*

male Indian standing to the left of the semi-circle of women, who was apparently making a speech and wildly gesticulating. After the fuel was consumed they filled in the pit again and placed two large stones on the center of it. Then the women filed slowly away towards the house, but the leader, seeming to think she had forgot something, suddenly stopped and returned to the General and placed a small coin in his hand, and then a number of the others did the same until the amount of their contributions amounted to the sum of two dollars.

Pico then delivered a speech that, according to the visitor, was "quite a moral lecture. On inquiring of him the meaning of this part of the performance, he informed me that many years ago he was elected their chief, and that on such occasions as this they made him a present, but that he always returned it a thousand fold."[32]

---

32. *Los Angeles Daily Star,* June 23, 1874. Evidently, the visitor was Josephine Maclay Walker, who circa 1920 wrote an account similar in words and style to the newspaper article. See "Reminiscences of General Andrés Pico," MC 506 (A+B) Typescript, The Huntington Library.

This tradition would soon vanish, because Senator Charles Maclay, who purchased much of the rancho in 1874, intended to subdivide his property. According to the visitor, Maclay was not "disposed to sell a large quantity to any one party, as he says, and very truthful too, that a hundred families who devote themselves to farming, each with a small capital will not only be more beneficial to the country but to himself also." Maclay was "receiving letters daily from all parts of the State and country making inquiries in regard to his lands and lands generally of Southern California, and that a great many express themselves as desirous of making their future home in Southern California."[33] A week later the visitor again wrote to the *Star*, this time predicting that "in a few years San Fernando will be adorned with groves and orchards. It will become the site of a resort of seekers after health. It is removed from everything which can, in a sanitary point of view, be considered deleterious."[34]

Long before this occurred, most of San Gabriel's estancias had been turned into ranchos.[35] But the disposal of the mission itself did not go smoothly. In his memoirs, Pico mentioned that he sold the mission but "it did not become effective."[36] He probably was referring to the rejection of an offer by José Antonio García on behalf of thirty-three New Mexicans.[37] When Andrés Pico and Juan Manso arrived at the mission in early July 1845 to take inventory, they were rebuffed by Father Tomás Eleuterio Esténaga who refused to surrender the mission until ordered to do so by his superiors. A few days later, however, when a circular arrived at the mission directing all the missionaries to turn over their establishments to the commissioners, Esténaga relented.[38]

---

33. *Los Angeles Daily Star*, June 23, 1874.
34. Ibid., June 30, 1874.
35. For land distribution in Southern California, consult Conner, *The Romance of the Ranchos*.
36. Cole and Welcome, eds., *Don Pío Pico's Historical Narrative*, 145.
37. Bancroft, *History of California*, 4: 635n13.
38. Engelhardt, *San Gabriel Mission*, 237–39.

Unsure of their future, the neophytes were particularly disturbed when Majordomo Juan Pérez told them that they would be kept in greater subjection than before and would never be free. Later, the neophytes were assured that the government had no intention of keeping them in slavery.[39] Approximately three hundred Indians remained at the mission.[40]

In 1845 Henry Dalton accepted the post of mayordomo, and in February 1846 he informed Governor Pico's secretary that only twenty-nine or thirty head of cattle remained and that "the property is in complete ruin. It has neither implements nor tools of any kind. Consequently it will be with much difficulty to make any improvement both for said lack as also for lack of hands."[41] That month 140 Indians signed a petition and sent it to Pico. They pointed out the abuses suffered at the hands of the priests, administradores, and mayordomos and asked that an Indian pueblo be formed from mission lands. In March the commission on missions recommended that it not be converted into a pueblo because of its large debts. The issue should be settled by the governor.[42] The issue, however, was rendered moot at mid-year when Hugo Reid and William Workman bought the mission and surrounding lands. They promised to pay the seven thousand pesos debt and support the padre who would remain on the property.[43] It is difficult to determine what the neophytes thought of the new owners, but at the end of June 1846, Reid told Abel Stearns that "the Gabrielinos are behaving very badly. Some remedy must be done to make them obey."[44]

Upon the death of Father Esténaga in early 1847, Father Blas Ordaz took charge of the mission itself and Manuel Olivera became the overseer of mission property. In May the remaining Indians protested against Olivera's arbitrary acts and called for his removal. They insisted that if he were replaced, the neophytes

---

39. Bancroft, *History of California*, 4: 637n14.
40. Jackson, *Indian Population Decline*, 173.
41. Quoted in Engelhardt, *San Gabriel Mission*, 223.
42. Dakin, *A Scotch Paisano*, 119–20.
43. Ibid., 120.
44. Hugo Reid to Abel Stearns, Uva Espina, June 25, 1846, Abel Stearns Collection, sc Box 530. See also Dakin, *A Scotch Paisano*, 121.

that Father Esténaga had allowed to leave the mission would return. Evidently, Ordaz had failed to establish control over the neophytes because in August he asked the alcalde of Los Angeles to instruct them to repair the church and curate's house.[45] The recent death in May of Juan Pérez perhaps freed them to express their defiance.[46]

With the establishing of the State of California, the Indians came under the authority of a different kind of officer. In 1850 the California legislature passed "An Act for the government & protection of the Indians," which placed Indians under the control of local authorities. Article one stated that "Justices of the Peace shall have jurisdiction in all cases of complaints, by, for, or against Indians in their respective townships in this state." Other articles were more specific. The justice of the peace had the right to punish "chiefs or principal men by reprimand or fine, or otherwise *reasonably chastise them*," if their group or village refused to obey the laws. He could require leaders to bring to him "Indians charged or suspected of offenses." And only he had the right to punish an individual Indian who had committed a crime against a white man. An unemployed Indian frequenting taverns and living an "immoral" life could be arrested on the complaint of any citizen. If convicted, he could be "sold" to the highest bidder to work off his fine.[47]

Evidently the local justice of the peace of the San Gabriel township failed to enforce the law regarding non-Indians. The *Star* reported in late 1851 that "certain persons" were converting to their own use timbers, tiles, and other materials belonging to the mission. As many as four large dwelling houses had been constructed from these materials and "some of the mission buildings have been unroofed by parties who have appropriated to themselves the materials." A complaint had been lodged with the district attorney because the mission had become the property of the

---

45. Bancroft, *History of California*, 5: 628–629n2. Olivera (or D'Olivera) was a Portuguese immigrant married to Rufina, a neophyte.
46. Dakin, *A Scotch Paisano*, 125–26.
47. "The Statutes of California," in Harlow, ed., *The City of the Angels*, 37–40. The township was a six-mile square track of county land with judicial authority in the hands of a justice of the peace.

United States government. In the same edition the county district attorney posted a notice warning "all persons against further trespass upon said buildings, as it becomes my duty to see the law enforced against all offending. Until the property of the mission is disposed of by Congress, it is the duty of the officers of the law to keep the same from waste and injury, in the hands of those venerable men to whose pious care the same has been entrusted."[48]

In March 1852 Benjamin Hayes and his wife, Emily Martha Hayes, visited the mission, the latter noting that the church was "in good repair, but most of the other buildings have fallen down." The orange grove was "a remnant of what it was, yet a pleasant sight, large trees hanging full of fruit." Pear and olive orchards had also survived. They contacted early settlers Benjamin Wilson and Michael White, both of whom had obtained land once attached to the mission.[49]

After abandoning Rancho Muscupiabe in the Cajon Pass because of Indian hostility, White and his wife María moved near the mission in 1843. María was a daughter of Eulalia Pérez, former llavera at the mission.[50] As noted by Mrs. Hayes, White was married to a Californio who "appears to be a fine woman." The Whites lived in an adobe house about a mile and a half from the mission. They raised pigs and chickens, manufactured vinegar, and grew green peas in their garden which was tended by an Indian.[51] White also served as justice of the peace at San Gabriel township. On March 29 he convicted José Valenzuela of horse stealing, sentenced him to two months in jail, and ordered him lashed thirty-nine times on the bare back. The Mexican escaped before the sentence was imposed. For stabbing Cayetano Rico twice on the arm, White convicted Amarante Corrante of assault and battery, fined him thirty-two dollars, and confined him to the jail until the fine was paid. A few days later, the citizens of San Gabriel, probably operating under the Act of 1850, hanged an Indian for murdering

---

48. *Los Angeles Star*, November 8, 1851.
49. "Mrs. Hayes to a sister," Los Angeles, March 13, 1852, in Wolcott, ed., *Pioneer Notes, 1849–1875*, 88–89.
50. White, *California All the Way Back*, 39, 39n13, 68.
51. "Mrs. Hayes to a sister," March 13, 1852, in Wolcott, ed., *Pioneer Notes*, 89.

another Indian. The *Star* reported on April 3 that "the one murdered was a fine sober lad; the other a great scamp."[52]

Going unpunished were three Americans who on June 13 raped some Indian women in their village. As reported in the *Star*,

> One of the women, who had been an invalid for years, was nearly strangled by one of the party, because she would not conform to his wishes. The noise and cries brought together a large number of Indians, who would assuredly have killed him, had he not fled and escaped. We learn that the Indians have been well advised what to do in case of another assault, and it is only to be regretted that the names of these three sons of liberty cannot be ascertained. Shame on the man who will take advantage of the helpless and degraded condition of these Indians, and their ineligibility to appear as witnesses, to ill treat them, and render their condition, if possible, more forlorn than it now is.[53]

In July, however, a Mexican was lashed sixty times for stabbing an Indian.[54]

Longtime resident and former justice of the peace Hugo Reid must have witnessed these local events and probably had a say in the legal decisions. The Los Angeles Census of 1850 identified him as a merchant, age thirty-nine, whose property was worth $12,500. Living with him were his wife Victoria, her sons from a previous marriage, Carlos and Felipe, Felipe's wife, and two other persons including two grandchildren.[55] Before his death in December 1852, Reid composed a series of articles for the *Star* about the Indians he knew so well. Collectively called "Los Angeles County Indians," the first "letter" was published on February 21. From his wife Victoria, a Tongva, and from the neophytes at San Gabriel, Reid had absorbed considerable information. His titles included "Lodges," "Language," "Government, Laws, and Punishments," "Religion and Creed," "Food and Raiment," "Marriages," "Births and Burials," "Medicine and Diseases," "Customs," "Traffic and Utensils," "Sports and Games," "Tradition," "Tradition and Fable," and "Legend." These letters cover much of traditional Tongva culture and

---

52. *Los Angeles Star*, April 3, 1852.
53. Ibid., June 26, 1852.
54. Ibid., July 31, 1852.
55. Newmark and Newmark, eds., *Census of the City and County of Los Angeles*, 89.

represent a true ethnography of these people. In "First Arrival of the Spaniards," "Conversion," "First Missionary Proceedings," "New Era in Mission Affairs, "Better Times," "Decay of the Mission," and "Finis," Reid wrote about their post-contact history.[56] Ironically, a few days before "First Missionary Proceedings" was published in which Reid mentioned that the neophytes who fled San Gabriel often returned to steal its stock, he and Michael White had been on a campaign against Indians who had stolen sixty animals from the mission.[57]

In his last letter, published on July 24, he summed up the condition of the Indians remaining near his residence. Noting the deterioration of their traditional culture, he lamented that they were no longer as articulate in their language as once was the case. This was largely because they no longer attended councils once held frequently "in which their wise men spoke with eloquence suited to the occasion, using more dignity and expression, which naturally elevated the minds of all and gave a tinge of better utterance even in ordinary conversation."[58]

Nevertheless, some customs remained: "There are two families at this day whose bad feelings commenced before Spaniards were even dreampt of and they still continue yearly singing and dancing against each other. The one resides at the Mission of San Gabriel and the other at San Juan Capistrano; they both lived at San Bernardino when the quarrel commenced. During the singing they keep stamping on the ground to express pleasure they would derive from tramping on the grave of their foes. Eight days was the duration of the song fight."[59]

Four leaders remained at San Gabriel, but they retained only the authority to hold feasts and to regulate some of the affairs associated with the church. The Indians practiced two religions,

---

56. The letters have been republished several times, the most accessible being Heizer, ed., *Indians of Los Angeles County;* and Dakin, *A Scotch Paisano*, 220–86. The letters are also discussed in McCawley, *The First Angelinos*, 205.
57. *Los Angeles Star,* June 26, 1852.
58. Reid, "Los Angeles County Indians," in *Los Angeles Star,* July 24, 1852; Heizer, ed., *Indians of Los Angeles County,* 102.
59. Reid, "Los Angeles County Indians," in *Los Angeles Star,* April 10, 1852; Heizer, ed., *Indians of Los Angeles County,* 38.

one of custom, and another of faith. Naturally fond of novelty, the Catholic one serves as a great treat—the forms and ceremonies an inexhaustible source of amusement. They don't quarrel with their neighbor's mode of worship, but consider their own the best. The life and death of our Saviour is only, in their opinion, a distorted version of their own life. Hell, as taught them, has no terrors. It is for whites, not Indians, or else their father would have known it. The Devil, however, has become a great personage in their sight; he is called *Zizu*, and makes his appearance on all occasions. Nevertheless, he is only a bugbear and connected with the Christian faith; he makes no part of their own. The resurrection they cannot understand, but a future state of spiritual existence is in accordance with their creed.[60]

The Indians continued to consume the foods of their ancestors as well as those introduced by the Spanish. Their clothing had changed but only recently had the cloak made of rabbit skins "become a novelty." Marriage was conducted in the church but vows, "I am sorry to say, are not very binding, although many examples of strict fidelity exists." Women experienced the same purification procedure after childbirth as in pre-contact times, with the exception of those who were "in the services of whites at their first parturition." Shamans had lost "much in their ability both of predicting events and doing harm; although instances of sickness occasionally occur of which they stand the blame." Shell-bead money, a currency shared by Indians and whites a decade before, was "extremely scarce, and hoarded from one year to another to use at their church ceremonies."[61]

Reid concluded the series by acknowledging he had "refrained from touching on politics. The Administrators I have left to work out their own salvation—and dates, with statistics, I leave to those possessed of abler pens to furnish an account of, and of which there is a fine field open to write about—confining my self entirely to the titles of these letters."[62] But if Reid had no political purpose in writing the letters, others saw in them information that could

---

60. Reid, "Los Angeles County Indians," in *Los Angeles Star*, July 24, 1852; Heizer, ed., *Indians of Los Angeles County*, 101–2.
61. Reid, "Los Angeles County Indians," in *Los Angeles Star*, July 24, 1852; Heizer, ed., *Indians of Los Angeles County*, 102–3.
62. Reid, "Los Angeles County Indians," in *Los Angeles Star*, July 24, 1852; Heizer, ed., *Indians of Los Angeles County*, 103.

be used to help all the Indians of California. On July 24, 1852, when the *Star* published the final letter, it also noted that the series had "attracted much attention, and we have received applications from different parts of the State for copies of the *Star* containing these letters."[63] Two weeks later an individual calling himself "Philo" informed the *Star* that he hoped the letters would serve to ameliorate the condition of the Indians: "No doubt every philanthropist, upon the perusal of those letters has asked, if nothing can be done from the prospective and permanent welfare of this unfortunate race."[64]

When asked by Edward F. Beale, the Superintendent of Indian Affairs for California, to prepare a report on the condition of the Indians, an Indian agent passed on the task to Judge Benjamin Hayes. Hayes noted in his diary entry of January 1, 1853 that "in the afternoon, finished the map to accompany the report of Indian Agent (Benj. D. Wilson).... This Report is of date December 26, 1852, prepared by me, at his instance, from information derived from Don Juan Bandini, Hon. J. J. Warner, and Hugo Reid, Esq."[65] In what is apparently a first draft of the document, Hayes, included two appendixes. The first dealt with the Indians' languages; the second was "a series of essays touching their ancient customs and connection with the missions: both documents from the pen of the late Hugo Reid, Esq., a resident here of twenty years, an accomplished scholar, and whose opportunities of knowing the Indians perhaps exceeded those of any other person in the State. In his death they have lost a zealous friend, who might have been eminently useful to them at this time."[66]

---

63. *Los Angeles Star*, July 24, 1852.
64. Philo to editors, n.d., *Los Angeles Star*, August 14, 1852.
65. Benjamin Hayes, Diary, January, 1, 1853, in Wolcott, ed., *Pioneer Notes*, 94.
66. [Benjamin Hayes] to Edward F. Beal, Los Angeles, December 30, 1852, "The Indians of Southern California," 3–4. This report (minus the appendices which evidently have been lost) is in the The Bancroft Library. It is in the handwriting of Benjamin Hayes but is not signed. Edited by John Walton Caughey, the report was published in book form in 1952 as *The Indians of Southern California in 1852: The B. D. Wilson Report and a Selection of Contemporary Comment*. Unaware of the original, Caughey based the book on a series articles published by the *Los Angeles Star* in July 1868. The appendices and the sentence mentioning them were not included in the book and articles.

Hayes's report contained important ethnographic and historical information regarding the Indians of Southern California, especially the Cahuillas, Serranos and Luiseños, and presented a plan for their protection and management. On January 15, 1853, the editors of the *Star* reviewed the report. They maintained that its publication would be "an important addition to the cause of science" and insisted that its ideas "could be put into operation here most effectually."[67] Some of its ideas were in fact implemented by Beale when in 1853 he established the first permanent reservation in California in the southern San Joaquín Valley.[68] Reid's letters, therefore, served a larger purpose than just providing the readers of the *Star* with interesting information. By alerting the public to the deplorable conditions under which the Indians presently lived, the letters stimulated efforts to ameliorate those conditions.

The implementation of federal Indian policy, however, came too late to improve the lot of the few Indians remaining at San Gabriel, although Victoria Reid managed to survive on her own. After the death of her husband, she sold Huerta de Cuati to Benjamin Wilson. It consisted of a vineyard of 25,000 vines, several fruit orchards, three horses, seven oxen, two carts, wine-making equipment, and household furnishings.[69] For the remainder of the 1850s and through most of the 1860s, she lived at the mission and paid special attention to young Laura Evertsen King. "Generous to a fault" is how she remembered Victoria, "and if I did not come to visit her every day she would send her servant to see what kept me from her." King usually found her "on the ground just outside the corridor of the house, directing her Indian servant to make 'tortillas.' Seated before a small fire, dressed in a costly gown of black satin, with an embroidered shawl of crepe around her shapely shoulders, daintily taking the broiled beef in her fingers, she would give me a lesson in Indian etiquette. Not all the dainty dishes of a king's banquet could equal the unforgotten flavor of

---

67. *Los Angeles Star*, January 15, 1853.
68. The influence of the report is discussed in Phillips, *"Bringing Them under Subjection,"* 81–110.
69. Chávez-García, *Negotiating Conquest*, 77.

that simple supper. While eating she would tell me stories, and give me rules for social life, the principles of which might well be engrafted among the rules of social life today." King spent hours upstairs reading the literature Reid left behind, but Victoria, troubled over the education he had given their son and daughter, deemed it a "waste of life to learn from books what she had already learned from nature." And one thing she learned from nature was to fear earthquakes, never venturing to the second story of her house.[70]

King described the setting in which Victoria lived:

> The main street or roadway of the Mission San Gabriel ran about a mile and three-quarters from the church in shape like a reclining letter L, the lines of the long shank of the letter-shaped street vanishing among the live-oak trees to the north of the Mission. On one side and between rows of willows, ran the zanja which watered the "milpas" of Indians. And on either side of the street were the "jacals" or huts built of adobe and thatched with tule, which was cut in the lake near Pasadena, tied in bundles, dried in the sun, and bound on the roofs with thongs of the same, making a picturesque and weather-proof covering. There dwelt the remnant of the Mission Indians. They planted corn, beans, pumpkins, peas and chiles.[71]

Although some of the local Indians found temporary work at and near the mission, one called Capitán successfully labored for himself. The mocking birds he raised built their nests in the space between the top of the adobe walls and the thatched roof of his house. "His birds were his pets," recalled King, "and ate from his hands and sat upon his shoulders." When ready for market, he put the birds in a pail or a cage made of reeds and walked to Los Angeles. Because there was "a very slight difference in the feathers of the wings, it was an easy matter to pass upon a novice a female bird. The female birds do not sing." But Capitán was always "reliable in his dealings with customers."[72]

---

70. King, "Hugo Reid and his Indian Wife." See also Dakin, "Hugo Reid, Humanitarian," and Newmark, *Sixty Years*, 165.
71. King, "Capitán and Tin Tin," 139.
72. Ibid., 139–40.

Aftermath

The Indian, however, lived in an environment offering familiar temptations. Horace Bell visited the mission in the early 1850s and identified three grog shops, all run by Americans, that catered to the local Indians and vagabonds. One, called the "Headquarters," was situated at the southwest corner of the mission building and also served as a jail. Another, managed by Frank Carroll, was located in a cottage in the orange grove and also served as a court house. All three did "a smashing business, especially on Sundays, when from early dawn till late at night these devil's workshops would be surrounded by a mass of drunken, howling Indians. About sundown the smashing business would begin in good earnest; that is to say, these gentle aboriginal Christians would commence to smash in each other skulls. Now you see the kind of *smashing* business carried on by our three honorable countrymen in addition to getting the Indian's coin."[73]

On a Sunday night late in November 1853 a "smashing" took place. After getting drunk and arguing with Salvador early in the day, José hid in some bushes until dark and then sprang on his foe, striking him over the head with an ax. Salvador died a short time later. Apparently, the justice of the peace was absent or looked the other way when the local Indians hanged José.[74] The hanging was probably the one witnessed by Horace Bell, who recounted a white man telling him that he thought it was "rich" that Indians had adopted the white man's system of justice.[75]

In mid-1855, approximately fifty Indians still remained at the mission.[76] A few of them were noticed by William Ingraham Kip when he visited San Gabriel in October: "The single priest remaining here—a Frenchman speaking no English—took us into the sacristy and showed us the rich fabrics, heavy with gold embroidery—remains of their former glory—and probably brought originally from Spain. We entered the large church, once filled with their Indian converts, but now of a size entirely useless.

---

73. Bell, *Reminiscences of a Ranger*, 84.
74. *Los Angeles Star*, December 3, 1853.
75. Bell, *Reminiscences*, 83.
76. *Los Angeles Star*, July 7, 1855.

Several children were on their knees before the chancel, who went on with their devotions without seeming to notice our party. The eldest was reading aloud from some devotional book, while the others responded at intervals. The heavy stone walls of the church were hung with the usual pictures."[77]

After Sunday Mass, attended by Indians and whites, cock fights and horses races took up much of the afternoon. Those remaining at their houses were entertained by the strolling mission choir. As recalled by King, "It was composed of four musical instruments, flute, violin (some were rude enough to call it a fiddle,) triangle and drum. The principal object of the choir was the collection of tithes, which everyone was very willing to pay after listening to the music for an hour.... The music was wild and weird, and helped to pass an otherwise long and lonely Sunday afternoon."[78]

Occasionally fiestas were held on week days, as was the case on a Tuesday in June 1856. "The good people of San Gabriel Mission... announced a 'gran combate' between a bull and a bear, a bull fight and sundry other sports of the kind," reported the *Star*. "A large number of people were attracted to the spot, some in carriages, some on horses, and others a foot, which created no little bustle and excitement in that usually peaceful village." Things, however, did not go according to plan. One of the two bears escaped, and the other demonstrated no inclination to engage the bull. "Consequently, the fight was only between horsemen and the bulls; and notwithstanding the expertness of the riders, some of the poor horses were badly gored by the infuriated bulls." One bull was fought on foot and if "the sharp horns of the quadruped" had not been sawed off, "the 'torero' would have been dispatched in short order."[79]

Probably in attendance were several American merchants who had found the village an attractive place to conduct business. Arriving from Cleveland in 1853, Nathan Tuch opened a store and married an Indian woman. According to Harris Newmark,

---

77. Kip, *The Early Days of My Episcopate*, 209.
78. King, "Capitán and Tin Tin," 140.
79. *Los Angeles Star*, June 28, 1856.

notwithstanding "the difference in their stations and the fact that she was uneducated, Tuch always remained faithful to her, and treated her with every mark of respect." Cyrus Burdick, originally from Iowa, was elected constable in 1855, and ran a store for eight or nine years. J. S. Mallard operated a small business, and Mrs. Evertsen, Laura King's mother, also managed a store.[80]

The stores, or *tiendas* as King called them, were located near the church where Indians purchased blankets, handkerchiefs, and aguardiente. Regarding the sale of the latter, she was conflicted whether to blame it on the cupidity of the *tenderos* or on the weakness of the Indians. The results were not in question.[81] Vividly remembered was an Indian called Tin-Tin, who all week long "labored faithfully and conscientiously, but on Sunday morning he would be seen by those on their way to church with his head in the ditch, dragged there by some friend, to cool him off for Monday's work. He was a fine specimen of the Indian, as he was, and should be but for the civilization of the white man; being tall and straight, and well built. But what constitution could stand 'fire water' and exposure week after week? In his prime he was taken to the ditch for the last time, a victim of his appetite, and the greed of the white man."[82]

---

80. Newmark, *Sixty Years*, 89–90.
81. King, "Pinacate," 133.
82. King, "Capitán and Tin Tin," 140. For information about the Indians of the San Gabriel towards the end of the nineteenth century, consult Holder, *About Pasadena*. For a summary of the book, see Forbes, "Indians of Southern California in 1888," 71–76.

CHAPTER 12

Violent Vineyards

In January 1847 Edwin Bryant entered Los Angeles with a U.S. military contingent that had recently negotiated the surrender of Mexican forces during the Mexican-American War. Not particularly impressed with the layout and the buildings, Bryant nevertheless observed a thriving agriculture community "with numerous vineyards and gardens, enclosed by willow hedges. The gardens produce a great variety of tropical fruits and plants. The yield of the vineyards is very abundant; and the large quantity of wines of good quality and flavor, and *aguardiente*, are manufactured here. Some of the vineyards, I understand, contain as many as twenty thousand vines." Bryant also observed an abundance of corn, wheat, frijoles, onions, potatoes, and red peppers but was struck by the lack of mills, "the universal practice of Californian families being to grind their corn by hand." Thus, flour and bread were scarce.[1] In mid-March Stephen C. Foster, a member of the Mormon Battalion, another American military unit that invaded California, noted that "on Los Angeles Street were some 300 or 400 Indians, the laborers in the vineyards, who had taken a holiday to witness our entry."[2]

---
1. Bryant, *What I Saw in California*, 405–6.
2. Foster, "Reminiscences: My First Procession in Los Angles, March 16, 1847," 50.

Initially, the American military authorities, led by Colonel Jonathan D. Stevenson, allowed the ayuntamiento to continue regulating the affairs of the town, and the management of the Indian residents occupied much of its time.³ Because of the rowdiness taking place in the Indian village of Pueblito, in February 1847 the ayuntamiento considered removing it farther away from the town. The issue was referred to a special committee.⁴ The following month members of the ayuntamiento recommended that all those employing Indians house them on their premises "in order to check their excesses." Those not steadily employed were to be granted title to land at the edge of the city in the form of house lots.⁵

On June 3 the members discussed a proposition from the síndico recommending that the Indian alcaldes be required to request in writing permission to hold "reunions and diversions" in their settlements. On the night of a gathering, the alcaldes were to show the permit to the constable on duty in the settlement, who was to ensure that its terms were strictly enforced. No white person would be allowed to attend and would be fined $1.50 for the first offense and $3.00 for the second. If a person had to "search for his servant, or have some other business in such places, it shall be his duty to apply to their constable." Moreover, if any person, or an Indian in his employ, introduced "fermented liquors" into the Indian settlements, he would have his products confiscated and would be fined $3.00 dollars for each offense.⁶

At a session of the ayuntamiento on October 10, Rafael Gallardo submitted a petition seeking the removal of the Indians from Pueblito because of their scandalous conduct. Until then a citizen guard was to be stationed at the village every Saturday to prevent visits by non-Indians.⁷ On November 8 the ayuntamiento passed an ordinance authorizing the destruction of Pueblito. This

---

3. The beginnings and structure of the American city government are discussed in Hunter, *The Evolution of Municipal Organization*, 9–41.
4. Minutes of the Ayuntamiento, February 24, 1847, Los Angeles Archives, 4: 275.
5. Ibid., March 13, 1847, 2: 430–31.
6. Ibid., June 3, 1847, 4: 368–70.
7. Ibid., October 30, 1847, 4: 497.

required housing servants and workers on their employers' premises, relocating self-sufficient Indians outside the town limits in widely separated settlements, and assigning vagrants of either sex to public works projects or confining them in jail.[8] Two weeks later the síndico reported to the ayuntamiento that Pueblito had been razed and its inhabitants relocated east of the pueblo. Twenty-four dollars had been appropriated to assist the Indians in moving.[9] As the American military authorities were soon to realize, however, the destruction of Pueblito accomplished little as many Indians remained in camps scattered throughout the town. In February 1848, Colonel Stevenson ordered First Alcalde Stephen C. Foster to break up the camps.[10] Because Foster and José Vicente Guerrero had been appointed first and second alcaldes by Stevenson, they probably made some effort to disperse the Indians, but the results are unknown.[11]

Keeping those convicted of crimes incarcerated proved to be another problem facing Foster. Los Angeles had no jail, so criminals were housed in an old building that was clearly unsuitable for the task.[12] Escape was not difficult, especially for Juan Antonio, a neophyte from San Gabriel or San Fernando, who for the previous fifteen years had been an active stock raider and had been charged with murder and burglary. Caught several times, he always managed to free himself.[13] Captured again, he was brought before Foster on charges of horse stealing. Foster described him as "a full-blooded California Indian . . . , a man about forty years

---

8. Ibid., November 8, 1847, 4: 507–8.
9. Ibid., November 20, 1847, 4: 510. In December, María Armenta, the wife of José Bermúdez, petitioned the ayuntamiento for the lot where Pueblito had been located. Her husband being seventy-nine years of age, María did most of the work. She raised grain and corn near San Bernardino and transported her products in carretas to Los Angeles. She needed the lot to corral her oxen. Her petition was granted. See Beattie and Beattie, *Heritage of the Valley*, 43.
10. Cook, *Conflict*, 472n22.
11. Foster, "Eve of the Gold Rush," 1: 16; Bowman, *Los Angeles: Epic of a City*, 149.
12. "Los Angeles Correspondence," Los Angeles, Dec. 1850, in *Daily Alta California*, January 20, 1851.
13. Stephen Clark Foster to Governor [Bennett Riley] Los Angeles, May 13, 1849, Archives of California, Unbound Documents, CA 63, The Bancroft Library.

old and five feet seven or eight inches in height." After two weeks in confinement, Juan Antonio broke his handcuffs and the fetters and the bar connecting them, bored a hole through the adobe wall of the building, and fled to the north. The day that he escaped, Indians stole sixty horses from a rancho six miles from town and about ninety horses from Rancho Ex-mission San Fernando. The following day a rancho in the Santa Clara Valley lost fifty head and Juan Antonio was spotted among the stock raiders.[14]

For Juan Antonio the excitement of Los Angeles proved to be irresistible. In April 1849, while attending a game of peon, he was arrested by the Indian alcaldes. Calling him a sorcerer and a very bad man, the alcaldes turned him over to Foster, who summoned a jury that day. Witnesses accused Juan Antonio of various offenses, including horse stealing and robbing the church of a sacred vessel. The prisoner pleaded guilty and the jury recommended execution.[15] Under Mexican law condemned prisoners were executed by firing squad, but the local American military commander rejected any participation because only soldiers were executed that way. He recommended hanging but Foster knew of no one in the town with expertise in that procedure. A solution was found when the military commander ordered one of his soldiers to assist Foster. The soldier, an Irishman, was reluctant to undertake the task but agreed to teach the technique to whomever Foster selected. Foster found an Indian volunteer and offered him $2.50, the money to come from city funds, and an additional $2.50 from Foster's own pocket if the Indian performed well.[16]

Foster recounted that "the Indian was a *vaquero* accustomed to ropes and knots, and was an apt scholar. The first lesson was to teach him how to make a hangman's knot, which the Indian soon learned to do as dexterously as the Irishman. . . . I acted as interpreter in all, and it struck me as absurd. Seven years before I had been a schoolmaster in Virginia, teaching *hic, haec, hoc*, to the dull sons of Virginia planters, and here I was in Los Angeles acting as

---
14. Foster, "Eve of the Gold Rush," 2: 29.
15. Ibid.
16. Ibid., 30.

interpreter to an Irish soldier whilst he taught the science of Jack Ketch to a California Indian!"[17]

On May 10 a guard of soldiers escorted Juan Antonio, who "manifested the utmost coolness," to the scaffold. A pole propped in the ground secured the trap door. A rope was tied to the pole.

> There was a large concourse of spectators, as it was the first execution by hanging that ever took place in Los Angeles. The entire Indian population turned out, and among them Juan Antonio had no friend. They all feared him.... I told the Indian alcalde to order that as many Indians as could take hold of the rope to do so. It being forty feet long there were at least forty Indians that took hold of it, when I raised my right hand to give the word to pull away. I watched the priest carefully; he was very nervous and excited; neither he nor myself had ever seen an execution in our lives. I saw that both the priest and the Indian executioner stepped back from the condemned. The executioner folded his arms and stood as cooly as if he were looking at a bullock he had tied. The priest raised his right hand; I raised mine; a sudden rush of forty Indians pulled the pole from under the trap and Juan Antonio fell. He gave two or three convulsive leaps (from the scarcity of timber it had been impossible to brace the scaffold, and it shook so that we all expected it would fall). The priest and executioner could scarcely keep their feet.

Juan Antonio was buried in the Catholic cemetery. Foster kept the hinges of the trap door as a memento of the execution. They had been fashioned by a San Gabriel neophyte.[18]

Foster also had to deal with the hordes of immigrants passing through the pueblo on their way to the gold fields in Central California. Some of the immigrants remained in the pueblo while others returned after failing to strike it rich. But all of them transformed Los Angeles into one of the most volatile and lawless towns in the American West. Writing to a friend in March 1849, a military officer mentioned that "the Pueblo has changed much since you left. It is now thronged with Soldiers, Quartermaster's men, Sonoranians, Etc, the most vicious and idle set you ever beheld. Gambling, drinking, and whoring are the only occupations, and they seem to be followed with great industry,

---
17. Ibid., 30–31.
18. Ibid.; Foster to Governor [Riley], Los Angeles, May 13, 1849.

particularly the first and second. Monte banks, cock fights, and liquor shops are to be seen in all directions." Missing, however, were the Californios: "You never see them parading about on their fine horses as formerly."[19]

Benjamin Hayes, who arrived in Los Angeles in February 1850, observed a town in transition but one that was still culturally Mexican and Indian. He attended Mass at the plaza church and witnessed the burial of an Indian who had died the previous day and who was interred beneath the floor of the church. Although the graveyard was nearby, for "what reason the deceased was entitled to this distinction I did not learn." Few men were in attendance, but there were "many women, many of them richly dressed, graceful and handsome. The whole scene, 'American' by the side of 'Mexican'... Indian and white, trader and penitent, gayety, bustle and confusion on the one side and religious solemnity on the other, was singular to me." At the conclusion of the service, an Indian stood at the door chanting in a language Hayes did not understand and "many in passing placed their alms in his hand."[20]

Politically, Los Angeles quickly became American. The first state legislature under American rule passed in March 1850 "An Act to Provide for the Incorporation of Cities." And on April 4, an act to incorporate Los Angeles became law. It stated that "All that tract of land included within the limits of the Pueblo de Los Angeles, ... shall henceforth be known as the city of Los Angeles." The act stipulated that the corporation assume all the rights, claims, and powers of the pueblo in regard to property and would be subject to all the liabilities incurred by the ayuntamiento. The first session of the common council, as the new city government was called, convened in early July.[21]

---

19. "Los Angeles in 1849, A Letter from John S. Griffin, M.D.," Los Angeles: Privately Printed, 1949. On August 19, 1851, the *Daily Alta California* commented on the disappearance of the Californios from the streets of San Francisco: "Three years ago, in this city, the Californian and his horse constituted as important a feature, and as characteristic a commonplace, as any peculiarity incidental to daily life in San Francisco. He was a feature and a figure in the thronging population, and seemed identified with the scenes of these shores. He has lost that identity—is missed from the crowded streets—is no more a part of us."
20. Wolcott, ed., *Pioneer Notes*, 71–72.
21. Guinn, "The Passing of the Old Pueblo," 115; and Guinn, "From Pueblo to Ciudad," 220.

Los Angeles in 1853.
From *Reports of Explorations and Surveys.*

The Indians of Los Angeles were affected both by the actions of the common council and the policies of the State of California. Because the federal government had yet to assert its authority over Indian affairs through the implementation of the reservation system, the state introduced its own Indian policy. The act of 1850 placing Indians under the control of local authorities stated that

> any Indian able to work and support himself in some honest calling, not having wherewithal to maintain himself, *who shall be found loitering and strolling about, or frequenting public places where liquors are sold, begging, or leading an immoral or profligate course of life,* shall be liable to be arrested on the complaint of any resident citizen of the county, and brought before any Justice of the Peace of the proper county, mayor or Recorder of any incorporated town or city who shall examine said accused Indian, and hear the testimony in relation thereto, and if ... satisfied that he is a vagrant ... he shall make out a warrant ... authorizing and requiring the officer having him in charge or custody, to hire out such vagrant within twenty-four hours to the best bidder, by public notice, given as he shall direct, for the highest price that can be had for any term not exceeding four months.[22]

---

22. Abstract of "An Act for the government & protection of Indians," *The Statutes of California*, in Harlow, ed., *The City of the Angels*, 39.

Imitating the legislature, the common council issued an ordinance in August 1850 stating that "when the city has no work in which to employ the chain gang, the Recorder shall by means of notices conspicuously posted, notify the public that such a number of prisoners will be auctioned off to the highest bidder for private service."[23]

Some of those arrested paid their fines and thus were spared the indignity of the auction. In fact, the local government met part of its operating expenses with the revenues collected from Indians. On October 2, 1850, the common council authorized the recorder to pay the Indian alcaldes one *real* (twelve and a half cents) out of every fine collected from an Indian brought to jail. And they quickly took advantage of this economic opportunity. On November 27 the council appropriated $15.75 for the alcaldes. At the rate of eight Indians to the dollar, evidently these officials had rounded up well more than 100 souls, of whom 126 had paid their fines or had their fines paid for them.[24]

Seldom were Mexicans or Americans brought to justice for committing crimes against Indians, although two were tried in 1850. Fernando Vacquites was arrested in July for assaulting an Indian woman. According to a witness, "I heard the woman, Rosa, crying out loud when looking up I saw Fernando Vacquites have Rosa in the water. He had his hand in her hair and was hitting her in the ribs and cursing her. Afterwards I saw him knock her down with his fist and then punch her with a stick about 18 inches long and 2 inches thick." The defendant admitted the testimony was true, except for the part of his striking her with the stick. The case was dismissed, although Vacquites had to pay court costs. In September, Juan de Dios de García was found guilty of beating an Indian woman named Josefa for refusing his advances. He was fined one dollar.[25]

Victims of crime were not limited to Indians. The same night in December that an Indian was arrested for murdering a female

---

23. Session of August 16, 1850, in Robinson, ed., "The Indians of Los Angeles," 172.
24. Minutes of the Common Council, October 2, November 27, 1850, Archives of Los Angeles, 1: 87; Guinn, "The Passing of the Old Pueblo," 117.
25. Quoted in Woolsey, "Crime and Punishment," 82.

companion, a Sonoran killed a Californio. Although the ethnicity of the twelve prisoners who broke out of the "jail" that month was not identified, apparently most were either Mexicans or Americans. Three had been convicted of murdering a man named Callahan. This third jail break in the past two months prompted a citizen to complain that not only had the common council made no effort to construct a true jail, it paid twelve (sometimes forty) dollars a day to those guarding the building, "and yet the prisoners all manage to escape."[26]

Most of those killing Indians never saw the inside of the "jail" because they were fellow Indians. Many died at games of peon where aguardiente was usually consumed in large amounts. Producing enormous excitement and extravagant betting for players and bystanders, the games were hotly contested. In March 1851 a fight erupted at a game between one group of Indians and Cahuillas. Joseph Lancaster Brent recalled that the dead "all had their heads mashed beyond recognition, which is the sign manual of Indian murder."[27] Eugene Upton recorded the same fight. Four of the dead "have laid exposed to the gaze of the passers by throughout the day. Many more are reported in a dying condition in consequence of the severe wounds received during the affray. They fought with hatchets, knives, clubs, stone, &c."[28]

In May the coroner conducted three inquests. Although a jury concluded that an Indian named Bisante, originally from San Diego, had drowned in the zanja, the *Los Angeles Star* reported that he had first been "beaten insensible by some persons unknown" before being dumped in the ditch. The body of a woman (probably an Indian), "cut and lacerated in a most shocking manner," was discovered in the San Gabriel River, but the jury found no facts to indict anyone and returned a verdict of "death by violent means inflicted by some person or persons unknown." While attending

---

26. "Los Angeles Correspondence," Los Angeles, Dec. 1850, in *Daily Alta California*, January 20, 1851.
27. Brent, *The Lugo Case: A Personal Experience*, 8.
28. Eugene Upton, March 21, 1851, Scrapbook No. 7. California Historical Society Library, San Francisco. The *Daily Alta California*, a northern California newspaper, mentioned the fight on April 4, 1851, the information probably coming from a copy of the *Los Angeles Star*.

a game of peon, a Mexican "came to his death in consequence of blows inflicted upon his head." The jury "recommended the establishment of a night police, as a measure calculated to prevent the recurrence of similar crimes."[29]

In late October a leader of the Cahuillas living in the pueblo sought permission from the marshal to play peon. Citing an ordinance prohibiting the playing of peon within the city limits, the marshal turned down the request. The Indian, however, got permission from Alcalde Juan Sepúlveda to hold a game near the cemetery in front of the house of a Mexican, José María Ibarra. To keep order Sepúlveda assigned six Mexicans to patrol the area. During the evening an Indian named Coyote got into an argument with Ibarra's wife over a bottle of liquor. When Coyote attempted to take the bottle by force, Ibarra intervened and subdued the Indian. Five or six Indians secured his release and attempted to set fire to Ibarra's house. As many as one hundred Indians drove off the Mexican patrol. Sepúlveda, who was in the area, dashed back to the pueblo for help and returned with seven Americans. They and the Mexicans attacked the Indians, killing eight and arresting twenty-one who had taken shelter in Ibarra's house. The marshal fined each of those arrested one dollar and ordered that each be lashed twenty-one times.[30] Before the punishment was carried out, however, Juan Antonio, Chief of the Mountain Cahuillas, and several followers entered the city to inquire into the arrests. The marshal released the prisoners to Juan Antonio and he and his men immediately departed for their homeland. The incident prompted the *Star* to remind its readers that "*peon* has always been a fruitful source of disturbance when held within the limits of the city, and it is only a few months since that it brought on an affray in which some five or six Indians were killed."[31]

In February 1852 the *Star* reported the deaths of two Indians: "One was found upon the premises of Lorenzo Leek & Co., and

---

29. *Los Angeles Star*, May 17, 1851.
30. *Daily Alta California*, November 13, 1851. The article was copied from the *Los Angeles Star* of November 1, 1851.
31. Ibid.

was manifestly killed by aguardiente. The other was stabbed and cut in various places, but all inquiries were unsuccessful in ascertaining the perpetrators of the murder."[32] In July four Indians stole a barrel of aguardiente from Matthew Keller. They were caught and tried. Each received twenty-five lashes and they were fined the cost of the prosecution.[33] That month the Indian servant of Julián Valle was found near of the house of José López, his throat cut and body disfigured. Attributed to "death by violence from persons unknown," his murder exhibited all the signs of that induced by aguardiente.[34] When two Indians were severely wounded in a fight during a game of peon in August, the editors of the *Star* commented that "it excites some surprise that such assemblages are permitted."[35] Although statistics are lacking, the rising degree of violent and criminal behavior may have been in part a result of an increasing unemployment rate.[36] When John Russell Bartlett entered Los Angeles in 1852, he "saw more Indians about this place than in any part of California I had yet visited. They were chiefly 'Mission Indians'.... They are a miserable squalid-looking set, squatting or lying about the corners of the streets, without occupation."[37]

By this time, the common council had contracted with J. D. Hunter of San Bernardino to construct a proper jail. The building was to be thirty by fifteen feet in which the lower story was to be of stone, three feet thick. The jailer would reside on the upper floor made of adobe. The cost was to be seven thousand dollars and the building completed in five months.[38] The jail was probably operating in early 1853 when the editors of the *Star* exclaimed:

> The wretched, worthless wo-begone Indians who, as regularly as Sunday comes around, occupy our city prison on charges varying from

---

32. *Los Angeles Star*, February 21, 1852.
33. Ibid., July 17, 1852.
34. Ibid., July 10, 1852.
35. Ibid., August 14, 1852.
36. Mexican and American violence in the pueblo is discussed in Blew, "Vigilantism in Los Angeles," and in Woolsey, "Crime and Punishment."
37. Bartlett, *Personal Narrative of Explorations*, 2: 82.
38. *Los Angeles Star*, August 7, 1852.

drunkenness to stealing, making disturbances in the streets, stabbing &c., were last Monday employed by the city authorities in the healthful and benevolent occupation of clearing away the rubbish which has been accumulating for a long time in the streets, and the result of their labors is certainly an improvement in the general aspect of affairs. The plan adopted seems to be an admirable one, and it is to be hoped it will be continued. If Indians will get drunk and kick up a row, why let them work it out. If white men do the same why—"let 'em rip."[39]

In March 1853, the *Star* reported that every Sunday morning "our streets are filled with drunken Indians, male and female.... Who knows how or where they procure the rotgut stuff that makes them thus? One thing, however, is known, namely: that they are beastly drunk, and further, that there is a heavy fine for vending liquor to them; but we do not know, with these hundred abominations staring our whole community in the face, in broad daylight every Sunday, that efforts are made to discover who has done it."[40] Apparently some efforts were made, because during the first week in May 1853 the district attorney was kept especially busy prosecuting those accused of selling liquor to Indians. A. W. Timm and Peter Collins were fined $20.00 each. Alexander Ramón and Eugene Agaia were also fined $20.00 each but had to pay court costs as well. Alexander Ramón's fine and costs came to $41.00.[41] Curtailing the sales proved to be an impossible task, because, as noted by Benjamin Hayes, "in some streets of this little city, almost every other house is a grog-shop for Indians."[42]

The violence continued. In March 1853, an Indian named Juan assaulted Juana Ibarra, a Mexican woman. According to her testimony, Juan raped her a short distance from the pueblo while she was on her way to her home on Arroyo Seco Street. As of early April, Juan, confined to jail, was waiting for a grand jury to decide his future.[43] Intoxication or "a visitation of God" was a jury's verdict regarding the death of Bacilio, a Christian Indian. In

---

39. Ibid., February 12, 1853.
40. *Daily Alta California*, March 31, 1853, from the *Los Angeles Star*.
41. *Los Angeles Star*, May 14, 1853.
42. Caughey, ed., *The Indians of Southern California*, 22.
43. *Los Angeles Star*, April 2, 1853.

early June his body was found near the zanja at the upper end of the city. A priest performed last rites.[44] Whether the Indian who attacked an elder Mexican named Valdez was also drunk is not known, but his behavior points in that direction. According to the *Star*, the Indian inflicted a severe knife wound on the Mexican's head. Valdez fled to the house of Stephen C. Foster, "warding off with his blanket many blows which the Indian struck." There, the Indian attacked Foster who would have been wounded without the intervention of his servant. Both men disarmed the Indian and turned him over to the authorities.[45]

In June the jailer shot an Indian who was attempting to smuggle tools to an Indian prisoner. The ball glanced off the Indian's skull and he was expected to recover. An investigation was to follow.[46] In September the *Star* reported that twenty-five Indians "supposed to be drunk" had been arrested and brought to the jail. But no sooner had the marshal "turned his back then crash! went the door, and the Indians scattered in every direction, up every street in town." Confounded at the possibility of heading off so many fugitives, the marshal stood "solemnly silent, and when the last fugitive had disappeared, gave utterance to a sigh and wended his way homeward."[47] Later, the newspaper condemned the practice of arresting and fining drunken Indians:

> It has long been the practice with the Indians of this city, to get drunk on Saturday night. Their ambition seems to be to earn sufficient money, through the week, to treat themselves handsomely at the close of it. In this they only follow white examples; and like white men, they are often noisy about the streets.—It has also been the practice with the City Marshal and his assistants, to spend the Sabbath in arresting and imprisoning Indians, supposed to be drunk, until Monday morning, when they are taken before the Mayor and discharged on paying a bill of two dollars and a half each, one dollar of which is the fee of the Marshal. Sometimes of a Monday morning we have seen the Marshal marching in a procession with twenty or twenty-five of these poor people, and truly, it is a brave

---

44. Ibid., June 18, 1853.
45. Ibid., June 4, 1853.
46. Ibid., June 18, 1853.
47. Ibid., September 17, 1853.

sight—Now, we have no heart to do the Marshal slightest prejudice, but this leading off Indians and locking them up over night, for the purpose of taking away one of their paltry dollars, seems to us a questionable act.[48]

Most of the arrests took place in Calle de los Negros, which James Woods, an Episcopal minister, called "a perfect hell on a Sabbath afternoon. That is the place of assemblage for poor low drunken Indians." A better name for the "City of Angeles" would be the "City of Demons." On November 12, 1854, Woods wrote in his journal that even though he had been in the town "only two weeks, there have been it is said eleven deaths, and only one of them a natural death—all the rest by violence." Most of those killed were Mexicans and Indians. On November 19 he mentioned that two Mexicans had been shot the previous night, "one mortally, the other slightly."[49]

On November 16, 1854, a grand jury of the "City of Demons" summed up its proceedings by announcing that it had issued three indictments for murder, two for larceny, one for forgery, and one for assault with the intent to commit murder. It asserted, moreover, that "the evil existing in this community" grew out of the "sale of ardent spirits." Because nearly all the crimes committed daily by Indians resulted from this sale, the grand jury chastised the common council for not taking action to end it. And it identified the worst offenders. The owners of taverns in Calle de los Negros called "Monte Pío" and "New World," the latter "being one of the greatest nuisances now in the community," were unknown. But identified were Alexander Delique, Pedro María, Ferrio Abilia, and J. B. Guernod.[50] In March the following year the marshal arrested Vicente Guerrero and Birando Sunega for selling liquor to Indians. Guerrero paid a fine of $30.00 and was released. Arrested a short time later, he paid another fine—this one for $200.00—and was again released. Sunega was fined $35.00 and freed.[51] Extraordinary profits resulting from a huge volume in sales must account for the retailers sustaining such heavy fines.

---

48. Ibid., December 3, 1853.
49. Bynum, ed., "Los Angeles in 1854–5," 70, 74, 83.
50. *Southern Californian*, November 16, 1854.
51. *Los Angeles Star*, March 31, 1855.

Violent Vineyards

The vineyard of Tomás Sánchez seems to have been a particularly violent place. Before their removal to Pueblito, Indians had resided next to his property at Ranchería de Poblanos. On January 11, 1855, the *Star* reported that an inquest had been held on an Indian whose body was found in the vineyard. He was about eighteen years old and apparently was from San Diego. Found naked except for a pair of socks on his feet, his head was bruised and smashed as though the deed had been done with stones. Evidently, "he was murdered by Indians during the night previous, as the occupants knew nothing of the affair."[52] Early the following month the vineyard was the scene of another fight in which two Indians died. "Such occurrences have become so frequent of late," noted the *Star*, "that it causes very little notice or remark, excepting from those who are engaged in doleing out to these poor miserable creatures intoxicating drinks, until they are lost to all sense of right or wrong, and fight and murder one another." Causing more notice was the body of a Frenchman found in the same vineyard. He died from blows to the head with a club or stone. According to the *Star*, he had recently arrived from Clarksville, Texas, where "he leaves a wife and family."[53]

In mid-March the editors of the *Southern Californian* found in the murder of Juan an opportunity for a bit of whimsy. The Indian "departed for the happy hunting grounds of the red man on Tuesday night last. He was discovered near the residence of Don. Casildo Aguilar, with a deep stab in his breast, which showed that his sudden flitting from the scenes of his childhood was not entirely the result of choice."[54] That month James Woods came across an Indian girl dying near the vineyard of William Wolfskill. An old man and woman, apparently her parents, were tending to her. Woods later learned that when her Mexican employer discovered that his young servant was terminally ill, he dumped her there, apparently to avoid burial expenses.[55] The six Indians jailed late in March for assault with the intent to do bodily harm

---

52. Ibid., January 11, 1855.
53. Ibid., February 8, 1855.
54. *Southern Californian*, March 14, 1855.
55. Bynum, ed., "Los Angeles in 1854–5," 81.

would have their fines of $25.00 each canceled only if they worked for the public for not more than six months.⁵⁶

Indian arrests and in particular deaths allowed the editors of the *Southern Californian* to continue their witty obituaries. In May they wrote: "The past few days have dissipated the half formed impressions that Los Angeles was about becoming shorn of her well earned notoriety for blood-letting,—Until recently no really sanguinary affairs have been enacted—excepting of course an occasional case of 'dead Indians.'" But the times now were "tolerable good for killing. Two poor redskins have passed from among us to the happy hunting grounds; two of the 'light haired' race have paid the penalty for their misdeeds in the Monte." It reminded the editors of the old days when one would rise on "the second day of the week and view the lifeless remains of humanity quietly sleeping by the way side in the calm repose of death."⁵⁷

In a more serious mood the following month, they insisted that one purpose of the recently founded Tejón Reservation in the southern San Joaquín Valley was to accommodate the Indians who lived in and near Los Angeles.⁵⁸ But as explained by Superintendent of Indian Affairs Thomas Henley, who visited the city in December, this was a minority position. "If it were practicable or desirable in their demoralized condition, to remove them to the Reservation," he wrote the Commissioner of Indian Affairs, "it could not be accomplished, because it would be opposed by the citizens, for the reasons that in the vineyards, especially during the grape season, their labor is made useful and is obtained at a cheap rate." The only thing that could possibly be done for them would be "an agreement with the Municipal Authorities, to have them removed a short distance from the city, and prohibited from returning to it without permission from a properly authorized Agent, under whose protection they could perform the labor in the vineyards, and be protected in the reception of their pay."⁵⁹

---

56. *Los Angeles Star*, March 31, 1855.
57. *Southern Californian*, May 30, 1855.
58. Ibid., June 20, 1855.
59. Thomas Henley to George W. Manypenny, December 18, 1855, Letters Received at the Office of Indian Affairs, 1824–81, California Superintendency, Microcopy 234, Roll 35, United States National Archives.

Henley, a superintendent ever conscious of the rising costs of managing Indians, failed to follow up on his proposal.⁶⁰

With neither federal protection nor local control, the Indians had no one to turn to. Julius Froebel arrived in September and commented on the indifference of the citizenry to Indian violence:

> The fact of Indians being found dead in the streets at morning was scarcely thought of sufficient importance to constitute a case for a serious investigation. Those of the Indian tribes of California who have passed through the discipline of the ancient missions, and had acquired a certain civilization by this school, have sunk very deep in almost every respect since they have been left to themselves. In the streets of Los Angeles they could be seen gambling, intoxicated, quarreling among each other, and often in the most disgusting situations. There were, however, other classes of the population not much above these wretches, under a moral point of view. Almost every night pistols were fired in the street under my windows, in consequence of disputes originating in gambling-houses and other places of ill repute.⁶¹

Horace Bell assessed the system in which the Indians were caught:

> Los Angeles had its slave mart, as well as New Orleans and Constantinople—only the slave at Los Angeles was sold fifty-two times a year as long as he lives, which did not generally exceed one, two or three years, under the new dispensation. They would be sold for a week, and bought up by the vineyard men and others at prices ranging from one to three dollars, one-third of which was to be paid to the peon at the end of the week, which debt, due for well performed labor, would invariably be paid in *aguardiente*, and the Indian would be made happy until the following Monday morning, having passed through another Saturday night and Sunday's saturnalia of debauchery and bestiality. Those thousands of honest, useful people were absolutely destroyed in this way.⁶²

Despite its social chaos, Los Angeles continued its economic expansion. According to the state census of 1852, eighty-five vineyards

---

60. Concerning Henley's cost consciousness see Phillips, *"Bringing Them under Subjection,"* 153–78.
61. Froebel, *Seven Years' Travel,* 568–69.
62. Bell, *Reminiscences of a Ranger,* 35–36.

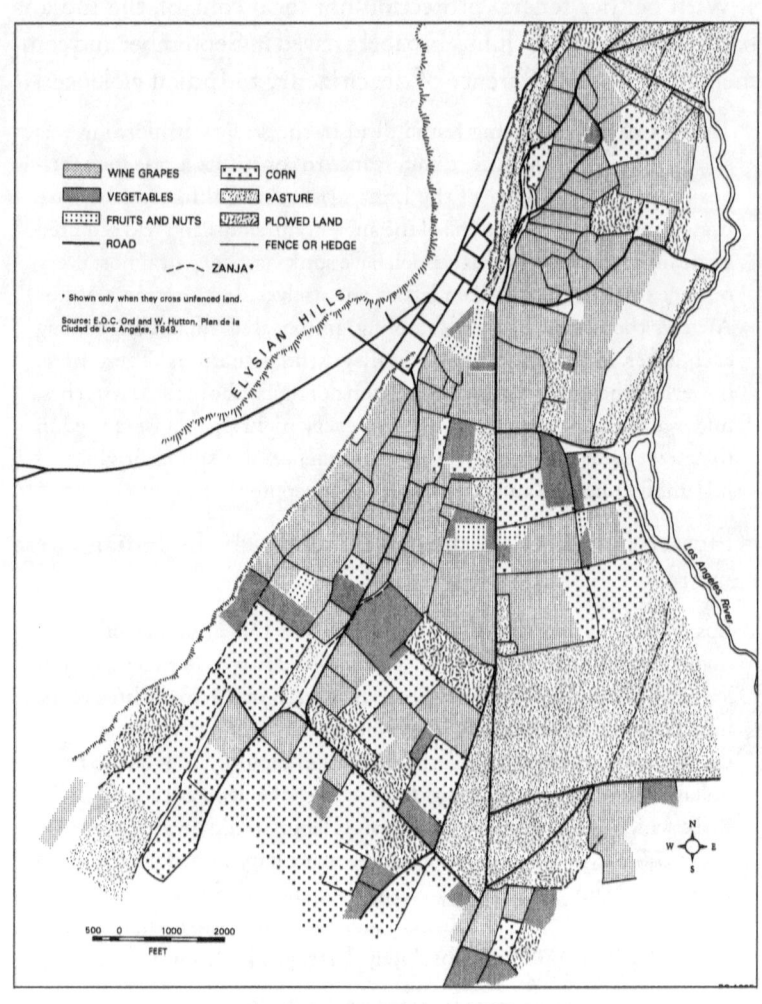

Agricultural Lands of Los Angeles, 1849.
Map by Blake Gumprecht; used with permission. *Reproduced from*
The Los Angeles River: Its Life, Death, and Possible Rebirth
(*Baltimore: Johns Hopkins University Press, 1999*).

were located within the city limits, another twenty in the county. Each of the 450,000 vines produced five pounds of grapes. Annually, Los Angeles manufactured 2,000 barrels of brandy and 2,000 of wine.[63] In August 1852 one lot of grapes shipped to San Francisco sold at eighty cents per pound, but by the end of October, the price on average had dropped to twenty-two cents.[64] In mid-January the following year, the *Star* reported that 5,825 packages of grapes, each weighing between fifty and one hundred pounds, had been shipped from San Pedro. But the grape speculators had lost money "the past season, sufficient to deter most of them from engaging in the fruit trade another season." The cost of freight was too high, the steamers too unreliable.[65]

William Blake probably knew nothing of the pueblo's economic situation when on November 1, 1853, he entered Los Angeles. But what he observed impressed him greatly:

> It is not possible for me to present a faithful and complete representation of the agricultural capabilities and resources of this region—a region which enjoys the advantages of a most genial climate and fertile soil. It is also impossible, in this place, even to enumerate the variety of fruits and vegetables that can be abundantly produced here with great ease. The most important production of the soil, at this time, is the grape, which is raised in immense quantities in the suburbs of the town and at adjoining ranchos.... Many of these vineyards are very extensive, and are said to contain from 25,000 to 30,000, and 40,000 vines....
>
> These vines are planted about five feet apart, and are not trained on supports of espaliers, but are kept closely trimmed, and are not allowed to spread or rise over about four feet from the ground. This produces a stout, thick vine, which does not require support. Many of the vines were six and eight inches in diameter. These vines bear enormous bunches of fruit, weighting from one to three pounds and more.

A harvest was under way, the vineyards being "traversed in all directions by laborers, bearing baskets of the fruit to the packing-sheds, where it was spread out in large piles upon clean white cloths,

---

63. Abstract of the Census of 1852 of the State of California, *Journal of the Senate*, 4th sess., Doc. 14, 1853, 19–20.
64. *Los Angeles Star*, August 28 and October 30, 1852.
65. Ibid., January 15, 1853.

laid down on the hard ground or upon floors. Boxes of redwood, capable of holding about sixty pounds, are used for their reception, and the clusters are carefully laid in with clean saw dust."[66]

Captain E. D. Townsend visited Los Angeles in October 1855 and was especially impressed with the vineyards of Jean-Louis Vignes, Benjamin Wilson, and William Wolfskill. He noted in his diary that Wolfskill's vineyards appeared "to be the most extensive and in the best order. Indian labor is chiefly used in gathering the grapes for market and for the wine press." Townsend also mentioned that "experiments are being made with presses of various kinds as substitutes for treading out the wine, which operation I saw a large Indian performing at Don Luis's."[67] Although Townsend anticipated the replacement of Indian labor with technological innovations, the four hundred Indians residing in the city remained for the time indispensable.[68]

At a harvest vividly remembered by a resident, "the grapes were placed in huge shallow vats placed near the 'sanja' or water ditch. The Indians were made to bath their feet in the sanja and then step into the vats where they trod rhythmically up and down on the grapes to press out the juice. Quite a number of Indians were in the vat at one time. The juice was drained off into larger vats, where it was left to stand until fermentation. Then it was clarified, aged and bottled or barreled. The process used seemed not to interfere with the appreciation of the fine California wine."[69] Harris Newmark recalled a less pleasing result. Wearing only loincloths and laboring in the early fall when the temperature was at its peak, the Indians "tramped with ceaseless tread from morn till night." But the sweat of the Indians dripping into the vats "in no wise increased my appetite for California wine."[70]

In 1857 Los Angeles shipped to San Francisco 250,000 gallons of wine.[71] A major contributor to the increase in exports was

---

66. Blake, *Report of the Geological Reconnaissance*, 77–78.
67. Edwards, ed., *The California Diary*, 105–6.
68. Harlow, ed., *The City of the Angels*, 28.
69. Lenz, ed., "Memories of Caroline van der Leck Lenz," 197–98.
70. Newmark, *Sixty Years, 1853–1913*, 202–3.
71. Warner, Hayes, and Widney, *An Historical Sketch*, 114.

the firm of Kohler and Frohling. Charles Kohler resided in San Francisco, where he managed a wine cellar. J. Frohling contracted with growers in Los Angeles to harvest their grapes.[72] William Wolfskill, for example, sold his grapes on the vine and allowed the purchaser the use of his mills, presses, and cellars. Wolfskill received a certain price per gallon of wine once it had passed its first fermentation.[73]

Although lasting only a few days, the harvesting of a large vineyard called for a sizable labor force well trained and managed. In October 1859, a visitor to Wolfskill's vineyard observed forty hands hard at work,

> two thirds of whom are engaged in picking and hauling the grapes; the balance are at work about the presses or in the cellars. The grapes are cut off by the stem from the vine and carried in baskets to the crossroads running through the vineyard and turned into tubs holding from 150 to 200 pounds (or as large as two men can easily handle,) which are hauled in one-horse carts to the press where they are weighed, and then turned into a large "hopper," which has an apron, or strong wire seive, through which they are "stemmed," the stems being thrown out before the grape is mashed, when the latter is run through a mill, consisting of two grooved iron cylinders, so gauged as to run as closely as possible together with out mashing the seeds. The grooves of one cylinder are longitudinal, and of the other, spiral. This method is quicker, less laborious, and far more decent than the old way of "treading out" the grapes, which in a measure has passed away, as it should.... By it the mere crushing of the grape is done by two men more easily, than probably ten men could do the same work by any of the old methods of trampling, malls, or what not.
>
> After being ground, the pommace runs down into a vat, on the bottom of which is a grating through which the juice of the grape runs, whence it is conveyed into tubs for white wine. The pommace is taken directly to spiral screw presses and subjected to moderate pressure, the runnings from which make *pale* or *yellow wine*, like sherry. The grape skins are then put into large tubs to ferment six or eight days for red wine, or longer, when the residue of their vinous property is extracted in *auguardiente* [sic] for distillation. Four men are employed by Mr.

---

72. Bancroft, *History of California*, 7: 48–49n8.
73. *Transactions of the California State Agricultural Society*, 287. See also Wilson, *William Wolfskill*, 169.

Frohling in cleaning off the stems. This they do by pressing the grapes through the "sifter" with their hands. Two men turn the mill by cranks; two feed the hopper; one weighs the grapes; three or four attend to the wine as it comes from the mill and the presses; five or six do the pressing and carry off the pommace to the fermenting vats; one, two or three attend to washing, cleansing and sulphuring of grapes; three teams are constantly employed in hauling the grapes. Every night all the presses and appliances used about them are all washed thoroughly to prevent acidity. Everything that comes in contact with the grapejuice from the time the grape is bruised till it reaches the cask, is kept as pure as an abundance of water and hard scrubbing can make it.

Five days of labor resulted in 160,000 pounds of harvested grapes which were turned into 10,000 gallons of wine, exclusive of the considerable amount of pomace that was to be distilled into brandy.[74]

Changing economic conditions in Northern California contributed to a increased emphasis on wine production. Harris Newmark mentioned the competition from grape growers residing near San Francisco who "began to interfere with this monopoly of the South and, as, a consequence, the shipment of grapes from Los Angeles fell off." The decline of the fresh fruit trade, however, led to an increase in the making and exporting of wine, "and several who had not ventured into vineyarding before, now did so, acquiring their own land or an interest in the establishments of others."[75] The number of grape vines in Los Angeles County had increased from 600,000 in 1857 to 1,650,000 the following year.[76] By October 1858, however, the small producers were being squeezed out by the large operators who purchased the crops of the growers. According to the *Star*, "the wine manufactured will be less general, but probably more carefully attended to."[77] The quantity of aguardiente produced that season is not known, but as the retail liquor business thrived, the Indian crime rate may have increased.

---

74. Anonymous, "Letter from Los Angeles," Los Angeles, October 24, 1859, in *San Francisco Evening Bulletin*, October 27, 1959.
75. Newmark, *Sixty Years*, 199–200.
76. *Transactions of the California State Agricultural Society*, 312–13.
77. *Los Angeles Star*, October 23, 1858.

In late January and early February 1859, a grand jury addressed the problem of intra-Indian violence and questioned the policy of granting police powers to the Indian alcaldes. As reported in the local press, the jury concluded "that the employment of Indians by civil authorities—more especially of this city—has been, and is daily productive of evil and deserving of unqualified condemnation. The Indians thus selected and clothed with a brief and *illegal* authority, are in no respect in advance of the mass of their degraded race." The Indian officials were often more drunk than those they arrested, and there was incontestable proof that "offenses against the good order and peace of the community, have been the result of the ignorant and brutal officiousness of Indian Alcaldes in intermeddling not alone with individuals of their own race, but in many instances with those, who, neither by education or instinct, are disposed to tamely submit to the pretensions of beings whom they cannot but despise."[78]

The grand jury insisted that "it did not wish to be understood as reflecting in any manner upon the civil authorities: they are but continuing a system which has ever, in this city been the practice—and by custom, come to be regarded as an integral part of our local government." It recommended

> that steps should be taken for the removal from the city of all vagrant Indians—male and female. Of the latter class more especially, a large number are daily and hourly encountered on every street and corner—in every conceivable state of intoxication, disease and misery; without any abode, and eking out a precarious existence from the proceeds of crime and licentiousness. Stringent vagrant laws should be enacted and enforced, compelling such persons to obtain an honest livelihood or seek their old homes in the mountains.[79]

Evidently, the recommendations were ignored, because late in the year the very thing the grand jury complained about was still taking

---

78. Unidentified newspaper article, probably the *Los Angeles Star* of January or February 1859, in Benjamin Hayes Scrapbooks, vol. 46.
79. Ibid.

place. In October 1859 a fight erupted between two Indians, José and Juan. Juan was expected to recover from a knife wound; José was to stand trial.[80] Two months later, the *Star* reported that two Indian women with too much to drink "began fighting with each other, pulling hair, tearing dresses, rolling and sprawling on the ground; their struggles brought them to the edge of a bank leading to the zanja, down which they impotently rolled, each with a firm hold of the other's hair. A more disgusting sight could not have been exhibited."[81] In May 1860, an Indian informed a Mr. Laventhal that his servant had been killed the previous night in the upper part of the city and that he had come to take his place.[82] "Last Sunday, our vigilant City Marshal and his assistants brought *forty one* Indians to the station-house, generally on charges of drunkenness," reported the *Star* in June. "We do not know whether the officers are becoming more vigilant, or the aborigines more dissipated."[83]

No wonder William H. Brewer condemned Los Angeles in December as a place where "every prospect pleases and only man is vile." From a resident, he learned that fifty to sixty murders per year were common, but "some think it odd that there has been no violent deaths during the two weeks that we have been here."[84] A few of the violent deaths were legally sanctioned. Tomás, who had been convicted of murdering his wife and daughter on the Tejón Reservation, was sentenced to be hanged on September 27, 1859.[85] He escaped but was quickly captured and confined to his cell.[86] Judge Benjamin Hayes set the date of his execution for January 4, 1860, to allow Tomás time to receive religious instruction. Hayes knew that the Indians on the reservation feared Tomás and wished him dead. And Tomás confessed to Father Blas Raho that he had come to Los Angeles to kill one of the Indian alcaldes and two other Indians and that he was ready to die.[87]

---

80. *Los Angeles Star*, October 22, 1859.
81. Ibid., December 17, 1859.
82. Ibid., May 5, 1860.
83. Ibid., June 30, 1860.
84. Brewer, *Up and Down California in 1860–1864*, 13–14.
85. Benjamin Hayes, Diary, January 5, 1860, in Wolcott, ed., *Pioneer Notes*, 184.
86. *Los Angeles Star*, September 3, October 1, 1859,
87. Benjamin Hayes, Diary, January 5, 1860, 184.

Because Tomás exhibited signs of being either an imbecile or insane, some members of the community were not sure execution was in order. Hayes was troubled on both practical and moral grounds. He was convinced that the punishment would not serve the Indians on the reservation, "none of whom, I suppose, would be present, and, perhaps, not a half dozen of them would ever hear of the event." And he thought the twelve men he ordered the sheriff to assemble to determine the state of the Indian's mind would find Tomás insane and recommend life in prison. Hayes informed Tomás's attorney, whom he had appointed, that "there should be a commutation of punishment," but the attorney failed to attend the meeting. Declared sane, Tomás received the death sentence.[88] Evidently, hangings were no longer the spectacle they once were, because his warranted only a brief comment from the *Star*: "On Tuesday last, a miserable, imbecile looking creature, Tomás, an Indian, was executed in the jail yard . . . ; the jury agreed that he was a proper subject for the operation of the law and he was operated upon accordingly."[89]

Because he was an outsider, Tomás was probably not counted in the census of 1860 that identified 443 Indians residing within the city limits.[90] And within those limits an increasingly diversified population was taking shape. William H. Brewer observed "a mixture of old Spanish, Indian, American, and German Jews; the last two have come in lately."[91] One of those referred to may have been Wolf Kalisher, a Polish Jew, who seems to have been more enlightened than many regarding the Indians of the city. About 1861 he hired Olegario, a Luiseño from San Diego County, although in what capacity is not known. Olegario and Kalisher became good friends, the Indian gaining from him much knowledge about the American political system, which in time he would put to good use.[92] Later, Olegario worked for Matthew Keller who maintained a huge vineyard and orchard near the center of

---

88. Ibid., 185.
89. *Los Angeles Star*, February 4, 1860.
90. *Population Schedules of the Census of the United States, 1860*.
91. Brewer, *Up and Down California*, 13.
92. *Los Angeles Star*, September 3, 1871; Carrico, "Wolf Kalisher," 100–102.

the city. A visitor to Keller's property noted in early 1861 that the grower expected to produce from 40,000 to 50,000 gallons of wine and 5,000 gallons of brandy, which would bring $2.50 per gallon in San Francisco. "The season is now commencing, and some dozen men—principally Indians—are employed picking and carrying the grapes, and assisting in the manufacture." Their wages of fifty to seventy cents per day were virtually the same as in 1853.[93]

Growers such as Keller were soon to experience a shortage of Indian labor. In November 1862, a few cases of smallpox were identified in Los Angeles.[94] To contain the disease the common council divided the pueblo into five districts. A commissioner was appointed to inspect each person in each house in each district. A flag was attached to every house containing the infected and in late January 1863, flags were flying throughout the town. The *Star* admitted having no information on district one, but district two was in "a favorable condition," with fifteen cases "of a mild type" and only twenty persons yet to be vaccinated. But the disease continued unabated in the third and fourth districts, especially in the fourth. At least two hundred cases of small pox had been identified and about one hundred persons had died.[95] On February 21, the *Star* provided statistics regarding those infected in four of the five districts. Again, the fourth district was the most contaminated, 150 cases identified and only twenty-one persons vaccinated.[96]

The disease, of course, respected no race or class, but social and economic factors largely determined its demographic impact. An American resident concluded that the Indians "succumbed *en masse*" because their constitutions and been undermined by years of dissipation.[97] According to Harris Newmark, "The dread disease worked its ravages especially among the Mexicans and Indians, as many as a dozen of them dying in a single day; and these

---

93. John Quincy Adams Warren to editors, *American Stock Journal*, March 1861, reprinted in Gates, ed., *California Ranchos and Farms, 1846–1962*, 94–95.
94. *Los Angeles Star*, November 22, 1862.
95. Ibid., January 31, 1863.
96. Ibid., February 21, 1863.
97. King, "Reminiscences of San Gabriel," 59.

sufferers and their associates being under no quarantine, and even bathing *ad libitum* in the *zanjas*, the pest spread alarmingly."[98] By early March 1863 the number of cases had decreased sharply, and because of the efforts of the commissioner, opposition to vaccination among a portion of the population had been overcome.[99]

Those Indians surviving the epidemic continued to purchase aguardiente, but those selling it became increasingly regulated. In 1865 the city produced 600,000 gallons of wine worth $450,000 and 70,000 gallons of brandy worth $140,000.[100] In July the following year the common council amended an ordinance to require all proprietors of all establishments where "spirituous, vinous or malt liquors are retailed" to pay a monthly license of $10.00. Each was to "keep a quiet and orderly house, and not permit drunken Indians to be in or about the same." Selling or giving Indians intoxicating liquors of any kind was prohibited. Any breech of the conditions would result in the license being rescinded and the house abated as a nuisance. Furthermore, anyone selling wines in a restaurant or brewery had to pay a monthly license of $3.00, and anyone keeping a business house where liquor was sold and who permitted consumption on the premises was deemed a retailer and had to pay a license of $10.00 per month.[101]

The increasing regulation of its major industry perhaps encouraged growers to expand and diversify. As proudly noted by the *Star* in May 1868,

> The lines of the city of Los Angeles contain a body of land five and a-fourth miles square, comprising some of the finest soil in the State of California. Until within the last year or two, the great bulk of this tract was unimproved land, but latterly, by the introduction of water facilities, the whole of it presents a surface, almost uninterrupted, of vineyards, orchards, and grain fields, dotted, at brief intervals, with neat

---

98. Newmark, *Sixty Years*, 322.
99. *Los Angeles Star*, March 7, 1863.
100. *Los Angeles Semi-Weekly News*, September 21, 1866.
101. Ibid., July 31, 1866.

and comfortable houses of its owners. The district is watered by the Los Angeles river, utilized by means of numerous zanjas, or water courses, which distribute the water over the entire surface of land.[102]

The *Star* reported two years later that fifty miles of zanjas were "carrying the water from the river to every part of the city, for the purposes of irrigation." Moreover, the 1,000,000 bearing vines produced "every variety of grape grown in Europe and the Atlantic States."[103]

With this horizontal expansion came problems. Writing to the *Star* at the end of 1868, an individual noted that wages for day laborers had doubled during the past few years and lamented the time "when Indian labor could be had as required." Because the introduction of new industries had produced competition in the labor market, the grape grower should diversify "by introducing some other source of industry, to be carried on in unison with his wine-making, which will enable him to give employment throughout the year to laborers, instead of about two months—that is, a few weeks in the winter season in pruning the vine and plowing the vineyard, and again in the autumn, in harvesting the grapes." If silk culture were introduced, laborers would find year-round employment, feeding the silk worms in May after having pruned and plowed the vineyards. Therefore, growers should plant one fifth of their lands in mulberry trees. Because silk raising was "light business," Indian women and children of eight or nine and older would do most of the work.[104]

Early the following year the *Star* reported that it was "the intention of a number of gentlemen to associate, or at all events, cooperate in this business; so that, their plantation adjoining, they will form a community by themselves, wherein the various processes of the business, including reeling, will be conducted." The editors predicted that "there is no doubt whatever of the success

---

102. *Los Angeles Star*, May 23, 1868. For an overview of the development of the zanjas, see Hoffman and Stern, "The Zanjas and the Pioneer Water Systems."
103. *Los Angeles Star*, August 16, 1870. For more on the zanjas, see the *Star* of August 27, 1870.
104. Albert Brewster to editors, *Los Angeles Star*, December 12, 1868.

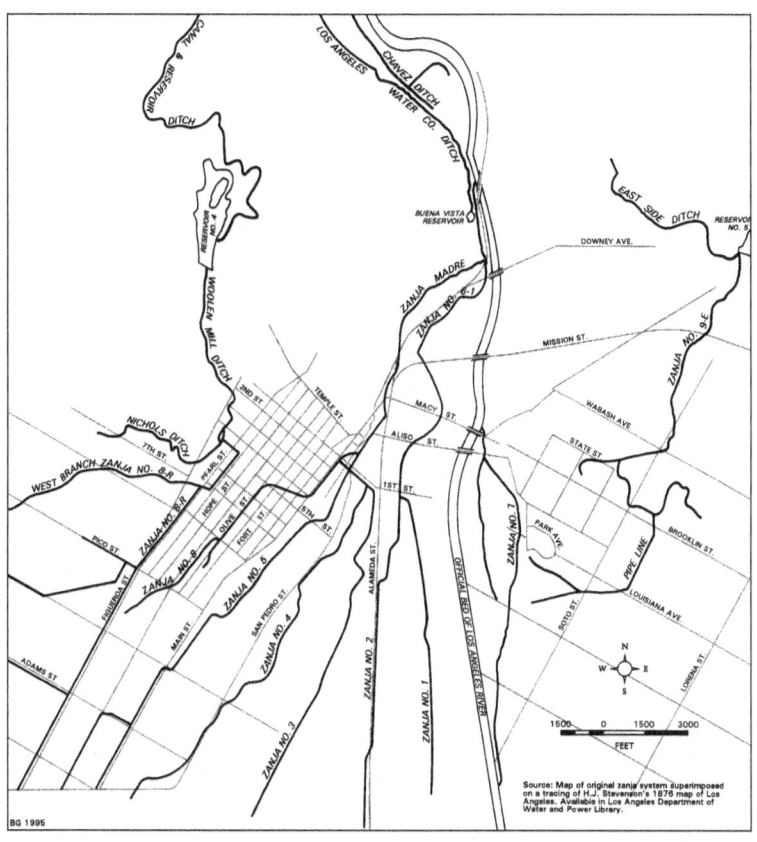

Zanja System of Los Angeles circa 1880.
Map by Blake Gumprecht; used with permission. *Reproduced from
The Los Angeles River: Its Life, Death, and Possible Rebirth
(Baltimore: Johns Hopkins University Press, 1999).*

TABLE 10. AGRICULTURAL EXPANSION IN
LOS ANGELES COUNTY, 1867–1868 (IN ACRES)

	1867	1868
Land enclosed	17,300	23,200
Land cultivated	15,000	19,950
Wheat	800	765
Barley	4,400	5,840
Rye	35	40
Corn	5,300	6,000
Buckwheat	50	65
Peas	20	22
Beans	600	715
Castor beans	113	60
Potatoes	1,000	1,000
Sweet potatoes	50	52
Onions	25	30
Hay	320	750
Tobacco	15	16
Broom corn	25	30

Source: Adapted from *Los Angeles Star*, September 5, 1868, and September 18, 1869.

of such undertaking. The market is the world; and our citizens should be foremost in supplying its wants."[105] In October, however, the *Star* noted that the industry suffered from a want of reelers, although a woman with this expertise was at work on one farm and was willing to teach her skill to those interested.[106] Millions of silk worms and larvae were imported from France and Japan, and hundreds of mulberry trees were planted, but the industry that might have kept some Indians permanently employed died as quickly as it was born.[107]

By this time, Los Angeles was also rising vertically. The *Semi-*

---
105. *Los Angeles Star*, February 13, 1869.
106. Ibid., October 16, 1869.
107. Cleland, *Cattle on a Thousand Hills*, 177–80.

Weekly News of May 1, 1866, summed up how new construction was bringing an earlier period to an end. After mentioning that William Wolfskill had commenced grading a lot on Main Street for a new store in brick that was destined to be "one of the largest and most substantial structures south of San Francisco," the editors pointed out that "one by one the old adobe buildings, the relics of a former and more incomplete age of civilization, are giving way to a more useful and ornamental class of buildings."[108] As recalled by Ludwig Louis Salvator, "not until 1867–8 did the city began to grow rapidly and show decided progress in the erection of handsome houses, fine buildings and substantial brick shops, hotels, schools, banks and factories which sprang up at the time as if by magic."[109] At the end of 1868 Los Angeles could claim five grist mills, one steam powered saw mill, and three quartz mills, all powered by 1,775 inches of daily water flow. A twenty-mile railroad had been completed to San Pedro.[110]

That year Los Angeles County produced 1,111,200 gallons of wine and 85,800 gallons of brandy, by far the most of any county in California.[111] With fewer vines than Sonoma County, which at 348,136 gallons was the second largest producer, it made more wine because there was little demand for grapes.[112] But federal revenue laws were especially harmful to those manufacturing brandy. A capacity tax was based on the assumption that a still that held one hundred gallons could produce thirty-four gallons of brandy each day and would remain in operation seven days per week. But the grape juice usually had to be run through the still at least twice, and no still operated more than once a day. The producer had to pay a tax on the full capacity of the still, even if it were in operation only part of each day. Moreover, after the first one hundred barrels of brandy, the producer was taxed four dollars on each additional barrel.[113]

---

108. *Los Angeles Semi-Weekly News*, May 1, 1866.
109. Salvator, "A Flower from the Golden Land," 2: 43.
110. *Los Angeles Star*, September 18, 1869.
111. Ibid.
112. Ibid., February 5, 1870.
113. Ibid., October 16, 1869.

On October 10, 1869, the mayor, common council, board of supervisors, wine and brandy manufactures, and citizens at large held a meeting and drafted a memorial to the Commissioner of Internal Revenue in Washington, D.C. In part, the memorial pointed out that the laws imposed a capacity tax of such a high percentage that their stills could not turn a profit.[114] Because of the law, the firm of Kohler and Frohling had thrown away enough grape pomace to produce 2,500 gallons of brandy.[115]

At this juncture in the city's economic history, the editors of the *Los Angeles Daily News* questioned a long-standing labor practice. In an article published on February 11, 1869, and titled "Labor the Great Necessity of Los Angeles," they identified the problem, offered a solution, and found blame.

The problem:

> The great necessity of any agricultural county is labor—active, intelligent laborers who invest the savings from their earnings in farms and lots, and build houses that identify them with the permanent interests of the county. Experience and history has proven that in all countries where the labor has been performed by intelligent men, who settle with their families, and by the earnings of a few years acquire sufficient means to procure themselves homesteads, and surrounded with the comforts if not the luxuries of life—Prosperity and progress had made rapid and permanent strides; schools are built up and sustained; good morals and habits are cultivated, and improvement takes the place of languor and decay. In this portion of the State and particularly in this county, the great bulk of the labor has been performed by Indians, who are at best but inferior laborers, totally void of that interest in the welfare of the community. . . . They build no houses, own no lands, pay no taxes, and encourage no branch of industry; their scanty earnings at the end of the week being spent for rum in the lowest purlieus of the city, where scenes of violence occur, particularly on Saturday and Sunday nights, that would disgrace barbarism itself. During eighteen years, in which they have in a very indifferent manner performed the labor of this county,

---

114. Ibid.
115. Ibid., July 30, 1870. To inspect the quantity and alcoholic content of brandy, the internal revenue agent who was stationed in Los Angeles would send a "gauger" to the vineyards. Once the brandy was approved and the taxes paid, revenue stamps were pasted on the barrels and they were ready for shipment and sale. See Rose, *L. J. Rose of Sunny Slope*, 82.

scarcely a single one of them has become a tax-payer, and nothing has been added to the county by them save the debt and public expenditure in punishing them by the courts for murders and robberies committed in their drunken and phrenzied debauches. They have filled our jails, have contributed largely to the filling of our State prison, and are fast filling our graveyards, where they must either be buried at the public expense or be permitted to rot in the streets and highways.

The solution:

It is time that the men of wealth and influence in this county should take some steps to encourage a different and more useful class of laborers, who will combine the qualities of good and useful citizens to that of good laborers. By consulting the census returns of 1860, we find that this country contained a population of two thousand and fourteen Indians, male and female, who subsist (their living is a bare subsistence) by their daily labor. There can be no question but the number is greatly reduced, as deaths from disease, exposure and violence greatly exceed the increase of the race when brought in contact with any form of civilization. If they had been sent to reservations and their places supplied, ten years ago, with two thousand intelligent white laborers, at least two-thirds of that number would to-day be land owners; their number would have been doubled, and a large and valuable accession of the population made to the independent yeomanry of the county; farms and hamlets would have covered the now barren plains, schools, churches and other evidences of a high order of civilization, would have occupied the sites of ungainly *Rancherias*; and peace, intelligence and happiness would dwell where now misery and squalor reign supreme.

The blame:

[T]he Indian being constantly brought into competition with that class of labor that would be most beneficial to the country, checks immigration and retards the prosperity of the county. It is of no use for our leading farmers to say they took Indian labor from necessity; that other labor could not be had, &c.; they have made no effort to induce other labor to come to their assistance, as the absence of labor exchanges, agricultural societies and other means of encouraging laborers abundantly proves, but have contented themselves to use the county jail for nearly twenty years as an intelligence office from which to gather information concerning the class of laborers mostly employed by them.[116]

---

116. *Los Angeles Daily News*, February 11, 1869.

Clearly overlooking the important contributions of the Indians to the agricultural expansion of the county and obviously unable to understand the cultural reasons for Indian debauchery, the editors, nevertheless, put the blame squarely on those who perpetuated the system. Moreover, they were correct in predicting that Indian labor had no place in the future of the pueblo, especially in its industrial development. What they failed to know, however, was that the "problem" of Indian labor would not be solved by "men of wealth influence" encouraging "a more useful class of laborers," but by forces even more powerful.

In late 1868 smallpox had again appeared in the county. Some Indians, such as Olegario, simply fled.[117] Others remained in the region and fell victim to the disease. Perhaps the most prominent victim was Victoria, Hugo Reid's widow. The last member of the village of Comicrabit, she was buried at Mission San Gabriel on Christmas Eve, 1868.[118] By mid-May 1869, the Los Angeles authorities claimed the disease was under control.[119] On May 22 the *Star* identified twelve individuals with the disease, five being confined to the hospital. "In all, but three Americans have been affected. All cases not in the hospital are isolated, and their locality designated by a yellow flag."[120] At month's end only two more Americans had contracted the disease but several Mexicans and Indians had been infected. They refused hospitalization and two Indians had died.[121]

The number of Indians who perished in the epidemic is impossible to calculate, but thereafter, accounts of Indian behavior, so long a tragic topic of interest, virtually disappeared from Los Angeles newspapers. Perhaps to compensate for the absence of drama, the editors of the *Star* turned to the past. In July 1868 they began publishing Benjamin Hayes's report on the Indians of Southern California. "We reprint this document for its intrinsic value," they explained, "and not for any bearing it may have had on

---

117. *Los Angeles Star*, September 3, 1871.
118. Dakin, *A Scotch Paisano*, 200.
119. *Los Angeles Star*, May 15, 1869.
120. Ibid., May 22, 1869.
121. Ibid., May 29, 1869.

the system pursued by Government in its treatment of the Indians. It is well worth preserving, and will be found very useful to a full understanding of the early history of this portion of the State. It suggests a melancholy reflection upon the destiny of the red man, when one contemplates the scattered remnants of what were once numerous nations."[122] On February 6, 1869, they began reprinting Hugo Reid's letters about the Indians of Los Angeles County.[123] And a week later they referred to a copy of the *Star* of 1851 which brought them "back to the 'good times' of California, but it also reminds us of the dangers and hardships which the pioneers of even this favored clime had to undergo, in building up an American community in Southern California." Much of the "good old times" dealt with the crushing of an Indian uprising.[124]

When contemporary Indians were mentioned it was usually to announce the death of prominent individuals, to notify the public about the suspicious movements of Indians in the interior, or to comment on the arrival of Indians who had come to the pueblo to speak with local authorities or Indian agents.[125] Those from beyond the area seeking work also received some attention. The *Star* reported in October 1871 that in the employ of Matthew Keller were Olegario and several Luiseños from San Diego County.[126] An article of November 3, 1875, announced that a band of Luiseños from San Diego County would soon arrive to participate in the grape harvest.[127] The following year Ludwig Luis Salvator noted that Luiseños, Cahuillas, Juaneños, and Fernandinos traveled to Los Angeles in August to trade or hire out as laborers. "Many of them are fairly well educated and can read and write Spanish. Some of the sons of the chieftains speak English."[128] Los

---

122. Ibid., August 1, 1868.
123. Ibid., February 6, 1869. For the earlier reference to the letters see the *Star* of July 23, 1859.
124. Ibid., February 13, 1869.
125. See, for example, *Los Angeles Star*, February 9, 1869; November 27, 1869; September 3, 1871; and the *Los Angeles Herald*, September 18, 1875, in Bowman Scrap Book II, 103, California Room, Los Angeles Public Library.
126. *Los Angeles Star*, October 3, 1871.
127. Unidentified newspapers article, November 3, 1875, in Bowman Scrap Book II, 102.
128. Salvator, "A Flower from the Golden Land," 1:18.

Angeles, it seems, was now importing its Indian labor. In the city they found work in the vineyards, orchards, and fields now encompassing nearly 5,000 acres of land irrigated by a vastly expanded zanja system.[129]

The Indian workers, however, made up only a tiny percentage of the workforce. According to the federal census of 1870, only 219 Indians remained in Los Angeles County.[130] Although the figure is much too low for the county, it might approximate the number of Indians then in the city. The population of Los Angeles that year totaled 5,728, of which 2,160, or 37.7 percent, were Spanish-speakers. Of the latter, 444 were employed, 355 being manual laborers.[131] Clearly, Spanish-speakers had replaced Indians as the main labor force in the city. But with the extension of the Southern Pacific Railroad from San Francisco to Los Angeles in 1876, English-speakers began to arrive in large numbers and soon would become the dominant labor force. Between 1870 and 1880, the population of Los Angeles nearly doubled.[132]

The extent to which Los Angeles had changed culturally and architecturally is evident in the 1876 Centennial Celebration of the Declaration of Independence. Displays of bunting adorned the opera house, theater, stores, hotels, and residences. Through arches built over Main Street came the Los Angeles Guard, Veterans of the Mexican War, the French Benevolent Society, carriages carrying various dignitaries, Fire Engine Company Number One, the hook and ladder truck, a car containing thirteen young ladies representing the thirteen original colonies, another with thirty-eight representing the states, the Butchers Association, miners and their mules, various orders, including the Knights of Pythias, the Independent Order of Odd Fellows, the Ancient Order of Hibernians, the Irish Literary Society, and the Irish Temperance Society.[133]

---

129. Gumprecht, *Los Angeles River*, 70–71.
130. Cook, *Population of the California Indians, 1769–1970*, 55.
131. Griswold del Castillo, *The Los Angeles Barrio*, 35, 53.
132. Gumprecht, *Los Angeles River*, 83.
133. Warner, et al., *An Historical Sketch*, 142–45; Newmark, *Sixty Years*, 499–501.

Violent Vineyards 295

Also marching in the parade, an observer recalled, were "half a dozen representatives of the noble red man of the forest, who, with their lay figure of Capt. Jack of the Modocs, contributed not a little to the hilarity of the occasion."[134] Perhaps those caught up in the "hilarity of the occasion" failed to realize that the Indians may have been reminding the whites that a few years before, during the Modoc War, Captain Jack and his supporters had inflicted severe causalities on the U.S. Army.[135]

---

134. Warmer, et al., *An Historical Sketch*, 145.
135. Several books have been written about the Modoc War. Still one of the best is Murray, *The Modocs and Their War*.

CHAPTER 13

A Useful People

When Charles Edward Pancoast and companions rested at Rancho Santa Ana del Chino in 1849, its owner, Isaac Williams, provided them with all the grapes and meat they could consume but would not sell them any vegetables. Pancoast noted that the rancheros failed to cultivate sufficient vegetables for their own use and that Indians grew the garden crops.[1] Williams employed between seventy-five and one hundred persons, most being Indians who raised melons, onions, corn, and Irish potatoes.[2]

Regarding Indians as food producers, Benjamin Hayes, an astute observer of Indian affairs in Southern California, had much to say:

> Considered in their relation to agriculture, in this part of California, these Indians are the only farmers living here, besides the Americans who have come into the country since the war, and a very few who were here before. The California "Spaniard," (so to speak) loves his fiery steed—not the plough. Many such a *ranchero*, rich in cattle and "goodly

---

1. Hannum, ed., *A Quaker Forty-Niner*, 269.
2. Evans, *Mexican Gold Trail*, 174, 177. The work force on Rancho Chino remained remarkably stable for nearly twenty years. In 1844, sixty-seven Indians were identified as working on the rancho. See Northrop, ed., "The Los Angeles Padrón of 1844," According to the *Los Angeles Star* of May 31, 1862, about one hundred Indians resided on the rancho.

acres," by the ten thousand, must go to his Indian neighbor hard by on the ranch, if he would dine today on his maize or *frijoles*! This remark is made, subject only to isolated exceptions, and as authorizing a general inference much more favorable to the Indian than my incidental description of him, merely as a farm-laborer; for, in a multitude of instances on the numerous ranchos, even where he neither owns land, nor claims more than a casual occupancy, he is more than a *peon* (servant). A very independent and useful producer is the Mission Indian, in such case, whose house and furniture need no insurance, but without whom a *rancho* [ranchero] would eat much less bread and vegetables!"[3]

Hayes also acknowledged that "the Indian laborers and servants are 'domesticated;' mix with us daily and hourly; and, with all their faults, appear to be a necessary part of the domestic economy. They are almost the only house or farm servants we have. The San Luiseño is most sprightly, skillful, and handy; the Cahuilla plodding, but strong, and very useful with instruction and watching." Although an Indian farm hand occasionally earned from eight to ten dollars per month, few received that much. These low wages, claimed Hayes, kept them employed because "no white man here, whether American, Sonoranian, or Californian, will work for such wages, nor anything like it." Better wages would not necessarily make the Indian a better man. With more money, he would only further pursue "his evil tastes" of drinking and gambling. "But let us remember, these same Indians built all the houses in the country, and planted all the fields and vineyards. There is hardly any sort of ordinary work for which they do not show a good-will." Soon they might "rank with the best Californian and Sonoranian in all the arts necessary to their physical comfort. They teach the American, even, how to make an adobe (sun-dried brick), mix the *lodo* (mud mortar), put on the *brea* (pitch) for roof. . . . They understand the mysteries of irrigation, the planting season, and the harvest."[4]

Although Hayes correctly identified the importance of Indians as producers, workers, and instructors, he failed to mention that

---
3. Caughey, ed., *The Indians of Southern California*, 60.
4. Ibid., 21–22.

the rancheros relied heavily on Indian-produced vegetables and crops, in part because the gold rush created a great demand for beef. José Dolores Sepúlveda explained that "the rancheros did not cultivate as much land in these years because the price of cattle was very high."[5] Rounding up sufficient animals to drive north presented no problem, but getting them to the mines entailed considerable risk. In late 1850, Henry Dalton of Rancho Azusa sent a herd north, some 2,500 head that were managed by several vaqueros. Because it was too late in the season to reach the gold fields, they halted along the Kaweah River and built a corral. In January 1851 Kaweah Indians under the command of a chief called Francisco attacked and killed the vaqueros and six American immigrants who were in the area and fled with the herd. The loss forced Dalton out of the cattle exporting business. Thereafter, he maintained a herd of only three hundred head to support local needs.[6]

By driving cattle on the hoof to a market rather than exporting only their raw products to maritime merchants, Dalton was engaging in a new economic enterprise similar to that undertaken by more famous American ranchers of later years. Activities such as this prompted the editors of the *Daily Alta California*, a San Francisco newspaper, to compare the American rancher and his business acumen to the Mexican ranchero and his social obligations. The Californio

> does not partake of the same active desires and prospects which we all seek, in the round of daily toil and care. His requirements are altogether different. He lives, moves, and thinks in a different sphere—sees and feels by another medium. He is unlike by preference as well as different by birth, education and intellect. He never can be of us, or with us, in any of the changing events of our fast existence. We are emphatically "ahead of his time," and he knows it, feels it, and is not moved by it. He dislikes the velocity with which we think and act, and to all our great

---

5. José Dolores Sepúlveda, Testimony, in The Anaheim Water Company, et al., Plaintiffs and Respondents vs. The Semi-Tropic Water Company, et, al, Defendants and Appellants, in the Superior Court of Los Angeles County, State of California, 1883, 298–99.
6. Hafen, ed., *Letters of Lewis Granger*, 30–31. See also Jackson, *A British Ranchero in Old California*, 137–39; and Phillips, *Indians and Indian Agents*, 120–21.

"strokes of policy," our whole course of achievements and successes, our entire scheme of prosperity and destiny, he is alike indifferent. . . .

The Rancheros, who still inhabit many districts of California, particularly in the southern part of the State—their herds and their homes, as they enjoyed them before the conquest of the country, are as dear to them to-day as ever; but rather than conform to American manners and customs, and take an active part in the business developments of the State, they would sacrifice their property and surrender their homes to the encroachments of their American neighbors, and retire from the scenes of their nativity.[7]

What the editors failed to understand was that several herds of the 17,000 head of cattle Los Angeles County sent north in 1852 belonged to Mexican land owners and were herded by Indian vaqueros.[8]

According to the state census of 1852, grazing throughout the now vastly expanded county were 12,173 horses and 65,051 head of beef cattle. The census identified 4,091 non-Indians, mostly Mexicans and Americans, and 4,193 Indians (2,778 males and 1,415 females) of which 1,864 were over twenty-one years of age.[9] The individual taking the federal census of Los Angeles County failed to count Indians on several ranchos that obviously employed them, but he was able to identify twenty-two residing on Rancho Los Cerritos. Seven of the Indians were children under the age of twelve. Clearly, the Indians had families, but among the seventeen non-Indians, only two were twelve years old and under. All were Mexicans from California, except the mayordomo, José Simón Roca, who was from Spain. Another Spaniard and a Hawaiian also resided on the rancho. On Rancho Los Alamitos, Indian families seem to have been the main social group. Of the thirty-three Indians in residence, fourteen were twelve years old and younger. It is not known whether Indians reoccupied Povuu'nga, where

---

7. *Daily Alta California*, August 19, 1851.
8. *Los Angeles Star*, August 7, 1852; Cleland, *Cattle on a Thousand Hills*, 105.
9. Abstract of the Census of 1852 of the State of California, *Journal of the Senate*, 4th sess., Doc. 14, 1853, 19. In 1851 the state legislature greatly expanded Los Angeles County, extending it westward to the coast, eastward to the state line, northward to the Tehachapi Pass, and southward to San Juan Capistrano.

Chinigchinich appeared, but evidently its location was near the ranch house.¹⁰

Some of the Indians working on this rancho probably attended the rodeo witnessed by Horace Bell in 1853 at Rancho San Joaquín: "The Machados of La Ballona, the Picos from San Fernando and San Diego, the Dominguez, the Sepulvedas of Palos Verdes, the Lugos from everywhere, the Avilas of Tahauta, Centinela, and Aliso, the Sanchez, the Ocampo, and the Cotas, the Stearns, Rowlands, Reeds, Williams, the Yorbas of Santa Ana, and the Temples of Puente and Cerritos, all were there." Vaqueros, numbering close to one hundred, divided 30,000 head of cattle into herds belonging to the rancheros. They branded calves and then herded the cattle to the owners' ranchos.¹¹

With a surplus of cattle and numerous workers to manage them, the rancheros had no difficulty in exporting 25,000 head in 1853.¹² The price of beef cattle, ranging from $25.00 to $32.00 per head and some cows going for $40.00 per animal, probably stimulated more Mexicans to take an active part in the business developments of the state. But when prices dropped, the risks outweighed the rewards, and after 1854 the number of herds sent north dropped off.¹³ Loss of revenue soon would hurt many of the Mexican rancheros of California in unexpected ways. The U.S. Land Act of 1851 forced all landowners to prove title to their properties. The cost of hiring lawyers and traveling to San Francisco to argue their cases resulted in many of them selling or subdividing their estates. The rancheros of Southern California would retain their properties and maintain a life style based on cheap Indian labor a bit longer than their compatriots in the north, but their days were numbered.¹⁴

---

10. Newmark and Newmark, eds., *Census of the City and County of Los Angeles*, 78–80. Why the census taker identified fifty-five Indians residing at Ranchos Los Cerritos and Los Alamitos but failed to list them on others such as Rancho Santa Ana del Chino, where large numbers resided, remains a mystery. The possibility of reoccupation is suggested by Stephen O'Neil in "The Acjachemen in the Franciscan Mission System," 229–30.
11. Bell, *Reminiscences of a Ranger*, 300–301.
12. *Los Angeles Star*, June 4, 1853.
13. Gates, *California Ranchos*, 17–18. The rise and fall of the cattle boom, including Mexicans driving their herds north, is discussed in Cleland, *Cattle on a Thousand Hills*, 102–16.
14. Cleland, *Cattle on a Thousand Hills*, 35–40; Pitt, *Decline of the Californios*, 104–19.

Holding on longer were American landowners such as Abel Stearns. Originally from Massachusetts and a naturalized Mexican citizen, Stearns had purchased Rancho Los Alamitos in 1842.[15] Once part of the Nieto concession, it consisted of 28,512 acres, on which grazed 10,000 head of cattle, 700 horses, and 1,100 sheep.[16] In 1852 Stearns hired Charles Henry Brinley as administrator of the rancho. As did other administrators, Brinley occupied a social stratum between the owner and the mayordomo who managed the vaqueros and other workers. Brinley's duties were to supervise the raising of the cattle, to manage the rodeos on surrounding ranches, to order the matanza, to supervise the processing of fat, the tanning of hides, and the converting of tallow into soap. Although he did not flog his workers, Brinley failed to establish amicable relations with them, in part because he also ran the company store. For example, when a worker sought a pair of shoes, Brinley passed the request on to Stearns. Once approved, Brinley deducted the cost of the shoes from the worker's wages. Thus with every purchase or money lent him, the worker got further and further into debt. When the vaquero Andrés Duarte quit his job in mid-October 1852, he owed $1.40 for stirrup irons, 70¢ for cigars, and $5.00 in cash, all of which was deducted from his wages of $20.00.[17]

The Indian and Mexican workers, however, were not without options. In April 1852 Guadalupe (his single name suggests he was Indian) refused to participate in a rodeo unless paid two dollars a day or three if he provided his own horses. Another worker offered to use his own horses for five dollars a day. Brinley refused their demands and was five men short for the rodeo. Yet, if he thought the worker deserving, Brinley granted him higher wages, as in July 1852 when he increased an Indian's pay to $1.00 per day. On another occasion, he hired Querino who had fled from an impending flogging at nearby Rancho Los Cerritos, the property of John Temple. Later, Brinley told Stearns that Querino was "a

---

15. Cleland devoted an entire chapter to Stearns. See 184–207.
16. Ibid., 193.
17. Hough, "Charles Henry Brinley," 179.

good boy and is the only servant that has been upon this ranch during my stay here, who has shown himself at all times prompt, and ready to do anything to the best of his ability." Brinley also bragged that he would secure all of Temple's workers because his mayordomo was "too much of a Sultan among them, much to their disgust."[18] In August 1852, Brinley recommended that Stearns appoint someone to attend the auction taking place in Los Angeles on Mondays and "buy me five or six Indians."[19]

Brinley's need to "buy" Indians indicates a decline in his workforce, a situation he claimed was common on the surrounding ranchos. Because he was shorthanded and thus forced to manage the flocks of sheep himself, Brinley told Stearns that if he could hire workers "in whom one could have confidence, I should feel happier to say the least—but I am convinced that 'razon' and 'indio' is a distinction without a difference—that all are capricious and unreliable." In November 1852, when most of the remaining vaqueros served notice of quitting, Brinley insisted that the mayordomo, Francisco Rodríguez, was somehow responsible. Stearns blamed Brinley for mismanagement, but Brinley claimed he lacked the authority to truly manage the ranch and had, in fact, been too lenient with his workers. At the beginning of 1853, Brinley left the employ of Stearns. Rodríguez remained as mayordomo.[20]

Although relations between management and labor were much more amicable on Rancho Cucamonga, the working conditions troubled a member of a U.S. surveying expedition. He wrote in 1854 that the vineyard appeared to belong "to a Californian, living at a great distance off, who had placed these people here to look after it. They were evidently very poor, and lived in rude log huts, and a few others, not much larger than hay-cocks, were occupied by Indians who called themselves Kavias [Cahuillas], and were little insignificant-looking fellows who, in their scanty ragged clothing appeared the picture of misery. They stand much

---

18. Ibid., 176–79.
19. Charles Henry Brinley to Abel Stearns, Alamitos, August 30, 1852, Abel Stearns Collection, SG Box 11. See also Hough, "Charles Henry Brinley," 177.
20. Hough, "Charles Henry Brinley," 177–78.

in the position of serfs, and are bound, for a consideration of a small quantity of bad food, to labour in the vineyard, and perform any other work for the proprietor."[21]

Although the Indian workers at Rancho Cucamonga apparently sowed no grain during 1855, they harvested 300 bushels of peaches and 200 of pears. From the two vineyards containing 13,000 vines, they picked 202,500 pounds of grapes. Those employed on Rancho Jurupa that year produced 500 bushels of barley and 2,300 of corn, as well as 1,000 of onions and 500 of beans.[22] Most likely Cahuillas, they attended to 10 work horses, 50 mares, 20 milk cows and calves, 135 other cows and calves, 50 head of beef cattle, 200 of young cattle, and 1,200 sheep.[23]

The Indians working for Isaac Williams on Rancho Chino harvested 500 bushels of barley in 1855. Williams's garden was limited but his orchard was doing well. He continued to raise horses, cattle, hogs and sheep.[24] The following year, a visitor noted that Williams employed the Indian leader of the nearest band as his head cattle drover and a dozen or two vaqueros. While at the rancho he saw the leader arrive at the ranch house at sundown, hat in hand, to report on the day's work.[25] For the previous few years Williams's sheep had gone unsheared because no one was available to do the work.[26] Finally, Williams hired a shepherd at $5.00 a day but he had trouble getting Indians to work for him even for wages, and whites demanded too much. "Scarcely anything was left of the 13,000 acres of cultivated land, and the orchards and vineyards," wrote Julius Froebel. "The Colonel's possessions now consist only of his land, with 10,000 head of cattle, and a few thousand sheep feeding on it." But "better breeds" of sheep had recently been introduced and promised "great results in every way."[27]

---

21. Lieutenant A. W. Whipple, March 19, 1854, "Extracts from the preliminary report by Lieutenant A. W. Whipple, 1854," in Robert Stockton Williamson, *Reports of Explorations and Surveys*, 5: 134.
22. V. Johnson Herring to S. H. Marlette, San Bernardino County, October 25, 1855, *Annual Report of the Surveyor-General*, 290–94.
23. "Assessment of Louis Roubidoux in 1854," in Hornbeck, *Roubidoux's Ranch in the 70s*, 86.
24. Herring to Marlette, October 25, 1855.
25. Harlow, ed., *The City of the Angels*, 13.
26. Black, *Rancho Cucamonga and Doña Merced*, 243.
27. Froebel, *Seven Years' Travel*, 547–48, 566–67.

To those intending to replace cattle with sheep, nature lent a helping hand. At least 10,000 head of cattle perished in Los Angeles County in the severe drought of 1856. In April the *Los Angeles Star* reported that "the teeth of the cattle have this year, been so dull that they have been able scarcely to save themselves from starvation."[28] Ignacio del Valle recalled having never seen such a condition in thirty years. Two hundred head of cattle died daily in the county, and as soon as one died, the vaqueros would skin it, the hide being worth $2.00.[29] The cattle industry never fully recovered from the drought and a corresponding decline in the market value per animal.[30]

Of more consequence to Indians, however, was the impact the drought had on the environment. Many Indians still relied on acorns but they were in short supply and fish were absent from the streams. Indians were unable to raise sufficient amounts of corn, beans, and vegetables, prompting the editors of the *Star* to predict that "to save themselves from starvation they will no doubt be committing depredations on the stock of the rancheros, which may lead to hostilities against the poor savages. . . . The distribution of a few cattle, with blankets and other necessities, would enable the wandering tribes to pass our short winter, when they would be enabled to shift for themselves in the spring which, it is to be hoped, will be more auspicious than the two last seasons."[31] Evidently, no such distribution took place.

Indians "permanently" employed on the ranchos fared better. In August 1856 military officer Edward O. C. Ord, visited the eastern ranchos. At Rancho Cucamonga he observed Indians adding an extension to the owner's adobe house. Working "pretty well," they demonstrated "some skill in this rude & ancient masonry." But Ord was conflicted regarding a system he considered to be peonage. The Indians were "by state laws held in bondage by the owners of large estates, as the slaves are in the south—excepting that the slave, being a saleable chattel, always producing something, it is to

---

28. *Los Angeles Star*, April 26, 1856, quoted in Cleland, *Cattle on a Thousand Hills*, 109–10.
29. Hayes, Diary, December 13, 1856, in Wolcott, ed., *Pioneer Notes*, 153.
30. Cleland, *Cattle on a Thousand Hills*, 110.
31. *Los Angeles Star*, November 29, 1856.

the interest of the owner to keep him in good health and working order, as much as it is not to abuse a 1000 or 1200 dollar horse. But the Indian here, or Peon, is only saleable or buyable for debts due, which he must work out, and when the purchaser or owner has no more work for him, he ceases to credit him, drives him off." Still, the peonage system worked "very well at least for the cattle owners & vine growers.... Besides, the Indians are better fed on the ranchos than on government reservations & they prefer to stay there. So we might as well let the poor wretches have the choice of masters."[32]

In his report Ord elaborated on the system in which the Indians where caught: "The overseer of a large ranch, has but to be a 'Justice of the Peace' and he is enabled to buy and keep Indian servants as he may want them, and to punish them at discretion, within a limit. The system thus legalized provides labour in a hot climate where otherwise there would be none, and it being a continuation of the system to which the Indians were accustomed under the Mexican rule, it works well. Each of the large cattle ranchos near Los Angeles and San Bernardino has from fifteen to thirty Indians permanently occupied on it."[33]

In October 1857 an Indian agent detected distinctions between Indians residing in Los Angeles and San Bernardino counties, the latter carved from the former in 1853. Traditional villages were virtually absent in Los Angeles County. The Indians resided on the ranchos "in the capacity of Vaqueros, servants and farm hands generally. On all the Ranches they have allotted to them as much ground as they wish to cultivate with which they appear contented and have no complaints to make, at least none of which I could learn." In San Bernardino County, Indians also worked on the ranchos but many lived in traditional villages or practiced "a wandering life." They were dependent on the acorns which were in greater abundance than in previous years.[34] That year another

---

32. Harlow, ed., *The City of the Angels*, 12–16.
33. Ibid., 32.
34. J. J. Kendrick to Thomas Henley, San Diego, October 19, 1857, Letters Received by the Office of Indian Affairs, 1824–1881, Microcopy 234, California Superintendency, Roll 35.

A Useful People

Indian agent observed Cahuillas living in the San Gorgonio Pass, who "supported themselves comfortably by raising vegetables in small gardens of their own cultivation, with the addition of mesquite beans, which to a great extent abound in that valley." They have done this, moreover, "without the aid of the general government."[35]

By this time the federal government had established five reservations in Central and Northern California and was seeking to found more in Southern California. Because it lacked sufficient water, timber, and suitable farming land, and because much of it was occupied by American squatters, the San Gorgonio Pass was eliminated as a possible site. But Rancho Chino and ranchos in San Diego County were still being considered. Since 1852 when they were first promised reservations, the Indians of the region had been waiting for land and federal assistance.[36]

According to the census of 1860, in huge San Bernardino County, which extended to the Colorado River, Indians outnumbered whites 3,028 to 2,523. Between 1850 and 1860, however, the number of Indians recorded in Los Angeles County had dropped from 3,693 to 2,014.[37] Some of the reduction resulted from the creation of San Bernardino County which reduced the county to one third of its former size.[38] There were simply fewer Indians to be counted. But during the same ten year period, the number of acres improved for agriculture in Los Angeles County increased from 2,648 to 20,600.[39]

The increased acreage provided opportunities for some and problems for others. Harris Newmark recalled that, "small as was the population of Los Angles County at about this time, there

---

35. J. W. Denver to Thomas Henley, Washington, D.C., August 14, 1857, *Report of the Commissioner of Indian Affairs*, 407.
36. Thomas J. Henley to Charles E. Mix, San Francisco, February 18, 1858. Letters Received by the Office of Indian Affairs, 1824–1881, California Superintendency, 1849–1880, Photocopy 234, Roll 36. Indians not receiving the land they were promised is discussed in Phillips, *Chiefs and Challengers*, 69–70, 119–24.
37. Cook, *Population of the California Indians*, 55.
38. Beck and Haase, *Historical Atlas of California*, 62; Elliot, *History of San Bernardino and San Diego Counties*, 83.
39. Fogelson, *The Fragmented Metropolis*, 56.

was nevertheless for a while an exodus to Texas, due chiefly to the difficulty experienced by white immigrants in competing with Indian ranch and vineyard laborers."[40] The American immigrants also had to contend with increasing numbers of Sonorans, many of whom found employment on the ranchos situated along the Santa Ana River. S. Haley recalled that in 1862 on Cañón de Santa Ana "a good many Sonoranians and Indians" and "laboring Californians" were engaged in cultivating. "I do not think there was any land cultivated there which was not irrigated." After he moved on to Santiago de Santa Ana in 1864, Haley observed "a great many more Sonoranians on that side of the river than there had been." Arriving when the entire region was then in the throes of a drought, the Sonorans rented and cultivated plots of lands.[41]

North of the Santa Ana, Indians remained the predominant work force, although some Mexicans, probably Sonorans, increasingly found work there. Members of the State Agricultural Society who visited the region in 1858 reported that seventy-five persons resided on Rancho Chino, "including workmen, vaqueros, women and children, Spanish, and Indians; to feed which, the proprietor slaughters four beeves per week."[42] A passenger on the Butterfield Overland stage, while resting at the rancho that year, questioned why the land was not put to better use. The landowners "prefer to grow rich without doing any work. They have plenty of meat ready at hand and can buy what they want by selling stock. Many of them buy wheat and corn, while their lands would produce abundant crops with the greatest ease." Although the proprietor of Chino owned $300,000 worth of cattle, "yet at our breakfast, here, we had neither butter nor milk, without which the merest hod carrier in New York would think his meal incomplete. Their cattle dot the plains for miles around, and their land could produce everything; but they have not even the comforts of a Massachusetts farmer among the rocky hills." He could only imagine "what a different

---

40. Newmark, *Sixty Years*, 266.
41. S. Haley, testimony, in The Anaheim Water Company vs. The Semi-Tropic Water Company, 322–23. See also Stephenson, *Don Bernardo Yorba*, 94.
42. *Transactions of the California State Agricultural Society*, 290.

spectacle these fertile valleys would present were they peopled by some of our sturdy, industrious eastern farmers."[43]

Industrious eastern farmers would arrive in due time but in the meantime, Indians remained the work force on Rancho Azusa. There they often manifested the same inclination to drink as did those living in Los Angeles. The daily work records attest to this fact. On Sunday, December 26, 1858, for example, it was reported that all the Indians were drunk and that the carpenter (apparently an American or Mexican) had shot an Indian in the face "inflicting a very dangerous wound." The carpenter was confined to his room.[44] From January through March the following year Indians were reported being drunk on Sundays and on many Mondays they were too sick to work. Yet, Tuesdays through Saturdays they attended to their duties—chopping wood, breaking horses, and maintaining the vineyard.[45] Although some Indians resided on his rancho as a permanent work force, Henry Dalton also relied on those who worked intermittently. In 1859 he noted that the Mountain Cahuillas, led by Juan Antonio, were "constantly going and coming[.] Sometimes there were 20, sometimes there were none, it depended on their wants." Dalton also hired Desert Cahuillas under the command of Cabezón.[46] Of the 121 individuals residing on the rancho in mid-1860, 41 were Indians.[47]

Dalton's work reports for 1860 are silent, but on Saturday, November 3, 1861, they state that Indians were building houses for themselves. On Saturday, November 23, they worked on a fence, hauled stakes, and cleaned wheat. The following day, however, some stole aguardiente from the still and got drunk. None showed up for work on Monday. In mid-December, Dalton caught

---

43. Ormsby, *The Butterfield Overland Mail*, 112.
44. "Daily Occurrences at Azusa," vol. 2, December 26, 1858, Henry Dalton Collection, DL 1139.
45. Ibid., January–March 1859.
46. Deposition of Henry Dalton in George McCougall, claimant vs. the United States. In the United States Court of Claims, at Washington, D.C. Special files of the Office of Indian Affairs, 1807–1904, Special File 266, Microcopy 574, Roll 73. United States National Archives.
47. Population Schedules of the Census of the United States, 1860, Microcopy 653, Roll 59, Washington, D.C., United States National Archives.

and punished an Indian for stealing flour, but he failed to identify those who broke into his store and stole some wine. On January 9 Indians were reported putting in poles and roofing the privy. One plowed, two chopped wood, and the rest gathered cuttings in the vineyard. Two weeks later Indians broke into the store and stole two gallons of liquor.[48] Because most of the Indian workers were Mountain Cahuillas, Dalton had to trod a fine line when it came to dealing with their chief, Juan Antonio. Thus, when Juan Antonio arrived on Dalton's rancho on June 16, 1862, demanding that an individual named Guaty be turned over to him, Dalton promptly delivered the Indian. Apparently Guaty had killed one of Juan Antonio's men. Given Juan Antonio's reputation for strict justice, Guaty's fate, most likely, was execution.[49]

Whether the approximately fifty Indians working on nearby Rancho La Puente were also subjected to Juan Antonio's authority is not known, but they performed valuable service for its owner, William Workman. They managed 3,000 head of cattle and 600 horses, and tended to 10 acres of peach, pear, and apple trees, and vines, figs, and pomegranates. They probably made up the main work force that built a church for Workman. Constructed with bricks in the Gothic style, it was forty-eight by twenty-four feet inside; its sixteen inch walls with six abutments rose nineteen feet, its steeple an additional fifteen feet.[50]

On Santa Gertrudis, Indians tended to 3,000 head of cattle, 300 to 500 horses, and flocks of sheep.[51] But as on the other ranchos, some drank too much. In mid-April the body of an Indian named Mateo was found dangling from a limb of a sycamore tree. An investigation concluded that he had hanged himself. The *Star* reported that Mateo "was not only known as a faithful and obedient servant, but one who was not inclined to drink. On this

---

48. "Daily Occurrences at Azusa," vol. 4, November–December 1861, January–March 1862, Henry Dalton Collection, DL 1141.
49. "Daily Occurrences at Azusa," vol. 4, June 16, 1862, Examples of the punishment inflicted by Juan Antonio can be found in Phillips, *Chiefs and Challengers*, 52–53.
50. John Quincy Adams Warren to editors, *American Stock Journal* 3 (June 1861) in Gates, ed., *California Ranchos*, 110–12.
51. Ibid., 109.

occasion, however, a bottle two-thirds full of ardent spirits was found near the body."[52] If other Indian workers on Rancho Santa Gertrudis drank, it did not prevent them from digging a six mile zanja from the San Gabriel River and four separate ditches to irrigate 7,000 fruit trees.[53]

They also produced a unique product. By 1861 their employer had introduced a variety of sorghum called broom corn. From the panicles, a dozen or more Indians manufactured brooms. According to a visitor, John Quincy Adams Warren, the brooms "appear to be of excellent quality."[54] Near the town of El Monte, F. W. Gibson also raised broom corn, and recently had manufactured 3,000 brooms, but it is not known if they were produced by Indians.[55] Exclusive of the corn, it cost 11¢ to manufacture a broom, and a dozen brooms sold for $3.00.[56] At the end of 1862, Los Angeles County had 680 acres of broom corn under cultivation.[57]

Warren also visited Rancho Cucamonga where he observed 150,000 vines growing on 150 acres. The vineyard was irrigated by four small zanjas that were fed by a larger one that tapped a spring half a mile away. "The wine made here is the most celebrated in the country, on account of its peculiar, rich flavor, being some twenty per cent above Los Angeles wine in saccharine matter." The harvest of the past season had resulted in about 20,000 gallons of principally white wine. The Indian workers also harvested large numbers of prickly-pears, the juice of which they "highly esteemed" for its "delicious flavor."[58]

From May 1862 to March 1867, J. W. Gillette served as clerk of the vineyard and storekeeper. Also working on the ranch were a superintendent and his assistant, a foreman, a blacksmith, a carpenter, two Hawaiian cooks, a few Mexicans, and Indians from Temecula, San Luis Rey, and the desert. At the time of the grape

---

52. *Los Angeles Star*, April 13, 1861.
53. Warren to editors, *American Stock Journal* (June 1861): 109.
54. Ibid.
55. Ibid., (April 1861): 100.
56. Newmark, *Sixty Years*, 261–62.
57. *Los Angeles Star*, February 28, 1863.
58. Warren to editors, *American Stock Journal* 3 (July 1861): 116.

harvest, the number of Indians often swelled to seventy. Payment was in dry goods and provisions. On request, Indians also were paid in calico, overalls, combs, mouth organs, and aguardiente. "The Sabbath was a day of debauchery with many," remembered Gillette, "and it was woeful file that lined up for work Monday morning. A few were wise, and went away to their tribal homes fat, well clothed and contented."[59]

Robert S. Carlisle, now owner of Rancho Chino, presented a bottle of "Cocomungo" to a military officer when he and his unit bivouacked on his property in 1862. "This wine is the most celebrated in the Southern country," wrote a soldier, "and I am positive if the connoisseurs in this article could only test its qualities, they would use none other." He observed "cattle in such herds as would defy all human calculation to arrive at an accurate idea of the numbers." At a "distance from the house are the quarters of the Indian servants—about one hundred in number. They are exceedingly quiet, inoffensive and obedient, and are used principally to herd the stock and assist in any department of the ranch necessary."[60]

Missing from the rancho were sheep, although several ranchers had turned to this animal. In 1859 Los Angeles County exported 159,896 pounds of wool.[61] Three years later that number had increased to 597,039 pounds. The *Star* reported in late September 1862 that "there is no interest in this portion of the country which has made such vast strides in improvement and progress as sheep farming." Capitalists as well as small farmers had engaged in the business which was destined "to attain proportions which none now can even approximate." Because such "a fine animal requires no more care and attention than common stock, it is strange that all do not cultivate the finer qualities of wool." Prominent wool growers of the county included "Messrs. Corbitt & Dibblee, who have invested a large capital, and have the very finest animals, on the San[ta] Anita Rancho." To the eight to ten thousand sheep already on the ranch, more were being added. In 1862, 597,039

---

59. Gillette, "Some Indian Experiences," 158–59.
60. Anonymous to editors, *Sacramento Daily Union*, n.d., reprinted in the *Los Angeles Star*, May 31, 1862.
61. *Los Angeles Star*, February 4, 1860.

pounds of wool were shipped from San Pedro. The producers sold their fine wool to exporters at 22¢ per pound. In New York it was resold at about 30¢ per pound. Of the twenty-five individuals exporting wool that year, thirteen had Spanish surnames, and some were well known Californios, such as Felipe Lugo, Pío Pico, and Ignacio Palomares.[62] Obviously, Mexicans as well as Americans, had adapted to new economic opportunities.

Floods, disease, and drought, however, disrupted the local economy.[63] Those shifting from cattle to sheep did so at the most opportune time. The heavy rains that saturated the San Bernardino Valley in the winter of 1861 were followed in January by a heavy snow runoff in the mountains. The Santa Ana River turned into a deluge that destroyed the small farming community of San Salvador at Agua Mansa. No one died, however.[64] Down river, some of the ranchos, including Santiago de Santa Ana and Los Alamitos, were inundated. The town of Anaheim, although four miles from the river, came under four feet of water. Several of its vineyards were damaged. One person was swept away and drowned.[65] Large numbers of cattle also perished.[66]

The smallpox epidemic that followed hit the Cahuillas particularly hard. The *Star* reported on February 21, 1863 that Juan Antonio had contracted the disease and that the Cahuilla had fled their village of Sahatapa in the San Timoteo Canyon, leaving their chief behind. Shortly after, five Indians died, including Juan Antonio.[67] Two years later, an Indian agent reported that the Cahuilla, now under the leadership of Manuel Largo, numbered 703 men, women, and children, possessed 60 horses and cows, 200 hundred sheep, and were "much scattered."[68]

Dispersal took place as a drought again struck the region.[69] On

---

62. Ibid., September 27, 1862.
63. For an account of the destruction, see Cleland, *Cattle on a Thousand Hills*, 117–37.
64. Vickery, *Defending Eden*, 67–68.
65. Guinn, "Exceptional Years," 36.
66. Cleland, *Cattle on a Thousand Hills*, 130.
67. *Los Angeles Star*, February 21 and 28, 1863.
68. W. E. Lovett, Special Indian Agent, to Superintendent of Indian Affairs Austin Wiley, n.p., n.d., [1865], *Report of the Commissioner of Indian Affairs*, 124.
69. No rain fell during the fall and winter of 1862 and the spring of 1853. Cleland, *Cattle on a Thousand Hills*, 130–31.

January 23, 1864, the *Star* explained that "owing to the unusual drought, little or no farming has been commenced, while the prospects of the ranchero are gloomy in the extreme. During the present winter only two rains have occurred, one in November, and a slight shower in January.... The hills are now as red and arid as we ever saw them." On some ranchos one half of the stock perished from hunger.[70] The *Semi-Weekly News* recorded the same scene: "The cattle of Los Angeles County are dying so fast in many places.... that the large rancheros keep their men busily employed in obtaining hides. Thousands of carcasses strew the plains in all directions, a short distance from this city, and the sight is harrowing in the extreme. We believe the stock interests of this county, as well as the adjoining counties, to be 'played out' entirely. Famine has done its work, and nothing can now save what few cattle remain on the desert California ranches."[71]

The drought convinced many ranchers to either diversify or subdivide. Some turned to grains and fruits, others cashed in.[72] An individual writing in December 1865 to the editor of the *Semi-Weekly News* maintained that "stock raising has heretofore been a great drawback to agriculture in this county, but the decline in the price of cattle for the last few years has induced many of the land owners to dispose of their lands in small bodies to cultivators of the soil, which has added greatly to the revenues and population of the county. The wisdom of this policy is seen and felt, and it is hoped will be still further pursued. The emigration of industrious farmers, with their families, from the Atlantic States will be great for years to come."[73]

And come they did. The end of the Civil War released thousands from military service and some sought a new life in California. The settlers demanded small farms which put pressure on the ranchers to subdivide their estates. Thus in 1867 began the first of several real estate booms that would greatly subordinate stock raising to crop growing. In just thirteen years the number

---

70. *Los Angeles Star*, January 23, 1864.
71. Quoted in Cleland, *From Wilderness to Empire*, 294.
72. Guinn, "Exceptional Years," 37; Guinn, "Los Angeles in the Late Sixties," 63–64.
73. *Los Angeles Semi-Weekly News*, December 8, 1865.

A Useful People

of farms in Los Angeles County would total 1,940 and would be valued at $12,099,000. The farms would harvest $1,865,000 worth of produce.[74] Because industrious farmers needed fewer workers than did rancheros, there seems to be a correlation between an increase in fruit farming and the rise in Indian unemployment.[75]

Unemployment may also have increased as land owners shifted from one animal over another. As the numbers of cattle declined in Los Angeles County, those of sheep increased. In 1866, cattle totaled 17,252 head, but in 1867 the number dropped to 12,530. During the same period, sheep increased from 135,000 to 148,700.[76] Wool production went from 450,000 pounds in 1867 to 620,000 pounds in 1868.[77] Some of the vaqueros may have found work as shepherds and shearers, but it is difficult to assess how flexible they were in "dismounting" to labor. In other areas of Latin America, their counterparts did not always adjust very well to economic transitions.[78]

Tending sheep required fewer workers than managing an equal number of cattle. And even though figures are lacking, some vaqueros may have been released in 1869 when Rancho San Pedro ended the annual matanza. The owners had turned to sheep raising, and in a few years about 11,000 sheep would be browsing on the rancho. They were sheared twice a year, each sheep producing about eight pounds of wool per clip. Each of the thirty shearers received 4½¢ per sheep, averaging forty sheep per day. All were Mexicans.[79]

San Pedro would survive longer than many ranchos, but subdividing the great estates had already become a common practice. In 1860 immigrant J. L. Rose had bought 1,300 acres of Rancho San Pasqual for a little more than a dollar per acre. On the section of the estate known as La Presa were the remains of the dam built by the neophytes of Mission San Gabriel. A few years later he purchased 640 acres of Rancho Santa Anita for $5,000 and thus

---

74. Cleland, *Cattle on a Thousand Hills*, 172–75; Bancroft, *History of California*, 6: 522.
75. Elliott, *History of San Bernardino and San Diego Counties*, 88.
76. *Los Angeles Star*, September 5 and 12, 1868, September 18, 1869.
77. Ibid., September 18, 1869.
78. See Slatta, *Cowboys of the Americas*, 28–67.
79. Gillingham, *The Rancho San Pedro*, 225–26. Franklyn Holt, "The Los Angeles and San Pedro," 327–48.

participated along with other buyers in the reduction of the old rancho from 13,000 to 8,000 acres. Rose acquired the additional land to meet the increasing demand for his wines and to experiment with new varieties of grapes. Two hundred and fifty acres of the newly acquired land were cleared and planted with Blaue Elben and Burger vines.[80]

As recalled by Rose's son, clearing the land of chaparral, cactus, elders, sagebrush, and large weeds was done by a dozen or fifteen "Mexicans and domesticated Indians, who with their families lived at the Rancheria, near La Presa," where the old village of Akuuronga was located. Young Rose detected little difference between Mexicans and Indians: "Their modes of living were the same. They fraternized readily and frequently intermarried." Their village, however, exhibited distinctly Indian characteristics:

> The Rancheria, as we called the place where the workmen lived, was a plot of ground about five acres in extent. Their small huts were made of tule (bulrush), which grew in the swamp near by. The tule was stood upright six inches in thickness for the sides of the house, held in place by thin willow rods within and without, fastened together by pieces of raw cowhide. The roofs were made of the same material and construction. Mother earth was the floor. Their picturesque little abodes were proof against rain and were warm and comfortable. For a kitchen, a lean-to made of brush, open on one side was built—stoves were rarely used, but in their stead a number of flat stones conveniently placed about the fire to support the cooking utensils.[81]

The need for more workers forced J. L. Rose in 1871 to recruit members of another racial group then making itself felt in the Los Angeles region—the Chinese. His son remembered that the arrival of twelve Chinese created "quite a commotion amongst the native laborers, but it was purely curious and not resentful. The two factions soon fraternized and had a fine time trying to teach each other a few words of their respective languages, of which mixture they made a fine jargon."[82] Whether the Chinese participated

---
80. Rose, *L. J. Rose of Sunny Slope, 1827–1899*, 52–55, 81–84.
81. Ibid. 55.
82. Ibid, 81. The emergence of Chinese labor in California is discussed in Richard Steven Street, *Beasts of the Fields*, 235–57.

A Useful People

in the harvest of late 1872 is not known, but the Indian and Mexican workers certainly did. From his vineyard of 130,000 vines, Rose produced 40,000 gallons of port wine and manufactured 12,000 gallons of brandy.[83] As explained by young Rose, the distillation and manufacturing of brandy had become increasingly sophisticated. Once the wine was

> boiled in copper stills, the vapor evolved, condensed by passing through a copper coil immersed in a large vat of continually cooled water. The product is crystal white and about one hundred and eighty proof, which is reduced to one hundred by the addition of pure water. Whiskey and brandy absorb their color from the charcoal on the inner side of the barrel staves which are charred during construction. As a means of hastening the coloring process of our brandy, we added a very small amount of syrup made by burning white sugar; this also added a slight characteristic flavor. "Rose's Sunny Slope Brandy" was a staple article with wholesale druggists all over the country. None was just like it. This little dash of syrup—the story of which never before has been publicly known—no doubt had something to do with it.[84]

In noting that the Indian and Mexican workers were "bibulously inclined," Rose implied that some of the brandy fell into their hands, but unlike that taking place on other ranches, consumption was limited mainly to Saturday nights.[85] How they obtained the liquor is not known, but Benjamin Wilson of Lake Vineyard clearly sold wine and brandy (he called it cognac) by the bottle and gallons to his Indian workers. Although sixteen of the seventeen workers purchasing liquor in 1869 used single names, suggesting they were Indians, Wilson, like most of the rancheros at this time, probably employed Mexicans as well.[86] Neither Rose nor Wilson identified the origins of the Mexican workers but many probably came from Sonora. By the 1870s, Sonorans had largely replaced Indians as the work force throughout Los Angeles County. They

---

83. Unidentified newspaper article, probably the *Daily Alta California* of February 23, 1873, in "Missions of California," CC-23, Benjamin Hayes Collection, The Bancroft Library.
84. Rose, Jr., *L. J. Rose of Sunny Slope*, 80–81.
85. Ibid., 54.
86. Lake Vineyard Wine Company, Account Sheet and Miscellaneous Papers, Benjamin Wilson Papers, WN 524, The Huntington Library.

found work as domestics, vaqueros, tradesmen, and gamblers, or took what was available.[87]

Indians, however, remained the dominant work force in San Bernardino County. The 1870 census failed to include the number of Indians in the county, but it was probably much higher than the 658 recorded for 1880.[88] Some of the Indians were the Cahuillas who had departed the San Timoteo Canyon after the death of Juan Antonio in 1863 and who had resettled on the section of Rancho Jurupa that Louis Ribidoux had acquired in 1847. Located at the foot of Rubidoux Mountain on the Santa Ana River, the settlement became known as the Spring Ranchería. By 1870 the Cahuillas and some Serranos had constructed a substantial village of rectangular houses made of brush and batten-board. And for the next two decades they hired out as laborers to the whites, especially to those developing the town of Riverside. As wage earners they purchased American-made commodities—can foods and clothing—but grew vegetables in small gardens along the river.[89]

They also worked on the rancho. As recalled by Adelaide Rubidoux Estudillo, the Indians and her father got on well together: "The Indians who did the work on the rancho were the Cahuillas and Serranos. They lived in brush houses along the river a short distance from our house. Mother was for a long time afraid of these Indians, and she would not let us go near them for fear they would steal one of us. There was no reason for her fears. My father provided liberally for the Indians and treated them well. And they were friendly to him until the last." Later, after they had left the rancho, the Cahuillas would return once a year, "make camp on the river, and remain several months, picking and drying the elderberries and blackberries that were then plentiful all along the river. Father had two beeves killed for them daily as long as they stayed."[90]

---

87. Standart, "The Sonoran Migration," 348. For an analysis of Mexican workers in Los Angeles, see Griswold del Castillo, *The Los Angeles Barrio*, 30–61.
88. Cook, *Population of the California Indians*, 55.
89. Goodman, "Spring Ranchería," 49–50.
90. Adelaide Rubidoux Estudihlo [Estudillo], Statement. In Bowman Scrapbook, Bibliography, vol. 1, pt. 1, Calif. Folio FR 920.079 S433 A–L, Los Angeles Public Library, 63. Supposedly, the statement was printed in the *Los Angeles Times Magazine* sometime in 1917, but a search failed to locate it.

Charles Nordoff visited the area in 1872 and in a popular book about California mentioned that "the farm laborers are chiefly Indians. These people, of whom California has still several thousand, are a very useful class. They trim the vines; they plough; they do the household 'chores;' they are shepherds, and trusty ones too, vaqueros, and helpers generally. Mostly, they live among the whites, and are their humble and, I judge, tolerably efficient ministers. Near San Bernardino, at any rate, I found that it was thought a great advantage for a man to 'have' Indians." Nordoff was struck that "in California parlance a man 'has' Indians, but he 'is in' sheep, or cattle, or horses."[91]

Approaching the Rancho La Laguna, Nordoff observed "open shanties" which he took for cattle sheds, but discovered they were the houses of the Indian workers. The owner acknowledged "having" Indians and paying each $15.00 per month. At his store, situated in the front room of his adobe house, "he dealt out calicoes, sugar, coffee, and other dry goods and groceries, besides grape-brandy, to his Indians and any others who chose to come." The owner said that his Indian workers were a "useful people" and quiet but Nordoff found them noisy. Sleep was difficult because "it was nearly twelve before the Indians, our neighbors, ceased their chattering and singing. They began again at four; and by five—before daylight—I arose and found these uneasy spirits sitting around the fire talking." Later in the day, he witnessed one of these "spirits," a vaquero on a "mere pony," lasso a bull with such skill that he "did not know which most to admire, the horse, or the man who had so thoroughly taught it."[92]

Special Indian Agent John G. Ames visited the San Bernardino area the following year and spoke with several Indian leaders including Manuel Largo, chief of the Mountain Cahuilla. They were living in the Cahuilla Valley, where, because of its elevation, stock raising took precedent over crop growing. Ames recommended that five to ten thousand acres of land be purchased for them near the base of the San Bernardino Mountains. The

---

91. Nordhoff, *California for Health*, 149, 155.
92. Ibid., 149–54.

Indians told him "of their willingness to labor, and say they neither intended nor wish to be a burden to the Government." Ames was convinced that "if the opportunities above suggested are afforded them, they will themselves soon defray all the expenses of the agency charged with their care. More than this, I cherish the hope that they will at no distant day become prosperous and independent agricultural communities."[93]

That "distant day" was a long time dawning but in 1875 President Ulysses S. Grant, by executive order, created nine small reservations in San Diego County and six more the following year. In 1877, to administer to all the Indians in Southern California, the Mission Indian Agency was established.[94] That year, however, the vast majority of the Indians of Southern California resided not on reservations but on lands owned by others. As reported by an Indian agent:

> Most of the larger ranchmen have about them one or several families, whom they permit to build their slight houses on the corners of the ranch, or on grounds adjoining, and in addition allow the use of water sufficient to irrigate a garden, which such Indians often cultivate. These Indians do most of the ordinary work of the ranches.... They live more or less comfortably, as the proprietor of the ranch to which they are attached is a humane or just man, or hard-hearted and a cheat.... The interests of the ranchmen generally dictate treatment at least fair enough to prevent his Indians from moving away from him. This class of Indians is pretty large. They have no difficulty in securing enough food and comfortable clothing, and some of them have learned to be thrifty and prudent.

But as acknowledged by the agent, no matter how well treated or provisioned, the Indian workers remained tenants without legal recourse. They could neither make contracts nor sue to collect wages.[95]

---

93. "Report of Special Agent John G. Ames in Regard to the Condition of the Mission Indians of California, with Recommendations," *Annual Report of the Commissioner of Indians Affairs*, 29–41.
94. *San Diego Union*, January 23, 1876. See also Edward Everett Dale, *The Indians of the Southwest*, 85–87. For the founding of reservations in San Diego County, consult Carrico, *Strangers in a Stolen Land*, 135–48.
95. J. E. Colburn to Commissioner of Indian Affairs, San Bernardino, August 15, 1877, *Annual Report of the Commissioner of Indian Affairs*, 36.

CONCLUSION

Crosscurrents

Because interpretative and definitional crosscurrents have often muddied the waters regarding the peoples and institutions discussed in this book, it now remains to dive beneath the surface in search of clarity and perspective. The positions taken by several scholars are examined, and the role of the Indian as worker is analyzed. Analysis, however, sometimes produces conclusions not anticipated or even welcomed. As advocated in the introduction, the researcher must cultivate curiosity and remain open to surprise.

Surprising to many might be the fact that for about a century a few thousand Indians managed by small numbers of Spaniards, Mexicans, Europeans, and Americans launched and sustained an economic revolution based on crop growing and stock raising that radically altered a truly vast area of Southern California. And without the wealth that the expansion produced, the region's industrial development would have been delayed. Thus from this perspective, the pueblo, rancho, and mission become more than romantic or tragic institutions of a distant and colorful past, but economic institutions that initiated a process that continues to the present.

Any analysis of the role of Indians in the economic expansion of the region must include an acknowledgment that they participated in the alteration of the landscape. To those viewing Indians as ecologists, such an admission might be dismissed as a post-contact aberration. They consider pre-contact Indians as either passive stewards of a vast, pristine nature park or as active but careful managers of a delicate environment from which its resources were obtained with minimal labor. Those of a more realistic school have drawn on archaeological evidence to conclude that prior to contact, populations sometimes declined, the quality of health often fluctuated, and food resources were not always available. Droughts, floods, and fires altered the landscape; wars, personal violence, dietary changes, migrations, and disease affected the inhabitants. From this perspective, the post-contact environmental disruption of the Los Angeles region was hardly unique.[1] It was, however, rapid and massive and as noted achieved by relatively few people. After a century of expansion, the land carried only a few more thousand people, mainly non-Indians, than it did around 1770 when it was occupied by Mukat's People and the followers of Chinigchinich. That year the Indian population was approximately 14,500. The census of 1870 put the entire population of Los Angeles and San Bernardino counties at 19,297.[2]

During the following decades, industrialization and urbanization reduced the visual evidence of the region's first century to the old section of Los Angeles, to some impressively reconstructed rancho adobes, and to the magnificently restored missions. No longer the wine-growing center of California, the pueblo has metamorphosed into a metropolis of vast dimensions.[3] No longer raising cattle by the thousands and employing Indians by the hundreds, the ranchos have evolved into cities, many bearing the names of the estates that preceded them.[4] No longer functioning as colonizing institutions, the missions have been transformed

---

1. This issue is discussed in Raab, "Political Ecology of Prehistoric Los Angeles," 23–37. For environment change affecting a neighboring people, see Gamble, *The Chumash World at European Contact*, 32–36.
2. O'Neil, "The Acjachemen in the Franciscan Mission System," 142–44; Elliott, *History of San Bernardino and San Diego Counties*, 33.
3. See Fogelson, *The Fragmented Metropolis*.
4. See Robinson, *Ranchos Become Cities*.

into parish churches, research centers, art depositories, and tourist attractions.[5] Defenders and denigrators of the mission system have benefitted from the restoration of the missions and the preservation of the documentation produced in them. But some members of both factions have used the documentation to advance their own agendas rather than to address important historical issues. By focusing either on "bad" or "good" missionaries, for example, they have overlooked the importance of Indians in sustaining the system that the missionaries introduced.

Scholars have also overlooked the continuity of labor linking the pre- and post-contact periods. At the missions, the neophytes received training in a variety of crafts and thus produced a variety of products. But acquiring new skills did not necessarily result in the loss of old ones. Learning to produce wool clothing on looms did not eliminate the ability to manufacture rabbit-skin robes. Learning to work in adobe did not replace knowledge of the tule's utility. New tools and techniques may have replaced old ones, but for millennia Indians had been inventing new tools and experimenting with ways to best manage the environment. In time, of course, some skills were lost and some individuals born at the missions may never have mastered them.

In the spheres of food procurement and food production, the continuity of labor is also evident. The gentiles who first met the missionaries provided them with a variety of foods they had procured through traditional modes of labor. Their labor practices are not what changed but rather the destination of their products. Food procurement, moreover, never ceased at the missions, and when droughts or other calamities disrupted food production, it became an important means of survival. Moreover, the transition from one mode to another presented few difficulties. To the harvesting and processing of wild foods such as acorn was added the harvesting and processing of domesticated foods such as barley. To use a more obvious example, picking berries was not much different from harvesting grapes. To the hunting and processing of wild

---

5. Weber, "San Fernando, Rey de España: Its Role in the New Millennium," 383–400; Pauley and Pauley, *San Fernando Rey de España*, 313–21.

animals such as deer was added the slaughtering and processing of domesticated animals such as cattle.

The continuity of work from village to mission, it should be noted, did not necessarily translate into the contentment of work, merely that the transition may not have been as difficult as sometimes is thought. Nevertheless, prior to colonization, food procurement was seasonal. This resulted in an intermittent rather than a steady effort. In the mission, food and commodity production called for a continuous effort in which labor was divided into units of time: years into months, months into weeks, weeks into days, and days into hours. For Indian women, whose work had always been continuous, the transition may have been less dramatic than for men, who once enjoyed considerable leisure time. In fact, the time women spent laboring per day may have been less in some missions than in some villages.

Suggesting such a possibility is a far cry from defending the mission system. Without question and rightly so, the mission remains the most controversial institution founded by the Spanish in their colonies, and classifying it has produced some confusion. For example, according to Francis F. Guest, "In the Spanish mission there was something of the Spanish monastery, the Spanish hacienda, the Spanish guild, the Spanish town, the Spanish hospital, the Spanish school, and even the Spanish family."[6] Mission social structure also resembled that found in institutions where a small, supervisory staff controls a population majority, such as boarding schools, penitentiaries, and slave plantations. This point was made in an article I wrote postulating that social structure produced the Indian discontent that determined the demise of the mission system. By emphasizing structure over function, however, I overlooked the role of Indian labor in perpetuating the system.[7] In an essay that in part challenged my conclusions, Clement W. Meighan asserted that the mission might be compared to "a corporation-owned estate" from which the Indians, whom he called serfs, could not be separated.[8] But David Sweet seems to

---

6. Guest, "Cultural Perspectives," 33.
7. Phillips, "Indians and the Breakdown," 291–302.
8. Meighan, "Indians and California Missions," 197.

be agreeing with me when he wrote: "In practice, the mission was more like the slave plantation or the highland hacienda than like the semi-independent *pueblo de indios* of the colonial core areas, and more like the prison/reform school or the military base than like any other modern social institution."[9]

According to Sherburne F. Cook, the mission formed a communal system in which "the labor contributed by the individual went into a common pool from the resources of which the worker received his support—food, shelter, clothing, and other necessities." In theory, all the products the workers produced were for their benefit and ultimately they would inherit the system they created. But the system was defective because recently incorporated neophytes failed to comprehend that their immediate labor would produce remote results. "Consequently, in order to set up a workable scheme, the church administrators were obliged to exercise a coercion which rapidly induced the development of a full-scale forced labor system." As a result, Indians equated labor with punishment.[10]

Cook makes some excellent points but he emphasized the static over the dynamic; that is, he defined the missions when they were fully developed and thus failed to account for their development. Over time the Indian workers may have come to realize that their work had long-term consequences and thus did not always equate labor with punishment. And coercion did not inevitably evolve into forced labor.

Regarding limited physical movement, forced labor, physical abuse, denial of property rights, and restrictions on technological development, Laurence H. Shoup and Randall T. Milliken have found similarities between the mission system and chattel slavery. But they noted that the mission system differed from chattel slavery in that Indians were not sold, children were not separated from their parents, and the neophytes had some legal rights. The mission system also shared similarities with feudalism in that people were restricted in their physical movements, they were forced to labor, and they had no property rights. But feudalism differed from the

---

9. Sweet, "Ibero-American Frontier Mission," 19.
10. Cook, *Conflict*, 301.

mission system in that physical abuse was uncommon and populations remained steady. Shoup and Milliken's conclusion that the mission system was "similar to feudalism" but in practice "resembled slavery" exemplifies the difficulty in defining it.[11]

Other scholars also insist that slavery or something akin to it characterized mission labor. To Robert Archibald, "The California missions were not agents of intentional enslavement, but rather rapid and therefore violent social and cultural change.... The result in many cases was slavery in fact although not in intent."[12] To Steven Hackel, "Indian laborers at the missions were neither enslaved nor indentured servants; in essence, they were a semicaptive labor force."[13]

Labor historian Richard Street has classified the Indian workers not by what they were but where they worked. "Inside workers" built things, butchered cattle, made shoes, plastered walls, and served as pages and assistants to the missionaries. "Outside workers" were the field hands who were spread over the countryside laboring in the fields, gardens, vineyards, and orchards. Those who became vaqueros managed sheep, cattle, horses, and mules.[14]

Street, however, failed to account for the social complexity of the mission, in particular the hierarchy of work. Pages held a higher status than those butchering cattle, even though both were "inside workers." And lumping the vaquero with the gardener as an "outside worker" ignores the elite status he held at his mission. Moreover, many of the fields, vineyards, gardens, and orchards were adjacent to the mission compound, so not all field hands were spread over the countryside. During the harvest and rodeos, "inside workers" often lent a hand and butchering occurred not in the compound but where the cattle were slaughtered. Although a denigrator of the mission system, Street acknowledged the importance of the Indian workers and resisted calling them "slaves."

---

11. Shoup and Milliken, *Iñigo of Rancho Posolmi*, 82–85. Even *In Land and Society in Colonial Mexico*, the classic study of the hacienda, Francois Chevalier is a bit inconsistent, identifying the system as serfdom at one time and the Indian workers as peons at another. See pages 69 and 278.
12. Archibald, "Indian Labor at the California Missions," 181.
13. Hackel, *Children of Coyote*, 281.
14. Street, *Beasts of the Field*, 25.

Attempts at defining rancho labor have also led to confusion. Charles Dwight Willard determined in 1901 that "the actual labor of the country was performed by the Indians, who were held in servitude, and may be compared to negro slaves of the southern states. The upper class Spaniards [Mexicans] may be compared in an industrial sense to the slave holders of the south.... and, finally the lower class Californians may be likened to the poor whites of the slave states."[15] With a limited secondary literature upon which to draw, in 1946 Carey McWilliams cited Willard, but what may have sounded profound then, seems simplistic today.[16] Still, decades later Tomás Almaguer, after rejecting numerous labels applied to the rancho, reluctantly concluded that "if imprecise analogies must be drawn," then life on the rancho was strikingly similar "to that of life on an American southern plantation."[17] A more balanced assessment, however, comes from Douglas Monroy: "Though the rancho system had certain characteristics in common with other socio-economic systems in North America, neither chattel slavery nor market structures adequately describe the way Californios organized production or their social relations."[18]

"Peonage" is the term most often applied to rancho labor. Cook claimed that peonage was "developed by the ranchers and other large landowners. Here the motive of mutual benefit was completely absent. To be sure, large groups of workers might be aggregated in a single economic unit, but the fruits of their efforts, particularly regarding capital improvements, were almost completely absorbed by the overlord himself." Although the workers received "wages," usually in the form of homes, food, and commodities, the landlord controlled the distribution of these benefits. "Moreover," Cook continued, "in order to maintain the flow of undependable and transient Indian labor, coercion was usually resorted to. This might take the form of innocent persuasion, or economic pressure through control of food reserves, or out-and-out kidnapping and slavery."[19]

---

15. Willard, *The Herald's History of Los Angeles*, 183.
16. McWilliams, *Southern California: An Island on the Land*, 52.
17. Almaguer, "Interpreting Chicano History," 489.
18. Monroy, *Thrown Among Strangers*, 100.
19. Cook, *Conflict*, 302.

As with the missions, Cook failed to account for the origins and development of the ranchos. Late in the history of a rancho, most of the capital improvements probably did benefit the rancheros. But to claim that mutual benefits for the Indian workers were completely absent overlooks the initiative many of them exhibited on the ranchos, such as growing their own crops. By controlling the distribution of many commodities, some rancheros forced their workers into debt, but peonage was not universal. Moreover, Cook's claim that coercion was used to control undependable and transient Indian labor implies that the labor was, in fact, undependable and transient. Perhaps it was on some ranchos, but not on most of them in the Los Angeles area. Innocent persuasion may have stimulated some Indians to work harder, but it is hard to imagine the rancheros controlling food reserves to achieve the same end.

As an institution employing Indians, the town has remained beyond the purview of most scholars. An exception is Cook who noted that free labor operated on a small scale in the towns prior to the American takeover of California. Indians could "accept or relinquish employment" in the open market and when working receive "fair compensation." The pueblos needed Indian labor and the gentiles were the ones sought. "In the beginning, the labor market thus created was free and competitive, since demand exceeded supply and inducements were necessary in order to get an adequate number of workmen." But there was "a growing reluctance on the part of wild natives to come in as day labor. This attitude was due to harsh treatment, lack of adequate remuneration, and fear of involuntary conversion. Insufficient voluntary labor meant that the civilian employers went into the field and compelled natives to offer their services." Thus, the early "advantage held by the natives due to a labor shortage was by this means eliminated, and free employment reduced to a minimum."[20]

By claiming that before the American annexation free labor operated on a small scale and was limited to gentiles, Cook overlooked important data. Even before secularization some neophyte fugitives entered Los Angeles to sell their labor. After secularization many

---

20. Ibid., 302–3.

"liberated" neophytes saw in the pueblo opportunities for work that existed nowhere else except on the ranchos. Cook also was mistaken to claim that over time the Indians, fearing harsh treatment and inadequate pay, had to be induced to work as day laborers. In Los Angeles, too many workers competed for too few jobs.

At one time or another, Indians in Los Angeles, at the missions of San Gabriel and San Fernando, and on the ranchos, have been identified as "slaves," "wards," "vassals," "peons," "serfs," or "inmates." While some of the terms may fit better than others, all hinder an understanding of the initiative the Indians exhibited in seeking work, the changing relations between the workers and their employers, and the freedom many Indians possessed to simply leave if they so chose. Undoubtedly, the terms will continue in use, but by emphasizing exploitation over productivity, they make it difficult to comprehend the Indians' participation in the economic expansion of the Los Angeles region. There is, however, a neutral term that fits all adult Indians—"workers." If Indians are perceived first as workers and then as victims, their economic importance becomes more apparent and appreciated. Victimization—to be exposed and condemned—has many degrees, and seldom were the victims without choices. Depending on time circumstance, they could be efficient or lazy, reliable or untrustworthy, humble or defiant, loyal or rebellious.

Within the authoritarian social structures the priests forged at Missions San Fernando and San Gabriel, the neophytes exhibited all of these characteristics. Those structures clearly defined management and labor. Management consisted of the priest, mayordomos, and other office holders. Along with soldiers and artisans and their families, they formed a small minority of a mission's population. The responsibilities of management involved not just the guidance and inspection but also surveillance and punishment. A few of the more acculturated members of the majority allied themselves with management as aids, assistants, artists, and especially alcaldes. In fact, some of the alcaldes became so important and powerful that they might be considered middle management. Because social identity was ascriptive and cultural in base, however, even they were prevented from transferring into the dominant group.

While racial barriers persisted, social stability was imposed at the two missions. And once the major building projects had been completed and labor routines firmly established, working conditions may have improved and thus the degree of coercion may have decreased. Because San Gabriel became one of the most prosperous and one of the most heavily populated of all the twenty-one missions founded in California, it is difficult to believe that this could have been achieved only by forced labor and the fear of punishment. Clearly, the managers had the authority to determine when and for how long the neophytes labored and the power to inflict punishment on those who disobeyed. Discontent sometimes turned violent and punishment at times was excessive but fugitivism and prolonged demonstrations were rare.[21] Moreover, there is no evidence that life in the missions led to docility as maintained by some denigrators of the system.[22]

Most of the Indians at this mission apparently worked efficiently, and some such as the vaqueros worked willingly, especially during the second half of its existence. Denigrators of the mission system may disagree with this conclusion, but identifying efficiency does not mean approving of the system under which it was achieved. Furthermore, even if labor at San Gabriel devolved from the coercive to the merely compulsory, it would be a mistake to assume this process was similar at all the mission of California. The degree of coercion at some missions may have remained relatively constant, as perhaps was the case at San Fernando which had fewer neophytes and a shorter history than its neighbor. At other missions it may have increased.

No matter the degree of coercion, maintaining the educational, occupational, religious, and political inequalities inherent in the system occupied much of management's time. Keeping neophytes at

---

21. Neither San Fernando nor San Gabriel experienced mass withdrawals of Indians as occurred at some of the missions along the Central California Coast. See Phillips, *Indians and Intruders, 1769–1849*.

22. See for example, Bouvier, *Women and the Conquest of California*, 149.

the missions depended in large part on the managerial skills of the missionaries and their assistants. But they often had to deal with rapidly changing economic and political circumstances over which they had no control, such as the secularization of the missions. Secularization did not legally free the neophytes, but it served as a catalyst to freedom. It allowed them to make decisions regarding how best to reorder their lives. Some remained to claim the land collectively promised to them; others petitioned for individual land grants; some found work on the ranchos; others moved into the pueblos.

Whereas the working conditions at the missions may have forced the most discontented to leave, those in Los Angeles enticed the most enterprising to enter. Indeed, long after the mission system had ended, thus releasing the neophytes, the pueblo continued to replace and displace its Indian workers. Therefore, there was a certain continuity of Indian labor in Los Angeles from its Spanish beginnings, through its Mexican phase, and into the American period.[23] Initially, most of those seeking work were gentiles who lived in their own villages, where they governed themselves, practiced traditional ceremonies, maintained a strong family life, and worked for the pobladores at their discretion. Their basic mode of survival remained food procurement. As the vecino population increased and the land on which they grew their crops and grazed animals expanded, the Indians had no choice but to withdraw from the area or remain in villages reduced in size and numbers. The generally amicable relations forged between the settlers and Indians began to change rapidly in the 1830s as neophytes increasingly replaced gentiles as the predominant labor force. From their villages and camps within the Los Angeles district, Indians were recruited to work in the settlers' houses, fields, and vineyards.[24] In

---

23. Most studies of Indians working in urban settings are set in the post-1850 period and share similarities with Los Angeles at that time in its history. See Carrico, *Strangers in a Stolen Land*, 77–85; and Hurtado, "Indians in Town and Country," 37–51.

24. The Indian village (in its different locations) shares similarities with Indian towns created by the Spanish throughout New Spain from where labor was recruited and often exploited. Some scholars would call it a satellite of the metropolis and argue that by providing cheap labor to the metropolis, it was kept in a state of perpetual underdevelopment. See Weber, *Bárbaros*, 102, 106, 112, 211, 255; Wolf, *Europe and the People Without History*, 145–49, 367–68; Knack and Littlefield, "Native American Labor," 36–44; Frank, "The Development of Underdevelopment," 17–31; Jorgensen, "Indians and the Metropolis," 67–113.

the missions Indians were collectively governed; in Los Angeles they were individually managed.

Providing labor was not the only function of the main village wherever it was located. As a refuge for Indians recently arrived and for those released by their employers, the village may have served to reestablish friendships, strengthen kinship ties, and maintain reciprocity arrangements. Even with its violence and alcohol-related disorders, the village allowed Indians to engage in activities, especially at night after laboring for others during the day, more in keeping with their traditional past than with their restricted present.

As the growers produced more wine and brandy than they could export, a retail liquor business emerged that catered to newly arrived neophytes. It is hardly coincidental, therefore, that the arrival of the newcomers, the expansion of this business, and the rise of intra-Indian violence took place simultaneously. A labor system that had haphazardly employed gentiles evolved into one that systematically exploited neophytes. Nevertheless, because Indians were under few restrictions regarding where and when they worked, because they could leave and enter the pueblo largely at will, and because they had choices regarding their personal behavior, the labor system under which they worked was nominally a free one.

Americans modified the system. State and local laws allowing the marshal to arrest drunken and vagrant Indians ensured that the auctions held on Monday mornings would provide the growers with laborers. By paying their Indian workers in aguardiente, the vineyardists ensured that many would be arrested for drunkenness and thus recruited the following week by growers who paid their fines. Consequently, unlike the Spanish who arrived with no plans to incorporate Indians into the pueblo, the Americans established a legal precedent for retaining the Indians already there. If Indians equated labor with punishment, it may have been more pronounced in the pueblo than in the nearby missions.

The conclusion to be drawn, therefore, is that "free" labor in the American city of Los Angeles was far more detrimental to the workers than was compulsory or even coercive labor at the Spanish missions. By not belonging to an institution where discipline was enforced and some security provided, they had little protection from blatant exploitation. To those Americans who saw the violence and dissipation resulting from the exploitation as detrimental to the development of the city, the system was an anathema. Despite the protests emanating in the press, nothing was done to ameliorate the condition of the Indians, simply because the growers would have none of it. But this kind of system could not be maintained over the long run, because labor recruitment depended in large part on the perpetuation of Indian social instability. The Indians, it seems, were caught not so much in a vicious circle as in a downward spiral from which some escaped physically but few survived culturally.

Conditions differed significantly on the ranchos. Initially, few gentiles went to work on a full-time basis on the first ranchos founded in the Los Angeles area. And those who did sold their labor. Indians could choose where and when to work, and the turnover rate on many ranchos may have been high, especially as populations dispersed. Until secularization, most of the ranchos in the region remained little more than grazing tracts, and thus large numbers of workers were not needed. The breakup of the missions, however, resulted in a dramatic increase in the number of ranchos and thus a corresponding increase in the need for workers. Neophytes, most from the southern missions, supplied this need. In a short time they became the region's dominant labor force. Without neophyte labor, it is difficult to imagine the Mexican rancho becoming the socially and economically important institution it did. Upon the twin foundations of private land ownership and Indian labor evolved the quintessential Southern California rancho famous in fiction and history.[25]

At its fully developed stage, the rancho formed a social, economic, and political community that was hierarchical and paternalistic. But even though the rancheros possessed the power to reward and

---

25. The most famous fictional account of a Mexican rancho is Jackson, *Ramona*.

punish, they lacked the authority of the Spanish missionaries. Unlike the priests who sought the souls and labor of their charges, the rancheros sought only their labor. As long as their employees showed up at sunrise, they cared little about what they did after sunset. Only through a system of social and economic reciprocity were the most successful rancheros able to secure and maintain Indian labor. The ranchero was not just the Indians' employer—he might also be their friend, kinsman, fictive chief, or military leader.[26] It must be assumed that those vaqueros defending the ranchos and pursuing the stock raiders did so out of loyalty to the rancheros for whom they worked. But when vaqueros clashed with raiders, the rancho changed from a relatively peaceful institution to one that inadvertently fostered inter-Indian enmity. The raids also fostered Mexican-American military cooperation, especially after the U.S. invasion. A common enemy gave former enemies, at least temporarily, a common cause.

Long before Americans realized that Southern California was a land of opportunity, "outsiders" had already reached that conclusion. Whether coming from New Mexico to trade or from Utah to raid, members of both groups sought to obtain the wealth the ranchos produced in such great quantities. Through skill and careful planning, New Mexicans, Utes, and Paiutes engaged in economic enterprises designed to obtain a particular product. The New Mexicans exchanged woolen goods for animals that were eagerly sought in their homeland. By consuming, trading, and riding the animals obtained by the raid, the Utes and Paiutes often made better use of these animals than did the rancheros themselves.

The Indian workers on some of the large ranchos often made better use of land than did their employers. The considerable freedom that the rancheros allowed their Indian workers enabled them to grow on their own plots vegetables and in some cases grain which they consumed, exchanged, or sold. In fact, on the large ranchos, Indians consumed a large part of the grain meat, and brandy their labor produced. The result was the binding of Indians and some

---

26. Wolf and Mintz, "Haciendas and Plantations," 391–92.

rancheros in a system of economic interdependence. Because several of the rancheros in the region were naturalized Mexican citizens and because most of the first American rancheros conformed to the Mexican model, ethnicity or nationality apparently had little to do with how well a rancho was run. Rather, the managerial skills of the rancheros determined efficiency.

Throughout California, relations between rancheros and their Indian workers varied considerably. But unlike the situation on some ranchos in Northern California, there is little evidence that those in the Los Angeles region were terribly oppressive.[27] Ranchos located near the ex-missions tended to employ displaced individuals and their families, most of them neophytes. Drawing on skills acquired at the missions, they utilized Spanish and Mexican material items, produced and consumed a variety of introduced foods, and attended Mass if not regularly, at least from time to time. To manage individuals on these ranchos, especially after the American annexation of California, a system of social control developed that often was reinforced by coercive measures. Several rancheros became justices of the peace and inflicted corporal punishment on Indians suspected or convicted of crimes. Those who maintained stores on their estates and allowed for payment on credit clearly instigated economic dependency. But not every worker went into debt and some fled without paying.

In the eastern part of the region, the rancheros also hired individual neophytes but some collectively employed Indians who had never resided at a mission. Under the control of their own leaders, they remained politically independent, maintained kin organizations, built their lodges as in the past, consumed wild game and plants as well as domestic crops and animals, and conducted traditional spiritual ceremonies. Thus on some ranchos, Indian culture survived, although aspects of that culture, especially the economic, changed.

❊ ❊ ❊

---

27. See Silliman, *Lost Laborers*.

Despite the disabilities under which they labored and the deplorable depths to which many sank, for over a century the Indians of the Los Angeles region contributed in instrumental ways to the agricultural, mainly "horizontal," expansion of the Los Angeles region. Although largely excluded from its industrial or "vertical" development, they and all the Indians of Southern California continued to provide important labor for farmers, ranchers, and growers well into the twentieth century. From their hovels on the outskirts of towns, bands of itinerant grape pickers and sheep shearers departed seasonally to work on nearby ranches and farms and in Los Angeles, Anaheim, and San Diego. Some men raised grain and animals which they sold to whites, while others worked as cowboys and day laborers. Some women turned their ancient expertise of weaving baskets and manufacturing pottery into commercial enterprises, while others produced lace so intricate that it astounded those purchasing it.[28]

Residing in a region destined to attract large numbers of people from the eastern United States and northern Mexico, however, the Indians were eventually overwhelmed by those quite willing to undertake the work they had long monopolized. Of course, the phenomenon of workers of one culture competing with and replacing those of another—a process that continues today—comes as no surprise even to those only remotely familiar with California's labor history.

Perhaps less known is the irony of that history. Whereas the missionaries and rancheros of Southern California long ago lost their estates, Cahuillas, Serranos, and other Indians of the region now reside on reservations created from the lands that the intruders once claimed. Even some Tongva, once thought by whites to be extinct, have emerged to announce their presence and declare their intentions.[29]

---

28. See Carrico and Shipek, "Indian Labor in San Diego County," 198–217; and DuBois, "The Indian Woman as Craftsman," 391–93. For a first hand account of Indian at work in San Diego County, see Brown, "Indian Grape Pickers in California," 554–58.
29. Consult Jurmain and McCawley, *O, My Ancestor*; Valdez-Singleton, "Surviving Urbanization"; Trafzer, *The People of the San Manuel Indian Reservation*; and Bean and Bourgeault, *The Cahuilla*.

Glossary

Acequia	Irrigation ditch, term used less in California than zanja
Administrador	Individual in charge of a mission during secularization
Adobe	Sun-dried brick made of sand, clay, and straw; a dwelling or construction made of such bricks
Aguardiente	A brandy distilled from grapes
Albérchigo	Cling-stone peach tree
Alcalde	Mayor or magistrate, often a member of a municipal council; an Indian leader elected by the neophytes at his mission
Almud	Dry measure equal to 4.275 quarts
Arroba	Bulk weight equal to about twenty-five pounds
Arroyo	Creek or stream
Asistencia	Mission outpost with resident neophytes but not a permanent priest. Sometimes called a visita
Atole	Cooked ground, dry grains mixed with water. A staple at the missions
Ayuntamiento	Town council
Bali	Notched stick used to brand animals
Barzón	Strip of braided leather or twisted fiber

Brea	Pitch, rosin, tar, bitumen, asphalt
Caballada	A herd of about twenty-five horses, to be ridden rather than used as draft animals
Caballero	Horseman, gentleman
Californio	A Mexican born or raised in California
Cañada	Gully or ravine
Cañón	Ravine, gorge, canyon
Caporal	Overseer of a rancho who works for a mayordomo
Carreta	Ox drawn two-wheeled cart
Ciudad	City
Comal	Griddle
Comandante	Military commander
Comisionado	Noncommissioned officer with judicial authority in a pueblo
Convento	Main mission building
Cotón	Woolen shirt or blouse worn by neophytes
Cuartillo	About a pint of liquid
Cuera	From the word *cuero* which means "hide" or "leather." Sleeveless, leather armor jacket worn by soldiers.
Dehesas	Pasture lands of a pueblo
Diegueños	Originally Indians attached to Mission San Diego, but now a tribal/linguistic group called Kumeyaay
Dormitorio	Mission dormitory for boys and unmarried young men
Ejidos	Distant pasture lands of a pueblo
Enramada	Arbor, shed
Era	Bed, plot, or patch of ground for cultivation
Escolta	Squad of soldiers assigned to a mission
Estancia	Farm or rancho of a mission
Fanega	A dry measure of weight of about 1.6 bushels and a measurement of land equivalent to 8.8 acres

Feria	Fair
Frezada	Wool blanket, brought to California from New Mexico after 1830
Gabrielinos	Originally Indians attached to Mission San Gabriel but now a tribal/linguistic group called Tongva
Gente de razón	People of reason, as the civilian Spanish-speaking people of California called themselves
Gentil	A gentile or non-baptized Indian
Hacienda	A large estate, a term used more in Mexico proper than in California
Huerta	Garden or orchard
Indianilla	Printed calico
Inválido	Retired soldier, but not necessarily one with a disability
Isleño	Island Indian
Jabonería	Mission soap factory
Jacal	Indian lodge often made of tules
Jáquima	Hackamore or bitless bridle
Jerga	Coarse woolen cloth produced at the missions, from which the neophytes made tunics, blouses, and petticoats
Juaneños	Originally Indians attached to Mission San Juan Capistrano but now a tribal/linguistic group
Juez de campo	Field judge, the official in charge of rodeos and in settling cattle disputes (see ch. 4)
Juez de paz	Judge or justice of the peace, an official with local judicial authority
Legua	League equal to about 2.6 miles
Llavero(a)	Keeper of the keys at a mission
Llaves	Keys
Lodo	Mud or mud-mortar

Luiseños	Originally Indians attached to Mission San Luis Rey, but now a tribal/linguist group
Manada de yeguas	A herd of between twenty-five and sixty breeding mares led by a stallion
Mano	Stone for grinding seeds and grains on a metate
Manta	Coarse cotton cloth; a blanket
Manteca	Tallow droppings from butchered cattle; lard
Matanza	Massive stock killing, usually cattle but sometimes horses
Matrona	Matron who supervised unmarried Indian women and girls in their mission dormitory
Mayordomo	Foreman or supervisor at a mission or on a rancho
Metate	Slab of stone on which acorn seeds, corn, and other grains were ground
Mochila	Leather blanket thrown over the saddle, through which the pommel and cantle protrude
Monjerío	Mission dormitory for girls and unmarried women
Montadura	Accoutrements for a vaquero's horse
Neófito	Neophyte or baptized Indian
Olla	Pottery jar with a small mouth for storing seeds and hauling water
Paisano	Fellow countryman
Palizada	Palisade or stockade
Panocha	Coarse brown sugar molded into small cakes
Peon	Indian gambling game
Peón	Unskilled, often exploited worker
Peso	Monetary unit equivalent to the dollar (see ch. 4)
Pinol(e)	Parched corn, ground and mixed with sugar and water to be drunk
Piñón	Pine nut
Plaza	Town square, fortified town

Glossary

Poblador	Settler usually in a town
Poblano	Settler
Pozole	A thick soup served at the missions consisting of cornmeal, beans, meat, and other ingredients
Pozolera	Mission kitchen. *Pozolera(o)* can also mean the person who cooks in the *pozolera*.
Presa	Dam
Presidio	Fort housing a military garrison
Propios	Municipal grazing lands to be rented or leased
Ranchería	An Indian settlement of one or more villages
Ranchero	Rancher or farmer
Rancho	Either a mission estancia or a track of land consigned or granted to an individual
Real	Unit of currency of eight to a peso
Realengas	Royal town lands from which settlers received plots
Reata	Leather braided rope for roping cattle and other animals
Regidor	Either a Spanish, Mexican, or Indian councilman, the latter elected by the neophytes at his mission
Rejón	Stick
Rodeo	Roundup of stock, usually cattle
Sala	Reception room or parlor in a mission's convento
Sarape (serape)	A small blanket worn over the shoulders
Sebo	Tallow
Síndico	Town attorney or advocate/representative of a mission
Sitio de ganado mayor	One square league of 4,316 acres
Solar	House lot in a town
Sonoran (Sonoranian)	Resident of Sonora, who often became a second-class citizen in Mexican California
Suerte	Track of town land on which to grow crops
Taparabo	Strip of woolen cloth like a breechclout

	wrapped around the waist and under the legs of a male neophyte
Te Deum Laudamus	A traditional Latin hymn of praise to God
Tule	Bulrush used by Indians and others as a building material. The Spanish word derived from Náhuatl *tullin*.
Vaquero	Cowboy or ranch hand, often an Indian
Vara	Measurement of length just under a yard
Vecino	Civilian, usually a resident of a pueblo
Visitador general	An inspector from the government or the church
Zanja	Irrigation ditch or canal
Zanja madre	Main or mother ditch
Zanjero	Official in charge of maintaining the zanjas

Bibliography

Primary Sources

The Bancroft Library, University of California, Berkeley
  Archive of California. Unbound Documents. C-A 63.
  Alvarado, Juan Bautista. "History of California." Vol. 1. Translated by Earl R. Hewitt. C-D 1.
  Hayes, Benjamin. Benjamin Hayes Scrapbooks. Vol. 39.
  Hayes, Benjamin. "Reminiscences." C-E 81: 3.
  Lorton, William B. "Diaries." Vol. 8. C-F 190.
  Schuerman, James Wall. "Letters." 1842–1851. 84/73c.
  Vallejo, Mariano Guadalupe. "Historical and Personal Memoirs Relating to Alta California." Translated by Earl R. Hewitt. C-D 18–22.
California Historical Society, North Baker Research Library, San Francisco, California
  Upton, Eugene. "Scrapbook no. 7."
The Huntington Library, San Marino, California
  Anonymous. "Chaguanosos and Horse Stealing in California in the Forties." George William and Helen Pruitt Beattie Collection. B-15.
  Copy book of legal cases in Los Angeles, 1840–1850. Vol. 1. HM 38278.
  Dalton, Henry. "Daily Occurrences at Azusa." Vols. 1, 2, 4, 5.
  Dalton, Henry. Indian Books-Wages and Accounts for Indian Employees on Azusa Ranch, Vols. 1, 2, 4, 5. Henry Dalton Collection. DL 1138, 1139, 1141, 1142.
  Stearns, Abel. Abel Stearns Collection. Box 11, 32, 34, 45, 53, 69.
  Walker, Josephine Maclay. "Life and Personal Reminiscences of General Andrés Pico." MC 506.

Wilson, Benjamin. Benjamin Wilson Collection. WN 1805.
Los Angeles City Library, Los Angeles, California
Estudihlo [Estudillo], Adelaide Rubidoux. Statement. Bowman Scrapbook, Bibliography. Vol. 1, pt. 1. Calif Folio fr 920.0794 S433 A–L.
Los Angeles County Museum, Los Angeles, California
Los Angeles City Archives, Office of the City Clerk. Prudhomme Collection. Vols. 1, 2, 3, 4, 6.
Santa Bárbara Mission Archive-Library, Santa Bárbara, California
Bandini, Juan. "Letter of Bandini to an Unnamed Missionary on Indian Turbulence." CMD 3629.
Pico, Pío. "Proclamation of P. Pico on Viticulture." Los Angeles, September 6, 1845. CMD 3996.
Seaver Center for Western History Research, Natural History Museum of Los Angeles
Alcalde Court Records. Vol. 7.
University of California at Los Angeles
Excerpts from Archives of Ayuntamiento, City of Los Angeles, California, 1832–1847. Miscellaneous Manuscript Collection. Collection 100, Box 117. Special Collections.

GOVERNMENT DOCUMENTS

Abstract of the Census of 1852 of the State of California. *Journal of the Senate*, 4th sess., 1853, Doc. 14.
Ames, John G. "Report of Special Agent John G. Ames in Regard to the Condition of the Mission Indians of California, with Recommendations." *Annual Report of the Commissioner of Indian Affairs to the Secretary of the Interior for the Year 1873*. U.S. Government Printing Office, 1873.
Blake, William P. *Report of a Geological Reconnaissance in California*. New York: H. Ballière, 1858.
Colburn, J. E. "Letter to Commissioner of Indian Affairs, San Bernardino, August 15, 1877." *Annual Report of the Commissioner of Indians Affairs to the Secretary of the Interior for the Year 1877*. U.S. Government Printing Office, 1877.
Fall, John C., et al. "Report of Visiting Committee to Examine Farms, Orchards, Vineyards, Nurseries, Mines, Mining, etc." *Transactions of the California State Agricultural Society during the Year 1858*. Sacramento: John O'Meara, State Printer for California, 1859.
Letters Received by the Office of Indian Affairs, 1824–81, California Superintendency, Microcopy 234, Roll 35. National Archives and Records Administration, Washington, D.C.

Lovell, C. S. "Report in Relation to the Cahuilla Indians." *Reports Received Pertaining to Indian Customs, 1853–54*. Pacific Division. Register of Letters Received and Sent. National Archives and Records Administration, Washington, D.C.

Lovett, W. E. "Report of Committee on Indian Affairs, Assembly Session, 1867–68." Benjamin Hayes Scrapbooks, 39, The Bancroft Library, University of California, Berkeley.

Stanley, J. Q. A. "Temecula Meeting." *Report of the Commissioner of Indian Affairs to the Secretary of the Interior for the Year 1865*. U.S. Government Printing Office, 1865.

Williamson, Robert Stockton. *Reports of Explorations and Surveys to Ascertain the Most Practicable and Economical Route for a Railroad from the Mississippi River to the Pacific Ocean*. Vol. 5. Washington, D.C.: A. O. P. Nicholson, Printer, 1856.

10th Military District. Pacific Division Records. Letters Received, 1847–51. Microcopy 210. Rolls 3, 4, 6. RG 98. National Archives and Records Administration, Washington, D.C.

NEWSPAPERS

Daily Democratic State Journal, 1853
Los Angeles Semi-Weekly News, 1866
Los Angeles Star, 1851–1870
Sacramento Daily Union, 1852
San Bernardino Weekly Patriot, 1861
San Francisco Daily Alta California, 1851–1853
San Francisco Daily Herald, 1851–1852
Southern Vineyard, 1858–1859

DISSERTATIONS, THESES, AND UNPUBLISHED SOURCES

Altschul, Jeffrey H., Martin R. Rose, and Michael K Lerch. "Man and Settlement in the Upper Santa Ana River Drainage: A Cultural Resources Overview." Statistical Research: Technical Series No. 1, 1984.

The Anaheim Water Company, et al., Plaintiffs and Respondents vs. The Semi-Tropic Water Company, et al., Defendants and Appellants. Transcript on Appeal in the Superior Court of Los Angeles County, State of California, 1883. Long Beach City Library, Long Beach, California.

Frierman, Jay D. "The Ontiveros Adobe: Early Rancho Life in Alta California." Pacific Palisades, Calif.: Greenwood and Associates, 1982.

Goodman, John D. II. "Spring Ranchería: Archaeological Investigations of a Transient Cahuilla Village in Early Riverside California." M.A. thesis, University of California, Riverside, 1993.

Guest, Florian F. "Municipal Institutions in Spanish California, 1769–1821." Ph.D. diss., University of Southern California, 1961.

Johnson, John R. "The People of *Quinquina*: San Clemente Island's Original Inhabitants as Described in Ethnohistoric Documents." Santa Barbara Museum of Natural History, 1988.

King, Chester. "Ethnographic Overview of the Angeles National Forest: Tataviam and San Gabriel Mountain Serrano Ethnohistory." Vancouver: Northwest Economic Associates, 2004.

O'Neil, Stephen. "The Acjachemen in the Franciscan Mission System: Demographic Collapse and Social Change." M.A. thesis, California State University, Fullerton, 2002.

———. "The Appearance of Mountain Cahuilla at the Bernardo Yorba Rancho de Cañón de Santa Ana, on the Santa Ana River." Unpublished paper, 2008.

———. "The Appearance of Mountain Cahuilla Rancherías in the Mission San Juan Capistrano Baptismal Registers, for Stacie Wilson and her thesis." Unpublished paper, 2008.

Rumble, Josephine, compiler. "History: The Mill Creek Zanja, San Bernardino County, State of California, 1819–1937." Works Progress Administration Project No. 3428, 1937.

Wilson, Stacie L. "A GIS Based Analysis of Prehistoric and Post-Contact Mountain Cahuilla Settlement and Subsistence Patterns." M.A. thesis, Northern Arizona University, 2008.

BOOKS

Almaguer, Tomás. *Racial Fault Lines: The Historical Origins of White Supremacy in California*. Berkeley: University of California Press, 1994.

Anonymous. *Visit to Los Angeles in 1842: Unpublished Narrative of Commodore Thomas ap C. Jones, U.S. Navy*. First published in the *Daily Alta California*, April 18, 1858. Los Angeles: Privately Printed, 1960.

Archibald, Robert. *The Economic Aspects of the California Missions*. Washington, D.C.: Academy of American Franciscan History, 1978.

Atherton, Faxon Dean. *The California Diary of Faxon Dean Atherton, 1836–1839*. Ed. Doyce B. Nunis, Jr. San Francisco: California Historical Society, 1964.

Bailey, L. R. *Indian Slave Trade in the Southwest: A Study of Slavetaking and the Traffic of Indian Captives*. Los Angeles: Westernlore Press, 1966.

Bibliography

Bailey, Paul. *Walkara: Hawk of the Mountains*. Los Angeles: Westernlore Press, 1954.
Bancroft, Hubert Howe. *California Pastoral, 1769–1848*. San Francisco: The History Company, 1888.
———. *History of California*. 7 vols. San Francisco: The History Company, 1884–1890.
Barrows, David Prescott. *The Ethno-Botany of the Coahuilla Indians of Southern California*. Ed. Harry W. Lawton, Lowell John Bean, and William Bright. Banning, Calif.: Malki Museum Press, 1967.
Bartlett, John Russell. *Personal Narrative of Explorations and Incidents in Texas, New Mexico, California, Sonora, and Chihuahua: Connected with the United States and Mexican Boundary Commission during the Years 1850, '51*, Vol. 2. New York: D. Appleton and Company, 1854.
Bean, Lowell John. *Mukat's People: The Cahuilla Indians of Southern California*. Berkeley: University of California Press, 1972.
Bean, Lowell John, Lisa Bourgeault, and Frank W. Porter. *The Cahuilla*. New York: Chelsea House Publishers, 1989.
Bean, Lowell John, and William Marvin Mason, eds. *Diaries and Accounts of the Romero Expeditions in Arizona and California, 1823–1826*. Los Angeles: Ward Ritchie Press, 1962.
Bean, Lowell John, and Katherine Siva Saubel. *Temalpakh: Cahuilla Indian Knowledge and Usage of Plants*. Banning, Calif.: Malki Museum Press, 1972.
Bean, Lowell John, Sylvia Brakke Vane, and Jackson Young. *The Cahuilla Landscape: The Santa Rosa and San Jacinto Mountains*. Menlo Park, Calif.: Ballena Press, 1991.
Beattie, George William, and Helen Pruitt Beattie. *Heritage of the Valley: San Bernardino's First Century*. Oakland: Biobooks, 1951.
Beck, Warren A., and Ynez D. Haase. *Historical Atlas of California*. Norman: University of Oklahoma Press, 1974.
Beebe, Rose Marie, and Robert M. Senkewicz, eds. *Lands of Promise and Despair: Chronicles of Early California, 1535–1846*. Berkeley and Santa Clara: Heyday Books and Santa Clara University, 2001.
———, trans. and eds. *Testimonios: Early California Through the Eyes of Women, 1815–1848*. Berkeley: Heyday Books, 2006.
Beechey, Frederick. *Narrative of a Voyage to the Pacific and Beering's Strait: To Cooperate with the Polar Expeditions, Performed in His Majesty's Ship Blossom, Under the Command of Captain F. W. Beechey, in the Years 1825, 26, 27, 28*. London: Henry Colburn and Richard Bentley, 1831.
Beeler, Madison S., ed. *The Ventureño Confesionario of José Señán, O.F.M.* University of California Publications in Linguistics, Vol. 47. Berkeley: University of California Press,1967.

Beilharz, Edwin A. *Felipe de Neve: First Governor of California.* San Francisco: California Historical Society, 1971.

Bell, Horace. *On the Old West Coast: Being Further Reminiscences of a Ranger, Major Horace Bell.* Ed. Lanier Bartlett. New York: Grosset and Dunlap Publishers, 1930.

———. *Reminiscences of a Ranger or Early Times in Southern California.* Santa Barbara: Wallace Hebberd, 1927.

Black, Esther Boulton. *Rancho Cucamonga and Doña Merced.* Redlands, Calif.: San Bernardino County Museum Association, 1975.

Boscana, Gerónimo. *Chinigchinich: A Revised and Annotated Version of Alfred Robinson's Translation of Father Gerónimo Boscana's Historical Account of the Belief, Usages, Customs, and Extravagancies of the Indians of this Mission San Juan Capistrano Called the Acagchemem Tribe.* Banning, Calif.: Malki Museum Press and Morongo Indian Reservation, 1978.

Bouvier, Virginia Marie. *Women and the Conquest of California, 1542–1840: Codes of Silence.* Tucson: University of Arizona Press, 2001.

Bowman, Lynn. *Los Angeles: Epic of a City.* Berkeley: Howell-North Books, 1974.

Boynton, Margaret, and Francisco Patencio. *Stories and Legends of the Palm Springs Indians.* Palm Springs: Palm Springs Desert Museum, 1969.

Brackett, F. P. *History of Pomona Valley California with Biographical Sketches of the Leading Men and Women of the Valley Who Have Been Identified with its Growth and Development from the Early Days to the Present.* Los Angeles: Historic Record Company, 1920.

Brent, Joseph Lancaster. *The Lugo Case: A Personal Experience.* New Orleans: Searcy and Pfaff, Ltd., 1926.

Brewer, William H. *Up and Down California in 1860–1864: The Journal of William H. Brewer.* Ed. Francis P. Farquhar. Berkeley: University of California Press, 1966.

Brooks, George R., ed. *The Southwest Expedition of Jedediah S. Smith: His Personal Account of the Journey to California, 1826–1827.* Glendale, Calif.: The Arthur H. Clark Company, 1977.

Brown, Alan Kelsey, ed. *A Description of Distant Roads: Original Journals of the First Expedition into California, 1769–1770 by Juan Crespí.* San Diego: San Diego State University Press, 2001.

Brown, John Jr., and James Boyd. *History of San Bernardino and Riverside Counties with Selected Biography of Actors and Witnesses of the Period of Growth and Achievement.* Madison: Western Historical Association, 1922.

Browne, J. Ross. *Crusoe's Island: A Ramble in the Footsteps of Alexander Selkirk with Sketches of Adventure in California and Washoe.* New York: Harper and Brothers, 1864.

Bryant, Edwin. *What I Saw In California*. Lincoln: University of Nebraska Press, 1985.

Caballería y Collell, Juan. *History of San Bernardino Valley from the Padres to the Pioneers, 1810–1851*. San Bernardino: Times-Index Press, 1902.

Camarillo, Albert. *Chicanos in a Changing Society: From Mexican Pueblos to American Barrios in Santa Barbara and Southern California, 1848–1930*. Cambridge: Harvard University Press, 1979.

Carosso, Vincent P. *The California Wine Industry, 1830–1895: A Study of the Formative Years*. Berkeley: University of California Press, 1951.

Carrico, Richard. *Strangers in a Stolen Land: Indians of San Diego County from Prehistory to the New Deal*. 2nd ed. San Diego: Sunbelt Publications, 2008.

Carvalho, Solomon Nunes. *Incidents of Travel and Adventure in the Far West*. Ed. Bertram Wallace Korn. Philadelphia: The Jewish Publication Society of America, 1954.

Caughey, John, ed. *The Indians of Southern California in 1852: The B. D. Wilson Report and a Selection of Contemporary Comment*. San Marino: The Huntington Library, 1952.

Caughey, John, and LaRee Caughey, eds. *Los Angeles: Biography of a City*. Berkeley: University of California Press, 1976.

Chávez-García, Miroslava. *Negotiating Conquest: Gender and Power in California, 1770s to 1880s*. Tucson: University of Arizona Press, 2004.

Chevalier, François. *Land and Society in Colonial Mexico: The Great Hacienda*. Trans. Alvin Eustis. Berkeley and Los Angeles: University of California Press, 1963.

Christensen, Erwin O. *The Index of American Design*. New York: The MacMillan Company, 1959.

Cleland, Robert Glass. *The Cattle on a Thousand Hills: Southern California, 1850–1870*. 2nd ed. San Marino: The Huntington Library, 1951.

———. *El Molino Viejo*. San Marino: Ward Ritchie Press, 1950.

———. *From Wilderness to Empire: A History of California, 1542–1900*. New York: Alfred A. Knopf, 1944.

———. *The Irvine Ranch*. 1952. Ed. Robert V. Hine. 3rd ed. San Marino: The Huntington Library, 1962.

———. *Pathfinders*. San Francisco: Powell Publishing Company, 1929.

Cohen, Chester G. *El Escorpión: From Indian Village to Los Angeles Park*: Woodland Hills, Calif.: Periday Co., 1989.

Cole, Martin, and Henry Welcome. *Don Pío Pico's Historical Narrative*. Trans. Arthur P. Botello. Glendale, Calif.: The Arthur H. Clark Company, 1970.

Collins, Kate, ed. *Desert Hours with Chief Patencio*. Palm Springs: Palm Springs Desert Museum, 1971.

Conner, Palmer. *The Romance of the Ranchos.* Los Angeles: Title Insurance and Trust Company, 1939.

Cook, Sherburne F. *The Conflict between the California Indian and White Civilization.* Berkeley: University of California Press, 1976.

———. *The Population of the California Indians, 1769–1970.* Berkeley: University of California Press, 1976.

Coronel, Antonio Francisco, *Tales of Mexican California.* Ed. Doyce B. Nunis, Jr. Trans. Diane Avalle-Arce. Santa Barbara: Bellerophon Books, 1994.

Costo, Rupert, and Jeannette Henry Costo, eds. *The Missions of California: A Legacy of Genocide.* San Francisco: The Indian Historian Press, 1987.

Craig, Donald, ed. *William Robert Garner: Letters from California, 1846–1847.* Berkeley: University of California Press, 1970.

Cramer, Esther. *La Habra: The Pass Through the Hills.* Fullerton, Calif.: Sultana Press, 1969.

Crosby, Harry W. *Antigua California: Mission and Colony on the Peninsular Frontier, 1697–1768.* Albuquerque: University of New Mexico Press, 1994.

Crouch, Dora P., Daniel J. Garr, and Axel I. Mundigo. *Spanish City Planning in North America.* Cambridge: MIT Press, 1982.

Cutter, Donald C., trans. and ed. *Writings of Mariano Payeras.* Santa Barbara: Bellerophon Books, 1995.

Dakin, Susanna Bryant. *The Lives of William Hartnell.* Stanford: Stanford University Press, 1949.

———. *A Scotch Paisano in Old Los Angeles: Hugo Reid's Life in California, 1832–1852, Derived from his Correspondence.* Berkeley: University of California Press, 1939.

Dana, Richard Henry. *Two Years Before the Mast and Twenty-four Years After.* New York: Collier and Son Corporation, 1937.

Davis, William Heath. *Seventy-five Years in California.* San Francisco: John Howell, 1929.

Dawson, Nicholas. *California in '41, Texas in '51.* Austin and New York: Jenkins Publishing Company, 1969.

Diamond, Jared. *Guns, Germs, and Steel: The Fates of Human Societies.* New York: Norton and Company, 1997.

Duflot de Mofras, Eugène. *Travels on the Pacific Coast,* Vol. 1. Trans. and ed. Marguerite Eyer Wilbur. Santa Ana, Calif.: The Fine Arts Press, 1937.

Duggan, Marie Christine. *The Chumash and the Presidio of Santa Bárbara: Evolution of a Relationship, 1782–1823.* Santa Barbara: Santa Barbara Trust for Historic Preservation, 2004.

Duhaut-Cilly, Auguste. *A Voyage to California, the Sandwich Islands, and Around the World in the Years 1826–1829*. Trans. and ed. August Frugé and Neal Harlow. Berkeley: University of California Press, 1979.

Dumke, Glenn S. *The Boom of the Eighties in Southern California*. San Marino: The Huntington Library, 1970.

Dwinelle, John W. *The Colonial History of San Francisco*. San Diego: Frey and Smith, 1924.

Edwards, Malcolm, ed. *The California Diary of General E.D. Townsend*. Los Angeles: Ward Ritchie Press, 1970.

Elliott, Wallace W. *History of San Bernardino and San Diego Counties California with Illustrations*. Riverside, Calif.: Riverside Museum Press, 1965.

Ellison, William Henry, ed. *The Life and Adventures of George Nidever [1802–1883]*. Berkeley: University of California Press, 1937.

Engelhardt, Zephyrin, O.F.M. *The Missions and Missionaries of California*. 4 vols. San Francisco: The James H. Barry Company, 1908–1915.

———. *San Buenaventura: The Mission by the Sea*. Santa Barbara: Mission Santa Barbara, 1930.

———. *San Fernando Rey: The Mission of the Valley*. Chicago: Franciscan Herald Press, 1927.

———. *San Gabriel and the Beginnings of Los Angeles*. Chicago: Franciscan Herald Press, 1927.

———. *San Juan Capistrano Mission*. Los Angeles: The Standard Printing Co., 1922.

Engstrand, Iris H. W. *William Wolfskill, 1798–1866: Frontier Trapper to California Ranchero*. Glendale, Calif.: The Arthur H. Clark Company, 1965.

Evans, W. B. *Mexican Gold Trail: The Journal of a Forty-Niner*. Ed. Glen S. Dumke. San Marino: The Huntington Library, 1945.

Fages, Pedro. *A Historical, Political, and Natural Description of California by Pedro Fages: Written for the Viceroy in 1775*. Trans. Herbert Ingram Priestley. Ramona, Calif.: Ballena Press, 1972.

Farris, Glenn, ed. *The Diary and Copybook of William E. P. Hartnell, Visitador General of the Missions of Alta California in 1839 and 1840*. Trans. Starr Pait Gurcke. Santa Clara, Calif. and Spokane: California Mission Studies Association and The Arthur H. Clark Company, 2004.

Fogelson, Robert M. *The Fragmented Metropolis: Los Angeles, 1850–1930*. Berkeley: University of California Press, 1967.

Font, Pedro. *Font's Complete Diary: A Chronicle of the Founding of San Francisco*. Trans. and ed. Herbert Eugene Bolton. Berkeley: University of California Press, 1933.

Forbes, Jack D. *Warriors of the Colorado: The Yumas of the Quechan Nation and Their Neighbors*. Norman: University of Oklahoma Press, 1965.

Forbis, William, H. *The Cowboys*. New York: Time Life Books, 1973.

Francis, Jessie Davies. *An Economic and Social History of Mexican California, 1822–1846, Vol. 1, Chiefly Economic*. New York: Arno Press, 1976.

Frémont, John Charles. *Memoirs of My Life*, Vol. 1. Chicago and New York: Belford, Clark and Company, 1887.

Fried, Morton H. *The Evolution of Political Society: An Essay in Political Anthropology*. New York: Random House, 1967.

Froebel, Julius. *Seven Years' Travel in Central America, Northern Mexico, and the Far West of the United States*. London: Richard Bentley, 1859.

Gates, Paul W. *California Ranchos and Farms, 1846–1862, Including the Letters of John Quincy Adams Warren of 1861, Being Largely Devoted to Livestock, Wheat Farming, Fruit Raising, and the Wine Industry*. Madison: The State Historical Society of Wisconsin, 1967.

Gates, Paul W., and Clement W. Meighan, eds. *As The Padres Saw Them: California Indian Life and Customs as Reported by the Franciscan Missionaries, 1813–1815*. Santa Barbara: Santa Barbara Mission Archive-Library, 1976.

Geiger, Maynard, O.F.M. *Franciscan Missionaries in Hispanic California, 1769–1848: A Biographical Dictionary*. San Marino: The Huntington Library, 1969.

———. *Mission Santa Barbara, 1782–1965*. Santa Barbara: Franciscans Fathers of California, 1965.

Gerstacker, Friedrich. *Scènes de la Vie Californienne*. Trans. Gustave Revilliod. Geneva: Imprimerie de Jules-Gme Fick, 1859.

Gibson, Wayne Dell. *Tomás Yorba's Santa Ana Viejo, 1769–1874*. Santa Ana, Calif.: Santa Ana College Foundation Press, 1976.

Gillingham, Robert Cameron. *The Rancho San Pedro: The Story of a Famous Rancho in Los Angeles County and of its Owners the Domínguez Family*. Los Angeles: Cole-Holmquist Press, 1983.

González, Michael J. *This Small City Will Be a Mexican Paradise: Exploring the Origins of Mexican Culture in Los Angeles, 1821–1846*. Albuquerque: University of New Mexico Press, 2005.

Griswold del Castillo, Richard. *The Los Angeles Barrio, 1850–1890: A Social History*. Berkeley: University of California Press, 1979.

Guinn, J. M. *A History of California and an Extended History of Los Angeles and Environs*, Vol. 1. Los Angeles: Historic Record Company, 1915.

Gumprecht, Blake. *The Los Angeles River: Its Life, Death, and Possible Rebirth*. Baltimore and London: The Johns Hopkins University Press, 1999.

Gutiérrez, Ramón A., and Richard J. Orsi, eds. *Contested Eden: California Before the Gold Rush*. Berkeley: Published in association with the California Historical Society by the University of California Press, 1997.

Bibliography 353

Haas, Lisbeth. *Conquests and Historical Identities in California, 1769–1936*. Berkeley: Published in association with the California Historical Society by the University of California Press, 1995.

Hackel, Steven W. *Children of Coyote, Missionaries of Saint Francis: Indian-Spanish Relations in Colonial California, 1769–1850*. Chapel Hill: Published for the Omohundro Institute of Early American History and Culture, Williamsburg, Virginia, by the University of North Carolina Press, 2005.

Hafen, LeRoy R., ed. *Letters of Lewis Granger: Reports of the Journey from Salt Lake to Los Angeles in 1849, and Conditions in Southern California*. Los Angeles: Glen Dawson, 1959.

Hafen, LeRoy R., and Ann W. Hafen, eds. *Journals of Forty-Niners, Salt Lake to Los Angeles*. Lincoln: University of Nebraska Press, 1998.

———. *Old Spanish Trail: Santa Fé to Los Angeles*. Glendale, Calif.: The Arthur H. Clark Company, 1954.

Hannum, Anna Paschall, ed. *A Quaker Forty-Niner: The Adventures of Charles Edward Pancoast on the American Frontier*. Philadelphia: University of Pennsylvania Press, 1930.

Harlow, Neal. *Maps and Surveys of the Pueblo Lands of Los Angeles*. Los Angeles: Dawson's Book Shop, 1976.

Harris, Benjamin Butler. *The Gila Trail: The Texas Argonauts and the California Gold Rush*. Ed. and ann. Richard H. Dillon. Norman: University of Oklahoma Press, 1960.

Hardwick, Michael R. *Changes in Landscape: The Beginnings of Horticulture in the California Missions*. Orange County, Calif.: The Paragon Agency, 2005.

Heizer, Robert F., ed. *The Indians of Los Angeles County: Hugo Reid's Letters of 1852*. Los Angeles: Southwest Museum, 1968.

Heizer, Robert F., and Albert B. Elsasser, eds. *Original Accounts of the Lone Woman of San Nicolás*. Ramona, Calif.: Ballena Press, 1976.

Hittell, Theodore H. *History of California*, Vol. 2. San Francisco: Pacific Press Publishing House and Occidental Publishing Co., 1885.

Hornbeck, David. *California Patterns: A Geographical and Historical Atlas*. Palo Alto, Calif.: Mayfield Publishing Company, 1983.

Hunter, Burton L. *The Evolution of Municipal Organization and Administrative Practice in the City of Los Angeles*. Los Angeles: Parker, Stone and Baird Company, 1933.

Hurtado, Albert L. *Indian Survival on the California Frontier*. New Haven: Yale University Press, 1988.

Hutchinson, C. Alan. *Frontier Settlement in Mexican California: The Híjar-*

Padrés Colony, and Its Origins, 1769–1835. New Haven and London: Yale University Press, 1969.

———, trans. *Manifesto to the Mexican Republic*. Berkeley: University of California Press, 1978.

Iverson, Peter. *When Indians Became Cowboys: Native Peoples and Cattle Ranching in the American West*. Norman: University of Oklahoma Press, 1994.

Jackson, Donald, and Mary Lee Spence, eds. *The Expeditions of John Charles Frémont, vol. 1, Travels from 1838 to1844*. Urbana, Chicago, and London: University of Illinois Press, 1970.

Jackson, Helen Hunt. *Ramona: A Story*. New York: Grosset and Dunlap, 1912.

Jackson, Sheldon G. *A British Ranchero in Old California: The Life and Times of Henry Dalton and the Rancho Azusa*. Glendale and Azusa, Calif.: The Arthur H. Clark Company and Azusa Pacific College, 1977.

Jackson, Robert H. *Indian Population Decline: The Missions of Northwestern New Spain, 1687–1840*. Albuquerque: University of New Mexico Press, 1994.

Jackson, Robert H., and Edward Castillo. *Indians, Franciscans and Spanish Colonization: The Impact of the Mission System on California Indians*. Albuquerque: University of New Mexico Press, 1995.

Janssens, Agustín. *The Life and Adventures in California of Don Agustín Janssens, 1834–1856*. Ed. William H. Ellison and Francis Price. San Marino: The Huntington Library, 1953.

Johnson, John R. *The Chumash Indians after Secularization*. Bakersfield, Calif.: California Mission Studies Association, 1995.

Johnston, Bernice Eastman. *California's Gabrielino Indians*. Los Angeles: Southwest Museum, 1962.

Jones, Oakah L., Jr. *Los Paisanos: Spanish Settlers on the Northern Frontier of New Spain*. Norman: University of Oklahoma Press, 1979.

Jurmain, Claudia, and William McCawley. *O, My Ancestor: Recognition and Renewal for the Gabrielino-Tongva People of the Los Angeles Area*. Berkeley: Heyday Books, 2009.

Kenneally, Finbar, ed. *Writings of Fermín Francisco de Lasuén*. 2 vols. Washington, D.C.: Academy of American Franciscan History, 1965.

Kip, William Ingraham. *The Early Days of My Episcopate*. New York: Thomas Whittaker, 1892.

Kroeber, Theodora, Albert B. Elsasser, and Robert F. Heizer. *Drawn from Life: California Indians in Pen and Brush*. Socorro, New Mexico: Boolean Press, 1977.

La Pérouse, Jean-François de Galaup, comte de. *Voyage Round the World, Performed in the Years 1785, 1786, 1877, and 1788 by the Boussole and Astrolabe.* Vol 1. New York: Da Capo Press, 1968.

Langum, David J. *Law and Community on the Mexican California Frontier: Anglo-American Expatriates and the Clash of Legal Traditions, 1821–1846.* Norman: University of Oklahoma Press, 1987.

Laylander, Don. *Early Ethnography of the Californias, 1533–1825.* Archives of California Prehistory, Vol. 47. Salinas, Calif.: Coyote Press, 2000.

Levi-Strauss, Claude. *Structural Anthropology.* Trans. Claire Jacobson and Brook Grundfest Schoepf. New York: Doubleday and Company, 1967.

Lewis, Henry T. *Patterns of Indian Burning in California: Ecology and Ethnohistory.* Ballena Press Anthropological Papers, No. 1. Ramona, Calif.: Ballena Press, 1973.

Lichine, Alexis. *Alexis Lichine's Encyclopedia of Wines and Spirits.* New York: Alfred A. Knopf, 1968.

Lightfoot, Kent G. *Indians, Missionaries, and Merchants: The Legacy of Colonial Encounters on the California Frontiers.* Berkeley: University of California Press, 2005.

Martin, Douglas, D. *Yuma Crossing.* Albuquerque: University of New Mexico Press, 1954.

Mason, William M. *Los Angeles Under the Spanish Flag: Spain's New World.* Burbank: Southern California Genealogical Society, 2004.

———. *The Census of 1790: A Demographic History of Colonial California.* Menlo Park, Calif.: Ballena Press, 1998.

Matsumoto, Valerie J., and Blake Allmendinger, eds. *Over the Edge: Remapping the American West.* Berkeley: University of California Press, 1999.

McCawley, William. *The First Angelinos: The Gabrielino Indians of Los Angeles.* Banning, Calif.: Malki Museum Press; Novato, Calif.: Ballena Press, 1996.

McClellan, Guy R. *The Golden State: A History of the Region West of the Rocky Mountains.* Philadelphia: William Flint and Company, 1876.

McGroarty, John Steven, ed. *History of Los Angeles County.* Chicago and New York: The American Historical Society, 1923.

McWilliams, Carey. *Southern California: An Island on the Land.* New York: Duell, Sloan and Pearce, 1946.

Miller, Henry. *Account on a Tour of the California Missions.* Los Angeles: Book Club of California, 1952.

Miller, Robert Ryal. *Juan Alvarado: Governor of California, 1836–1842.* Norman: University of Oklahoma Press, 1998.

Möllhausen, Baldwin. *Diary of a Journey from the Mississippi to the Pacific Coast with a United States Expedition,* Vol. 2. Trans. Percy Sinnett. London: Longman Brown, Green, Longman and Roberts, 1858.

Monroy, Douglas. *Thrown among Strangers: The Making of Mexican Culture in Frontier California*. Berkeley: University of California Press, 1990.

Mora, Jo. *Californios: The Saga of the Hard-riding Vaqueros, America's First Cowboys*. Garden City, New York: Doubleday, 1949.

Neuerburg, Norman. *The Decoration of the California Missions*. Santa Barbara: Bellerophon Books, 1987.

Newmark, Harris. *Sixty Years in Southern California, 1853–1913*. Ed. Maurice H. and Marco R. Newmark. Los Angeles: Dawson's Book Shop, 1984.

Newmark, Maurice H., and Marco R. Newmark, eds. *Census of the City and County of Los Angeles California for the Year 1850, Together with an Analysis and Appendix*. Los Angeles: The Times-Mirror Press, 1929.

Nordhoff, Charles. *California for Health, Pleasure, and Residence*. Berkeley: Ten Speed Press, 1973.

Nunis, Doyce B., Jr., ed. *The Founding Documents of Los Angeles: A Bilingual Edition*. Los Angeles: The Historical Society of Southern California and the Zamorano Club, 2004.

Ogden, Adele. *The California Sea Otter Trade, 1784–1848*. Berkeley: University of California Press, 1975.

Ord, Edward O. C. *The City of the Angels and the City of the Saints or A Trip to Los Angeles and San Bernardino in 1856*. Ed. Neal Harlow. San Marino: The Huntington Library, 1978.

Ormsby, Waterman L. *The Butterfield Overland Mail: Only Passenger on the First West-bound Stage*. Ed. Lyle H. Wright and Josephine M. Bynum. San Marino: The Huntington Library, 1962.

Osio, Antonio María. *The History of Alta California: A Memoir of Mexican California*. Trans., ed., and ann. Rose Marie Beebe and Robert M. Senkewicz. Madison: The University of Wisconsin Press, 1996.

Palóu, Francisco, O.F.M. *Historical Memoirs of New California*, Vols. 2, 3, and 4. Ed. Herbert Eugene Bolton. Berkeley: University of California Press, 1926.

———. *Palóu's Life of Fray Junípero Serra*. Trans. and ann. Maynard J. Geiger, O.F.M. Washington, D.C.: Academy of American Franciscan History, 1955.

Pattie, James O. *The Personal Narrative of James O. Pattie*. Lincoln: University of Nebraska Press, 1984.

Pauley, Kenneth E., and Carol M. Pauley. *San Fernando Rey de España: An Illustrated History*. Spokane: The Arthur H. Clark Company, 2005.

Perissinotto, Giorgio, ed. *Documenting Everyday Life in Early Spanish California: The Santa Barbara Presidio Memorias y Facturas, 1779–1810*. Santa Barbara: Santa Barbara Trust for Historic Preservation, 1998.

Phelps, William Dane. *Alta California: 1840–1842. The Journal and Observations of William Dane Phelps, Master of the Ship "Alert."* Ed. Briton Cooper Busch. Glendale, Calif.: The Arthur H. Clark Company, 1983.

Phillips, George Harwood. *"Bringing Them under Subjection": California's Tejon Indian Reservation and Beyond, 1852–1864.* Lincoln: University of Nebraska Press, 2004.

———. *Chiefs and Challengers: Indian Resistance and Cooperation in Southern California.* Berkeley: University of California Press, 1975.

———. *Indians and Intruders in Central California, 1769–1849.* Norman: University of Oklahoma Press, 1993.

Phillips, Ulrich Bonnell. *Life and Labor in the Old South.* Boston and Toronto: Little, Brown and Company, 1963.

Pitt, Leonard. *The Decline of the Californios: A Social History of the Spanish-Speaking Californians, 1846–1890.* Berkeley: University of California Press, 1968.

Quaife, Milo Milton, ed. *Kit Carson's Autobiography.* Lincoln: University of Nebraska Press, 1935.

Raup, Hallock Floyd. *San Bernardino, California: Settlement and Growth of a Pass-site City.* University of California Publications in Geography, Vol. 8, No. 1. Berkeley: University of California Press, 1940.

Rawls, James J. *Indians of California: The Changing Image.* Norman: University of Oklahoma Press, 1984.

Remy, Jules, and Julius Benchley. *A Journey to Great-Salt Lake City,* Vol. 2. London: W. Jeffs, 1861.

Revere, Joseph Warren. *A Tour of Duty in California; Including a Description of the Gold Region.* New York: C. S. Francis and Company, 1849.

Ríos-Bustamante, Antonio. *Mexican Los Angeles: A Narrative and Pictorial History.* Encino, Calif.: Floricanto Press, 1992.

Ríos-Bustamante, Antonio, and Pedro Castillo. *An Illustrated History of Mexican Los Angeles, 1781–1985.* Los Angeles: University of California, Chicano Studies Research Center Publications, 1986.

Robinson, Alfred. *Life in California during a Residence of Several years in that Territory.* Santa Barbara: Peregrine Press, 1970.

Robinson, John W. *The San Bernardinos: The Mountain Country from Cajón Pass to Oak Glen: Two Centuries of Changing Use.* Arcadia, Calif.: Big Santa Anita Historical Society, 1989.

Robinson, William Wilcox. *The Indians of Los Angeles: Story of the Liquidation of a People.* Los Angeles: Glen Dawson, 1952.

———. *Land in California: The Story of Mission Lands, Ranchos, Squatters, Mining Claims, Railroad Grants, Land Scrip, Homesteads.* Berkeley: University of California Press, 1948.

———. *Los Angeles: A Profile.* Norman: University of Oklahoma Press, 1968.

———. *Los Angeles: From the Day of the Pueblo.* Intro. Doyce B. Nunis, Jr. San Francisco: California Historical Society, 1981.

———. *Ranchos Become Cities.* Pasadena: San Pasqual Press, 1939.

———. *The Story of San Fernando Valley.* Los Angeles: Title Insurance and Trust Corporation, 1967.

Rojas, Arnold R. *The Vaquero.* Santa Barbara: McNally and Loftin Publishers, 1964.

Rolle, Andrew F. *California: A History.* New York: Thomas Y. Crowell Company, 1963.

———. *Los Angeles: From Pueblo to City of the Future.* 2nd ed. San Francisco: MTL Inc., 1995.

Romo, Ricardo. *East Los Angeles: A History of a Barrio.* Austin: University of Texas Press, 1983.

Rose, Leonard John. *L. J. Rose of Sunny Slope, 1827–1899: California Pioneer, Fruit Grower, Wine Maker, Horse Breeder.* San Marino: The Huntington Library, 1959.

Russell, John. *Personal Narrative of Explorations and Incidents in Texas, New Mexico, California, Sonora, and Chihuahua.* Vol. 2. New York: D. Appleton and Company, 1854.

Sánchez, Nellie Van de Grift. *Spanish Arcadia.* San Francisco: Powell Publishing Company, 1929.

Sánchez, Rosaura. *Telling Identities: The Californio Testimonios.* Minneapolis and London: University of Minnesota Press, 1995.

Sandos, James A. *Converting California: Indians and Franciscans in the Missions.* New Haven: Yale University Press, 2004.

Schuetz-Miller, Mardith, K. *Building and Builders in Hispanic California, 1769–1850.* Tucson: Southwestern Mission Research Center; Santa Barbara: Santa Barbara Trust for Historic Preservation Presidio Research Publication, 1994.

Service, Elman R. *Primitive Social Organization: An Evolutionary Perspective.* New York: Random House, 1962.

Shaler, William. *Journal of a Voyage Between China and the North Western Coast of America Made in 1804 by William Shaler.* Intro. Lindley Bynum. Claremont, Calif.: Saunders Studio Press, 1935.

Shinn, George Hazen. *Shoshonenan Days: Recollections of a Residence of Five Years among the Indians of Southern California, 1885–1889.* Glendale, Calif.: The Arthur H. Clark Company, 1941.

Shipek, Florence Connolly. *Pushed Into The Rocks: Southern California Indian Land Tenure, 1769–1986.* Lincoln: University of Nebraska Press, 1987.

Shoup, Laurence H., and Randall T. Milliken. *Iñigo of Rancho Posolmi: The Life and Times of a Mission Indian*. Novato, Calif.: Ballena Press, 1999.
Silliman, Stephen W. *Lost Laborers in Colonial California: Native Americans and the Archaeology of Rancho Petaluma*. Tucson: University of Arizona Press, 2004.
Simpson, George Sir. *Narrative of a Voyage to California in 1841–42*. San Francisco: Thomas C. Russell, 1930.
Simpson, Lesley Byrd, ed., and Paul D. Nathan, trans. *The Letters of José Señán, O.F.M., Mission San Buenaventura, 1896–1823*. Ventura, Calif.: John Howell Books, 1962.
Slatta, Richard W. *Comparing Cowboys and Frontiers*. Norman: University of Oklahoma Press, 1997.
———. *Cowboys of the Americas*. New Haven: Yale University Press, 1990.
Smith, Gerald A., and Clifford J. Walker. *Indian Slave Trade along the Mohave Trail*. San Bernardino: San Bernardino County Museum, 1965.
Stephenson, Terry E. *Don Bernardo Yorba*. Los Angeles: Glen Dawson, 1941.
Street, Richard Steven. *Beasts of the Field: A Narrative History of California Farmworkers, 1769–1913*. Stanford: Stanford University Press, 2004.
Strong, William Duncan. *Aboriginal Society in Southern California*. Banning, Calif.: Malki Museum Press, 1972.
Taylor, William B. *Drinking, Homicide, and Rebellion in Colonial Mexican Villages*. Stanford: Stanford University Press, 1979.
Tibesar, Antonine, O.F.M. *Writings of Junípero Serra*. Vols. 3 and 4. Washington, D.C.: Academy of American Franciscan History, 1956, 1966.
Trafzer, Clifford E. *The People of San Manuel*. Patton, Calif.: San Manuel Band of Mission Indians, 2002.
Tyler, Daniel Tyler. *A Concise History of the Mormon Battalion in the Mexican War, 1846–1847*. Chicago: Río Grande Press, Inc., 1964.
Van Nostrand, Jeanne, ed. *Edward Vischer's Drawings of the California Missions, 1861–1878*. Intro. Thomas Albright. San Francisco: The Book Club of California, 1982.
Vickery, Joyce Carter. *Defending Eden: New Mexican Pioneers in Southern California, 1830–1890*. Riverside, Calif.: Riverside Museum Press, 1977.
Von Langsdorff, Georg Heinrich. *Voyages and Travels in Various Parts of the World during the Years 1803, 1804, 1805, 1806, and 1807*, vol. 2. 1814. New York: Da Capo Press, 1968.
Walton, John. *Storied Land: Community and Memory in Monterey*. Berkeley: University of California Press, 2001.
Warner, Juan José, Benjamin Hayes, and Joseph Pomeroy Widney. *An Historical Sketch of Los Angeles County California*. Los Angeles: O. W. Smith, Publisher, 1936.

Watson, Douglas S., ed. *The Santa Fe Trail to California 1849–1852: The Journal and Drawings of H. M. T. Powell.* New York: Sol Lewis, 1981.

Webb, Edith Buckland. *Indian Life at the Old Missions.* Los Angeles: The Wayside Press, 1952.

———. *The Mission Villages or Rancherías.* Bakersfield, Calif.: California Mission Studies Association, 1998.

Weber, David, J. *Bárbaros: Spaniards and their Savages in the Age of Enlightenment.* New Haven: Yale University Press, 2005.

———. *The Californios versus Jedediah Smith, 1826–1827: A New Cache of Documents.* Spokane: The Arthur H. Clark Company, 1990.

———. *The Mexican Frontier, 1821–1846: The American Southwest under Mexico.* Albuquerque: University of New Mexico Press, 1982.

Weber, Francis J. *Mission San Fernando.* Los Angeles: Westernlore Press, 1968.

———, ed., *The Mission in the Valley: A Documentary History of San Fernando, Rey de España.* Los Angeles: Westernlore Press, 1968.

White, Michael. *California All the Way back to 1828.* Ed. Glen Dawson. Los Angeles: Glen Dawson, 1956.

Whitehead, Roy Elmer. *Lugo: A Chronicle of Early California.* Redlands, Calif.: San Bernardino County Museum Association, 1978.

Wierzbicki, Felix Paul. *California As It Is and As It May Be, or A Guide to the Gold Region.* New York: Burt Franklin, 1970.

Wilbur, Marguerite Eyer, ed. and trans. *Duflot de Mofras' Travels on the Pacific Coast,* Vol. 1. Santa Ana, Calif.: Fine Arts Press, 1937.

Willard, Charles Dwight. *The Herald's History of Los Angeles.* Los Angeles: Kingsley-Barnes and Neumer Co., 1901.

Winkler, Albert Julius. *General Viticulture.* Berkeley: University of California Press, 1965.

Wolcott, Marjorie Tisdale, ed. *Pioneer Notes from the Diaries of Judge Benjamin Hayes, 1849–1875.* New York: Arno Press, 1976.

Wolf, Eric. *Europe and the People without History.* Berkeley: University of California Press, 1982.

———. *Sons of the Shaking Earth.* Chicago: University of Chicago Press, 1959.

ARTICLES

Adam, V. G. "Notes on the Mission San Gabriel." *Annual Publications of the Historical Society of Southern California and Pioneer Register* 4 (2), 1898: 131–33.

Albers, Patricia C. "From Legend to Land to Labor: Changing Perspectives on Native American Work." In *Native Americans and Wage Labor: Ethnohistorical Perspectives*, ed. Alice Littlefield and Martha C. Knack. Norman: University of Oklahoma Press, 1996: 245–73.

Almaguer, Tomás. "Interpreting Chicano History: The World-System Approach to Nineteenth-Century California." *Review* 4 (3), 1981: 459–507.

Anonymous. "Sheep-Farming in California." *Overland Monthly* 8 (6), 1872: 489–92.

Archibald, Robert. "Indian Labor at the California Missions: Slavery or Salvation?" *The Journal of San Diego History* 24 (2), 1978: 172–82.

Avilés, Brian A., and Robert L. Hoover. "Two Californias, Three Religious Orders, and Fifty Missions: A Comparison of the Missionary Systems of Baja and Alta California." *Pacific Coast Archaeological Society Quarterly* 33 (3), 1997: 1–28.

Baer, Kurt. "California Indian Art." *The Americas* 16 (1), 1951: 23–44.

Baker, Charles. "Mexican Land Grants in California." *Annual Publications of the Historical Society of Southern California* 9 (3), 1914: 236–43.

Bakken, Gordon Morris. "Rancho Cañón de Santa Ana." In *Rancho Days in Southern California: An Anthology with New Perspectives*, ed. Kenneth Pauley. Studio City, Calif.: The Westerners, Los Angeles Corral, 1997: 207–23.

Barger, William J. "Furs, Hides, and a Little Larceny: Smuggling and Its Role in Early California's Economy." *Southern California Quarterly* 85 (4), 2003: 381–412.

Barrows, H. D. "California in the Thirties." *Annual Publications of the Historical Society of Southern California* 1894: 33–39.

———. "Michael White The Pioneer." *Annual Publications of the Historical Society of Southern California* 3 (4), 1896: 19–21.

———. "The Story of a Native Californian." *Annual Publications of the Historical Society of Southern California* 4 (2), 1898: 114–18.

———. "Water for Domestic Purposes versus Water for Irrigation." *Annual Publications of the Historical Society of Southern California* 8 (3), 1941: 208–10.

Bauer, Patricia M. "The Beginnings of Tanning in California." *California Historical Society Quarterly* 33 (1), 1954: 59–72.

Bauer, William, Jr. "'We Were All Migrant Workers Here': Round Valley Indian Labor in Northern California, 1850–1929." *Western Historical Quarterly* 37 (1), 2006: 43–63.

Bean, Lowell John. "The Wanakik Cahuilla." *The Masterkey* 34 (3), 1960: 111–19.

Beattie, George William. "San Bernardino Valley Before the Americans Came." *California Historical Society Quarterly* 12 (2), 1933: 111–24.

———. "San Bernardino Valley in the Spanish Period." *Annual Publications of the Historical Society of Southern California* 12, 1923: 10–28.

Beattie, Helen Pruitt. "Indians of San Bernardino Valley and Vicinity." *Southern California Quarterly* 35 (3), 1953: 239–64.

Beebe, Rose Marie, and Robert M. Senkewicz, trans. "Revolt at Mission San Gabriel, October 25, 1785, Judicial Proceedings and Related Documents." *Boletín: The Journal of the California Mission Studies Association* 24 (2), 2007: 15–29.

Belden, Joseph. "Pastoral California through Gringo Eyes." *Touring Topics* 22 (8), 1930: 40–47, 53–54.

Benedict, Ruth Fulton. "A Brief Sketch of Serrano Culture." *American Anthropologist* 26 (3), 1924: 366–92.

Bibb, Leland E. "Pablo Apis and Temecula." *The Journal of San Diego History* 37 (4), 1991: 257–71.

Blew, Robert W. "Vigilantism in Los Angeles, 1835–1874." *Southern California Quarterly* 54 (2), 1972: 11–30.

Bolton, Herbert Eugene. "The Mission as a Frontier Institution in the Spanish American Colonies." *American Historical Review* 23 (1), 1917: 42–61.

Botta, Paolo Emilio. "Observations on the Inhabitants of California, 1827–1828." Trans. Anne Milano Appel. *Boletín: The Journal of the California Mission Studies Association* 23 (2), 24 (1), 2006/2007: 59–76.

Bowman, Jacob N. "The Names of the Los Angeles and San Gabriel Rivers." *Southern California Quarterly* 29 (2), 1947: 93–99.

Boxt, Matthew A., and L. Mark Raab. "Pavunga and Point Conception: A Comparative Study of Southern California Indian Traditionalism." *Journal of California and Great Basin Anthropology* 22 (1), 2000: 43–67.

Bynum, Lindley, ed. "Los Angeles in 1854–5: The Diary of Rev. James Woods." *The Historical Society of Southern California Quarterly* 23 (4), 1940: 65–86.

Camp, Charles L., ed. "The Chronicles of George C. Yount." *California Historical Society Quarterly* 2 (1), 1923: 3–66.

Carrico, Richard. "The Struggle for Native American Self-Determination in San Diego County." *Journal of California and Great Basin Anthropology* 2 (2), 1980: 199–213.

———. "Wolf Kalisher: Immigrant, Pioneer Merchant and Indian Advocate." *Western States Jewish Historical Quarterly* 15 (2), 1983: 99–106.

Carrico, Richard, and Florence C. Shipek. "Indian Labor in San Diego County, California, 1850–1900." In *Native American Labor: Retrieving*

History, Rethinking Theory. Ed. Martha C. Knack and Alice Littlefield. Norman: University of Oklahoma Press, 1996: 198–217.

Carson, James H. "Early Recollections of the Mines, Tulare Plains, Life in California." In *Bright Gem of the Western Seas: California 1846–1852*, ed. Peter Browning. Lafayette, Calif.: Great West Books, 1991: 1–169.

Castillo, Edward D. "Blood Came from Their Mouths: Tongva and Chumash Responses to the Pandemic of 1801." *American Indian Culture and Research Journal* 23 (3), 1999: 47–61.

———. "Gender Status Decline, Resistance, and Accommodation among Female Neophytes in the Missions of California: A San Gabriel Case Study." *American Indian Culture and Research Journal* 18 (1), 1994: 67–93.

Chace, Paul G. "The Archaeology of 'Ciénaga,' the Oldest Historic Structure on the Irvine Ranch." *Pacific Coast Archaeological Society Quarterly* 5 (3), 1969: 39–55.

Chávez-García, Miroslava. "'Pongo Mi Demanda:' Challenging Patriarchy in Mexican Los Angeles, 1830–1850." In *Over the Edge: Remapping the American West*, eds. Valerie J. Matsumoto and Blake Allmendinger. Berkeley: University of California Press, 1999: 272–90.

Charles, W. N. "Transcription and Translation of the Old Mexican Documents of the Los Angeles County Archives." *Southern California Quarterly* 20 (2), 1938: 84–88.

Clark, Harry. "Their Pride, Their Manners, and Their Voices: Sources of the Traditional Portrait of the Early Californians." *California Historical Society Quarterly* 53 (1), 1975: 71–82.

Cook, Sherburne F., trans. and ed. "Expeditions to the Interior of California, Central Valley, 1820–1840." *Anthropological Records* 20 (5), 1962: 151–213.

———. "Smallpox in Spanish and Mexican California, 1770–1845." *Bulletin of the History of Medicine* 7 (2), 1939: 153–91.

Costello, Julia G. "Lime Processing in Spanish California: With Special Reference to Santa Barbara." *Pacific Coast Archaeological Society Quarterly* 13 (3), 1977: 22–32.

———. "Variability among the Alta California Missions: The Economics of Agricultural Production." In *Columbian Consequences, Vol. 1, Archaeological and Historical Perspectives on the Spanish Borderlands West*, ed. David Hurst Thomas. Washington, D.C.: Smithsonian Institution Press, 1989: 435–49.

Costello, Julia G., and David Hornbeck. "Alta California: An Overview." In *Columbian Consequences, Vol. 1, Archaeological and Historical Perspectives on the Spanish Borderlands West*, ed. David Hurst Thomas. Washington, D.C.: Smithsonian Institution Press, 1989: 303–31.

Coulter, Thomas. "Notes on Upper California." Reprint from the *Journal of the Royal Geographical Society*, 1835. Chicago: Aldine Book Company, 1925.

Cowan, Robert Ernest, ed. "Bancroft's Guide to the Colorado Mines." *California Historical Society Quarterly* 12 (1), 1933: 3–10.

Crandell, John. "Río Porciúncula: A New Perspective on the Former Environs of Los Angeles." *Southern California Quarterly* 81 (3), 1999: 305–14.

Cutter, Donald C. "Report on Rancho El Encino for State of California, Division of Beaches and Parks." *Southern California Quarterly* 43 (2), June 1961: 200–14.

Dakin, Susanna Bryant. "Hugo Reid, Humanitarian." *Southern California Quarterly* 31 (1–2), 1949: 53–59.

Davies, David, ed. "An Emigrant of the Fifties: The Letters of James Clark." *Historical Society of Southern California Quarterly* 19 (3–4), 1937: 99–120.

Davis, James T. "Trade Routes and Economic Exchange among the Indians of California." In *Aboriginal California: Three Studies in Culture History*, ed. Robert F. Heizer. Berkeley: University of California Press, 1963: 1–71.

Denhardt, Robert M. "The Role of the Horse in the Social History of Early California." *Agricultural History* 14 (1), 1940: 13–22.

Dixon, Keith A. "Reviving Puvunga: An Archeological Project at Rancho Los Alamitos." *The Masterkey* 46 (3), 1972: 84–92.

Dorland, C. P. "The Los Angeles River—Its History and Ownership." *Annual Publications of the Historical Society of Southern California* 3 (1), 1893: 31–35.

Drown, D. Bartlett. "Indian Grape Pickers in California." *Overland Monthly* 65 (6), 1915: 554–58.

Du Bois, Constance Goddard. "The Religion of the Luiseño Indians of Southern California." *University of California Publications in American Archaeology and Ethnology* 8 (3), 1908: 69–186.

Duggan, Marie Christine. "The Laws of the Market versus the Laws of God: Scholastic Doctrine and the Early California Economy." *History of Political Economy* 37 (2), 2005: 343–70.

Dumke, Glenn S. "The Masters of San Gabriel's Old Mill." *California Historical Society Quarterly* 45 (3), 1966: 159–65.

Ellerbe, Rose L. "The Mother Vineyard: A Glance at the Hectic History of Cucamonga Rancho." *Touring Topics* 20 (2), 1928: 18–20.

Engstrand, Iris H. W. "California Ranchos: Their Hispanic Heritage." *Southern California Quarterly* 67 (3), 1985: 281–90.

———. "Early Southern California Viniculture, 1830–1865." *Southern California Quarterly* 39 (3), 1957: 242–47.

Ettinger, Catherine R. "Hybrid Spaces, Indigenous Contributions to Mission Architecture." In *Architecture, Physical Environment, and Society in Alta California: Proceedings of the 22nd Annual Conference of the California Mission Studies Association*, ed. Rose Marie Beebe and Robert M. Senkewicz. Santa Clara, Calif.: California Mission Studies Association, 2005: 77–89.

———. "Spaces of Change: Architecture and the Creation of a New Society in the California Missions." *Boletín: The Journal of the California Mission Studies Association* 21 (1), 2004: 23–44.

Evans, William S., Jr. "California Indian Pottery: A Native Contribution to the Culture of the Ranchos." *Pacific Coast Archaeological Quarterly* 5 (3), 1969: 71–81.

Fairchild, Mahlon Dickerson. "A Trip to the Colorado Mines in 1862." *California Historical Society Quarterly* 12 (1), 1933: 11–17.

Farnsworth, Paul. "Missions, Indians, and Cultural Continuity." *Historical Archaeology* 26 (1), 1992: 22–35.

Farnsworth, Paul, and Robert H. Jackson. "Cultural, Economic, and Demographic Change in the Missions of Alta California: The Case of Nuestra Señora de la Soledad." In *The New Latin American Mission History*, ed. Erick Langer and Robert H. Jackson. Lincoln: University of Nebraska Press, 1995: 109–29.

Farnsworth, Paul, and Jack S. Williams. "The Archaeology of the Spanish Colonial and Mexican Republican Periods: Introduction." *Historical Archaeology* 26 (1), 1992: 1–6.

Farris, Glenn. "The Reyes Rancho in Santa Barbara County, 1802–1808." *Southern California Quarterly* 81 (2), 1999: 171–80.

Forbes, Jack D. "Indians Horticulture West and Northwest of the Colorado River." *Journal of the West* 2 (1), 1963: 1–14.

———. "Indians of Southern California in 1888." *The Masterkey* 33 (2), 1959: 71–76.

———. "The Tongva of Tujunga to 1801." *Annual Reports of the University of California Archaeological Survey* 8 (1), 1966: 137–50.

Ford, Henry Chapman. "Some Detached Notes by Henry Chapman Ford on the Missions of California." *California Historical Society Quarterly* 3 (3), 1924: 238–44.

Foster, Stephen Clark. "Los Angeles on the Eve of the Gold Rush," Part 1. *Touring Topics* 21 (7), 1929: 14–19.

———. "Los Angeles on the Eve of the Gold Rush," Part 2. *Touring Topics* 21 (8), 1929: 26–31.

———. "Reminiscences: My First Procession in Los Angeles, March 16, 1847." *Historical Society of Southern California* 1 (3), 1887: 46–52.

Frank, Andre Gunder. "The Development of Underdevelopment." *Monthly Review: An Independent Socialist Magazine* 18 (4), 1966: 17–31.
Frederick, M. C. "The Californian Montadura." *The California Illustrated Magazine* 4 (June–November), 1893: 179–86.
Frierman, Jay D. "The Pastoral Period in Los Angeles: Life on the Ranchos and in the Pueblo, 1800–1850." In *Historical Archaeology of Nineteenth-Century California*, ed. Jay D. Frierman and Roberta S. Greenwood. Los Angeles: William Andrews Clark Memorial Library, 1992: 3–52.
Garr, Daniel J. "Los Angeles and the Challenge of Growth. *Southern California Quarterly* 61 (2), 1977: 147–58.
———. "Planning, Politics, and Plunder: The Missions and Indian Pueblos of Hispanic California." *Southern California Quarterly* 54 (4), 1972: 291–312.
———. "A Rare and Desolate Land: Population and Race in Hispanic California." *Western Historical Quarterly* 6 (2), 1975: 133–48.
Gates, Paul W. "The California Land Act of 1851." *California Historical Society Quarterly* 50 (4), 1971: 395–430.
Geiger, Maynard, O.F.M. "The Building of Mission San Gabriel: 1771–1828." *Southern California Quarterly* 50 (1), 1968: 33–42.
———, ed. "Fray Rafael Verger, O.F.M., and the California Mission Enterprise." *Southern California Quarterly* 49 (2), 1967: 205–31.
Gentilcore, Louis R. "Mission and Mission Lands of Alta California." *Annals of the Association of American Geographers* 51 (1), 1961: 46–72.
Gifford, Edward Winslow. "Clans and Moieties in Southern California." *University of California Publications in American Archaeology and Ethnology* 14 (2), 1918: 155–219.
Gillespie, Archibald H. "Letter to Thomas Oliver Larkin, Los Angeles, April 7, 1847." In *The Larkin Papers: Personal, Business and Official Correspondence of Thomas Oliver Larkin, Merchant and United States Consul in California*, Vol. 6. Ed. George P. Hammond. Berkeley and Los Angeles: University of California Press, 1951–1953.
Gillette, J. W. "Some Indian Experiences." *Annual Publications of the Historical Society of Southern California and of the Pioneers of Los Angeles County* 6 (1), 1904: 158–64.
Greenwood, Roberta S. "The California Ranchero: Fact and Fancy." In *Columbian Consequences, Vol. 1. Archaeological and Historical Perspectives on the Spanish Borderlands West*, ed. David Hurst Thomas. Washington, D.C.: Smithsonian Institution Press, 1989: 451–65.
Griffin, John S. "Los Angeles in 1849: A Letter from John S. Griffin, M.D. to Col. J. D. Stevenson, March 11, 1849." Los Angeles: Privately Printed, 1949.

Gudde, Edwin Gustav, ed. and trans. "Edward Vischer's First Visit to California." *California Historical Society Quarterly* 19 (3), 1940: 193–216.

Guerra Ord, Angustias de la. "Occurrences in California as Told to Thomas Savage in Santa Bárbara by Mrs. Ord (Doña Angustias de la Guerra), 1878." In *Testimonios: Early California through the Eyes of Women, 1815–1848*, trans. and ed. Rose Marie Beebe and Robert M. Senkewicz. Berkeley: Heyday Books, 2006: 194–270.

Guest, Francis, O.F.M. "Cultural Perspectives on California Mission Life." *Southern California Quarterly* 65 (1), 1983: 1–65.

———. "The Indian Policy under Fermín Francisco de Lasuén, California's Second Father President." *California Historical Society Quarterly* 45 (3), 1966: 195–224.

———. "Junípero Serra and his Approach to the Indians." *Southern California Quarterly* 67 (3), 1985: 223–61.

———. "Mission Colonization and Political Control in Spanish California." *The Journal of San Diego History* 24 (1), 1978: 97–116.

———. "Municipal Government in Spanish California." *California Historical Society Quarterly* 46 (4), 1967: 307–35.

Guinn, J. M. "Exceptional Years: A History of California Floods and Droughts." *Annual Publications of the Historical Society of Southern California* 1 (5), 1890: 33–39.

———. "From Pueblo to Ciudad: The Municipal and Territorial Expansion of Los Angeles." *Annual Publications of the Historical Society of Southern California* 7 (1–2), 1907–1908: 216–21.

———. "How the Area of Los Angeles City was Enlarged." *Annual Publications of the Historical Society of Southern California* 9 (3), 1914: 173–80.

———. "In the Old Pueblo Days." *Annual Publications of the Historical Society of Southern California and Pioneer Register* 4 (3), 1899: 223–27.

———. "Los Angeles in the Adobe Age." *Annual Publications of the Historical Society of Southern California* 4 (1), 1897: 49–55.

———. "Los Angeles in the Late Sixties and Early Seventies." *Annual Publications of the Historical Society of Southern California* 1893: 63–68.

———. "Muy Ilustre Ayuntamiento." *Annual Publications of the Historical Society of Southern California and Pioneer Register* 4 (3), 1899: 206–12.

———. "The Passing of the Old Pueblo." *Annual Publications of the Historical Society of Southern California and of the Pioneers of Los Angeles County* 5, 1900–1902: 113–20.

———. "The Plan of Old Los Angeles." *Annual Publications of the Historical Society of Southern California* 3 (3), 1895: 40–50.

Guzmán, José María, Fr. "Guzmán's 'Breve Noticia.'" *California Historical Society Quarterly* 5 (3), 1926: 209–17.

Haas, Lisbeth. "Emancipation and the Meaning of Freedom in Mexican California." *Boletín: The Journal of the California Mission Studies Association* 20 (1), 2003: 11–22.

Hackel, Steven W. "Land, Labor, and Production: The Colonial Economy of Spanish and Mexican California." In *Contested Eden: California before the Gold Rush*, ed. Ramón A. Gutiérrez and Richard J. Orsi. Berkeley: Published in association with the California Historical Society by the University of California Press, 1997: 111–46.

———. "Sources of Rebellion: Indian Testimony and the Mission San Gabriel Uprising of 1785." *Ethnohistory* 50 (4), 2003: 643–69.

———. "The Staff of Leadership: Indian Authority in the Missions of Alta California." *William and Mary Quarterly* 54 (2), 1997: 347–76.

Haraszthy, Arpad. "Wine making in California." *The Overland Monthly* 7 (6), 1871: 489–97.

Harvey, H. R. "Population of the Cahuilla Indians: Decline and its Causes." *Eugenics Quarterly* 14 (3), 1967: 185–98.

Heizer, Robert F., ed. "A California Messianic Movement of 1801 among the Chumash." *American Anthropologist* 43 (1), 1941: 128–29.

Hewes, Gordon, and Minna Hewes. "Indian Life and Customs at Mission San Luis Rey." *The Americas* 9 (1), 1952: 87–106.

Hoffman, Abraham, and Teena Stern. "The Zanjas and the Pioneer Water Systems for Los Angeles." *Southern California Quarterly* 89 (1), 2007: 1–22.

Hoffman, Walter James, ed. "Hugo Reid's Account of the Indians of Los Angeles County, California." *Bulletin of the Essex Institute* 17 (1–3), 1885: 1–33.

Holt, Franklyn. "The Los Angeles & San Pedro: First Railroad South of the Tehachapis." *California Historical Quarterly* 32 (4), 1853: 327–48.

Hooper, Lucile. "The Cahuilla Indians." *University of California Publications in American Archaeology and Ethnology* 16 (6), 1920: 315–80.

Hoover, Robert L. "Some Models for Spanish Colonial Archaeology in California." *Historical Archaeology* 26 (1), 1992: 37–44.

———. "Spanish-Native Interaction and Acculturation in the Alta California Missions." In *Columbian Consequences, Vol. 1, Archaeological and Historical Perspectives on the Spanish Borderlands West*, ed. David Hurst Thomas. Washington, D.C.: Smithsonian Institution Press, 1989: 395–406.

Hornbeck, David. "Economic Growth and Change at the Missions of Alta California, 1769–1846." In *Columbian Consequences, Vol. 1, Archaeological and Historical Perspectives on the Spanish Borderlands West*, ed. David Hurst Thomas. Washington, D.C.: Smithsonian Institution Press, 1989: 423–33.

———. "Land Tenure and Rancho Expansion in Alta California, 1784–1846." *Journal of Historical Geography* 4 (4), 1978: 371–90.

———. "The Patterning of California's Private Land Claims." *Geographical Review* 69 (4), 1979: 434–48.

Hough, John C. "Charles Henry Brinley: A Case Study in Rancho Supervision." *Southern California Quarterly* 40 (2), 1958: 174–79.

Hudson, Dee. T. "Proto-Gabrielino Patterns of Territorial Organization in South Coastal California." *Pacific Coast Archaeological Society Quarterly* 7 (2), 1971: 49–76.

Hudson, Travis. "A Rare Account of Gabrielino Shamanism from the Notes of John P. Harrington." *Journal of California and Great Basin Anthropology* 1 (2), 1979: 256–62.

Hudson, Travis, and Thomas Blackburn. "The Integration of Myth and Ritual in South-Central California: The 'Northern Complex.'" *The Journal of California Anthropology* 5 (2), 1978: 225–50.

Hurtado, Albert L. "California Indians and the Workaday West: Labor, Assimilation, and Survival." *California History* 69 (1), 1990: 211.

———. "Indians in Town and Country: The Nisenan Indians' Changing Economy and Society as Shown in John A. Sutter's 1856 Correspondence." *American Indian Culture and Research Journal* 12 (2), 1988: 31–51.

———. "'Saved So Much as Possible for Labour:' Indian Population and the New Helvetia Work Force." *American Indian Culture and Research Journal* 6 (4), 1983: 63–78.

Hussey, John Adam. "Kit Carson at Cajón—Not Tejón." *California Historical Society Quarterly* 29 (1), 1950: 29–38.

Hutchinson, C. Alan. "The Mexican Government and the Mission Indians of Upper California, 1821–1835." *The Americas* 21 (4), 1965: 335–62.

Ivey, James E. "Secularization in California and Texas." *Boletín: The Journal of the California Mission Studies Association* 20 (1), 2003: 23–36.

Jackson, Robert H. "The Changing Economic Structure of the Alta California Missions—A Reinterpretation." *Pacific Historical Review* 59 (3), 1992: 387–415.

Johnson, John R. "The Indians of Mission San Fernando." *Southern California Quarterly* 79 (3), 1997: 249–90.

———. "The Various Chinigchinich Manuscripts of Father Gerónimo Boscana." In *San Diego, Alta California and the Borderlands: Proceedings of the 23rd Annual Conference of the California Mission Studies Association*, ed. Rose Marie Beebe and Robert M. Senkewicz. Santa Clara, Calif.: California Mission Studies Association, 2006: 1–19.

Johnson, John R., and David D. Earle. "Tataviam Geography and Ethnohistory." *Journal of California and Great Basin Anthropology* 12 (2), 1990: 191–214.

Johnson, John R., and William M. Williams. "Toypurina's Descendants: Three Generation of an Alta California Family." *Boletín: The Journal of the California Mission Studies Association* 24 (2), 2007: 30–55.

Jorgensen, Joseph G. "Indians and the Metropolis." In *The American Indian in Urban Society*, ed. Jack O. Waddell and O. Michael Watson. Boston: Little Brown, and Company, 1971: 67–113.

Kelsey, Harry. "A New Look at the Founding of Old Los Angeles." In *The Founding Documents of Los Angeles: A Bilingual Edition*, ed. Doyce B. Nunis, Jr. Los Angeles: The Historical Society of Southern California and the Zamorano Club, 2004.

Kindall, Cleve E. "Southern Vineyards: The Economic Significance of the Wine Industry in the Development of Los Angeles, 1831–1870." *Southern California Quarterly* 41 (1), 1959: 26–37.

King, Chester, and Thomas C. Blackburn. "Tataviam." In *Handbook of North American Indians, Vol. 8. California*, ed. Robert F. Heizer and William C. Sturtevant. Washington, D.C.: Smithsonian Institution, 1978: 535–37.

King, Laura Evertsen. "Captain and Tin Tin." *Annual Publications of the Historical Society of Southern California and the Pioneer Register* 4 (2), 1898: 139–40.

———. "Hugo Reid and His Indian Wife." *Annual Publications of the Historical Society of Southern California and the Pioneer Register* 4 (2), 1898: 111–13.

———. "Pinacate." *Annual Publications of the Historical Society of Southern California and of the Pioneers of Los Angeles County* 6 (2), 1904: 132–34.

———. "Reminiscences of San Gabriel." *Annual Publications of the Historical Society of Southern California* 11 (3), 1920: 58–62.

Knack, Martha C., and Alice Littlefield. "Native American Labor: Retrieving History, Rethinking Theory." In *Native Americans and Wage Labor: Ethnohistorical Perspectives*, ed. Alice Littlefield and Martha C. Knack. Norman: University of Oklahoma Press, 1996: 3–44.

Kroeber. A. L. "Ethnography of the Cahuillas Indians." *University of California Publications in American Archaeology and Ethnology* 8 (2), 1908: 29–68.

Lamar, Howard. "From Bondage to Contract: Ethnic Labor in the American West, 1600–1890." In *The Countryside in the Age of Capitalist Transformation: Essays in the Social History of Rural America*, ed. Steven Hahn and Jonathan Prude. Chapel Hill and London: University of North Carolina Press, 1985.

Langum, David J. "Californios and the Image of Indolence." *Western Historical Quarterly* 9 (2), 1978: 181–96.

Lawrence, Eleanor. "Caballos and Caballeros in Pastoral California." *Touring Topics* 23 (5), 1931: 12–16, 40.

———. "Mexican Trade between Santa Fe and Los Angeles, 1830–1848." *California Historical Society Quarterly* 10 (1), 1931: 27–39.

Lawton, Harry, W. "Agricultural Motifs in Southern California Indian Mythology." *The Journal of California Anthropology* 1 (1), 1974: 55–79.

Layne, J. Gregg. "Annals of Los Angeles: From the Founding of the Pueblo to the American Occupation." *California Historical Society Quarterly* 13 (3), 1934: 196–234.

———. "The First Census of the Los Angeles District." *Historical Society of Southern California Quarterly* 18 (3) 1936: 81–166.

Lelande, Harry J., ed. "Extracts from the Los Angeles Archives." *Annual Publications of the Historical Society of Southern California* 6, 1903: 242–52; 6, 1905: 242–53.

Lenz, Louise, ed. "Memories of Caroline van der Leck Lenz." *Southern California Quarterly* 36 (3), 1954: 192–213.

Lepowsky, Maria. "Indian Revolts and Cargo Cults: Ritual Violence and Revitalization in California and New Guinea." In *Reassessing Revitalization Movements: Perspectives from North American and the Pacific Islands*, ed. Michael E. Harkin. Lincoln: University of Nebraska Press, 2004: 1–60.

Livingston, M. M. "The Earliest Spanish Land Grants in California." *Annual Publications of the Historical Society of Southern California* 9 (3) 1914: 195–99.

Loughead, Flora Haines. "The Old California Vaquero." *Land of Sunshine* 5, 1896: 109–14.

Lugo, José del Carmen. "Life of a Rancher." *Historical Society of Southern California Quarterly* 32 (3), 1950: 185–236.

Magliari, Michael. "Free Soil, Unfree Labor: Cave Johnson Couts and the Binding of Indian Workers in California, 1850–1867." *Pacific Historical Review* 73 (3), 2004: 349–89.

Magnaghi, Emily B., and Russell M. Magnaghi. "The Agricultural Development of Mission San Fernando, Rey de España." In *Architecture, Physical Environment and Society in Alta California: Proceedings of the 22nd Annual Conference of the California Mission Studies Association*, ed. Rose Marie Beebe and Robert M. Senkewicz. Santa Clara, Calif.: California Mission Studies Association, 2005: 135–52.

Mann, Ralph. "The Americanization of Arcadia: Images of Hispanic and Gold Rush California." *American Studies* 19 (5), 1978: 5–19.

Mason, William M. "Fages's Code of Conduct toward Indians, 1787." *Journal of California Anthropology* 2 (1), 1975: 90–100.

———. "Indian-Mexican Cultural Exchange in the Los Angeles Area, 1781–1834." *Aztlán* 15 (1), 1984: 123–44.

McGarry, Daniel D. "Educational Methods of the Franciscans in Spanish California." *The Americas* 7 (3), 1950: 335–58.

McGinty, Brian. "Angelica: An Old California Tradition." *Vintage* 5 (1), 1975: 33–37, 58.

McKee, Irving. "The Beginnings of California Winegrowing." *Southern California Quarterly* 29 (1), 1947: 59–71.

Meighan, Clement W. "Indians and California Missions." *Southern California Quarterly* 69 (3), 1987: 187–201.

Merriam, C. Hart. "Village Names in Twelve California Mission Records." *Reports of the University of California Archaeological Survey* 74, 1968.

Mills, Elizabeth. "Old Indian Paintings at Los Angeles." *Overland Monthly* 38 (3), 1901: 766–77.

Miranda, Gloria E. "Racial and Cultural Dimensions of *Gente de Razón* Status in Spanish and Mexican California." *Southern California Quarterly* 70 (3), 1988: 265–78.

Monroy, Douglas. "The Creation and Re-creation of Californio Society." In *Contested Eden: California before the Gold Rush*, ed. Ramón A. Gutiérrez and Richard J. Orsi. Berkeley: Published in association with the California Historical Society by the University of California Press, 1997: 173–95.

Morgan, Edmund S. "Cultivating Surprise." *Huntington Frontiers* 1 (1), 2005: 6–7.

Nelson, Howard J. "The Two Pueblos of Los Angeles: Agricultural Village and Embryo Town." *Southern California Quarterly* 59 (1), 1977: 1–11.

Neuerburg, Norman. "The Indian Via Crucis from Mission San Fernando: An Historical Exposition." *Southern California Quarterly* 79 (3), 1997: 329–82.

Newmark, Marco R. "Calle de Los Negros and the Chinese Massacre of 1871." *Southern California Quarterly* 26 (2–3), 1944: 97–98.

Nunis, Doyce B., Jr. "The Franciscan Friars of Mission San Fernando, 1797–1847." *Southern California Quarterly* 79 (3), 1997: 217–48.

Ogden, Adele. "Alfred Robinson: New England Merchant in Mexican California." *California Historical Society Quarterly* 23 (3), 1944: 193–218.

Owen, Thomas J. "The Church by the Plaza: A History of the Pueblo Church of Los Angeles." *Southern California Quarterly* 42 (1), 1960: 5–28.

Pelzel, Thomas O. "The San Gabriel Stations of the Cross from an Art-Historical Perspective." *Journal of California Anthropology* 3 (1), 1976: 115–19.

Pérez, Eulalia. "An Old Woman and her Recollections." In *Testimonios: Early California through the Eyes of Women, 1815–1848*, ed. and trans. Rose

Marie Beebe and Robert M. Senkewicz. Berkeley: Heyday Books, 2006: 95–117.

Perkins, Arthur B. "Rancho San Francisco: A Study of a California Land Grant." *Southern California Quarterly* 39 (2), 1957: 99–126.

Phillips, George Harwood. "The Alcaldes: Indian Leadership in the Spanish Missions of California." In *The Struggle for Political Autonomy*, ed. Frederick E. Hoxie. Chicago: The Newberry Library, 1989: 83–87.

———. "Indian Paintings from Mission San Fernando: An Historical Interpretation." *Journal of California Anthropology* 3 (1), 1976: 96–114.

———. "Indians and the Breakdown of the Spanish Mission System in California." *Ethnohistory* 21 (4), 1974: 291–302.

———. "Indians in Los Angeles, 1781–1875: Economic Integration, Social Disintegration." *Pacific Historical Review* 49 (3), 1980: 427–51.

———. "The Stations of the Cross: Revisited, Reconsidered, and Revised (sort of)." *Boletín: The Journal of the California Mission Studies Association* 24 (2), 2007: 76–88.

Pleasants, J. E. "A Fourth of July at San Fernando in 1856." *Touring Topics* 22 (2), 1930: 49, 52–53.

———. "Los Angeles in 1856." *Touring Topics* 22 (1), 1930: 36–37, 56.

———. "Ranging on the Mohave River in 1864." *Touring Topics* 22 (3), 1930: 42–43.

Polley, Frank J. "Ship Building at the San Gabriel Mission." *Annual Publications of the Historical Society of Southern California* 3 (3), 1895: 34–39.

Preston, William. "Serpent in the Garden: Environmental Change in Colonial California." In *Contested Eden: California before the Gold Rush*, ed. Ramón A. Gutierrez and Richard J. Orsi. Berkeley: Published in association with the California Historical Society by the University of California Press, 1997: 260–98.

Rawls, James J. "Gold Diggers: Indian Miners in the California Gold Rush." *California Historical Quarterly* 55, 1976: 28–45.

Robinson, W. W. "Los Alamitos: The Indian and Rancho Phases." *California Historical Society Quarterly* 45 (1), 1966: 21–30.

———. "Our Spanish-Mexican Heritage." *The Masterkey* 39 (3), 1965: 3–11.

———. "The Indians of Los Angeles as Revealed by the Los Angeles City Archives." *Historical Society of Southern California Quarterly* 20, 1938: 156–72.

———. "The Indians of Yang-Na." *California History Nugget* 6 (6), 1939: 172–76.

———. "People vs. Lugo." In *Mexicans in California after the U. S. Conquest*, ed. Carlos E. Cortés. New York: Arno Press, 1976.

———. "The Spanish and Mexican Ranchos of San Fernando Valley." *Southwest Museum Leaflets* 31, 1966: 3–14.

Russell, William. "Reminiscences of Old Times: A Private's-Eye View of the Mexican War in California." *Historical Society of Southern California Quarterly* 33 (1), 1951: 5–36.

Rust, H. N. "Rogerio's Theological School." *Out West* 21, 1904: 243–48.

Sahlins, Marshall. *Stone Age Economics*. Chicago: Aldine Publishing Company, 1972.

Salvator, Ludwig Louis. "A Flower from the Golden Land." Trans. Marguerite Eyer Wilbur. *Touring Topics* 21 (1), 1929: 14–19, 48; 21 (2), 1929: 38–43, 48.

Sánchez, Federico. "Rancho Life in Alta California." *The Masterkey* 60 (2–3), 1986: 15–25.

Sánchez, Nellie Van de Grift. "The Days of a Rancher in Spanish-California." *Touring Topics* 22 (4), 1930: 22–29.

Sandos, James A. "Converting California: Indians and Franciscans in the Missions, 1769–1836." *Boletín: The Journal of the California Mission Studies Association* 20 (1), 2003: 5–10.

———. "Toypurina's Revolt: Religious Conflict at Mission San Gabriel in 1785." *Boletín: The Journal of the California Mission Studies Association* 24 (2), 2007: 4–14.

Seaman, Florence Josephine. "A Brief History of Rancho La Brea." *Annual Publications of the Historical Society of Southern California* 9 (3), 1914: 253–56.

Servín, Manuel P. "The Secularization of the California Missions: A Reappraisal." *Southern California Quarterly* 47 (2), 1965: 133–49.

Shepard, William Finley, trans. "California Prior to Conquest: A Frenchman's View." *California Historical Society Quarterly* 37 (1), 1958: 63–77.

Silliman, Stephen W. "Missions Aborted: California Indian Life on Nineteenth-Century Ranchos, 1834–1848." *Boletín: The Journal of the California Mission Studies Association* 21 (1), 2004: 3–22.

———. "Theoretical Perspectives on Labor and Colonialism: Reconsidering the California Missions." *Journal of Anthropological Archaeology* 20 (4), 2001: 379–407.

Singleton, Heather Valdez. "Surviving Urbanization: The Gabrielino, 1850–1928." *Wicazo* 19 (2), no. 2 (2004): 49–59.

Sleeper, Jim. "The Many Mansions of José Sepúlveda." *Pacific Coast Archaeological Society Quarterly* 5 (3), 1969: 1–38.

Standart, M. Colette, O.P. "The Sonora Migration to California, 1848–1856: A Study in Prejudice." *Southern California Quarterly* 58 (3), 1976: 333–57.

Stephenson, Terry E. "Tomás Yorba, his wife Vicenta, and his Account Book." *Quarterly of the Society of Southern California* 23 (3–4), 1941: 127–56.

Sweet, David. "The Ibero-American Frontier Mission in Native American History." In *The New Latin American Mission History*, ed. Erick Langer and Robert H. Jackson. Lincoln: University of Nebraska Press, 1995: 1–48.

Street, Richard Steven. "First Farmworkers, First Braceros: Baja California Field Hands and the Origins of Farm Labor Importation in California Agriculture, 1769–1790." *California History* 75, 1996/1997: 306–19.

Temple, Thomas Workman II. "The Founding of San Gabriel Mission." *Southwest Museum Leaflets* 36, 1971: 3–28; *The Masterkey* 33 (1), 1959: 103–12; *The Masterkey* 33 (4), 1959: 156–61.

———. "Toypurina the Witch and the Indian Uprising at San Gabriel." *The Masterkey* 32 (5), 1958: 136–52.

———, ed. "Two Letters from Sergeant José Francisco Ortega to Governor Felipe de Neve, September 4th and 5th, 1781." *Historical Society of Southern California Quarterly* 22 (1), 1940: 121–27.

Thomas, David Hurst. "Columbian Consequences: The Spanish Borderlands in Cubist Perspective." In *Columbian Consequences, Vol. 1, Archaeological and Historical Perspectives on the Spanish Borderlands West*, ed. David Hurst Thomas. Washington, D.C.: Smithsonian Institution Press, 1989: 1–14.

Thorne, Tanis. "The Death of Superintendent Stanley and the Cahuilla Uprising of 1907–1912." *Journal of California and Great Basin Anthropology* 24 (2), 2004: 233–58.

Timbrook, Jan. "Virtuous Herbs: Plants in Chumash Medicine." *Journal of Ethnobiology* 7 (2), 1987: 171–80.

Valle, Rosemary K. "James Ohio Pattie and the 1827–1828 Alta California Measles Epidemic." *California Historical Society Quarterly* 52 (1), 1973: 28–36.

Vallejo, Mariano Guadalupe. "Ranch and Mission Days in Alta California." In *Tales of California*, ed. Frank Oppel. Secaucus, New Jersey: Castle Books, 1989: 83–92.

Villegas, Isabelle, "San Fernando Mission, 1797–1825." *The Masterkey* 20 (1), 1946: 5–10.

Warner, J. J. "Reminiscences of Early California from 1831 to 1846." *Annual Publications of the Historical Society of Southern California* 7, 1907–1908: 176–93.

Webb, Edith Buckland. "Pigments Used by the Mission Indians of California." *The Americas* 2, 1945: 137–50.

Weber, Francis J. "The Stations at Mission San Fernando." *The Masterkey* 39 (1), 1965: 7–12.

———. "Toypurina the Temptress." *The Masterkey* 43 (2), 1969: 75–76.

Weiss, Michael. "Education, Literacy and the Community of Los Angeles in 1850." *Southern California Quarterly* 60 (2), 1978: 117–35.

Willoughby, Nona Christensen. "Division of Labor among the Indians of California." *University of California Archaeological Survey Reports* 6, 1963: 1–79.

Wilson, Benjamin D. "The Narrative of Benjamin Wilson." Appendix to Robert Glass Cleland, *Pathfinders*. San Francisco: Powell Publishing Company, 1929, 371–415.

Wilson, Florence Slocum. "The Flores Adobe." *The Masterkey* 43 (1), 1969: 4–21.

Wolf, Eric, and Sidney W. Mintz. "Haciendas and Plantations in Middle America and the Antilles." *Social and Economic Studies* 6 (3), 1957: 380–412.

Woodward, Arthur, ed. "Benjamin David Wilson's Observations on Early Days in California and New Mexico." *Annual Publications of the Historical Society of Southern California* 1934: 74–150.

Woolsey, Ronald C. "Crime and Punishment: Los Angeles County, 1850–1856." *Southern California Quarterly* 61 (1), 1979: 79–98.

Yorba, Antonio. "The Will of Antonio Yorba." *Orange County History Series* 2 (1), 1932: 89–93.

Index

"Act for the government & protection of the Indians, An," 247, 248–49, 265–66
Administradores: orders to, 164–65; duties clarified, 169–70; replaced by, 170
Adobe bricks, manufacturing of, 70
Ahwiinga (village): location of, 66; converted Indians from, 66
Albers, Patricia C., 16
Alcaldes (neophyte officers): advantages taken by, 73; cruelties demonstrated, 145, 146; elections restricted and resumed, 77–78; position created, 73; status of, 145
Alvarado, Juan (governor), 169–70
Alvarez, Pedro (supervisor), 138–39
Ames, John G. (Indian agent), 319–20
Archibald, Robert, 21, 326
Arrillaga, José Joaquín (governor), 117
Ávila, Francisco Xavier (settler), 100
Ayuntamiento: control over Indians expanded, 125–28; epidemic in, 193; liquor laws passed, 189–90, 192–93; organization of, 85; social problems in, 194–96; unruly Indians dealt with, 160–61
Azusa (rancho): Cahuillas work on, 231; Indian work records of, 309; stock lost to raiders, 212

Bancroft, Hubert Howe, 21
Bandini, Juan (ranchero): appointed administrador of San Gabriel, 169; concerned about Indian raids, 204; granted Rancho Jurupa, 169; problems with neophytes, 170–71
Barrows, David Prescott, 40, 43
Bell, Horace (settler), 255, 275, 301
Black Hawk (Indian), 186
Blake, William (surveyor): at San Fernando, 237–38; at Los Angeles, 277–78
Blew, Robert W., 27
Boscana, Gerónimo (priest), description of Tongva by, 46–48, 49, 51
Brewer, William (settler), 282

377

Brinley, Charles Henry (administrator), 302–303
Bryant, Edwin (traveler): at Los Angeles, 259; describes vaqueros, 221–22
Buenaventura (neophyte), threatens to kill Spaniards, 122
Bull-bear fights, 223–24
Bullfights: at Mission Dolores, 224–25; at San Gabriel, 256

Cabezón (Cahuilla chief), 209
Cahuilla: origins of, 37–38; economy of, 38–39, 40–41, 42–43; fight Mexicans, 166; raid San Bernardino, 166; on Rancho Azusa, 231, 309–310; on Rancho Cucamonga, 303–304; on Rancho Jurupa, 318; in Cahuilla Valley, 319–20; proposed reservation for, 336
California State Agricultural Society, 240
Calle de los Negros: taverns in, 272; violence in, 272
Cambón, Pedro Benito (priest), 59–60, 61–62
Cañón de Santa Ana (rancho): granted in, 161; Sonorans and Indians work on, 308; visited by Sepúlveda and Warner, 161–62
Capitán (neophyte), sells mockingbirds, 254
Carabantes, Salvador (carpenter), 131
Carson, James, H. (settler), 23
Carson, Kit (soldier), stationed in Cajon Pass, 211
Carvahlo, Solomon Nunes (traveler), 226

Castillo, Pedro, 29, 30
Centennial Celebration of the Declaration of Independence (1876), 294–95
Chaguanosos (stock raiders): identification of, 204–205; ranchos raided, 205
Chapman, Joseph (immigrant): builds schooner at San Gabriel, 153; in Los Angeles, 188
Chinese, on a rancho, 316
Chinigchinich (spirit), 43–44. See also Tongva
Cleland, Robert Glass, 21–22, 24
Cochimí (Baja California Indians): at San Gabriel, 63–64; importance of, 63–64
Colonization Act of 1824, 159; ranchos created from, 160–61; revised, 159–60
Cook, Sherburne F., 325, 327, 328–29
Coronel, Antonio Francisco (ranchero), 134, 223, 224
Costello, Julia G., 33
Crespí, Juan (priest): description of Tongva marriages, 53; meets Tongva, 58–59; names Los Angeles River, 58
Croix, Teodoro de (governor of Northern New Spain), 82
Cucamonga (rancho): Indians on, 303–304; size of herds on, 304; wine of praised, 311–12

Dalton, Henry (ranchero), 208, 217, 231, 246, 299, 309–10
Dana, Richard Henry (seaman): criticizes administradores, 173–74; at San Pedro, 227–28

Index

Davis, William Heath (settler), 220, 226–27, 278
Dawson, Nicholas, 224
De la Guerra Ord, Anguistias, 156–57
De la Guerra y Noriega, José (soldier), 110–11
Del Valle, Antonio (administrador), at San Fernando, 177–78; granted estancia 178; death of, 179
De Neve, Felipe (governor): advocates civilian settlements, 82; Indian alcaldes and rigidores appointed, 73
De Neve, Felipa Teresa and Felipe (Tongva), 82
De Portolá, Gaspar (soldier), 57
Deppe, Ferdinand (painter), 155
Disease: in Los Angeles, 193, 284–85, 292; in San Bernardino, 313; at San Fernando, 107; at San Gabriel, 131, 132; south of San Fernando, 99. *See also* Pneumonia; Smallpox; Syphilis; Venereal disease
D'Oliveria (Olivera), Manuel (immigrant): granted land at San Gabriel, 176; oversees property at mission, 246–47
Domingo, Juan (vineyardist): appropriates Indian land, 187; buys vacated Indian village, 196
Domínguez, Juan José (ranchero): horses of become wild, 89; petitions for land, 87
Drought: of 1856, 305; of 1864, 314
Duflot de Mofras, Eugène (seaman), 135, 192
Duhaut-Cilly, Auguste (seaman), 124–25

Dumke, Glenn S., 18
Durán, Francisco (father president): complaint issued to, 172; seeks support of neophytes, 179

Echeandía, José María (governor), emancipates neophytes, 162
El Encino (estancia), granted to Indian, 180
El Encino (rancho): becomes Mission San Fernando, 97; founded, 95–96
El Escorpión (estancia), 179–80
El Molino Viejo (mill), 134
Emilio Joaquín (neophyte), receives land near San Gabriel, 176
Enríquez, Antonio Domingo (artisan), at San Gabriel, 70
Esténaga, Tomás Eleuterio (priest): complains about Mexicans at San Gabriel, 171–72; death of, 245–46; initiates matanza, 156; introduces changes at mission, 174; supports neophytes, 176–77
Estudillo, Adelaide Rubidoux (daughter of ranchero), 311
Eustaquio María (Indian alcalde), at San Gabriel, 78
Ex-mission San Fernando (rancho): Butterfield Stage stops at, 240–42; feasts held at, 236, 243–44, 256; founding of, 236; leased, 234; sold, 235; end of, 245

Fages, Pedro (soldier and governor), 46, 51, 52, 60, 61, 64; allows neophytes to occupy a

Fages, Pedro (soldier and governor) *(continued)*, rancho, 95; forbids neophytes use of horses, 72; instructions to ranchero, 90; identifies site for Los Angeles, 81
Féliz, Vicente (comisionado), 85–86
Figueroa, José (governor), 163, 203
Font, Pedro (priest), 65
Foster, Steven C. (mayor): arrives in Los Angeles 259; tries and executes Indian prisoner, 261–63
Francis, Jessie Davies, 22
Francisco Andrés (Isleño), 121
Francisco de Lausén, Fermín (father president): justifies Indians using horses, 72; records founding of Mission San Fernando, 96
Francisco de Sarría, Vicente (priest): as father president, 137; at San Gabriel, 93
Francisco Papabubaba (neophyte), 180
Frémont, John C. (explorer), 219
Frierman, Jay D., 24, 31
Froebel, Julis (traveler): in Los Angeles, 275; at Rancho Chino, 304
Frohling, J. (grape contractor), 279

Gallardo, Rafael (settler), 266
García, Carlos (mayordomo), 140
Garner, William (settler), 201, 203
Geiger, Maynard, 18
Gentiles, definition of, 20
Grant, Ulysses S. (president), reservations created, 320

Greenwood, Roberta S., 24–25
Grijalva, Juan Pablo (ranchero), 92–93
Grizzly bears: hunted, 222–23; Indian spiritual views of, 52; pitted against bulls, 223–24
Gutiérrez, Manuel (carpenter and architect), 104
Guest, Francis, F., 324
Guinn, J. M., 27

Hackel, Steven W., 19, 326
Hartnell, William (visitor general): appointment of, 170; replaces administradores, 172–73; return of neophytes sought, 190–91; at San Fernando, 178–79; at San Gabriel, 170–71; at San Pedro, 148
Hayes, Benjamin (judge): holds trial of neophyte, 282–83; Indians as producers recognized, 297–98; Indian worker admired, 297–98; in Los Angeles, 264; observes taverns, 270; at San Fernando, 251–53
Heinrich Von Langsdorff, Georg (seaman), 133
Henley, Thomas (superintendent of Indian Affairs), 274
Hides, processing and manufacturing of, 147
Híjar, José María (colonist), 165–66
Hornbeck, David, 33
Horses: training of, 225–26; treatment of at missions, 71; treatment of on ranchos, 220–22

Ibarra, Francisco (priest): departs

and returns to California, 177–78; hordes products, 113; manages San Fernando, 110; problems with Santa Barbara presidio 111–12; supports Indian's land claim, 177

Janssens, Agustín (administrador): observes Indian raiders, 205; seeks Indians returned to mission, 91
José Antonio (neophyte), death of, 97
José de los Santos Juncos (neophyte), recalls life at mission, 153
José María (Cahuilla), baptized at Rancho Santiago de Santa Ana, 93
José Miguel Triunto (neophyte): granted land at Cahuenga, 180–81; death of, 181
Juan Antonio (Cahuilla chief): allies with rancheros, 266–67; death of, 313; in Los Angeles, 268; at Rancho Azusa, 310
Juan Antonio (neophyte), tried and executed in Los Angeles, 261–63
Juan Capistrano (neophyte), 76
Jurupa (rancho), Cahuillas work on, 318

Kalisher, Wolf (immigrant), 283
Keller, Mathew (vineyardist), 283–84, 293
Kip, William Ingraham (clergyman), 255
Kohler, Charles (vineyardist), 274

La Laguna (rancho), 319
La Perouse, Jean-Francois de (seaman), 133
La Puente (estancia): conflict over, 90; buildings at, 136; neophytes sent to, 136
La Puente (rancho): robbed of stock, 205; neophytes at 230; number of Indians on, 310
La Presa (dam): neophytes construct, 79; Indians living near, 175
La Purísima (mission), 155
Layne, J. Gregg, 26
Lightfoot, Kent G., 31–32
Lime: manufacturing at missions, 99; traditional processing of, 54
López, Claudio (mayordomo at San Gabriel): death of, 156; manages estancias, 134–35, supervises building of grist mill, 134–35
Los Alamitos (rancho): flooded, 313; Indians on, 302
Los Angeles: census of 1790, 115; census of 1830, 125; designated a city, 183; development of, 285–90; expansion of, 83–85, 285–88; founding of, 83–84; incorporation of, 264; labor problems at, 290–92; population of, 183–84; relations with Indians, 85–86; violence in, 275, 281–83
Los Angeles Church, 120
Los Angeles River: changes course, 123, 124; environment of 45–46; named by Crespí, 58
Los Cerritos (rancho), 302
Lovell, C. S. (soldier), 213–16

Lugo, Antonio María (ranchero): allies with Cahuilla, 206; buys Indian, 199; loses stock to raiders, 213; obtains ranchos in San Bernardino Valley, 206

Lugo, José del Carmen (ranchero), 70–71; describes bullfights, 224; describes rancho work routine, 229–30; describes rodeo, 226; describes work routine on estancias, 135; explains distinction between vaqueros, 144; observes hides at San Pedro, 148; witnesses flood and matanza in Los Angeles, 122–23

Lugo, José María (ranchero), 213

Manuel (neophyte), 180

Manuel Antonio (neophyte), 176–77

Manuel Largo (Cahuilla): becomes chief of Mountain Cahuilla, 313; wounded in campaign against stock raiders, 215

María de Echeandía, José (governor), hostile to missionaries, 112

Mariné, José: death of, 168; marries Eulalia Pérez, 167; seeks land at San Gabriel, 168

Maso, Juan (settler): receives lease at San Fernando, 234; takes inventory at San Gabriel, 245

Mason, William, 29

Matanzas: at Los Angeles, 127; end at San Pedro, 315

Mateo (Tongva), baptized at San Gabriel, 66

McCulloch, Hugh (trader), 148

McWilliams, Carey, 327

Medicine, traditional preparations of, 54

Meighan, Clement W., 326

Micheltorena, Manuel (governor), 180

Mill Creek Zanja: construction of, 138–39; repairing of, 138–40

Milliken, Randall T., 325–26

Missions. *See names of individual missions*

Mohaves: lose lives at San Buenaventura, 138; raid estancias, 131–32, 138

Möllhauser, Baldwin (traveler), 220

Monroy, Douglas, 25, 327

Moreno, Santiago (soldier), 70

Morgan, Edmund S., 30

Mukat (spirit), 37–38. *See also* Cahuilla

Muñoz, Pedro (priest), 104

Newmark, Harris (settler), 280, 284, 307

New Mexicans: arrive in California, 201–202; participate in slave trade, 202; relations with Indians, 202–203

Nicholás José (alcalde): appointment of, 73; organizes uprising, 75–76; plots to kill missionaries, 74; provides women to soldiers, 73–74; tried and imprisoned, 77

Nordoff, Charles, 319

Nuez, Joaquín Pascual (priest), 119

Odón Chihuya (neophyte), 179

Oligario (Luiseño), 283–84, 293

Olivera, Manuel. *See* D'Oliveria, Manuel

Ord, Antonio María (ranchero), 158
Ord, Edward O. C. (soldier), 305–306
Ordaz, Blas (priest), 246–47
Ortega, José Francisco (soldier), 84
Osio, Antonio María (settler), 158

Pancoast, Charles Edward (immigrant), 297
Patencio, Francisco (Cahuilla), 41–42
Paiutes: raid Rancho Ex-mission San Fernando, 241; raid ranchos, 214, 215–17
Palóu, Francisco (priest): describes founding of San Gabriel, 60; discusses inter-Indian situation, 64–65
Payeras, Mariano (father president), 119, 120, 139
Pedro (Cahuilla), baptized at Rancho de Santiago de Santa Ana, 93
Pedro (neophyte), at San Gabriel, 70
Pedro Celestino (alcalde), elected at San Gabriel, 78
Peon (gambling game): description of, 53; violence associated with, 267–68
Peonage, 327–28
Peraltla, Juan (ranchero), 92, 93
Pérez, Eulalia (supervisor), 156; appointed Keeper of the Keys, 143; claims land at San Gabriel, 167; describes duties, 41–44
Pérez, Juan Crespín (mayordomo): accused of wasting mission property, 173; appointment of, 173; death of, 249; upsets neophytes, 246
Phelps, William Dane (seaman), 191–92
Pico, Andrés (ranchero): in charge of fighting stock raiders, 212; conveys rancho to brother, 242–42; joins commission to dispose of missions, 234
Pico, Pío (governor): implements act to sell missions, 233–34; leases San Fernando, 234; meets with Utes, 210; sells San Fernando, 235
Pipimares (Island Indians): relocated to Los Angeles, 121; removed from settlement, 198–99
Pleasants, J. E. (traveler), 239
Plows, construction of, 70–71
Pneumonia, 97
Pobladores: arrival of, 83; land received, 83; responsibilities of, 83–84; subject to civil authority, 85
Povuu'nga (Tongva village), 43–44, 300–301
Pueblito (Indian village): created, 196; drinking in, 196–98; razed, 261

Quechans, 82

Ramírez, José Antonio (neophyte), 119
Ranchería de Poblanos: abandonment of, 195–96; founding of, 185
Ranchos. *See names of individual ranchos*

Reid, Hugo (immigrant): buys mission, 266; comments on alcaldes, 145; death of, 249; on death of Father Sánchez, 196; difficulty with Indians, 175; letters on Indians published, 249–52; marries Indian, 168; notes improvement at San Gabriel, 150; praises priest, 174; receives land at San Gabriel, 168; on recruitment of gentiles, 65–66; views of Tongva, 48, 49–50, 50–51, 53, 55
Revere, Joseph Warren (seaman), 220, 222
Reyes, Francisco (ranchero), 96
Ríos-Bustamante, Antonio, 27, 29, 30
Rivera y Moncada, Fernando (soldier), 82
Robinson, Alfred (supercargo): at San Fernando, 113; at San Gabriel, 150–52, 154
Robinson, W. W., 28–29
Rogerio Rocha (neophyte), 181
Rogers, Harrison (trapper), 146–47
Rolle, Andrew, 22
Román (neophyte), 180
Romero, José (soldier), 140
Rose, Leonard John (vineyardist): employs Indians, Mexicans, and Chinese, 316–17; products produced by, 317; purchases land, 315–16
Rufina (neophyte), 176

Sabino Pomasquimbet (neophyte), 70
Salazar, Alonso (priest), 116
Samuel (neophyte), 180

San Bernardino County, population of, 307
San Buenaventura (mission): assists San Fernando, 97; founding delayed, 63; Mohave Indians at, 138
San Diego (mission), 57, 156; neophytes in Los Angeles, 125; sends supplies to Los Angeles, 120
San Fernando (mission): expansion of, 99; estancias of, 99–100; founding of, 96–97; Indians flogged at, 107; Indian wall designs, 108–109; neophyte defiance at, 110; sends supplies to Los Angeles, 120
San Francisco (rancho), raided by Utes, 213
San Francisco Xavier (estancia), 100; crops damaged, 112–13; granted to, 178
San Gabriel (mission): cattle slaughtered at, 156–57; founding of, 59–60; Indian resistance to, 61–63; new location established, 67; new management at, 129–49; population of non-Indians, 166–67
San Juan Capistrano (mission), 156; sends neophyte workers to Los Angeles, 117; sends supplies to church in Los Angeles, 120
San Joaquín de Cahuenga (estancia): conflicts with Los Angeles, 105; crops damaged, 113; dam constructed at, 104–105; granted to Indians, 180–81
San José (rancho): animals stolen from, 215–16; conference with

Utes at, 210; horses stolen from, 203
San Luis Rey (mission): cattle slaughtered at, 158; neophytes from in Los Angeles, 125; sends supplies to Los Angeles, 120
San Nicolás Island, 185–86
San Pedro (rancho), 155; granted in, 89; horses escape from, 89; matanza ends, 315; workers at, 162
San Rafael (rancho): granted, 89; responsibilities to grantee defined, 90
Sánchez, José Bernardo (priest): at San Bernardino estancia, 139; changes policy at Mission San Gabriel, 149–51; death of, 156; releases land to settlers, 167
Sanchez, Miguel (priest), 92
Sanchez, Nellie van de Grift, 23
Sánchez, Tomás (vineyardist): land identified, 185; violence at, 273
Sandos, James A., 20
Santa Ana del Chino (rancho): considered for reservation, 307; granted, 161; products produced at, 304; soldiers stationed at, 213–14, 215
Santa Ana River: changes course, 124; described by priest, 57; region of, 45
Santa Anita (rancho): granted 92–93; Indian baptized on, 93; sheep introduced, 312–13
Santa Bárbara (mission): assists San Fernando, 97, 104; sends supplies to Los Angeles, 120
Santa Bárbara (presidio), 110–12
Santa Gertrudis (rancho), 155;
Indians employed on, 161; number of animals on, 161; part of Los Nietos, 91; population increase, 162
Santa María, Vicente (priest), explores San Fernando Valley, 95–96
Santiago de Santa Ana (rancho): Indians in debt at, 232; population of, 161; suicide on, 310–11; visited by, 161–62;
Secularization: articles of, 163–64; officers to implement, 164–65; views of, 21–22
Señán, José (priest), 104; blesses church at San Fernando, 96; concerns about Indians working for settlers, 115–16
Sepúlveda, José Dolores (ranchero): at Rancho Cañón de Santa Ana, 161; horses stolen from, 212
Serra, Junípero (father president): on appointment of alcaldes, 74; on treatment of Indians at San Gabriel, 62–63
Serranos: baptized at mission, 132; economy of, 41, 42–43; seek instruction in agriculture, 138; organization of, 39; raid San Gabriel estancias, 131; rejected by Tongva, 140
Sexton, Daniel (settler), 139
Shaler, William (seaman), 117
Sheep raising, expansion of, 304, 315
Silliman, Stephen W., 16, 17, 26, 32
Sinova, Francisco (soldier), at San Gabriel, 70
Smallpox, 193, 284–85, 292, 313

Smith, Jedediah (trapper), at San Gabriel, 146
Soap, manufacturing of, 148
Solá, Pablo Vicente de (governor), 137–38
Somera, Ángel (priest), 60
Sonorans: gamble with Indians, 175–76; raid ranchos, 203–204; replace Indians in Los Angeles County, 317
Spring Rancheria, 318
Stations of the Cross: painting of, 101–104; at San Fernando, 235
Stearns, Abel (ranchero): chases stock raiders, 212; problem with Indians, 302–303
Street, Richard, 326
Stevenson, Jonathan D. (soldier): governs Los Angeles, 260; seeks help of Californios, 211–12
Suñer, Francisco (priest), 117
Sweet, David, 19, 20
Syphilis, 107

Tac, Pablo (neophyte), 145
Tallow, 227
Tapia, Bartolomé (militia leader), 131–32
Tapia, Tiburcio (judge of Indians in Los Angeles), 127
Tapis, Estevan (father president), 118
Tataviam villages, 98
Thomas, David Hurst, 20–21
Tiburcio (Tongva), 98
Tiburcio Cayo (neophyte), 180
Tiles, manufacturing of, 99
Tin Tin (neophyte), 227
Tomás (neophyte, mason), 104
Tomás (neophyte), 282–83
Tongva: division of labor within, 51–52; environment of 44–46; food and products produced by, 50–51, 54; government of, 46–50; society described, 43–48, 52, 53, 55; survival of, 336
Tools, types at missions, 69
Townsend, E. D. (soldier): at San Fernando, 239; at Los Angeles, 278
Toypurina (Tongva): converted to Christianity, 76–77; organizes uprising at San Gabriel, 75–76; tried and sentenced, 76; death of 76–77
Triunto, José Miguel (neophyte), granted land, 180–81

United States Land Act of 1851, 301
Urbano Chari (neophyte): granted land, 179–80; leads Indians at Rancho El Escorpión, 236–37
Utes, raid ranchos, 210–14. *See also* Walkara

Valdez, Bacilio (regidor), 127
Vallejo, Mariano Guadalupe (ranchero), 222
Vaqueros: emergence of 72; skills displayed, 219–27; types of, 144; uniqueness of, 136–37
Venereal disease: in Los Angeles, 198; at San Gabriel, 132
Verdugo, José María (ranchero), granted land, 89–90
Victoria (Tongva): befriended by Laura Evertsen King, 253–54; marries Hugo Reid, 253; marries Pablo María, 141; death of 292
Vignes, Jean-Louis (vineyardist): begins commercial wine industry,

188–89; complains about Indian village, 196; size of vineyard, 191; seeks Indian land, 189
Villa, Francisco (settler), 167–68
Villegas, Isabel, describes feast at San Fernando, 236
Virmond, Henry (merchant), sends ships to Alta, California, 155
Vischer, Edward (painter): at Los Angeles, 192; paintings by, 224–25

Walkara (Ute chief): death of, 218; raids ranchos, 213, 215
Warner, J. J. (settler): notes activities of New Mexicans, 201; at Rancho Cañón de Santa Ana, 161–62
Warren, John Quincy Adams (immigrant), visits Los Angeles region, 311
White, Michael (ranchero): driven off property, 207; granted land near San Gabriel, 176; justice of the peace, 248
Willard, Charles, Dwight, 327
Williams, Isaac (ranchero): employs Indians, 304; employs Indian woman, 186; loses animals to stock raiders, 216; seeks soldiers stationed in the interior, 213; sells food to immigrants, 297
Wilson, Benjamin D. (ranchero): granted rancho, 253; Indian agent, 252; leads campaign against stock raiders, 208–209; at San Gabriel, 248; sells brandy to Indian workers, 317
Wolfskill, William (immigrant): builds schooner at mission, 153–54; constructs buildings in Los Angeles, 289; harvest described, 279–80; at San Gabriel, 201
Woods, James (minister), in Los Angeles, 272–73
Wool: garments made from, 72; production of, 72–73
Woolsey, Peter C., 29
Workman, William (ranchero), buys Mission San Fernando, 246

Yaanga (village): location of 82; end of, 119
Yorba, Bernardo (ranchero), granted Rancho Cañón de Santa Ana, 161–62
Yorba, José Antonio (ranchero), granted Rancho Santiago de Santa Ana, 92–93
Yorba, Tomás (ranchero): assists Father Esténaga at San Gabriel, 158; comments on Sonorans, 203–204
Yount, George C. (trapper), at San Gabriel, 151–52, 53

Zalvidea, José María (priest), 18; achievements assessed, 149; answers questionnaire, 132–33; baptizes Indians from San Bernardino, 132; described by contemporaries, 129–30; has mill built; 134; managerial skills demonstrated, 130–31; requested to live at San Bernardino, 206; transferred to Mission San Juan Capistrano, 149; undermines Indian religious leaders, 146
Zapatero (neophyte), relocates to San Joaquin Valley, 190

www.ingramcontent.com/pod-product-compliance
Lightning Source LLC
Chambersburg PA
CBHW020932180426
43192CB00036B/557